CONSTRUCTION
SPECIFICATIONS

CONSTRUCTION SPECIFICATIONS

JACK R. LEWIS

FCSI, Architect
Associate Professor
School of Architecture and Environmental Design
California Polytechnic State University

Prentice-Hall, Inc., Englewood Cliffs, New Jersey

Library of Congress Cataloging in Publication Data

LEWIS, JACK R.
  Construction specifications.

  Bibliography: p.
  1. Building-Contracts and specifications.
  I. Title.
TH425.L48   692'.3   74-16459
ISBN 0-13-169375-1

PRENTICE-HALL INTERNATIONAL, INC., London
PRENTICE-HALL OF AUSTRALIA, PTY. LTD., Sydney
PRENTICE-HALL OF CANADA, LTD., Toronto
PRENTICE-HALL OF INDIA PRIVATE LIMITED, New Delhi
PRENTICE-HALL OF JAPAN, INC., Tokyo

CONTENTS

PREFACE   xi

1 WHAT IS A SPECIFICATION?   1

    Summary, 7
    Questions, 7

2 DRAWINGS AND SPECIFICATIONS   9

    The Drawings, 9
    Drafting Symbols, 10
    Material Indication, 10
    Dimensions, 12
    Building Openings, 12
    Drafting Scale, 13
    Cross-Referencing, 14
    Schedules, 15
    The Specifications, 16
    Deviations, 16
    Architect-Contractor Cooperation, 18
    Standard Details, 18
    Drafting Notes, 19
    Reference Drawings, 19

CONTENTS

Checking Drawings, 20
Building Departments, 21
Summary, 21
Questions, 22

3 SOURCES FOR INFORMATION 23

Testing, 24
Product Catalogs, 28
Governmental Sources, 34
Trade Associations, 38
Other Sources, 39
Summary, 41
Questions, 41

4 TYPES OF SPECIFICATIONS 43

Closed vs. Open Specs, 43
The "Or Equal" Clause, 45
Manufacturer's Specifications, 46
Federal Specifications, 47
Commercial Specifications, 48
Performance Specifications, 49
Streamlined Specifications, 50
Preliminary Specifications, 51
Tabulation Specifications, 52
Summary, 52
Questions, 54

5 SPECIFICATIONS LANGUAGE 55

Mandatory Construction, 56
"Contractor" as Subject, 57
Punctuation, 58
Escape Clauses, 58
Words and Phrases, 59
Exact Word Meanings, 60
Summary, 61
Questions, 61

6 LEGAL DOCUMENTS – "BOILERPLATE" 63

Included Forms, 64
Announcement, 65

Invitation to Bid, 66
Description of Project, 66
Pre- Bid Qualification, 67
General Conditions, 67
Supplemental General Conditions, 68
Special Conditions, 69
Wage Scales, 70
Bid Forms, 70
List of Subcontractors, 71
Bond Forms, 71
Miscellaneous Forms, 72
Summary, 72
Questions, 73

7 THE UNIFORM SYSTEM 75

The Division, 77
The Section, 78
Division—Section, 79
The Filing System, 82
Cost Accounting Guide, 83
Index of Key Words, 83
Manufacturer- Contractor, 84
Acceptance, 86
Summary, 86
Questions, 87

8 WRITING A SPECIFICATION 89

Preliminary Review, 89
The Preliminary Specification, 90
Beginning Final Specifications, 92
Three—Part Section, 93
Paragraph Numbering, 98
Project-Page Identification, 99
Page Arrangement, 99
Drafting the Final Specification, 100
Material—Methods Research, 101
Check and Recheck, 102
The Last Look, 102
Summary, 103
Questions, 103

9 THE FEDERAL SPECIFICATION   **105**

The PDE, 105
Preliminary Survey, 106
Preliminary Submittal, 107
Waiting Period, 108
Manufacturer — Distributor, 109
Writing the Final Federal Spec, 110
Final Federal Specification, 111
Nonstandard Items, 112
Final Submittal, 112
Other Federal Work, 112
Summary, 113
Questions, 113

10 ALTERNATIVES, ADDENDA, AND CHANGE ORDERS   **115**

Alternates, 116
Unit Prices, 118
Addenda, 118
Change Order, 120
Summary, 121
Questions, 122

11 MECHANIZATION OF SPECIFICATIONS   **123**

The Systems Approach, 124
Catalog Retrieval, 125
Automatic Typewriters, 126
Computers, 128
Summary, 130
Questions, 130

12 REPRODUCTION METHODS   **131**

Carbon Paper, 132
Spirit Duplication, 133
Mimeograph Duplication, 134
Electrostatic Duplication, 134
Printing, 136
Computers, 137
Blueprinting, 137
Color Code, 138
Binding, 138
Preprinted Material, 140

Specification Covers, 140
Summary, 141
Questions, 141

13 MASTER SPECIFICATIONS   143

Cut-and-Paste Master, 143
The "Topsy" Master, 144
The Office Master, 145
The Government Master, 147
The Consultant's Master, 148
Purchased Masters, 149
MASTERSPEC, 149
COMSPEC, 150
Miscellaneous Masters, 151
Summary, 151
Questions, 152

14 CONSULTANTS   155

Specifications Consultants, 155
What the Specifications Consultant Does, 156
Training and Experience, 157
Who Are the Clients? 158
Consultants Office, 158
Consultants' Fees, 159
Consultants Consultants, 160
The Researcher, 161
Summary, 162
Questions, 163

15 THE FUTURE?   165

APPENDICES

A TYPICAL SPECIFICATIONS OF THE CSI   171

B MASTER SPECIFICATIONS   241

C SPECIFICATION REFERENCES   319

D BIBLIOGRAPHY   333

E ORGANIZATIONS   335

INDEX   337

PREFACE

Quite a few years ago while I still operated an office for the general practice of architecture, a very good friend of mine in a major west coast city urged me to move to his area and engage in the then comparatively new occupation of specifications writing as a free-lance consultant to other architects and engineers. With the great faith and energy of those tackling a new field, I accepted the challenge and over the next fifteen years developed a knowledge of specifications that has been both interesting and profitable to me and reasonably acceptable to my clients.

During those early days, I would have been hard-pressed to accurately describe the methods and sources of information in construction work. I was exceptionally fortunate, however, in having a grandfather who was a contractor. I was also aided by my inquisitiveness and strong interest in the processes of construction. About this time I was introduced to the then-new organization, *Construction Specifications Institute,* and its aims and possibilities for solving some of my problems and confusion through its publications and contacts. In more recent years, a chance meeting at an architectural convention channeled my efforts into the profession of college instruction in architecture with a specialty in specifications and office practice.

Searching for suitable texts for specification writing resulted in review of many books, most of which were out-of-date, written for the active professional, or not written for college instruction. Hence, this book; the arrangement and contents have been compiled in general as an expansion of notes and lecture material given over the past three years to groups of fourth-year students in a school of architecture.

A great many schools of architecture, engineering, or construction technology still do not have courses in specifications writing. Perhaps in the past this phase of the construction business was less important, since materials, their use, and installation were relatively simple and quite often completely covered by appropriate notes on the drawings. With the increased knowledge of construction, new materials, and new methods, this system no longer adequately assured the quality required. Specifications now must augment the drawings, not only in the "architectural" portions, but in the structural, mechanical, and electrical engineering fields and the various sections devoted to furnishing and equipping our construction projects. With this thought in mind, interested curriculum-makers and students made more specifications courses available in colleges of architecture and engineering.

Although this book has been principally devised for architectural students, the methods and information may with slight change or emphasis be equally applied to other construction-oriented instruction. The structural, mechanical, and electrical engineer working as consultant to an architect must (1) write his specifications to conform to the requirements of the architect and (2) adequately define his own requirements for materials and methods in his particular field. Civil-engineering works concerned with highways, dams, disposal systems, etc., also need specifications to compliment the drawings; even works concerned only with the manufacture of a material or product need properly specified materials, processes, and uses.

My association with the members of the *Construction Specifications Institute, American Institute of Architects, Producers Council, Associated General Contractors of America*, and the hundreds of manufacturers' representatives, subcontractors, and craft mechanics has been invaluable to me, and since I cannot thank them all individually, I appreciatively extend my thanks to them here. Without their cooperation, it would have been difficult to develop ability and interest. I hope that this effort to pass along some of this knowledge and experience will result in more student awareness and possible interest in the writing of good construction specifications.

My special thanks go to my daughter, Holly Kay Ramsey, and to her husband and children. Without her valuable help as typist, critic, and general reviewer, and the patient cooperation of her family, this book might never have been completed.

JACK R. LEWIS
San Luis Obispo, Calif.

1

WHAT IS
A SPECIFICATION?

What is a specification? The dictionary defines it as "A definite and complete statement, as in a contract . . . the precise method of construction."

Every day we use dozens or even hundreds of items, each of which requires a specification somewhere along the line. When we first get up in the morning we use water, soap, toothpaste, and towels; later we eat breakfast, using perhaps an electric toaster, coffee maker, and certain dishes; we go to work in automobiles or on bicycles; later we enjoy radio or television; of course most of this time we are covered with clothing. Each of these products has a specification, as do dozens more, generally set up by the original buyer and altered as needed by successive buyers or users. These specifications set requirements for quality and appearance, and as raw materials are manufactured into finished products new specifications are drawn up for these finished products. In the construction field we are more concerned with the last few words of the above definition, "**the precise method of construction,**" since we want to define the quality of various materials and the methods by which they are incorporated into the project. In this field a specification is regarded as augmenting or supplementing, with words, the drawings or other documents describing a project with lines or symbols.

In general the drawings indicate the project appearance, plans, elevations, and details by combinations of lines, dimension figures, certain established sections, and their relations to each other. Some types of work may also include descriptions of the properties of the materials that will provide the desired appearances; these descriptions make use of accepted symbols or actual lettered words. The use of words, however, is restricted to describing the materials or the installation, since it is difficult to indicate accurately on drawings (except at unreasonable drafting costs or in great detail) such things as gauges of metals, sizes of manufactured standard units, or how to install work in accordance with standard or special practices.

The specification, on the other hand, does not usually include drawings or symbols but best describes all of the work by using appropriate combinations of words that augment the drawings by stating the requirements of quality, testing, installation methods, and other factors not easily shown by lines or symbols. Also included in most "specs" are the *General Conditions, Special Conditions, Bond Forms, Bid Information, Wage Scales,* and similar necessary information, which might be lettered on the drawings but is obviously done more rapidly and easily by typewriter or other production methods. The term *specifications* has been used for a long time to indicate all written information, but there is an increasing trend towards the use of terms such as *construction manual* or *project manual,* where the *book* contains all the special information and bidding documents as well as the actual specification requirements for materials and their installation.

In later chapters we will outline and discuss all of the facets included in the *book,* types of format, sources for information, differences in procedures, and the actual production of the finished product. The offices or individuals, sooner or later, determine the procedures or methods they think best suit their own needs or, perhaps more properly, the needs of their clients as well as the contractors and suppliers involved in projects that are under the supervision of the office or individual. Considerable experience is needed to make these decisions, and the student or beginning spec writer should try to become familiar with as many different systems of writing, kinds of materials, and methods of installation as possible. Location and availability will in great measure help in this respect.

There is no easy way to obtain this information or ability. For many years the spec writer in offices would be one of the older men who had, it was assumed, the knowledge and experience gained in the "school of hard knocks." It is unfortunate that many times this did not work out to the advantage of either the man or the office. Many experienced architects, engineers, draftsmen, or inspectors either feel that the specifications are a very minor, uninteresting part of the construction documents or they lack the capability or enthusiasm to write specs well. With the increase in the number of available materials, new methods of production or installation, skills of the mechanics installing the work, and the increasingly complex legal aspects of the specifications, the ability to write specs requires more and more training and assumes more and more importance.

Many architectural schools, and at least an equal number of engineering schools offering courses in the civil, mechanical, electrical, and construction fields, are becoming more conscious of the importance of specifications and are establishing some instruction in this area. Although primarily it is the architect who is concerned with specifications, they are just as essential in describing similar requirements for the engineering aspects of building construction, roads, dams, and other types of construction work. The principles are the same in any case, so today we have an increasing number of younger men who are interested in the preparation of specifications and who have at least a speaking knowledge of the necessary methods and requirements, although actual experience certainly supplements this "book-learnin'."

Another item that has definitely affected the importance of construction specifications is the *legal* aspect. In the "good old days" many contractors personally operated their own businesses and knew the architect or engineer quite well, and vice versa. This situation had its faults, but it did permit an easier relationship when they worked together on a project. This circumstance is no longer widespread. Today many architect/engineer firms are quite large and their opposite numbers in the contracting field are equally large, reducing to a minimum any personal contact between them. Since interpretations by the courts are often different from those intended by the architect/engineer the specifications must now be considered, and written, as legal documents that not only tell the contractor what is intended but what will hold up in a possible court case. It is hoped of course that your specifications will never face this test, but the architect or engineer who draws up the specifications should certainly consider the possibility of such a case at all times.

Specifications are written to clarify the intent of the architect or engineer in a manner that will leave no doubt in the mind of the reader (usually the contractor, his subcontractor, mechanic, or supplier) as to what is intended. Specifications are not written for the reading pleasure of the owner. It is true that clients such as governmental

3

agencies, schools, large corporations, and similar "owners" quite often have staff architects or engineers who read and review specifications, but these people are simply acting in a professional capacity and are providing their knowledge as protection for the owner. Building officials also read specifications, but in most cases they do so only to see if the specs comply with the requirements of building codes and safety ordinances.

Every specifications writer needs to be an analyst where construction is concerned. By looking at a cardboard model or a designer's rendering he must be able to put together a fairly accurate preliminary specification, and by a thorough review of working drawings he must be able to clearly describe all materials and installation methods required to construct the project. A good spec writer must be able to look at a civil engineer's survey of a property and see in his mind's eye the order and amount of grading to be done, paving to be placed, landscape work to be finished, and all other site work to be accomplished. He must be able to look at a structural or architectural section of a building and visualize the foundation excavation required, the forms for concrete, the reinforcing, the mixing, placing, and finishing of concrete, the framing of the walls, their finishing, and even the extent of cleaning required. He must be able to mentally transfer himself to the project site and do the work in the order required, with the materials specified, and in the manner shown on the working drawings. While doing all of this he must keep in mind the *standard* methods versus *special* methods, the availability of materials, their cost, the labor required, and the possible legal interpretation of all that he writes. Superman? Well, not quite.

A good knowledge of drafting, or perhaps more correctly, a good interpretation of drafting, is necessary, since the drawings and specifications must complement each other. The experience gained from having actually worked in one of the construction trades is invaluable. The ability to make accurate comparisons of manufacturers' data and claims for products is essential, as is a reasonable aptitude for writing. There are many sources to assist him in these requirements, but an interest in the challenge of writing specifications must be innate or kindled in a really good spec writer.

The size, shape, color, or texture of a material, or the finished appearance of a project, are not the only interests or responsibilities of the specifications writer. Probably one of the most important and least clearly defined is the item of cost. Any spec writer could take almost any project and, without a feeling for cost budget, specify materials and methods that would make construction prohibitively expensive. With some regard for cost he could hold to the budget, still provide quality installation, and adjust quality or quantity of materials. As soon as a preliminary construction cost estimate has been arrived at the specifications writer should know whether it is an economy range job, general average range, or luxury range, and he can specify accordingly.

The progressive architectural or engineering office should value the knowledge and experience of its specifications staff enough to include a spec representative at client meetings and staff meetings along with the project manager and designer. Project managers with good specifications backgrounds are rarely available and could use the assistance of specifications personnel. One of the biggest mistakes made by many offices is to postpone the introduction of the specifications writer to the project until the working drawings are nearly finished and then expect him to cover all materials and costs that were predetermined by someone else.

Specifications are specially written for a particular job. True, there are some "canned" specifications that are designed to be reused on similar projects, and there are "master specs" that are meant to be guides or dummies for many kinds of jobs, but the usual situation is for a document to be written with one individual project in mind. When specifications are intended to be reused on similar projects, they are written to cover the major but more common items of construction. This type of specification is most often used in connection with low-cost residential or tract construction where a great deal of the typical requirement is in the specification, and the more specific items are called out on the drawings. These specifications are often preprinted and may be purchased from stationers or blueprinting firms.

Master specifications are at the other extreme from the small preprinted or stock specification. The aim of a master spec is to include complete data on every type of material and method of installation that might ever be required. This seems a formidable task (and it is) but many firms use master specifications either of their own writing or purchased from some other source and revised to suit their needs. Because wide variations in climate, codes, availability, and preference require differences in materials and installation methods, no "canned" master spec can possibly be satisfactory throughout the entire country and must be individualized to fit the conditions under which the construction will take place. Notice the phrase "conditions under which the construction will take place." This is very important, since there may, and probably will, be differences of opinion between office site and construction site, especially when large offices operate at considerable distances from home base.

Thus we come to the special specification. This is a combination of the more standard or common materials or methods and the unique conditions of the project. *It fits one project and one project only.* It includes all of the materials and methods needed for every operation and space encompassed by the project. In most cases the specifications will be compiled from earlier project specifications, master specifications, manufacturers' literature, and accepted office preferences. In some cases the contractor or owner will have something to contribute in the form of material preferences or cost considerations. Properly combined, all of these bits of information will provide the data needed by the specifications writer to write a document setting forth all of the requirements for one particular project.

In the foregoing paragraphs we have referred to the specifications writer as an individual. Although this may be true in small offices, it is definitely not the case in larger offices. In the smaller office doing residential or small commercial work, the architect himself is often the designer, draftsman, spec writer, and field inspector. He designs and draws as he proceeds with the project, adding notes to the drawings and keeping in mind the few items he must cover by some sort of specification. Quite the reverse is true in the large office, where the specifications department may consist of ten or fifteen writers, several typists, and perhaps a librarian. If the office has its own structural, mechanical, or electrical engineering departments, these departments too will have specifications writers for their portions of the work. The writer assigned to the project must be able to coordinate the work of others, collect and properly assemble the bits and pieces, and assume responsibility for their accuracy of form and content.

The medium-sized office usually employs consultants for the various engineering phases of their work. When this happens, the office spec writer has the responsibility of coordinating the work of several persons with whom he has only intermittent contact. Many engineering offices do not have specially trained specifications writers; their methods "just grew." This situation may produce engineering specifications that are quite unlike the architectural specifications, that repeat conditions, or that are so general in content they will fit any job, not the one at hand. Often the structural engineer consultant will provide only a list of material requirements, allowing or forcing the architectural specifications writer to draw up the structural portions based upon the engineer's notes.

It is vitally important for the specifications writer to keep in mind who the specifications are written for. The contractor who is to build the project is most concerned, since he will have to interpret a set of drawings and the specifications (neither of which he has usually seen before) into a cost estimate, a bid for the work, and final construction if his bid is accepted. The many subcontractors, mechanics, and suppliers are also concerned in this process, since their costs are based upon the materials specified and the methods of installation required. The architect/engineer is also interested, since inadequate specifications may result in poor construction, cost differences, and other difficulties during construction. The owner has an interest, but usually not a professional one. He employs the architect/engineer to provide this knowledge. The owner is primarily interested in developing a project that lies within his budget and meets his basic requirements for space, appearance, and usability. Others have an interest only in regard to meeting minimum code requirements, financing possibilities, insurance, and similar items.

SUMMARY

Let us now quickly review this chapter. A specification is a combination of words properly describing the quality of a product, its method of manufacture, its installation into a project, and, in some cases, a description of the final result or appearance. Information for specifications is obtained from many sources, depending upon the subject. The specifications for a can of beans (can, beans, packing, label) are quite different from those required for construction materials, yet both serve the same purpose in defining quality. Specifications must be clear, definite, comprehensive, and even complex in some cases, but as understandable to those using them as though they themselves had written them. Specifications have many forms but all should be correct, so that no misunderstanding is possible. They should say what they mean, and mean what they say, so there can be no doubt about the ultimate outcome.

QUESTIONS

1.1. What major requirements typically belong in a specification?
1.2. Why are specifications termed "legal documents?"
1.3. For whom are specifications primarily written?
1.4. What abilities must a good spec writer generally possess?
1.5. What control over costs of a project does the specifications writer have, if any?

2

DRAWINGS
AND SPECIFICATIONS

Construction drawings and construction specifications are intended to complement each other in order to present the full requirements for the project. The general rule, "if it's shown in one place, do not repeat it somewhere else," is a good one to keep in mind, but certain items must be more strongly emphasized to make this rule stick. There are parts that should *never* be shown on drawings (metal gauges, methods of installation, tests), *sometimes* shown on drawings (types of materials, concrete strength), or *always* shown on drawings (plans, dimensions, details, and elevations). These rules of thumb also apply to specifications. Since, ordinarily the drawings and the specifications are not produced by the same people, a mutual understanding of who does what is a must if the project is to be properly coordinated, both in the office and in actual construction. A good rule of thumb to follow is that "*drawings* indicate *quantity* and *specifications* indicate *quality*."

THE DRAWINGS

Drawings consist of an orderly collection of lines, circles, symbols, dimensions, and notes that depict the size, order, general appearance, and details of a project. The weight or thickness of a line denotes its importance, and the length of the line indicates its use or juncture with some other surface or termination. While the practice of drafting is pretty much uniform, each office has its own peculiarities of lettering style, location of dimensions, and designation of doors, windows, and other features. These individual preferences generally do not conflict with the specifications, since they are considered to be strictly *drafting* items.

Drawings are a graphic description of the work to be done; the size and shape of a project plus a general indication of materials, their location in the project, their connections or details, along with a number of diagrams that depict the mechanical and/or electrical portions required. The drawings are all drawn to some scale or equation, with an inch, foot, meter, or other unit as the common measure. Together with any perspective or isometric drawings, the entire portion of the work that might be labeled *drawings* give a pictorial idea of the project. The drawings however should not, and normally do not, include such items as gauges of metals, specific trade names of materials, descriptions of processes, methods of installation, testing requirements, and similar items. These are specifications items and are not generally included on drawings.

DRAFTING SYMBOLS

The use of various symbols to designate materials or parts of a system is quite normal in architectural and engineering practice, but there really is no accepted universal code for these symbols. Several national organizations, various drafting handbooks, and general practice use sets of symbols that may be considered standards, but each office will probably have its own lists of abbreviations and symbols that they think best fit their office. Quite often these are indicated in an *Office Manual of Practice* along with weight of lines, section designations, office procedures of various kinds, and similar information. Every effort should be made to use the same symbol to mean the same thing in all situations, but because consulting engineers may do the drawings for the structural, mechanical, or electrical portions of a project, a standard symbol in their work may mean something different in some other type of work.

MATERIAL INDICATION

Combinations of lines, dots, irregular shapes, and solid coloring is known as *hatching* or *cross-hatching* when used to indicate materials. In the past this method was extensively used and is still used today in many offices to differentiate wood from steel, concrete from masonry, and earth from other materials. The value of such techniques is questionable and certainly requires considerable drafting time to accomplish properly. Some of the more common and acceptable hatchings are shown in Figure 2.1. These were done by straight drafting, but similar symbols are available in adhesive backed or rub on types that may be faster to apply if hatching is actually necessary.

Hatching is only of value when two different materials are shown in detail side by side or in a combination that might be confusing to the reader. Indicating wood-framed walls in an all-wood frame building by carefully drawn wavy lines, or methodically cross-hatching masonry walls at a diagonal in the drawing of a building made entirely of brick or concrete block is a waste of time and expensive to the architect or engineer. A much simpler method, which achieves the same result, is a solid *poché* of the walls. If there is a small amount of a different material, such as a masonry pier at a wood-frame wall, the pier may be hatched and will then stand out in the drawing.

Hatching on the face of the drawing is at best a poor procedure, since, if changes are necessary, both the elaborate hatching and the adjacent drawn lines must be erased and carefully replaced. Poché should be applied to the reverse side of the drawing, or, if hatching is unavoidable, hatch lines should be drawn on the back side of the sheet; then, if changes are necessary, poché can be erased or changed easily

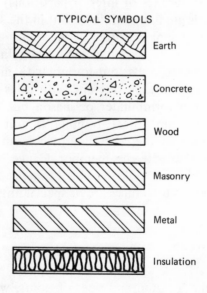

Figure 2.1 Typical symbols of some of the more common and acceptable hatchings used to indicate materials.

without changing a large area of drawn work. *Poché* is simply a solid shading of regular lead pencil or perhaps blue pencil. A paper stump shaped somewhat like a pencil is used to smooth the application, and some experience is required to evaluate the amount of poché required. Too little shading will not make the detail stand out, and too much may obliterate dimensions, arrows, or other indications when the drawing is printed.

DIMENSIONS

Dimensions on a drawing indicate the exact size of parts and should be accurately and prominently noted, since they control the size and shape of the project. Unfortunately, again there is no standard accepted method for dimensioning. In dimensioning *wood-frame buildings* the outer (length-overall) extreme is usually taken as the outside face of the stud rather than the extreme of the finished surface. This allows a little variation depending upon the finish material used (stucco, siding, shingles) and whether sheathing or rigid insulation is used. The most common practice in this country is to locate the interior walls by their center lines from the exterior stud face of the perimeter walls. In some areas, however, a different system indicates interior walls to one face of the interior stud, not to the centerline. In constructing a building by the first method (centerlines of interior partitions) the carpenter must of necessity cover his guiding chalklines, but in the second method they can be visible at one face or the other of the wall.

    Masonry and concrete buildings are usually dimensioned from the outer face of perimeter walls, out-to-out, with interior walls dimensioned to face of wall on each side and with thickness of wall shown. This is helpful to the formbuilder or mason but is slightly different from frame construction. Steel framing is still different. Steel is normally dimensioned to the centerline of columns or to a gauge line determined by the shape of the member. Gauge lines and centerlines are indicated in steel handbooks by exact dimension, but they should be checked where exact tolerances are of special importance.

BUILDING OPENINGS

Consideration of the location and sizes of doors, windows, and similar openings in the walls of a building again demonstrates to us the variations throughout drafting and construction practice. Windows and doors are manufactured to specific sizes, but again the material used or the methods of manufacture create some differences in dimensioning. Common practice in wood-frame construction is to dimension doors or windows to their centerlines; however this does not indicate the rough opening required. A window shown as 3⁻0 x 4⁻0 wood double-hung means that the net size of the wood sash, without the frame or clearance, is actually 36 in. wide by 48 in. high. The frame and any clearance will probably add at least 2 in. on each side, so the rough opening becomes 3 ft. 4 in. × 4 ft. 4 in. By using the centerline, plus adequate window details at large scale, the carpenter can allow for the rough opening required. Metal windows or doors installed in wood-frame have approximately the same requirements.

Masonry and concrete buildings usually have metal windows or doors included. The frames for these units are normally set by the mason or are set in the concrete formwork. Here the net size is particularly important, so these kinds of construction generally have openings shown to edge of opening, not to centerline. In masonry work, economies in construction may be realized by setting door and window openings as a module of the masonry unit. Locations in steel construction can be dimensioned either way, since the steel is usually only the frame, with some other material or system used to fill in the wall surfaces.

DRAFTING SCALE

In the United States, the foot is the unit on which measurements of length are based. Most other countries use the metric system based upon divisions of a meter, which is approximately thirty nine inches. Civil engineering in the United States uses the foot as a base unit, but divides it into tenths or hundredths of a foot or inch. Legislation introduced in 1972 will eventually change the foot-inch system into the metric system. This will take many years, since all manufacturing processes will have to be changed over, but a worldwide system may be the eventual result.

Most drawings are made to *scale*, that is at some ratio to the original or full size. Most sets of architectural or engineering drawings have portions shown at various scales, from ⅛ in. = 1 ft. 0 in.; ¼ in. = 1 ft. 0 in.; ½ in. = 1 ft. 0 in.; ¾ in. = 1 ft. 0 in.; 1 in. = 1 ft. 0 in.; 1½ in. = 1 ft. 0 in.; 3 in. = 1 ft. 0 in., and possibly full size or 12 in. = 1 ft. 0 in. Engineering drawings, primarily structural, are usually drawn at ½ in. = 1 ft. 0 in. or 1 in. = 1 ft. 0 in. Civil engineering drawings are normally at smaller scale, such as 1 in. = 20 ft. 0 in.; 1 in. = 40 ft. 0 in.; 1 in. = 100 ft. 0 in., etc., since they cover larger areas and a larger scale would make drawings nearly impossible. Architectural foundations, floor plans, elevations, and roof plans are usually depicted at ⅛ in. = 1 ft. 0 in. or ¼ in. = 1 ft. 0 in.; sections of buildings and some details at ¾ in. = 1 ft. 0 in.; and larger details at 1½ in. = 1 ft. 0 in. up to full size. In practice the information shown in a larger-scale drawing takes precedence over the same information shown in a smaller-scale drawing and a written dimension takes precedence over a scaled dimension.

CROSS-REFERENCING

Cross-referencing of architectural and structural drawings is almost a must. Since floor plans and elevations are usually drawn to a relatively small scale, any extensive and meaningful detail drawn at that same scale would be impossible to read properly. As mentioned before, these details are then drawn to a larger scale so as to be read more easily. In order to correlate the different scales, some type of cross-referencing system and proper symbols are required. Since the several parts of the complete set of drawings are usually spread over a number of sheets, it is necessary for a proper symbol to indicate the designation of both the sheet upon which the detail appears and the exact detail. Several types of reference symbols are shown in Figure 2.2.

Cross sections of a building attempt to show all, or most, of the conditions on a vertical or horizontal plane taken at the section line. To visualize this easily, think of a giant saw cutting the structure vertically from roof to foundation, or, in the case of a horizontal section, parallel to floors through all walls. These sections may be at small scale to show the relationship of various parts, or at larger scale to show details. See Fig. 2.2 for further clarification of section lines.

Another reference symbol often used is one indicating the several interior elevations of a room or space. Room elevations are normally drawn to ¼ in. = 1 ft. 0 in. or ½ in. = 1 ft. 0 in. scale and indicate what the various walls should look like when viewed from the center of the room. Usually at least four drawings are required, but in some cases the number may be reduced if a particular wall or walls have no special requirements. This is often the case when considering elevations of a residential bedroom, bath, kitchen, offices, halls, storage rooms, and similar spaces that are self-explanatory or duplicates of other rooms. Fig. 2.2 shows a possible floor plan and the referenced wall elevations indicated by the symbol in the center of the room.

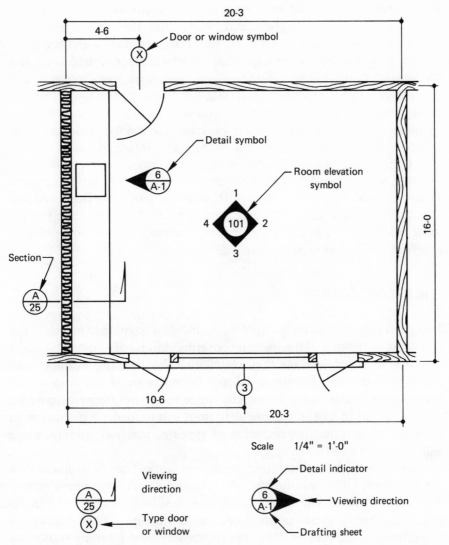

Scale   1/4" = 1'-0"

Figure 2.2. Several types of reference symbols used for cross reference in architectural and structural drawings.

SCHEDULES

For the specifications writer, *schedules* are possibly the most useful portions of a set of drawings. These include room-finish schedules, door and window schedules, equipment schedules, and various schedules for structural shapes or reinforcement, mechanical or electrical equipment. Unfortunately, schedules may be readily changed as ideas change, so they must be thoroughly checked to be sure they are reliable and haven't been altered. From a good room-finish schedule the specifications writer can tell accurately what materials are required for finish surfaces of floor, walls, ceiling, and in most cases trim, cabinets, and other items. From this knowledge and his own experience he will also know what materials or systems are necessary to support these finishes. In some cases the finish schedule may include colors, trade names or numbers, special requirements, and other useful information.

Other schedules are helpful in indicating sizes and types of doors and windows, materials for these items, and any special treatments. Reinforcement schedules show the sizes of bars, location, bending requirements, and similar details, and schedules of equipment often show physical sizes of units, power, venting, water, or drainage necessary, as well as manufacturers designations.

THE SPECIFICATIONS

Specifications have been interpreted in the past to include not only the actual specification information covering kinds of materials, their inclusion in the project and their installation, but also the legal forms of general conditions, supplemental conditions, special conditions, bid forms, bond forms, wage scales, etc. Since these later items are covered in some detail in Chapter 6, we shall limit this immediate discussion to the true specification requirements of types of material, quality, tests, and installation methods.

In general, all information regarding fabrication or manufacture quality, type, alloy, mix design, and similar details of a material should be a part of specifications and should *not* be shown on the drawings. In addition, the method or methods of installation, field testing or inspection, guarantees or warrantees, finishing, and cleaning should be included. These items should not overlap the information given on the drawings but should give additional detail. The method of connection, general location of materials, and, to a limited extent, the size and shape, as well as any other visual data should be shown on the drawings.

DEVIATIONS

In the past, specifications may not have been necessary as a separate document because of the more or less limited variety of materials, the local standard methods of installation, availability of materials, and the close personal contact between owner and builder or architect and contractor. To some extent this is still true today in limited localities or smaller types of projects, primarily residential. It is also very true in projects where the contractor or developer is building on speculation or for himself where a variable amount of freedom is desired to allow the builder to deviate from materials or to select others for which he may have a special buying power or personal preference.

In the case of the smaller residential project the architect may very well include all possible requirements for gauge of sheet metal, type material, grade and specie of lumber, thickness and face appearance of plywood and similar panel materials, and a great deal more of like information on his drawings. Concrete mixes, lists of plumbing fixtures by number, manufacturers names, and model numbers of various items may also be included, either by notes directly adjacent to the item or by tables or schedules on the drawings. When this is done the specifications shrink to a minimum size and quite often are stock-printed sheets outlining the standard requirements of codes or installation methods. All special conditions or material requirements are then indicated on the drawings. For minor projects there is nothing seriously wrong with this method, provided someone, the architect or the builder, is aware of the possible pitfalls due to the lack of a complete set of information and is able to compensate for this lack.

From the architect's standpoint this procedure is usually more costly, since the time consumed in lettering the information on the drawings is considerable. To offset this expense item some offices cut the standard drafting sheets into 8½ in. wide strips from top to bottom of the drafting sheet, have the information typed by the office stenographer on these sheets in their proper order, and then reassemble them with transparent tape. When these "specification" sheets are completed, they may then be printed and bound with the other sheets of drawings to form a complete set.

In the case of the speculative builder the conditions are somewhat similar but are determined by the latitude desired by the builder to substitute materials at will. Here the architect deliberately avoids detailed specifications of many products, or works very closely with the builder in the selection of them. This nondetailed specification allows the speculative builder an opportunity to select many materials on an availability or a cost basis. Since the primary objective of most speculative building is to produce a project at lowest cost for which there will be a market at a considerably higher sales price, the immediate substitution of reasonably similar products without the delays caused by the need for various approvals is desirable. Most often, the builder makes his selection based upon cost; this leaves the door wide open for considerable difference from what might originally have been intended by the architect.

ARCHITECT-CONTRACTOR COOPERATION

An increasing number of commercial projects are now underway where the contractor has been, or will be, selected prior to completion of the project documents. This is brought about by combinations of architect-engineer-contractor firms specializing in certain kinds of construction, or by the preference of an owner for a particular contracting company because of good past performance. This system has many advantages. The drawings, as well as the specifications, produced by the architect, are then guided by, or slanted toward, the methods and materials that the contractor has found to be most economical or easiest to install. By working closely with the contractor, the architect then can include only these items in his documents and may be able to reduce some portions of the specifications to material lists, leaving the installation methods to the contractor.

STANDARD DETAILS

Most specifications are reproduced for use on 8½ in. × 11 in. paper stock. Architectural or engineering offices that do a considerable amount of similar work quite often have *standard* details of repeated portions of the work also done on 8½ × 11 reproducible sheets, which are sometimes bound as a part of the specifications. These sheets, of course, are not specifications but drawings, however reproduced or assembled. They are a part of the *project manual* as are the *bid forms, bond forms*, and similar documents, yet the specifications writer must be fully aware of what they show so that he will not specify different materials or a different assembly of the detail. Even though they are accepted as *standard* details with the inference that they are identical on all projects, it must be quite apparent that minor changes do occur from one project to another. To this end a good review should be made of these details. Since these sheets are really drawings, they may often be bound separately from the specs or project manual, but the matter of coordination of details and materials shown remains a problem for the specifications writer.

DRAFTING NOTES

Regardless of the amount of cooperation between the drafting group and the specification writers there will usually be some questions about the information, or the lack of it, shown on the drawings. Ideally the specifications writer is a part of the team meeting with the owner along with the designer and the project manager. Actually this is usually not the case. In most situations, the specifications writer is notified about the project or has it dumped on his desk as a set of partially finished drawings at the 60 to 95 percent completed stage. As he reviews the drawings he is aware of details made by the draftsman, but they mean little or nothing to him, since he has no idea of the origin of the detail or the source of supply for the material. In addition, the draftsman may have been transferred to another project, left the office, or simply forgotten where he acquired the information shown on the drawing.

This confusion could easily be prevented. The draftsman or the project manager should have a system for keeping track of this information; this would be of great help to the specifications writer. Many draftsmen keep a list of details on a sheet of paper, giving the location of the detail on the drawings and the source of the information for those details. For example, "Sliding Door #1-XYZ catalog p. 53 type 100A" or "Drain cover–ABC Foundry–type 2024 C.I.-18 × 24." Together with the preliminary specifications and the notes the specifications writer has made during conferences or from conversations with designer or project manager, the final drafts of the specifications may be made. The drafting notes also help others working on the same project coordinate their efforts.

REFERENCE DRAWINGS

In the discussion on *drafting notes* we were concerned about detail drawings, made from manufacturers literature, showing the installation of a product as it should be in the actual project. This is usually the case, but occasionally a simple indication of a detail by lines or other symbols is drawn to small scale and is not enlarged or redrawn to indicate exact project conditions. Without some knowledge of the manufacturer, model or style number, size, or material, the specifications writer has but two choices; to search for some time until he finds the detail in some catalog, or to select one that may resemble the one at small scale. In either case he must then compare the proposed detail, not shown on the drawings, with the reference or symbol shown on the drawings and write his specification in a manner that will provide proper installation. This may lead to discrepancies between the ideas of the project manager and those of the specifications writer, discrepancies that could easily be avoided by proper notes from the project manager or attached to the drawings.

Another type of reference drawing is that provided by various manufacturing or trade associations. This is usually designed for use by mechanics installing or fabricating portions of the work and is at large enough scale and complete enough in detail to indicate the major problems that may be encountered. As with most standards, there is a tendency not to review these referenced details to make certain they fit the work perfectly but to assume that since they possibly cover all conditions, they do in fact do so. It is best to review all referenced drawings or other information and call any discrepancies with project requirements to the attention of the project manager. It is also good practice to write whatever information is necessary for correct and accurate specification directions for materials and installation.

CHECKING DRAWINGS

Checking drawings is possibly one of the least sought-after phases of any project development. In large offices special persons or groups do this work; in the smaller office perhaps the project manager or a senior draftsman does it; or perhaps no one does it on the assumption that each person has done his own checking. It requires an ability to visualize how the various pieces fit together, what the materials used will look like when installed, whether the structural, mechanical, or electrical systems can be installed as indicated, and a good knowledge of the governing building code that controls arrangement or materials. Whether the specifications writer is the one chosen to check will depend upon the office, but he certainly is in an ideal position to be of great help with little additional effort.

The specifications writer knows which materials or methods are proposed and should know if they comply with the code. He must of necessity review each plan, elevation, and detail so that any mistake or omission he sees can be easily noted for correction. He will almost always have a complete set of prints that have only minor work required for completion, including all of the engineering drawings. He is also an outsider by virtue of the fact that although he has a great deal of knowledge about the project, he has usually not worked on the drawings to the extent that he carries in his mind any of the detailing or requirements that should have been shown but somehow never were. A second checking is rarely amiss, so even if the office has a regular plan checker, the experienced specifications writer may be very helpful in catching errors before they leave the office.

BUILDING DEPARTMENTS

Nearly all incorporated cities or towns and most county or parish governments have some sort of building department offices that review applications for construction permits, check for code compliances, and collect fees. In most cases the applicable codes as well as the reviews are primarily concerned with aspects of health and safety and not usually with esthetics of a project. Custom and department requirements can vary greatly, since there are more than fifteen hundred codes in use throughout the U. S. Usually, however, proposed major buildings must be submitted with complete drawings as well as specifications. The experienced specifications writer should know the method of application for permits, the time required for review, and the procedure for *variance* or *use permit* if it is required. He also needs to know of other requirements by the fire marshall and others, such as, pollution control, soil erosion controls, or special engineering reviews.

SUMMARY

Working drawings and specifications *complement* each other and between them they should cover all conditions, materials, and requirements of the project. Although the specifications writer need not be an expert draftsman, a construction mechanic, or an expert writer, he should know how to read drawings, visualize the various construction steps, and be able to write reasonably well so that those reading his prose can understand what is required. As he becomes more experienced and proficient he should become more aware of building code requirements, costs of materials, and related work. As this proficiency builds up he will instinctively be able to visualize mentally the concealed parts of the construction, the processes by which the work will grow, the code requirements involved. He will also be able to quickly spot errors or other defects in the working drawings.

QUESTIONS

2.1. What two major kinds of information are indicated by the drawings?

2.2. What should the specifications indicate?

2.3. Is it possible to combine drawings and specifications in one document satisfactorily? How?

2.4. Is a detailed specification customarily provided in speculative or owner-builder contracts? Why?

2.5. Do you feel that 8½ in. × 11 in. sheets of standard construction details should be bound with the specifications? Explain.

2.6. Of what value are a draftsman's reference notes after he has drawn a detail?

2.7. Can you rely upon drafting details and specification notes supplied by manufacturers or trade associations?

2.8. Check procedures of your local building department and explain what happens when a building permit is applied for.

3

SOURCES
FOR INFORMATION

It should be obvious that the writer of specifications cannot, by any stretch of the imagination, have stored within his own memory a great deal of the information necessary to write a good specification. He will undoubtedly retain certain portions that have, by his experience, been repeated in past specifications, but he needs sources to augment this retained knowledge. Even if a master specification system is used, the information contained in it will need to be verified, changed, or supplemented for each project. Since the probability that projects such as hospitals, schools, or similar buildings will be identical is usually rather remote, specifications for these will also have to be changed as the situation demands. Therefore the specifications writer must know sources for information that will give him sound facts regarding products, installation, and related material that he can use to increase his already established knowledge.

These sources are numerous, and although some may be specialized, the majority are available for general use and can be relied upon by the specifications writer. In general they may be divided into a relatively few classes, namely testing methods, product standards, manufacturers catalogs, and trade association manuals. In each case the specifications writer must sift the information contained in the material to obtain that which applies to his particular project and section of the specification. This is sometimes rather difficult, but it must be done even with established standards, since many of these include a variety of materials or methods that may be acceptable as standards, but, because of availability, appearance, equality, or similar reasons, may not be used on a particular project.

In this chapter we will consider a typical sampling of source material, keeping in mind that *all are subject to revision* to make the information acceptable. In most cases the average architectural or engineering office will not have all of the types discussed readily at hand or may not have the clientele that would require all types. The specifications writer may supplement the office material with sources from his own private library or by occasional recourse to public libraries. Most public libraries, however, do not contain a great deal of this type of material. In addition, almost all printed material used as references by specifications writers is *dated* material, subject to continuous revisions and reissue and is therefore a greater burden upon a public library staff than most feel is warranted by the circulation it receives. This factor alone is a major drawback to the dependability of public library sources.

A word of caution is appropriate at this point to the office or specifications writer who may be thinking of establishing a library to contain immediately available reference material. A complete library, properly cataloged and readily available to office personnel, is a definite asset but requires both space and people to keep it operable. Nothing is more useless than an outdated catalog or report or one that has been misplaced or misfiled.

TESTING

Testing of materials, testing methods, and testing results are required in most specifications sections dealing with the structural materials used in a project. For the most part these are standards that have been established by industry committees, the various government agencies, or private enterprises recognized by the construction industry. The requirements reflect certain specific conditions that the tested materials must meet or exceed; the requirements may also indicate the exact procedures for the test methods to obtain these results. In either case a thorough inspection of the document or reference is necessary to insure that the project requirement is the same as that of the standard requirement. Two of the best known, and most used, of the testing organizations are the American Society for Testing and Materials (ASTM), and the Underwriters Laboratories Inc. (UL). ASTM has a much wider range of testing requirements than does UL, the latter being primarily concerned with fire safety, casualty hazards, and crime prevention. In general, ASTM does not do commercial testing itself but establishes the criteria for testing; the UL, on the other hand, does laboratory-controlled testing on typical components or equipment and provides a label service for the manufacturer of materials that successfully passes its testing procedures.

ASTM—American Society for Testing and Materials

ASTM describes itself as "An international, nonprofit, technical, scientific and educational society devoted to the promotion of knowlege of materials of engineering and the standardization of specifications and methods of testing." The reports of ASTM are referenced in construction documents as frequently as Federal Specifications or perhaps even more often. The *Book of ASTM Standards* (see Figure 3.1) consists of thirty-two parts or separate volumes and includes a wide variety of requirements and tests for manufactured

Rear:

Plastering Industry Promotion Bureau, San Francisco, Calif.
SWEETS 1972 Catalog (typical), Mc-Graw-Hill, New York.
SWEETS Light Construction 1970, McGraw-Hill, New York.
AEC Western Catalog, Times-Mirror Press, Los Angeles.
ASTM Standards (typical), American Society for Testing and Materials, Philadelphia, Pa.

Front:

ASTM Index to Standards, American Society for Testing and Materials, Philadelphia, Pa.
Structural Shapes, Bethlehem Steel Corp., Bethlehem, Pa.
Galvanized Reinforcement for Concrete, Zinc Institute Inc., New York.

Figure 3.1. Typical reference standards.

items such as petroleum products, textiles, automobile tires, plastics, soap, and most basic construction materials.

These reports are continuously updated and reissued, since about 30 percent of each part is new or revised with each review. Compliance with these standards by manufacturers is entirely voluntary, but such compliance provides a basis for comparison. The producer automatically gains prestige and users gain assurance when a manufacturer can say his product "complies with ASTM." A yearly *Index of Standards* is published, which lists all reports, tests, or papers both alphabetically and by designator numbers. This Index is almost indispensable to the professional specifications writer.

Reference to manufacturing or test requirements is by letter-numeral series such as *ASTM designator B-308* for *Aluminum alloy, standard structural shapes, rolled or extruded*. The basic designator, *B-308*, will be followed by a numeral such as *68* indicating the year of issue or by *68T* indicating a *tentative* issue of that date. As soon as a report has had a trial period for comment, it is revised and reissued without the *T* added. The original text and all changes are made by a committee selected from the industry specializing in the production of the material reported upon. Some reports and their designation of date may be several years old, but this simply means that revision was not deemed necessary since the original acceptance of the report. Copies of reports are available as single copies or in bound books of related materials. Since the complete set of documents includes many items never required in the average architect's or engineer's office, only about ten volumes relating to building products are normally considered. The same admonition regarding content of any report is again emphasized; however—*read the proper report to make sure it says exactly what you mean*!

ASTM references are usually not used on most residential or small commercial work, since only a few of these materials may require testing as indicated by local practice or building code. Larger commercial or industrial projects, schools, governmental construction, bridges, and specialized types of construction do however often require tests on concrete, reinforcement, steel, and many other items. Although the contractor who is building residential units has little use for a set of ASTM standards, the large construction companies engaged in multi-million-dollar programs use them regularly, since continual reference to ASTM requirements is made in specifications for these developments. With this thought in mind the specifications writer should then adjust his use of ASTM standards to the type and size of project and should preferably have a copy of the referenced document readily available to him to deal with any question of its meaning or conflict with the specifications as written by him. Since the various volumes are not published on a yearly basis or other regular schedule, but on a schedule determined by the amount of revision of previous documents, it is imperative that the architect-engineer as well as the constructor keep an up-to-date set for use. Membership in the society is open to individuals and organizations and includes discounts on documents as well as subscription to the monthly magazine and representation on appropriate industry committees.

Underwriters' Laboratories, Inc.

Founded in 1894, this nonprofit organization maintains and operates laboratories for testing of devices and systems. Four testing stations are maintained in the United States, each with its own specialized testing field, and more than 200 offices are located in other cities both here and abroad. Unlike ASTM, UL does not include such items as textiles, plastics, and soap except as they may be introduced as an element of a product undergoing UL testing. The primary fields of UL testing and inspection are *building materials, fire protection equipment, electrical appliances, electrical construction materials, hazardous location equipment, accident, automotive, and burglary protection equipment,* and *gas and oil equipment*, each covered by appropriate publications.

Testing of equipment or systems is done under strict laboratory conditions, and ratings are applicable only to *identical equipment or systems*. Listings of examinations are initially made on cards filed according to classification and guide number, and files containing these cards are maintained in the offices of principal boards of underwriters and inspection bureaus in the United States. Copies of these report cards are made available to the manufacturer of the product or system; a label service is also available. Of course, the manufacturer pays a fee for testing and a *follow-up* or *re-examination* service. These latter services tend to assure that the materials being manufactured *on production* are identical with those tested and approved. The label service provides the manufacturer with a visible identification on his product indicating type of material and serial or issue number. In addition to the card file, each general classification area has a booklet issued yearly, with bimonthly supplements, covering all materials tested and approved in that category. A caution here again; be certain that any tested-and-approved system is *identical* with one proposed before specifying any UL requirement. Any change voids the approval.

In order to follow a typical reference pattern let us look at the booklet on *Building Materials*. General classification is listed alphabetically, so we look at *Acoustical Materials*. Here we find a description of the requirements; *"fire hazard as shown . . . flame spread rating of 200 or less on both faces . . . in comparison with untreated red oak as 100 . . . Sound absorbing qualities, light reflectance, washability have not been investigated."*[1] Beneath these requirements are listed the various companies whose materials have been tested, each product identified by manufacturer's designation, and the results of tests for flame spread, fuel contributed, and smoke developed. These test results do not rate products as best, acceptable, or in any similar manner but do give results of tests that should be compared by the specifications writer. Where special integration of component parts is required, a simple sketch indicating these requirements accompanies the printed test outline. This again requires that the specifications writer properly compare UL arrangement with proposed project arrangement in order to compare "apples with apples."

Private Testing Laboratories

Testing laboratories as referred to in most construction documents are private corporations primarily organized to test materials for project requirements in accordance with some established standards such as those of ASTM. These laboratories are used for testing of concrete, reinforcing steel, steel structural shapes, and in some cases for soil or chemical tests. They charge a fee for their services, are usually under the direction of a registered engineer, and are usually dependable for the standard construction tests required. The specifications writer must spell out the number of tests required on each material, the standard (ASTM or ?) to be used, the time or place that samples should be taken, by whom (testing lab representative, contractor, job inspector, architect) and the distribution of the reports of the tests. Here again a word of caution; the architect-engineer should specify in detail the *number of tests* for each material. A statement that "all tests shall be paid for by the contractor" without telling him how many tests simply means that the contractor will guess at the number, crank some adequate amount into his bid, and either profit or lose by his guess. *Tell him what you expect!*

PRODUCT CATALOGS

Catalogs come in many shapes and sizes, give excellent, adequate, or even poor information, and may be combined as a sales implement with

[1] Underwriter's Lab Inc., "Building Materials List," 1969, p. 31.

some factual data. A great number of catalogs are devised by Madison Avenue advertising firms or by others who are more sales conscious than technically aware; these catalogs often contain color photographs and other material of little value to the specifications writer. Some of this literature may be of value to the design department, but the specifications writer needs more than the carefully photographed exterior of a major building to assist him in specifying the material used for the interior floor surfaces, acoustical treatment, or the plumbing items. Most offices will probably rely upon one or more of the several types of catalogs considered here, depending upon the kind of construction normal to their operation, volume of their business, space available for catalogs, and extent of their operating field, local, nationwide or international. A library of current manufacturers' catalogs is the mainstay of the specifications writer's reference material.

Sweet's Information Service

These catalog collections, probably the most used of all references, are simply volumes of manufacturers' printed catalogs, separated into various categories, indexed, and bound in convenient books. The series that will interest the specifications writer the most includes the *Architectural Catalog file*, the *Interior Design file*, the *Light Construction file* for small offices and some contractors, the *Industrial Construction file*, and possibly the *Plant Engineering file*. Canadian specifications writers should also have access to the *Canadian Construction Catalog file*. Most offices will have at least one of these files that best suits their type of business, but few offices will have all of them. In each case the general makeup is the same: catalogs supplied by each manufacturer are bound together with similar catalogs from other manufacturers of similar products. The various catalogs are not edited or changed in any way, so there is no uniform format for presentation nor any confirmation of claims made by manufacturers. Most of the manufacturers represented have nationwide distribution rather than local, and some of the firms with a wide variety of products have only token catalogs for their numerous materials. The cost of assembling and distribution is indirectly borne by the manufacturer, and the books are distributed at no charge to architectural or engineering firms doing more than a set minimum of business. Because of this required minimum many smaller offices do not receive the yearly editions and use older copies obtained from larger offices as their source of reference.

The use of the catalogs is quite simple. In earlier editions the catalogs were divided into thirty-eight sections arbitrarily set up by the assembler/publisher. These had no relation to any accepted specification format. Since 1971, the *Architectural Catalog file* has been arranged in the order of the *Uniform System*. Each volume has the same index in the front of the book, each indicating in separate listings the firm name, the product, and the trade name. Therefore, if a specifications writer knows any one of these he can easily find the correct catalog in the correct book. Since many offices may still be using the old system, let us look at an example for both the pre-1971 issues as well as those latter ones using the Uniform System divisions.

Pre 1971

Firm name: Roberts and Johnson Inc. 10C/Ro
Firm name is known but trade name is not. 10 indicates section 10; C indicates portion C; Ro is first two letters of company name.

Product: Insulation 10
Firm name or trade name not known. 10 will give catalog section for all types of insulation regardless of manufacturer.

Trade name: ELASTOFIBRE (insulation) 10C/Ro
Trade name is known but manufacturer is not. Same details of designator as for firm name.

Post 1971 (Uniform System)

Firm name: Timber Structures Inc. 6.5/Tim
This designation is basically the same as the old system except the section now is indicated by a decimal part of the sixteen divisions of the Uniform System. TIM are the first three letters of the firm name.

Product: Roof construction-wood Timber Structures 6.5/Tim
This is an improvement over the old system, as each firm is noted by name and division designator along with similar information for other companies producing a similar product.

Trade name: TIM-PLANK (heavy timber decking) 6.5/Tim
This identifier remains essentially the same as under the old system except for the decimal division number.

In addition to the three types of index in the front of each book there appears an index of firms, products, and trade names before each division in each book. These relate only to the following division and not to the entire book or file. With only a limited knowledge of the kind of product, a manufacturer's name, or a trademark name, it is possible to easily find an appropriate catalog, provided of course that the manufacturer has subscribed to Sweet's Catalog service. In addition to the manufacturer there are a number of trade associations with catalogs, and these may be located in the same manner, except they probably will not have a trade name since they represent a number of manufacturers.

Three major disadvantages are involved with Sweet's catalogs. First, the minimum value of construction designed by an office to be eligible to receive the catalogs is quite high, thereby eliminating a good many offices doing good work but not necessarily large projects. Second, most of the manufacturers who do not distribute nationwide are not included. This means some firms with good products locally available may have to be located by other means than use of Sweet's. Third, the various *manufacturers prepare their catalogs perhaps twelve to eighteen months before they are distributed* as Sweet's catalogs. Even with the shortest lapse this means that the references are out of date by this overlap time when they are received in the architectural or engineering office. Specified products may have been changed, model numbers rearranged, or the item may no longer be in production in this intervening time, causing problems and change orders during bidding or construction. A fourth problem occurs only with the free-lance specifications consultant. Since his office does not actually function as the *prime contractor* in the design of a building he cannot truthfully indicate that his office has participated in *x*-dollars of construction per year. This means that he is not presently eligible to receive Sweet's files but must rely upon those of his clients or an old set. This matter is currently being considered for change, since the specifications consultant possibly writes specifications for a larger volume of construction than many of the largest architect/engineer offices.

Local Catalog Collections

One of the disadvantages of Sweet's catalog file, as noted before, is the fact that few local manufacturers are represented. This has caused several *local* or area collections to be made into books similar to Sweet's catalogs. These generally are considerably smaller in volume than Sweet's but may be just as useful to the specifier. In some cases they may be even more useful, since they include only manufacturers whose product is *locally* available, which most often means lower prices caused by lower shipping costs; by the same token the availability often means less difficulty in shipping time, both of which should be important to the specifier.

One of the most prominent of the *local* catalog collections is the AEC book compiled by Mirror Press, Los Angeles, Calif. This collection was one of the first to use the *CSI 16 DIVISION* arrangement and is usually provided in one volume. Most of the included manufacturers' catalogs are small, seldom more than six or eight pages, and are representative of manufacturers in the southern California area who do not distribute their products outside of the western United States. Similar collections exist in other areas representing strictly local suppliers.

Manufacturers' Catalogs

With Sweet's catalogs and the local versions it might seem that few additional manufacturers' catalogs would be desirable; however, the reverse is true. Many manufacturers are not represented by either of the previously discussed methods or have such extensive fields of products that it is economically not feasible to pay a per-page fee for inclusion in Sweet's or other collections. Most of the larger manufacturers also have developed reliable and knowledgeable *manufacturer's representatives* who visit design offices at fairly regular intervals.

Individual manufacturer's catalogs usually contain more information than those from the same manufacturer bound in collections. More and more catalogs are being prepared in loose-leaf hard-bound binders for ease of handling and shelf storage. This allows easy updating of material by the manufacturer's representative or the design office. In some cases organizations have been formed that relieve the manufacturer of this chore by having attractive, educated girls distribute their literature and update their catalogs. Most manufacturers are now identifying their catalogs under the *Uniform System* (see Figure 3.2) so they may be most conveniently shelf-stored by division numbers. There still remain many small firms producing only a few items, all good in their respective field or unique in design or use, whose catalogs consist of only a few pages. These may be combined in binders for shelf reference or filed in manila folders for drawer storage, each prominently identified with proper division numbers.

A principal drawback in many manufacturer's catalogs is that they are produced for general advertising and do not present data conveniently to the architect or engineer. This means that careful selections and frequent updating of material is necessary to prevent unused catalogs taking valuable space. One way to reduce this volume and at the same time provide easily accessible information is through use of a collection of SPEC-DATA sheets.

32

Rear:

The Construction Specifier, Monthly magazine of the Institute.

Front:

The Uniform System for Construction Specifications, Data Filing and Cost Accounting.
Typical Monograph of CSI, Tooled Concrete Finishes, Construction Specifications Institute, Washington, D.C.

Figure 3.2. Construction Specifications Institute references.

SPEC-DATA Sheets

Around 1960 a program for the presentation of manufacturers' information was devised and copyrighted by Producers Council Inc., a national organization of producers of building products. For several reasons the system was never developed but was eventually sold to the Construction Specifications Institute, which expanded it and has continued it as a service to both manufacturer and specifier. Essentially it is a method of presenting, in concise form, information on building products of manufacturers, free of advertising and arranged in identical order in each case on a limited number of pages. A small fee is paid by the manufacturer to CSI for use of the copyright title and a review of format. Distribution is made by CSI to its members and by the respective manufacturers to others upon request.

Each SPEC-DATA is presented in ten parts, always in the same order: 1) product name; 2) manufacturer; 3) product description; 4) technical data; 5) installation; 6) availability and cost; 7) guarantee; 8) maintenance; 9) technical services; and 10) filing systems. The number of pages is generally limited to four with limited photographs or illustrations. None of the usual advertising illustrations such as pretty girls, dogs, scenery, or similar works of art are allowed. All information must be presented in as straightforward and simple a manner as possible. Pages are heavy stock 8½ in. × 11 in., printed black on colored paper, three-hole punched. They carry along the right-hand margin the Uniform System division number, date of issue, name of company, and name of product described. By the simple expedient of eliminating the advertising, SPEC-DATA becomes a quick, factual method for obtaining information. SPEC-DATA II is a further step for those who have microfilm scanning equipment available. Information Handling Services Inc. provides microfilm of the various available sheets.

The SPEC-DATA catalog is divided into the sixteen divisions, with separate sections under the division heading and with subheadings indicating products or methods. Part I lists the manufacturer by name, product by trade name, and date of issue of the SPEC-DATA sheet. Part II of the catalog lists the names and addresses of manufacturers alphabetically so that requests for sheets may be made directly to the manufacturer or through CSI by use of a request card which is included in the catalog.

GOVERNMENTAL SOURCES

The United States government is a good source of information, since nearly every department has both specialized and general publications. (See Figure 3.3) Of the latter, three are probably most used: Federal Specifications, Military Specifications, and Department of Commerce Standards. These number in the thousands and cover a wide variety of subjects, a great many of which have no relation to the construction industry. Copies of Federal Specifications and Military Specifications are supplied free to offices engaged in work that requires them, or they may be purchased for a small fee from the Government Printing Office. Commercial standards may be obtained from the Department of Commerce or the Government Printing Office. Other departments or bureaus that have available literature are the Department of Agriculture, the Wood Products Laboratory, the Indian Service Bureau, and the United States Postal Service. The United States Navy Public Works Department, the United States Army Corps of Engineers, NASA, and similar organizations use Federal or Military Specifications together with local variations.

Rear:

Index of Federal Specifications and Standards, Supt. of Documents, Washington, D.C.

Front:

Building Materials List, Underwriters' Laboratories Inc., Chicago, Ill.
Uniform Building Code, International Conference of Building Officials, Pasadena, Calif.
Standard Specifications, State of California, Dept. of Public Works, Div. of Highways, Sacramento, Calif.
General Industry Safety Orders, California Div. of Highways, Sacramento, Calif.
Construction Safety Orders, California Div. of Industrial Safety, Sacramento, Calif.

Figure 3.3. Government references.

Federal Specifications

These standards include requirements for minimum compliance to provide the materials indicated. The requirements generally allow a wide range of quality; thus the architect or engineer finds it difficult to design or specify to other than minimum standards. The gamut of subjects ranges from "Abrasive paste, dental, P-A-86a" to "Zinc-yellow, dry (paint pigment) TT-P-465," including specifications for canned fruit, typewriter ribbons, truck tires, and construction materials, among others. Each report is dated and identified with a three-component designator in the following order: an alphabetical symbol, the initial letter in the title of the specification, and a serial number. Revisions are made by the indication of a small letter following the serial number and a new date, both appearing in the upper right hand corner of the first page.

Federal specifications used for construction require careful reading and editing. Most contain every possible material or process that might produce the product in order to allow the utmost competition in bidding; the specifications writer must select only the portions applicable to the project. The text of the Federal Specification must be copied "cold" so far as possible when used in government work, so a thorough review is necessary. In addition to the use of Federal specifications for governmental work, they are referenced in many other specifications. Unfortunately some specifications writers use them more as standards without knowing their actual content.

As a supplement to some Federal specifications, local governmental facilities often issue their own revisions, because of differences in scope or process dictated by climatic or other conditions. Two of the most common of these are in relation to soil conditions (excavation, back-fill, compaction, landscape work) and roofing. These revised or local specifications take precedence over the national issue and should be read carefully and adhered to implicitly if possible.

Military Specifications

These are considerably more limited in scope than Federal specifications but still include items like ice cream mix, paint remover, kraft paper, as well as many construction items. Military specifications also have a three-part designator starting with MIL followed by the first letter of the subject and a number, such as "MIL-R-3423A roofing felt, in rolls, packaging of." Although Federal specifications are listed by the *first alphabetical symbol* in the government index, Military specifications are listed by *numerical sequence*. In general, Military specifications include more directions for crating or handling and fewer specifications for materials or their fabrication than do Federal specifications.

Military specifications are used in conjunction with Federal specifications and should have the same close review. In almost every case of a material or a condition of construction one or the other will apply and the specifications writer will often have to select the one that best defines the project conditions. Again, as in use of Federal specifications, the text of the official copy is to be copied "cold," with minimum revision in any part. Also, as is the case when using Federal Specifications, direct reference to the original source of requirements ("as required by MIL-R-3423A") is not desirable, so the specifications writer may need to rewrite portions in the style of someone else in order to have any continuity.

Bureau of Yards and Docks and Corps of Engineers

These two agencies are the primary representatives for the United States Navy and the United States Army respectively. Under their general supervision are area offices of *public works, facilities command,* and other titles whose principal operation is the selection of A/E's, review of drawings, and specifications for military construction in their areas, as well as the inspection of such construction. In the course of this planning and construction supervision, each has developed some additional *guides* that are to be used in connection with the writing of specifications for military construction. These guides, too, require close review, since many of them could spell trouble in big doses if the content were not cropped to meet the project requirements. A case in point is the Bureau of Yards and Docks 10Y-Metal Windows. This document includes the description and specifications for nearly every type of metal window ever made, in steel, aluminum, bronze, or other metals. In order to specify the correct project window, a major part of the entire document must be deleted.

Commercial Standards

These standards are produced by the United States Department of Commerce and are more like manufacturers' information than government specifications. They are in fact established standards for a considerable number of different items used in construction by which a manufactured product may be judged for quality or appearance. Commercial standards, or *commodity standards* as they are sometimes known, cover such products as wood doors, wood windows, plywood, and similar materials; they may include not only final appearance or function requirements but manufacturing methods and testing procedures as well.

Federal Housing Administration

The federal government has for years engaged in a program of mortgage insurance through this agency. The program is limited to residential and low-cost housing and requires that drawings and specifications for this work be processed through the FHA. They, like many other federal agencies, have specific requirements for materials and methods of installation. Combinations of Federal specifications, Military specifications, commercial standards, ASTM standards and others are used under specific restraints. The FHA issues guide handbooks for use by those who design residential units under the FHA program. Local housing authorities also often depend upon the rules and regulations of the FHA in their evaluations of proposed housing projects.

TRADE ASSOCIATIONS

There are many trade associations connected with the construction industry, both in the manufacture of the various products used and their design and installation. Nearly all of these associations issue publications useful to the specifications writer either in the form of standards, stock specifications, how-to-do-it bulletins, or similar material. (See Figure 3.4.) Since an association is composed of members from various companies, the literature available must be fairly open in content, accurate to allow all members to approve it, and specific enough to be useful. Sometimes the information presented in association publications can only be found through extensive research that may require data from several manufacturers and preparation of original comparisons.

The specifications writer will find most useful association booklets listing accepted sizes of materials, finishes applied to various metals,

Rear:

Designing with Wood, American Inst. of Timber Construction, American Plywood Assoc., Western Wood Preservers Inst., Western Wood Products Assoc., Manual of Millwork, Woodwork Inst. of California, Fresno, Calif.

Front:

Architectural Metals Finishes Manual, National Assoc. of Architectural Metal Manufacturers, Chicago, Ill.
Concrete Masonry Handbook, Portland Cement Assoc., Skokie, Ill.
Sound Control Construction, United States Gypsum Co., Chicago, Ill.
National Design Specifications, National Forest Products Assoc., Washington, D.C.
Design and Control of Concrete Mixtures, Portland Cement Assoc., Skokie, Ill.

Figure 3.4. Manufacturers' and Association references.

anodizing designations for aluminum parts, and lists of wood species available for structural as well as finishing use. Door and window associations have developed standards for size designations, wind and weatherproofing tests, and suggested best methods for installation. The glazed tile industry has compiled a large amount of data on proper installations; this data can almost be considered standards to be referenced by the specifications writer. The glass manufacturers do have such standards, which may be used by simple reference to require proper installation.

Since there are thousands of these associations in existence it is almost impossible to list them all, but some of the larger and more useful are listed in the Appendix of this book. A word of caution should again be repeated here in the use of standards or other material provided by associations—*read the material referenced in the specification*! It may not completely fit the requirements of the project, or it may have alternates generally acceptable to the trade but not specifically acceptable to the architect or engineer. Often trade association literature makes reference to Federal specifications or ASTM standards, so these also must be reviewed to be sure of proper meaning.

OTHER SOURCES

There are many other sources for information but the several listed below are neither governmental, manufacturing, or trade associations. They are nonprofit, construction-wide, regulatory or testing in origin, and have the stability and standing to be used with confidence as references by the strictest interpretation. Although these organizations are listed here last they are by no means last in importance; probably the reverse is true. As regulatory or testing groups they have a legal or quasi-legal standing and determine what may or may not be acceptable in construction work.

Building codes of one type or another are used to define most of the requirements for the health, safety, and welfare of those using buildings. At present there are approximately 1,500 separate building codes in use in the United States, with an equal or greater number of specialized codes for schools, hospitals, industry, and transportation. Because of this great number of codes it is impossible to discuss any one or several. The specifications writer must become familiar with his local code, together with any local revisions, in order to know which materials may be accepted for various uses. Special codes for the construction of schools, hospitals, etc., usually have additional requirements that are more comprehensive than the standard building code they supplement, and these should be thoroughly understood. The major codes list or otherwise restrict certain materials for certain uses, and often have a companion volume to the code that lists or describes the accepted materials. Manufacturers who develop new products or produce those that may not be on the *approved* list will submit test data and other information to the code authority for approval of their product. Services have been developed to provide card-file systems to distribute such approvals between publication dates of codes, and specifications writers should be aware of such approvals or rejections before incorporating questioned items into a specification.

Safety codes are governmental (usually state) requirements for protection of human life against fire, accident or extreme damage to property that are sometimes overlooked by specifications writers. These codes spell out the materials acceptable for elevator enclosures, stair wells, and boiler and heater rooms, as well as the precautions required to prevent accidents during construction. State or local fire marshals usually review the drawings and specifications for major buildings, and their interpretation of fire codes is a factor in determining acceptability of materials used. The designs of oil refineries, acid plants, explosives factories, and other high danger installations require a special review of all requirements.

Highway commissions have a special set of specifications for construction of sub-base, paving, culverts, bridges, guard rails, and other portions and devices directly related to highway construction. The specifications writer can make good use of these accepted specifications when setting forth requirements for grading, back-fill, earth compaction, paving work, and other highway-related construction. The subcontractor who normally does this work on a building project undoubtedly has done highway construction and knows the requirements and the references to them. When using these documents, however, it is still good practice to double check with the local offices of the highway department or local paving contractors for special requirements caused by soil conditions or climatic variances.

Insurance companies too have a big stake in the construction industry and have established definite requirements for safety, particularly fire safety. Safety of construction personnel is usually covered by state *Safety Orders*, which need not be cited in specifications, but, by specifying one type of material over another type, a specifications writer may considerably increase or decrease the amount of insurance premium that the building owner must pay. The premium is usually not set until application for insurance is made after the construction is completed, but by that time a major change in materials or their application is virtually impossible. A review of proposed materials with an insurance consultant before bid time is at hand is often a wise move.

SUMMARY

With experience the specifications writer will develop his own system of reliance upon several sources for information. These sources are greater than could possibly be given completely here or in any other book. It is possible to have too few and become case-hardened to any other influence, continuing to use only those most readily available or those that have caused the fewest problems. It is also possible to have too many sources, current-dated as well as past-dated, sources that are pertinent to the project and some that may be retained for that future "maybe" job. Nothing has been said in this chapter about reuse of old office specifications as a reference for new project specifications. This is an obvious source, since every specifications writer or A/E office sooner or later has an overabundance of old specs for reference. This is great—as long as only the acceptable information is used, the reference material is pertinent to the project at hand, and the mistakes are deleted or corrected. Too often elevator specifications from a ten-story office building are included in a hastily written specification for a one-story building, or masonry work is specified when a building is completely frame construction. *Make the specification fit the project. Read the standard before you use it.* It may not fit your project conditions, or worse yet, it may indicate the opposite from your requirements and intentions.

QUESTIONS

3.1. Discuss some advantages, and some disadvantages, in using Sweet's catalog files.
3.2. How is the information in a SPEC-DATA sheet arranged?
3.3. What are the principal specifications published by the United States government? How do they differ?
3.4. Do you feel that information in trade-association documents is reliable? Why?
3.5. Select a building product test report by ASTM and describe how to find it by title and by designator.

4

TYPES
OF SPECIFICATIONS

There are several types of specifications that the architect/engineer specifications writer should know, since each has its function. The proper type is usually determined by the use to which the material will be put, or in some cases by the agency or client for the project. The latter is especially true when the client is a governmental agency or speculative builder. Let us then investigate these types of specifications here.

CLOSED VS. OPEN SPECS

In general, most specifications can be classed as either *closed specifications* or *open specifications*, with a number of variations of each. For the most part it is the list of materials required for the work that determines *closed* or *open*. Simply stated, a *closed specification* is one in which only one material or process appears, or in which a description of a material is so detailed that only one product can qualify for use. The *open specification* on the other hand is one that allows the use of a number of products that the specifications writer deems equal and acceptable for the work.

An example of a *closed specification* may state: "Asphalt floor tile, 12 in. × 12 in. × ⅛ in., marbleized, grade *C*, as manufactured by XYZ Corp." This requirement would allow only floor tile made by the XYZ Corp., meeting the other qualities noted, and no other tile by any other manufacturer would be accepted. Another method of writing a closed specification is to call out peculiarities of manufacture or appearance in detail so that only one product could be supplied. An example of this might be: "Casings shall be 17 ga. galvanized steel sheet, factory prime coated 2.5 mils thick with ABC primer each side, baby blue color #1234, secured with $1\frac{1}{16}$ in. long by ¼ in. diameter flat head stainless steel screws at 3-$\frac{3}{16}$ in. o.c. etc." This example makes it possible for several manufacturers to provide the material, but only if they customarily produced the product that met all of the requirements or if they cared to produce on special order. The items that make this a closed specification are the requirement for 17 ga. metal and the rather detailed coating and fastening specified. Competitive products may meet several of the above requirements but perhaps only one manufacturer will meet all of the requirements.

Closed specifications are not necessarily undesirable, depending upon how they are used. A specification provided by a manufacturer is usually a closed specification or very near to it. This, of course, is to point out the special methods or materials that may not also be used by a competitive manufacturer. In the case of much remodeling or some work that must match existing work, the closed specification is desirable. In either of these cases the new work is to match that already in place, so only a matching product may be used. An example of a *good* closed specification would be "Electric clocks shall be 16 in. diam. type #1000 mfgd. by Eleco Clock Co. to match existing," where clocks in a school complex were required to be alike. This is often a concession to maintenance, since a number of different types of clocks would mean many different kinds of different repair parts to keep them operating. A closed specification is *bad* when it limits competition to the extent that costs are increased or when it allows only inferior prod-ucts that may not be completely familiar to the spec writer. Most manufacturers feel that a closed specification is usually not fair to competition—unless they happen to be the manufacturer specified. Owners also take a dim view of closed specifications, feeling that it allows or forces costs upwards.

An *open specification*, on the other hand, theoretically allows competition to supply a material or product within broad limits of equality. For example, the specification may state: "Asphalt floor tile,

12 in. × 12 in. × ⅛ in., marbleized grade *C* color as selected by architect, complying with requirements of Fed. Spec. SS-T-306." The requirements of Federal Specifications are set up by the United States government in an effort to eliminate trade names or particular manufacturers and to establish minimum standards for a wide variety of materials that may be used as long as they meet these standards. Another method is to name several brands or manufacturers of a product as: "Asphalt floor tile, 12 in. × 12 in. × ⅛ in., marbleized, grade *C* as manufactured by ABC Co.; Def Co.; G.Hi Co." In the first example the specifications writer has, by reference to a Federal Specification or similar standard, satisfied himself that any material meeting those standards will do the job. In the second example the specifications writer has selected three or more manufacturers whose product is familiar and would be acceptable.

THE "OR EQUAL" CLAUSE

At this point it would be a good idea to discuss the much maligned *or equal clause*, since it may tie in directly to open specifications. In the construction industry few items could actually be termed *equal*, since each product manufacturer tries to incorporate certain differences and supposed advantages over that of his competitor; yet the words *or equal* appear time after time in the requirements for materials and are in fact required by some states wherever public money is involved in the construction. This is of course an attempt to allow a wider choice among the products of taxpaying firms. Generally the use of *or equal* is a poor effort to allow bidding by all comers on a specified product selected beforehand. The burden of proving equality is usually on the supplier, but the architect or engineer involved must approve or disapprove substitutions or allow the contractor a free rein, with possible damage to the project resulting if substitutions are not relatively equal.

If the *or equal* clause must be used it is suggested that it be worded *or approved equal*, with approval for such substitution being in the hands of the architect or engineer. This can be required as a paragraph in the General Conditions or Supplemental Conditions, which should spell out exactly how submittals for *equal* consideration would be made and exactly who would approve such submittals. When a specifications writer does his research job properly on products he may favor, there should be no need to use *or approved equal*, since he has indicated the various manufacturers of those products he considers most nearly alike and acceptable to him by specifying these prior to stating *or approved equal.* Where such a phrase is required by law there is no alternative except to use it and then determine if any submitted substitutions are nearly equal.

MANUFACTURER'S SPECIFICATION

Many manufacturers of building materials have had specifications written for their various products as an assistance to the busy specifications writer and as a guide to potential purchasers of their material. These specs are most often written by professionals, but occasionally they are done by advertising agency people. In the first case the experienced specifications writer will carefully read for words or phrases that, if not found and omitted, might make a closed specification for the material, in favor of the manufacturer supplying the information. Specifications for special features of design, fabrication, or finish not provided by similar competitive products might be carefully worded to convey the idea that they were not so special that they excluded others. In the material provided by advertising agencies the data may range from very useful to complete junk; often this type of material is really not intended for the professional architect or engineer, but is simply meant to advertise to the general public.

In writing about manufacturer's specifications we should hasten to restate the reliance of the specifications writer upon the vast pool of knowledge available through the cooperation of the manufacturer's architectural representatives. For the most part these men and women are professionals in their fields, and even though they are constantly trying to stimulate increased sales of their particular employer's product, they have an excellent knowledge of their own products as well as those of their competitors. If a manufacturer's *guide specification* seems *closed* or incorrect, these manufacturers reps can usually be relied upon to clarify it, whether it is their own or that supplied by someone else.

Possibly the most important thing to remember about manufacturer's specifications is that they are written to sell their particular product by presenting the best qualifications, and in most cases they fail to mention any deficiencies. Most data supplied by manufacturers therefore must be suspect as *closed* unless the specifications writer uses it only as a guide and compares several guide specifications by different companies, on the same subject, and then writes his own information gleaned from these sources. This sifting and reassembling is obviously not necessary if a closed specification is desired for matching existing work or as an option of the client.

FEDERAL SPECIFICATIONS

As mentioned in Chapter 3, the United States government has a very complete, and somewhat complex, system of specification guides that are provided to the A/E specification writer for each project. These are both guides and masters from which to copy portions as they apply to the project. They are strictly *open* specifications, since no manufacturer's name or trade name is allowed and materials are required to meet the conditions set forth in the referenced Federal Specification. These requirements are quite lenient and allow both quality manufacturers and marginal manufacturers to supply materials. This means that the best quality will not usually be supplied on a project, since the manufacturer with the lowest price who is still able to meet the minimal requirements will get the work. The principal reason for having such an open specification is the same old story of giving everyone an equal chance, but there may be adequate reason to feel, at least among A/E's doing work for the government, that their efforts to produce a good design are often sabotaged when they realize that any or several products that have been incorporated may be summarily replaced by an "equal" but inferior product that barely meets the Federal Specification.

On rare occasions where a special product or system must be used on a governmental project, and that product is not included in a standard Federal Specification, or is required to match or exactly install in a special manner, the specifications writer may write his own requirements. In doing this he must refrain from manufacturer's or trade names and rely solely upon his written description. This description may include very precise phrasing to allow only one product, but it must be complete enough to rule out any others submitted. This portion then becomes a very closed specification within what essentially is a very open specification. This method may be legitimately used when matching existing work or when only one particular product will satisfy esthetic or operating desires.

One additional qualification contained in governmental specifications, either by direct statement or reference, is the prevention of use on a *public-financed* project of materials manufactured in some foreign countries. This ruling is the result of economic trade balances and political attitudes and applies even though the proposed product meets every Federal Specification requirement except place of manufacture. To further confuse the issue, there often is no clear-cut decision as to whether a finished product is *Mfg. in U.S.A.* Many companies in the United States have subsidiary plants in foreign countries manufacturing parts that are then shipped to the United States and finally incorporated into the finished product here. Is this then a product from a foreign country or is it a domestic product? To avoid embarrassment, the specifications writer should check in advance on any product that might be suspect of foreign manufacture.

COMMERCIAL SPECIFICATIONS

Commercial specifications (those not governmentally financed) may be either *closed, open*, or somewhere between. Since the money to build the project is not public money, there is no inherent requirement that all manufacturers be eligible to supply their products. In most cases commercial specifications would probably be classed as *modified open* or perhaps *modified closed*, depending upon individual preference. The specifications writer will select several manufacturers, usually at least three, whose product he is familiar with, the quality, appearance, or other features of which fit the project. The method of listing these manufacturers has already been given in the discussion on open specifications earlier in this chapter.

There is of course no legal deterrent to prevent a commercial specification for a project to be a closed one. Many times an owner has a preference for a particular product because of its good past performance on other projects. He may also be a stockholder in a manufacturing company and wishes to use that company's product. With the diversified combinations now found in industry it often happens that one company owns or is a subsidiary of another whose product it wishes to use. There is nothing wrong with writing a closed specification in these cases, provided the material proposed will do the job properly.

This commercial type of specification, or open type if you prefer, is most used in other than public-financed work today. The specifications writer, with some guidance from designers, office preference, location of the project, and materials available in that location, will determine to the best of his ability exactly which products will best meet the specific requirements of the project. In order to do this in a professional manner he will have to rely a great deal upon his experience. For this reason he should continuously keep himself up-to-date by using project inspector's reports to see if there were any problems the last time a material was used, by maintaining contact with contractor friends to see if they have had any purchasing, shipping, or installation problems with a certain product or method, and with manufacturers' representatives to determine if what he has been specifying is still the proper item or if it has been replaced by a newer one, a different model or an entirely new product.

One irritating factor that often creeps into poorly researched specifications is the local availability of a product. This may be particularly important where projects are at some distance from the home office where the specifications writer is actually working. For a project in California, the specifications might very well call for three products of similar quality but all manufactured on the east coast. If these products were not well represented by California distributors or manufacturer's warehouses there is every possibility that delays in delivery, model changes, or even basic design might occur to hold up completion of the project. This of course should not be, and usually is not, true of well-distributed or nationally warehoused products. Occasionally the reverse is true, when a specifications writer has a preference for a product, manufactured in his local area but not nationally distributed, that is specified for a project at some distant location. This makes for difficulties at the project site and usually brings requests for substitutions which could have been avoided. Many excellent products are manufactured in relatively small quantities by local operators who distribute in a regional area and these often offer advantages in delivery, price, or special fabrication.

PERFORMANCE SPECIFICATIONS

The foregoing types of specifications are generally considered descriptive in nature. They describe the material to be used and the methods of acceptable installation. In some cases there may be several equally good methods of installation, or the product or a part of it may be such that there is no general method available, or the project or material may not even exist. A specification written in a manner that sets forth all of the requirements the installation or product must meet but does not state how is called a *performance specification*. It allows the methods, and sometimes the material, to be selected by the contractor, who then assumes responsibility that the methods or materials he selects will produce the desired end result.

A number of architects and engineers prefer a performance specification, since it allows them to merely define the problem and the required result and does not require them to research materials or methods. The contractor prefers the performance-type specification, since it allows him to use his own ingenuity and favored material to obtain the results. The architect/engineer may not like a performance specification, since it takes the control of the material and methods to be used out of his hands and forces him to make the big decision to *accept* or *reject* after the work is an accomplished fact. The contractor may not like a performance specification, since it places all or most of the burden of determining how to achieve the end result on him, with final approval in the hands of someone else.

A special type of performance specification is one that is written, with the cooperation of contractors or suppliers, for a new or peculiar situation or where an installation or part of it may have unusual conditions. A case in point is a pumping plant or laboratory where pumps are required to instantaneously transfer gas or liquid from a very low temperature to a very high temperature. In this case a meeting between the parties involved and a thorough discussion of the details may be the basis for a performance specification written by the A/E, but done in a way that allows prospective suppliers or manufacturers to provide the pumps and the contractor to install them properly. Much of the space-program equipment is supplied on a performance specification, since actual manufacture may not even exist prior to proposed use.

The performance-type specification may sound like an easy way to write the project requirements by passing the buck to someone else, with the only responsibility being the acceptance or rejection if the materials and methods provide, or do not provide, the desired results. To some extent this is true; however, the specifications writer must generally do some research to see if the end result can be achieved or if he is dreaming about an impossible solution, for example, one with excessive costs or one that may be contrary to codes or normal operating methods. By conferring with manufacturers and contractors before he writes he may be able to avoid many such pitfalls.

STREAMLINED SPECIFICATIONS

While not perhaps a *type* of specification, but more accurately a *style*, there have been a number of attempts to shorten the actual length of the written specification. These have generally been classified as *streamlined specifications*, since they try to create a shorter version by eliminating certain words that may not be necessary to the required meaning. Where a normal sentence may be written as, "Millwork shall be accurately milled by the contractor to the details shown, with clean-cut mouldings and shall be scraped and sanded smooth, complete with mortise and tenon joints, and fastened in a manner to avoid any warping or splitting of material," (forty-two words), the streamlined revision may read "Millwork; accurately milled to details; clean cut mouldings; scraped and sanded; mortise and tenon joined; fastened to avoid warping or splitting." (twenty-one words: a 50 percent saving of words.).

In this example it is quite apparent which words have been omitted in the streamlined style. Since this is also a carefully selected example it cannot be considered as typical. The idea, of course, is to write in outline form instead of in complete sentence form. This is a good trick, provided you can do it so that there is no loss in the meaning. The streamlined form serves well in the specification of materials where a simple list may be adequate, but it is not the best form to adopt when describing methods. The additional possibility that the wrong word may be omitted, thus changing the meaning of the intent, is ever present. Consider that the specifications writer has a definite advantage over the specifications reader, in that he carries in his head what he intended to say in writing, while the reader has only the words he sees.

PRELIMINARY SPECIFICATIONS

A preliminary specifications too may not be easily classified as a *type* of specification nor even a *style*. It is exactly what the title implies, a preliminary or first listing of materials or methods required by the project. In the style of presentation it is most closely related to the streamlined specification, since it may be a simple listing of materials, incomplete reference to methods, tests, or other requirements, probably without *scope paragraphs* or *legal document* sections. Together with the designer, the specifications writer collects data on proposed materials and installation methods, suggests changes that may be due to cost, availability, or appearance, and coordinates these with the project manager and consultants. Normally the preliminary specification is only used as a guide in the office to acquaint the draftsmen and others of the types of materials to be used. In some cases however a preliminary specification is produced that is also meant to be distributed to the owner for approval or to a contractor who may have been selected to do the work without the requirements of competitive bidding. So far as type of specification is concerned, the preliminary may be open, closed, or any combination, so long as the many materials and methods to be used can be adequately described. The primary idea is to pin down as much information as possible so that all concerned will know what to use or expect.

TABULATION SPECIFICATIONS

This again is a style rather than a type of specification and is more closely related to the preliminary specification than to any other, except that it is used as a final specification. In its simplest form, as used by the Federal Housing Agency (FHA), it is preprinted, with headings and insert spaces for various items required on the project. Included are such items as *JOIST*_____, where the space is simply filled in with appropriate size and grade, or with *CONCRETE MIX*_____, which requires only mix ratio or ultimate strength inserted. Generally no complete sentences or descriptions of any methods are included. The methods to be used may be chosen by reference to standard methods of a governmental agency or trade association. The specifications are usually only a few pages long, are not very *tight*, and allow considerable variation by the builder. Strangely enough, many lending agencies require this type of FHA spec rather than a more complete or exacting one, possibly because it can be read more quickly, since it is much shorter, or because the agencies are not vitally interested in all the details of materials and methods that would be important to architect or builder.

SUMMARY

Let us now quickly review and summarize the various types or styles of specifications that have been discussed.

TYPE	PRINCIPAL FEATURES	ADVANTAGE/ DISADVANTAGE	WHERE USED
Closed	Limits material to one or few.	Limits competition. Allows architect to hold quality.	Manufacturer's specifications. Remodel work or where matching is required.

TYPE	PRINCIPAL FEATURES	ADVANTAGE/ DISADVANTAGE	WHERE USED
Open	Allows any material that meets requirements.	Allows competition. May include low quality items that barely meet requirements.	Government-financed projects. Commercial projects.
Manufacturer's	Information for writer. Usually *closed* type.	Source for information. Usually requires rewrite to eliminate *closed* aspects.	Information. May be copied in some uses.
Federal	*Open* type.	Requirements printed. May include many items not used. Used as master copy material.	As reference in other types. United States government work.
Performance	Specifies end result.	Allows contractor to select material and/ or method. Limits architect's control to *accept* or *reject*.	Commercial or experimental projects. Not on government projects.
Streamlined	Eliminates extra words. *Open* or *closed* type.	Reduces volume of paper. May mislead intent if wrong words eliminated.	Now becoming obsolete.
Tabulation	No sentences. Only requires notations in spaces.	Short. No methods described. Limits control of material.	Some governmental or speculative housing or lending agencies.

QUESTIONS

4.1. What are the two principal types of specifications called?

4.2. Manufacturers most often provide what type of specification material?

4.3. What type of specification is the normal Federal Specification?

4.4. Are closed specifications customarily used on commercial construction?

4.5. What is a *performance specification*?

4.6. Give an example of a *streamlined* specification sentence.

4.7. What is the primary use for a preliminary specification?

4.8. In what type presentation are preliminary specifications usually written?

4.9. What style or type is the so-called *FHA specification*?

4.10. Compare two opposite types of specifications.

5

SPECIFICATIONS LANGUAGE

In any book used as a guide for the writing of specifications there is usually some statement that the specifications writer need not have the ability of a brilliant author in order to produce a useful specification. To a great extent this is true, but the specifications must be able to convey to those reading them a clear, exact, and readily understood meaning of what is intended. Specifications should be written in as simple language as possible so that no misunderstanding of words is possible, and if technical terms are necessary, they should be those used in common practice and easily associated with local usage. Specifications that are not clear to the contractor or the subcontractor usually allow him to "add enough to cover it" in his bid and gamble that he has outguessed or can outtalk the A/E at a later date. There are three important *C*'s that are familiar to most specifications writers: *clear*, so that there is no ambiguity; *correct*, so that there can be no mistake from a technical point of view; and *concise*, to say what is necessary in as few words as possible in conjunction with the other two *C*'s.

With a reasonable command of the language, correct, intelligible, and readable specifications should not be too difficult to produce. Since we are primarily concerned with language in this chapter, it is assumed that a specifications writer has knowledge of materials and construction methods about which he can write. Good specifications are achieved when the written word most closely approximates the spoken word relating to the same subject. This involves proper grammar, use of words in their exact meaning, use of simple words rather than unfamiliar terms, and the avoidance of complicated sentence structures. Sentences should be short and to the point. Paragraphs should contain related information. Sections or other divisions should have the same subject matter.

Specifications are legal documents, and for that reason, if for none other, they should be clear and explicit. Because specifications are legal documents many writers feel that they must pepper their writing with words such as *aforesaid, heretofore, therefore, said so-and-so, previously indicated* that are associated with lawyer's jargon. Just the opposite is true. The simpler the language, the more easily it is understood. Ambiguous language in a specification usually means that the writer did not really know what to say. Phrases such as *to the satisfaction of the architect* or *additional tests may be required* indicate little and leave the contractor in the dark about what may actually be required. References to *smooth, hard, soft, textured,* and similar words carry little meaning unless there are accepted standards or some requirements are spelled out. *Hard* or *soft* may be specified in some relation to various standard tests; smooth means something different when used to describe a finish on concrete paving or on a walnut cabinet; *texture* is probably different to every plasterer. Unless the specifications writer tells the mechanic what he expects, there must be a difference in opinion of what is required, and this in turn often causes friction or outright disagreement.

MANDATORY CONSTRUCTION

Specifications are instructions to the contractor and suppliers of materials and should indicate exactly what is expected and what will be accepted. This means the specifications are mandatory upon the contractor. To be mandatory they must be imperative. One of the most controversial words used in specifications is the word *shall*, but it is entirely proper; it is a command or a demand if you wish, but it definitely tells the contractor that he is expected to do something. A number of writers are reluctant to be so demanding and use *will* or *to be*. These are vague terms and allow the reader a freedom to do or not to do if it is convenient to him.

Many times the use of the indicative mood, the passive voice, is the form most used in specifications. This accepts *shall* but may lead to production of longer sentences. The imperative mood uses fewer words, but it may be confusing if the *who does it* is not mentioned. For example, the indicative mood may be written as "The contractor shall set all screws with a screwdriver." This sentence tells *who* and *with what*, and is in the indicative mood, but it requires nine words. It may be shortened by use of the imperative mood without loss of meaning as in "Set all screws with a screwdriver." This saves three words; not much, perhaps, but the requirement hasn't changed, and a savings of three words in each of several hundred sentences, without loss of meaning, will reduce the volume of a specification.

The indicative mood is the normal language of specifications even if more words are used. In some regard this repetition of *shall* is monotonous, but it may be eliminated in specifying materials as indicated in the following: "Portland cement shall conform to ASTM-C-150, type I." This may be further shortened by inference, as follows: "Portland cement: ASTM-C-150, type I."

CONTRACTOR AS SUBJECT

One of the major principles to remember in connection with all construction documents is that legally there are usually only two parties to a construction contract, the owner and the contractor. From a legal standpoint the subcontractor, the material supplier, and the workman do not exist. We know that construction would be impossible without the help of others, but the prime contractor is the only one officially recognized, and he is responsible for all work of every kind in conformance with the requirements of the specifications. Therefore, it is never proper to refer to a workman or subcontractor as in the following examples:

INCORRECT: "The carpenter shall set all cabinets level."
INCORRECT: "The plastering contractor shall provide corner-bead at all corners."

These statements indicate that certain persons, in the opinion of the specifications writer, are to do the work required. Neither of those mentioned has a contractural relation with the owner, and the prime contractor may have an idea that someone other than those mentioned will do the work. This type of specification creates some ground for disputes between trades or subcontractors, circumvents the direct authority and responsibility of the prime contractor, and may make the A/E responsible for faulty work done in accordance with the word of the specifications. In the example given, the word *contractor* could have been substituted for *carpenter* or *plastering contractor*. The entire specification, however, is a part of a contract by which the contractor agrees to do certain work, so repeated reference to the contractor is superfluous.

There may be certain types of segregated work that will require a variation of the reference to a single prime contractor. When a construction contract is segregated into various parts, such as *General Construction, Elevators, Mechanical Work,* and *Electrical Work,* as is often the case in some publicly-financed projects, there must be a clear-cut indication of who does what. In this case there would be four prime contractors, each of whom could be referred to in other portions of the work. The specifications writer must be very careful to fully indicate which contractor he is considering, usually by a trade-contractor designation. In a case of this type it would be correct to write "Final line-voltage connection to motors, supplied and installed by the Elevator Contractor, shall be made as a part of the work of the Electrical Contractor."

PUNCTUATION

Punctuation is vitally important in the writing of specifications and may change the meaning of a sentence by its insertion or omission. With the increase in legal advice and interpretation by attorneys, the misplacement of a single punctuation mark may change the meaning of the specification. One method that might help to eliminate problems is to reduce the amount of punctuation. This, of course, may work hand in hand with shorter sentences, but extra care is necessary to insure that the sentence meaning is clear.

ESCAPE CLAUSES

Escape clauses, grandfather clauses, or other nondefinable phrases or clauses are the bane of the contractor who must use the specifications. These are often inserted to provide an out for the A/E when a definite statement is not easy to make or perhaps the exact requirement is not pinned down. Typical of these clauses are the following:

In the opinion of the architect . . .
As selected by the architect . . .
As the architect may direct . . .
To the satisfaction of the architect . . .

and similar phrases, all of which say practically nothing. These are termed *escape clauses* by the contractor who feels that the A/E is trying to evade his responsibility, and in most cases he is, or at least he is trying to. If the specifications writer can't say what he means he should not expect the contractor to second-guess him correctly.

WORDS AND PHRASES

The verbs *shall* and *will* have already been discussed. These are two of the most misused words in specifications. Remember that *shall* is a command, a positive statement, but *will* means maybe something will happen at someone's convenience.

Some other words that are open to interpretation are:

Any: implies a choice when no choice may be intended, for example: "Any surface not properly finished shall be removed and replaced." This could mean that not all improperly finished surfaces would be removed and replaced. In this particular case the use of the word *all* in place of *any* would be more appropriate.

Either: Again a "take-your-choice" word, for example: "Provide glass sidelights on either side of the door." The right side or the left side? Better instruction would be "Provide glass sidelights on both sides of the door."

Etc.: means "I'm not quite sure but I'll think of something more if it comes up." Think of the additional information and say it.

Intent: The contractor is not much interested in what was intended if some definite information of requirement is given. If the *intent* is not spelled out there may be a great difference in interpretation.

Must: Use *shall* instead. In addition to a difference in degree of obligation, must is often an irritating word to some people.

Same, Said: These words are carry-overs from attorney's language and do very little to clarify specifications. "The contractor shall inspect the work and repair any damage to same" can be made more positive by writing "repair all damaged work."

To be: In all of its various forms the verb *to be* is indefinite. Specifications are definite so avoid the use of this verb.

EXACT WORD MEANINGS

The correct use of words, or the correct word used, is of primary importance in writing of specifications. Misuse of words, double meanings, colloquial interpretation, or shortened or slang words may mean something different from what is intended. The daily exposure to radio, television, and advertising in general have caused many people to accept the misuse of words as correct usage. The specifier must be more correct and use words in their proper meanings.

Gage, Calk: These are but two examples of words that may be spelled in more than one way (gage = gauge; calk = caulk). There is nothing wrong with either spelling, but the writer should be consistent throughout the specification. If there is any doubt about accepted spelling it should be carefully checked with a good dictionary.

Non: Our English language is often confusing in that the identical meaning may be meant by two seemingly opposite words. For many years gasoline trucks were labeled *INFLAMMABLE*. This has exactly the same meaning as *FLAMMABLE*. The specifier should use *NONFLAMMABLE* if he means the opposite.

Balance, Remainder: These are often misused or used as synonyms. *Balance* is defined as "an instrument for weighing; a state of equilibrium." *Remainder* is defined as "anything left after the removal of a part; a remnant."

Remove and replace: This phrase is very common, especially in remodel work where existing work is to be removed and the same material reinstalled or new material installed. "Remove existing resilient floor and replace after repairing subfloor," means that the existing resilient flooring is to be saved and reinstalled. Usually what is meant is the existing material is to be replaced with new, but this must be made perfectly clear.

A workmanlike job: This means different things to different people. Many crafts have standards of workmanship, but these are not published and may be subject to considerable variation. The requirements for "a high-class job" or "a first-class job" should be spelled out. This also is confusing when top quality is not expected or required, so the specifier should describe what he wants in detail.

Pronouns: Pronouns can create ambiguities as illustrated by this old slapstick-comedy gag:
"I'll hold the spike with both hands and when I nod my head, you hit it with the hammer."
This instance of course is deliberate, but the misuse of pronouns or the question of what the pronoun refers to must be carefully considered.

SUMMARY

The specifications writer must be careful to write exactly what he means, in as few words as possible, and as specifically as his knowledge will allow. The use of certain words or phrases will almost automatically be avoided by many writers, but the continued misuse of words, poor sentence structure, and vague meaning of requirements should be avoided. The technical requirements and their specification are not usually confused by the specifications writer, but quite often the plain language needed to complete the documents is carelessly or inadequately composed. The only purpose of specifications is to help define the work required in language that is clear, correct, and concise.

QUESTIONS

5.1. What are the three words that should be considered as guiding every specification?
5.2. Define the words *shall* and *will* and explain the differences in their meanings.
5.3. Why should the various subcontractors or suppliers not be referred to in specifications?
5.4. When might it be necessary to refer to a subcontractor in the normal sense as a prime contractor?
5.5. What is an *escape clause*?

6

LEGAL DOCUMENTS
—BOILERPLATE

The title of this chapter may seem a little misleading at first glance, since all of the material included in *the book*, (announcements, bid and bond forms, various lists, and the specifications) are a part of the contract and individually do not have more or less legality. Within the construction industry however all of the material that is *not* specifications is often known as the *legal* part and in slang terms, *the boilerplate* or *front-end documents*. The actual preparation of the various forms and contracts involved is the work of a qualified attorney and considerable "nit-picking" has gone on over the past years as to just what the attorney or the A/E should do about these documents.

Most of the forms used in the construction industry today are the result of long and continuous review and rewriting by trade or professional organizations. These forms are at this date fairly well established and accepted. In each organization there are committees of professionals who, together with knowledgeable lawyers, insurance men, and others who might ultimately be concerned, consider any new suggestions or changes. The average specifications writer does not need to be a "legal eagle," but only needs to be sure that the forms he selects will do the job intended and provide the proper contractual relations between the parties involved. He can achieve this goal if he uses the forms provided by a construction industry organization. One of the pitfalls he must be aware of however is the overzealous owner's attorney, with limited construction knowledge, who might want to rewrite the standard forms to better protect his client. Very often this zeal for rewriting will void the normal agreement reached by the professional groups, so the specifications writer should stay with standard approved documents as much as possible.

INCLUDED FORMS

Each construction project is different and by these differences may require a different set of documents. The following outline will give some idea of the forms, lists, instructions, or conditions that will be needed for an average privately owned construction project. Many of these documents are standards of various organizations that may or may not be used without changes. The remainder almost invariably require revisions, additions, or outright original writing in order to fit them to the particular project at hand. If we exclude the abbreviated specifications often used by contractor-builders, most of the following portions of the "boilerplate" will be found in general use by A/E offices. Before we discuss each item we need to list those it is *possible* to use in a normal project.

1. Announcement of bid proposal (advertisement)
2. Invitation to bid
3. Description of project
4. Prebid qualification
5. General conditions
6. Supplemental general conditions
7. Special conditions
8. Wage scales
9. Bid form
10. Bid bond form
11. List of subcontractors
12. Performance bond form
13. Material bond form
14. Maintenance bond form
15. Specifications

In addition to those listed above a number of A/E offices also include the following, mostly to allow the contractor to see what he signs a contract for and to clarify any questions on the future use of some forms.

1. Owner/contractor blank contract
2. Contractor cost-breakdown form
3. Change order form
4. Contractor request-for-payment form

ANNOUNCEMENT

Announcements often take two forms: a short paragraph in a trade journal or newspaper, or a more formal announcement that can be sent to some contractors who may be interested in bidding the project. In the first case the announcement simply alerts prospective bidders that a project is on the boards, lists basic material, and gives a probable date for bidding. As an example:

> Architect John Jones of Sometown is working on drawings for a one-story factory building and offices for Acme Manufacturing Co. Floor area is 250,000 sq. ft. for manufacturing with 50,000 sq. ft. of offices, toilets, and supporting areas. Construction will be concrete slab floors, wood frame walls and roof, with asbestos vinyl floor tile, plaster, acoustic tile, metal doors and windows, glass, 4-ply built-up roof, paint, ceramic tile, elevated computer floors, electrical and mechanical equipment. Working drawings are expected to go to bid about 1 February, 19--.

These trade journal news items are consistently read by the contractor and allow him to make a selection of the ones he may want to bid on. These also are a help to the A/E, since many contractors may phone for advance reservations of sets of bidding documents. Subcontractors and suppliers are alerted so they may plan their operations for bidding on the project if they desire.

The second form usually is a bit more descriptive so far as materials are concerned and may include more information on site preparation, connection to existing work, special conditions, or other details. If the project is not financed by public funds this advertisement may be sent only to selected contractors as a prebid notice along with a list of possible bidders. This later list allows contractors to know who their probable competition will be and by this knowledge decide if they care to bid. In any case, either form of announcement gives the prospective bidders an opportunity to plan their future bid time, to review current work to determine if they can handle the project if they are low bidder, and to plan any changes in work force that might be required. For the preselected contractor who will build on any type of cost-plus or guaranteed-top figure, most of the previous type of announcement is superfluous. His announcement may very well be a simple letter asking him to stop in the office of the A/E to discuss the project, and all arrangements, dates, etc. will be worked out from there.

INVITATION TO BID

This is a formal invitation to bid rather than a general announcement and is usually bound in the *book* as a part of the required documents. This invitation is more explicit than the general announcement and usually includes a description of the site and the proposed construction, any special requirements, and, most important, the *closing date, time, and place for bids*. Although total estimated time for construction is usually given as a part of the contract, this time is also given in the invitation to help the contractor evaluate his potential time if he is awarded a contract. This form is one of several that may be duplicated in extra quantity to allow for one copy to be bound in the book and for additional copies to be sent by mail to prospective bidders. This invitation may also be sent to the owner so that he will be aware of the bid closing date and time and the time-of-completion.

DESCRIPTION OF PROJECT

This document is exactly what its title indicates, a complete description of the project. In many respects it overlaps the *invitation to bid* in project description. In fact this short document, usually not more than a page or two in length, is a condensation of a good part of the special conditions as well as the specifications. Where the *invitation* and the *announcement* briefly note the materials involved, the description covers them more thoroughly and makes some reference to their finish or installation. Usually a description does not include reference to ASTM, Federal Specifications or other standards. In some offices this section is not included, since the invitation may cover it adequately.

PRE-BID QUALIFICATION

In the past, *prebid qualifications* of contractor-bidders was not required. Local contractors were usually fairly well known, their past work was available for inspection, their finances could be easily checked, and their work force was known or could be easily evaluated. Since 1950 or thereabouts, this has been made increasingly difficult due to the increasing size of major contractor firms, by contractors bidding from outside the local area, by new builders with little previous record, and by the *broker-contractor*. Some of the old-time contractors have not kept up to date with new methods or the old principal has retired or passed away and the new management is interested in other types of construction.

The prebid qualification asks some very searching and personal questions of prospective bidders. Usually there are five major areas of inquiry: organization of the contractor; financial condition; past experience; equipment and labor force available; and work in progress. This information gives the A/E a good idea of the qualifications of proposed bidders, and, if required before bidding time, allows some selection of bidders, since privately financed construction does not require that any contractor can bid. Qualification information provided after bids are accepted is of little use, since it is then too late to eliminate anyone without becoming deeply involved in *judgment* and maybe something more serious. Prebid qualification forms are not usually bound into the *book* but are provided loose so that they may be returned to the A/E for evaluation before bidding time.

GENERAL CONDITIONS

The *General Conditions* for most architectural projects will simply be copies of the *American Institute of Architects Document A201*, latest edition, indicated by reference or perhaps by actual inclusion in the *book*. Engineering projects may use a similar form printed by the Consulting Engineers Council. Some A/E offices use their own general conditions, which they have developed over a period of years, but this should be done only with expert advice by an attorney familiar with construction practice, and any change should be carefully investigated before inclusion.

Samples of the AIA form A201 are not included here since they are available at national or local AIA offices and the latest revisions should be used. Copies in quantity are available from the national office but reproduction is prohibited by AIA copyright. The *General Conditions* are just that, conditions that apply *in general* to the project and include the following:

Article 1—Contract Documents

Article 2—Architect

Article 3—Owner

Article 4—Contractor

Article 5—Subcontractor

Article 6—Separate Contracts

Article 7—Miscellaneous Provisions

Article 8—Time

Article 9—Payments and Completion

Article 10—Protection of Persons and Property

Article 11—Insurance

Article 12—Changes in the Work

Article 13—Uncovering and Correction of Work

Article 14—Termination of the Contract

The document of the Consulting Engineers Council is somewhat similar in content but is divided into five parts, each with several sections.

Part 1—Legal and Procedural Documents and Bonds

Part 2—General Conditions of the Contract

Part 3—Special Conditions

Part 4—Detailed Specification Requirements

Part 5—List of Drawings

In actuality, only the first two parts apply as General Conditions in the printed form. Part three is listed as *Special Conditions* and will be discussed in later paragraphs; parts four and five are obviously not part of General Conditions.

SUPPLEMENTAL GENERAL CONDITIONS

The *General Conditions* in their printed form discussed above do not always exactly define the requirements of the A/E or the project. For this reason most projects have supplements to the printed *General*

Conditions and these supplemental conditions eliminate, change, or add portions that will bring the *General Conditions* to the correct requirements. Attention should be directed to keeping any changes supplemental and general in nature. *Special Requirements* relate strictly to *one project* and are not general in nature, and will be discussed later.

Modification of *General Conditions* should be arranged in the same order as the original *GC* items. Reference should be made to each article from the beginning with definite instructions to delete entirely, delete in part, change certain words or portions, or add as necessary. It would be virtually impossible to list all items that might be included as a part of *Supplemental General Conditions*, so each specifications writer should list the changes as they occur during the process of compiling the working documents and then rearrange them for his final documents.

SPECIAL CONDITIONS

Again the title of this paragraph accurately defines the content, *special conditions of the project that are not general and are not covered in other documents*. Some offices maintain that their supplemental general conditions are really special conditions and this may be so if they are written in that manner. Most usually however the *Supplemental General Conditions* are actually variations of the *General Conditions*, whereas *Special Conditions* are concerned with one project and one project only. An office may have some standard paragraphs that are used whenever applicable but paragraphs that do not apply should not be used any more than materials that are not used in a project should be included in specifications.

A few examples of *Special Conditions* are requirements for barricades and covered public walks, dust palliation, requirements for the continued use of utilities on remodel work, noise suppression (especially in school or hospital work), fire protection facilities, use of elevators, toilets, or existing parking, and burning of waste if allowed. In cities there is often a very special requirement for protection of the foundations of adjacent structures, buried public utilities, and access to streets or freeways by construction equipment. In engineering work the extent to which a street or highway may be closed or the amount of water diversion of a river are special requirements. Not all projects have a requirement for *Special Conditions*, but there should be a clear-cut separation between those conditions that might apply to any project and the special requirements for a particular project.

69

WAGE SCALES

A schedule of current approved wage scales for various trades that might be employed on a project are usually mandatory for publicly financed projects and are used more and more for privately financed work. Wage scales giving hourly rates, together with additional rates for medical, vacation, overtime, and other benefits are available from local trade union offices or may be obtained from the United States government. The responsibility of the specifications writer is to determine which trades apply to the particular project and eliminate the remainder. Do not try to change the rates, either up or down. These have been negotiated with the unions and are the minimums that are allowed. Contractors often pay key personnel more than minimum wages, but this is the contractor's business, and the specifications writer, owner, or A/E should not try to interfere. When proper selection of trades has been made, be certain that all rates shown on the union table are also included on the retyped sheet added to the project manual.

BID FORM

This document is the legally accepted form, supplied by the A/E, and used by every contractor submitting a bid for a project. There should be blank spaces left for date of bid, name of the bidder, bidder's address, bidder's phone number, name and address of the project (this is sometimes imprinted by the A/E), amount of bid both in words and figures, time for project completion, list of addenda received by the bidder, signature of authorized bidder representative, and type or license number of bidder. The usual wording includes a phrase indicating that "work shall be done in accordance with plans (or drawings) and specifications as provided by_____ architect," and some space should be allowed for any explanation of the bidder's deviation, if any, from such documents. The form should also include a statement that the bid will remain open and subject to acceptance by the owner for some period of time after bid opening. This period is normally thirty calendar days, although bids submitted for some publicly financed work will require a longer period.

In some bidding procedures there is a request for alternates for additions or deductions from the base bid. Most A/E offices will list these on the printed form in the same order that they have been called out in other documents and will include the words *add* and *deduct* at the value of each alternate. The inclusion of both of these words may seem superfluous when the A/E feels that it is obvious that the choice will be one or the other. However, the contractor may not agree or may prefer to not do the work involved in an alternate, so it is better to give him the opportunity to state his position. On projects where unit prices are required for yards of excavation, concrete, pile driving, paving, and similar work, the bid form should provide description and cost spaces for these items.

Most bid forms are bound in the project manual (the *book*) but this requires the bidder to remove the form and perhaps mutilate the bound copy in the process. If additional copies of this form are printed each bidder can receive two unbound copies, one for his actual bid and a copy for his file. A close scrutiny of the returned bid should be made for changes or deviations but this is usually not the responsibility of the specifications writer. On very small projects the bid form may be omitted and the bidder allowed to make his proposal on his letterhead.

LIST OF SUBCONTRACTORS

This is simply a list of subcontractors that the bidder proposes to use on the work if he is awarded the contract. On many jobs it is not required but if it is used it may operate in two ways. It more or less guarantees to the subcontractor that he was the successful bidder to the contractor for his specialized portion of the work, and it allows the A/E to review the list and possibly object to any who have been unsatisfactory on previous work. When a subcontractor is indicated on publicly financed work it is a delicate and often difficult matter for the prime contractor to change because of price-shopping or other similar reasons. If the A/E objects, it often means an increase in the bid amount, since the low bidder invariably uses the low subcontract bid.

BOND FORMS

The several bond forms indicated in the paragraph titled *Included Forms* may be made up in the A/E office, purchased from a professional organization, or accepted from a surety writing the bond. In any case they should be reviewed by knowledgeable professionals to insure that they fit the project and mean what they seem to say. In general, bond forms guarantee that a surety will provide money or services for a construction function in case the contractor fails to fulfill his obligation. Their inclusion in the project manual is usually only an indication of what is expected, and additional forms will be provided when contract signatures are required. The exception to this procedure is in the use of the *Bid Bond*, which is included with each bidders *Bid Form* at bid opening. On small projects or in unusual cases one or all of the bonds may be eliminated, but they do provide some protection to the owner if the contractor fails to perform properly.

MISCELLANEOUS FORMS

Other forms or variations of those listed may be included. Quite often the owner/contractor agreement is included to allow the contractor to see what obligations he may incur when he is asked to sign the contract. Occasionally, guarantee forms for build-up roofing, termite control, or similar long-range installations are also included. For segregated contracts, mechanical, electrical or similar separate bids, the prime contractor bidder may be furnished copies of the segregated contracts so that he may be able to evaluate those bids and include any work that he feels may be omitted or that will require extra cost to him.

SUMMARY

The *boilerplate* is as essential to the production of good construction documents as are the drawings or the specifications. Although they are not strictly specifications, neither are they drawings. They are normally bound in the project manual with the specifications; thus they have automatically become part of the work of the specifier. Many are repetitive on project after project and as a result may be taken for granted, but changes do occur and a good review should be made periodically. These are the parts that the legal professionals maintain are in their field and every effort should be made to insure that all of these documents are legally correct before they are used. The specifier should eventually develop enough business law knowledge to be able to spot errors, determine requirements, and provide any legal help necessary in the proper writing of these documents. An extra word of caution: when using standard printed forms be sure to use and specify the latest or current edition.

QUESTIONS

6.1. Discuss the possible differences between a project announcement and an invitation to bid.

6.2. List at least five *boilerplate* documents that you feel are important most of the time.

6.3. On what types or sizes of projects do you think *prequalification* is a good idea?

6.4. Read AIA form A201 *General Conditions* and list the items that you feel might need supplemental conditions.

6.5. List at least five *boilerplate* documents that you feel are in the text, that might occur on a major project.

6.6. Obtain a standard bid form, or write your own, and discuss the various important items included or omitted.

6.7. Talk to a subcontractor and a prime contractor about listing of subcontractors and discuss their reactions.

6.8. What happens when a contractor fails to complete a project he has a contract for?

6.9. Do you feel that the contractor should be provided with a copy of the owner/contractor agreement before bidding? Why?

6.10. Should the specifier actually write *boilerplate* material or should he require that the legal profession do this work? Explain.

7

THE UNIFORM SYSTEM

The problems of adequate and satisfying communication between architect and builder have always been present, but with the multitude of new products and methods appearing on the market after World War II these problems became unbelievably complex. It became quite evident that a more standardized system was required in construction specifications and the organization called the *Construction Specifications Institute* was formed in 1948 in Washington, D. C. to try to accomplish this result. Primarily local for the first few years, the CSI finally established chapters in New York and Chicago, but in 1953 the big growth started in California with the chartering of chapters in Los Angeles, then, in 1954, San Diego, Sacramento, San Francisco and others close behind. By 1960 there were approximately forty chapters throughout the United States, each voluntarily producing various guide specifications documents. Today, widespread interest in this organization has resulted in the establishment of more than 130 chapters throughout the United States, including 10 student chapters.

In past years no standardized arrangement for specifications was in use and each office developed its own system. This resulted in logical section sequences in some cases, but more often in a hit-or-miss order not coordinated with the actual construction or with other sections of the specification. Construction operations were usually not well organized, so that the work of one trade might be scattered through several sections or the normal work of several trades might be included in one section. This of course made it difficult for the contractor to perform properly and caused many misunderstandings. Some overhaul of the general field of specifications was in order and the CSI determined to provide the construction industry with a uniform method for organizing specifications.

After months of hard work, a *Tentative Proposal for a Manual of Practice for Specification Writing Methods* was presented at the 1961 CSI convention. This presentation had twenty divisions. A second rewritten draft, brought out in 1962, expanded the number of divisions to twenty-two with more mechanical and electrical portions. These early attempts to provide a format were derived from several hundred specifications, gathered from all over the country, that were tabulated by sections. Some were really not organized at all, with no attempt made to keep sections in any order as they occur in actual construction. By listing and relisting sections, the *division format* was finally developed for use.

In 1963 the Construction Specifications Institute published *The CSI Format for Building Specifications*, since revised and known as *The CSI Format for Construction Specifications* or simply as *the Format*. This presentation was reduced to sixteen basic divisions. During at least a part of the period required for this development the American Institute of Architects was also working on some ideas to update their Standard Filing System, in general use since 1920 but acknowledged as obsolete by most architects. In 1961 the Associated General Contractors of America Inc. published their *Suggested Guide for Field Cost Accounting* in an effort to establish a national cost accounting system. Each of these organizations recognized that their major interests were closely related to the interests of the others.

Shortly after publication of the *Format* a joint committee was formed including not only representatives of the Construction Specifications Institute and the American Institute of Architects but also the Associated General Contractors of America Inc., American Society of Landscape Architects, Council of Mechanical Specialty Contracting Industries Inc., and the National Society of Professional Engineers and Producers Council Inc. The early meetings were also attended by representatives of the Royal Institute of Architects of Canada, the Specification Writers Association of Canada, some interested representatives from various sections of the United States federal system, and miscellaneous others. After a slight revision of content, an agreement was reached by most of these organizations to adopt the *Format* and to publish it as a joint venture with the CSI.

In addition to the adoption of the *Format* as the guiding principle, it was determined to include in the publication three major parts that would be of value to all users. The first of these is the *Specification Outline*, which groups related work under *divisions* and *sections*; this outline will be discussed at greater length later in this chapter. The second is the *Filing System*, which provides a method for filing and retrieval of manufacturers' literature listed under one of the sixteen divisions. The third is the *Cost Accounting Guide*, an orderly arrangement of the various cost items of construction that are directly related to the identical or similar items of a specification. The publication encompassing all three of these parts is now known as *The Uniform System for Construction Specifications, Data Filing, and Cost Accounting*, or simply as *The Uniform System*.

THE DIVISION

The *Uniform System*, derived from the *Format*, lists sixteen *Divisions* organized to follow general construction progress on a project. These divisions are *fixed* major titles; they do not have specification material written under their headings and are not changed from project to project. Each division has an interrelation of four major categories— materials, trades, functions, or place relationship. Divisions should be *constant in sequence, short in name, and descriptive in title*. Since there are only sixteen divisions the specifications writer can easily memorize their sequence, number, and title.

The division arrangement is as follows:

Division   1—General Requirements

Division   2—Site Work

Division   3—Concrete

Division   4—Masonry

Division   5—Metals

Division   6—Wood and Plastics

Division   7—Thermal and Moisture Protection

Division   8—Doors, Windows, and Glass

Division   9—Finishes

Division 10—Specialties

Division 11—Equipment

Division 12—Furnishings

Division 13—Special Construction

Division 14—Conveying Systems

Division 15—Mechanical

Division 16—Electrical

THE SECTION

Under each division there may be one or many *sections* grouped together by a common factor that is directly related to the subject of the division. There may be as *many* sections as necessary under any *one* division. The section is complete in itself and includes only one item or type of construction. This encourages the preparation of smaller and more specific divisions of the work required and to some extent allows greater flexibility to add or subtract sections if the project changes. By this same token the contractor using this multi-divided specification has greater freedom in awarding subcontracts, since most of the small sections may be split or combined at his option. This method may lead to a somewhat greater number of sections than was used in the past and may add a few pages to the specification, but experience has shown that the end result is worth the effort.

One of the first concerns of the specifications writer is to review the drawings and other project data and try to determine the different materials or processes that will be required. By making a rough take-off, properly listing each material (section) under the correct division, the total number of sections is known.

The Uniform System indicates various sections as *broadscope* or *narrowscope*. The broadscope sections are those primary portions that occur most often under a division; for example, clearing of site, earthwork, or roads and walks under *Division 2—Site Work*. The narrowscope sections are those which further divide the work under any broadscope section such as demolition, structure moving, clearing and grubbing, which might be listed under the broadscope *Clearing of Site*. Not all specifications will separate easily into convenient broadscope or narrowscope sections, so most often there is a combination of these depending upon the type of construction and materials or processes involved.

In the preparation of a specification, the matter of adding or changing portions easily is of extreme importance. Under systems that encompass a considerable scope of work under one section this becomes difficult, since it often means rewriting part of the work and renumbering pages; an inconvenient process at best. The smaller, more specific section developed under the Uniform System should normally include only one material or process so that it can easily be revised; in most cases the pages of each section are numbered totally within that section (for example 2A-1 through 2A-6, 3A-1 through 3A-10) so that any change in the number of pages has little effect except within the section itself.

DIVISION-SECTION

Let us look at the possibilities in a typical division-section arrangement. Concrete work in some form is usually present on most projects and may encompass a number of sections on large projects. Specifications for this concrete work on a small project may possibly be contained totally in one broadscope section titled *Concrete Work*. This section would include requirements for a small amount of formwork, mixing, placing and curing of concrete, reinforcement, and related items, all under Division 3, perhaps as Section 3A. For a forty-story building of reinforced concrete we might have the following sections under Division 3—Concrete.

> DIVISION 3—Concrete
>> Section 3A—Concrete Formwork
>> Section 3B—Reinforcement
>> Section 3C—Cast-in-place Concrete
>> Section 3D—Precast Concrete
>> Section 3E—Cementitious Decks

All of these sections are broadscope since they indicate general areas of requirements within the division. A further breakdown of these same sections will give us narrowscope portions. Examples that might be considered under *Section 3D—Precast concrete* are, *Precast structural panels, Precast prestressed concrete,* or *Precast architectural concrete*. These subsections would further pinpoint requirements and might be identified as *Section 3D-1* or *Section 3E, 3F* etc. with *Cementitious Decks* becoming *3H*. The actual rearrangement would depend largely upon the use of a master specification having fixed indicators or a more flexible method.

The latest edition of *The Uniform System* includes a new numbering arrangement for the broadscope sections and a suggestion for any narrowscope sections that might be included under a broadscope section. This numbering system is based upon a five-digit indicator and may best be illustrated by the following example from Division 3 - Concrete.

03210	Steel Bars and Welded Wire Fabric
03310	Standardweight Concrete
03354	Heavy Duty Concrete Floor Finish
03431	Precast Prestressed Concrete
03521	Perlite Insulating Concrete Roof Decking

One disadvantage for this method may be that to follow it blindly is to add unnecessary sections or pages to the specification. The first and second digits indicate the division, the third digit indicates the broadscope section, and the last two digits indicate the narrowscope section within the broadscope section.

The preceding examples are all concerned with the *material*, concrete. Let us consider *Division 9—Finishes*. Here the various sections under the division have only a *process* as a mutual basis, namely, finishing the project. A typical example of sections under *Division 9* might be as follows:

DIVISION 9—Finishes

    Section 9A—Lathing and Plastering

    Section 9B—Gypsum Drywall

    Section 9C—Tile Work

    Section 9D—Terrazzo

    Section 9E—Acoustic Treatment

    Section 9F—Resilient Flooring

    Section 9G—Painting

    Section 9H—Wall Covering

These are all necessary to finish our imaginary project but have no one material common to all. All are broadscope, so again we may have narrowscope sections such as a division of *9A—Lathing and Plastering* into *Metal Lathing, Gypsum Lathing, Plastering, Stucco,* and *Acoustic Plaster. Section 9C—Tile* might be further divided into narrowscope sections titled *Ceramic Tile, Quarry Tile, Glass Mosaic,* or *Conductive Tile*. Subdivisions of other sections may be made in a similar manner or, in many cases, the broadscope title may actually be that of a normal narrowscope section such as *Section 9E—Quarry Tile* if no other tile work except quarry tile is included in the project. The important thing to keep in mind in regard to separation or combination of sections is whether the same trade does the work. Lathing and plastering could be combined; ceramic tile and quarry tile could be combined, too, if only a small amount of work was involved, but plastering and quarry tile sections should not be combined, since two different trades normally do this work.

This discussion brings us to the question of what to do if there is no work required under a division or a section. Let us first consider the division, since it is always present. A number of approaches have provided several methods to cope with this problem. One of the most common is simply to list only the divisions and sections *used* in the specification, omitting those that do not apply. This then brings up the point that the contractor may not be sure if the omission was intentional or an oversight. The burden is of course on the specifications writer to include sections for all required work and not to overlook any possibility. To some this is a rather sloppy way to work since it does leave some grounds for doubt, but in practice the contractor generally accepts the theory that if work is not indicated it is not required.

Other offices list every division but only those sections used. In case there is no work required (no elevator in a one-story building) the division is included in the Table of Contents, but it is simply marked *no work required, not required for this project, not used,* or similar notation. This indicates to the contractor or other readers that the division has not been overlooked. In a great many projects there will be no work required under Divisions 11 through 14. In engineering work a great many of the divisions may not be used; for example, a highway project would probably only use Divisions 1, 2, 3, 5, and 16 with remote possibilities for Division 4, part of 9, and perhaps 15. In a case of this kind there might be a considerable number of sections under each division used, but there would also be quite a few divisions marked *not used.* Although it may be repetitious, remember that the specifications should be written so that the contractor can interpret the intentions of the architect/engineer, and the inclusion of a few more words that clarify this intent are not superfluous.

Sections, on the other hand, are quite different. The number of sections under each division will vary from none to many, on different types of projects. Many offices using master specifications of some sort have the various portions of work permanently prenumbered (see the discussion of Division 9—Finishes). If all of these sections are required they are all listed, but if only *Lathing & Plastering,* and *Resilient Flooring* and *Painting* are required, only Sections 9A, 9F, and 9G would be listed. In a very few offices every standard section is listed on preprinted sheets of the Table of Contents and then marked *not required* where they do not apply to the project. Although this eliminates retyping the Table of Contents for each project it does require typing the *not required* notations, so it is a questionable time-saver. In other offices the sections are always in alphabetical order, so that the Sections noted above in *Division 9—Finishes* would appear as 9A, 9B, and 9C. There is nothing wrong with this except it requires diligence in watching the change in section numbers and makes automation of a section almost impossible because of the numerous changes required.

THE FILING SYSTEM

The filing and retrieval of literature in an A/E office is of utmost importance if efficient operation is to be maintained. Too often manufacturer's catalogs are simply placed on a shelf and a general hunt is required to locate a specific one. When the catalog is returned to the shelf, if it is at all, it might be placed in the first open spot rather than in its original position. Since most offices do not employ a librarian to keep order on the book shelves, a program with national recognition for doing this is important. The filing portion of the *Uniform System* provides a method, closely related to the *Specification Outline*, that allows literature and related material to be filed numerically under one of the sixteen division headings.

The correct classification, according to the *Uniform System*, will be assigned to the literature of any manufacturer who makes a request to the publishers of the *Uniform System*. This assignment has some specific requirements to be met, but in general it classifies the literature by division number for easy filing. It also provides for imprinting of the approved logotype, division number, specific title, and other useful filing information on the material. The important part of this system is the fact that a nontechnical clerk or office boy, who has limited knowledge of products, can correctly file literature by the preassigned designator or replace catalogs that have been used in the office for reference. With the advent of the *Uniform System* the American Institute of Architects declared their old filing system obsolete, although a number of offices still use it with increasing difficulty.

A major difficulty in using the *Uniform System* filing process arises because some manufacturers produce several, or perhaps hundreds, of items, all of which are described in a single book. If the manufacturer produces asbestos drainage pipe (Division 2), cement-fibre decking (Division 3), gypsum masonry units (Division 4), fibre-board sheathing (Division 6), roofing material (Division 7), curtain wall systems (Division 8), and asbestos water or soil pipe (Division 15), the information for all of these items may be contained in one hardbound catalog. The catalog can either be taken apart and the various portions refiled by some other method, or else the book, with all products included, can be filed under the most frequently used heading. A similar difficulty arises when unbound pages or single catalog sheets are provided but the manufacturer has not provided a way to contain them. Some offices use three-ring binders for storing this material according to categories, with several manufacturers represented in each binder. In some cases material is stored in standard filing cases but this, usually, is unsatisfactory since the individual pages can be lost, torn, or misfiled.

COST ACCOUNTING GUIDE

This portion of the *Uniform System* is primarily for the use of the contractor. It is arranged, with few exceptions, parallel and identical to the sections of the *Specification Outline* and is structured to be applicable to computer processing techniques. Each section is numbered with a five-digit designator; the first two numbers indicate the division and the second two indicate the section. Further breakdown is indicated by a decimal point and additional digits. The advantages of using a cost accounting system that closely parallels the specification system used cannot be overlooked and many contractors are using this method.

INDEX OF KEY WORDS

Although not a major innovation, the listing of key words as a part of the *Uniform System* is certainly worthwhile. Words are shown in three degrees of bold type according to their relative importance. Each word is also identified by division, complete with its section name. The experienced specifications writer will probably not use this list as much as the novice, but in either case it serves as a place to pinpoint a questionable subject with regard to specifications or filing.

These major parts then comprise the *Uniform System* in its entirety. For the person interested primarily in specifications, the *Specification Outline* and perhaps the filing system are most important.

The *Index of Key Words* is helpful in dealing with a question about a new or unfamiliar product or method, but the average specifications writer would seldom be called upon to use the estimating or project record portions. In Chapter 3 some of the sources for information referred to the number system for divisions, and a considerable number of manufacturers now indicate the proper location in the specification for their materials or systems. Now let us look at the use of the Uniform System as it relates to the manufacturer, supplier, and contractor.

MANUFACTURER-CONTRACTOR

Most building material manufacturers are fully aware by now of the *Uniform System* through the membership of their personnel in the CSI, the CSI Spec-Data program, requests for information from contractors, or by the general acceptance of the system by the construction industry. By using the *Uniform System* indicators the manufacturer provides the A/E as well as the contractor with easy access to his data. By matching indicators all parties can quickly see which materials are required, available, or may be considered on the project. This matching allows the manufacturer's representatives or suppliers to decide quickly and easily whether a material they handle is needed and thus avoid looking through the entire specification for a semi-hidden item.

From the contractor's viewpoint the *Uniform System*, properly used by the specifier, has many advantages. If the various requirements are properly located in the divisions, the contractor is able to divide the work among subcontractors more easily, and he can tabulate the work his own forces will do. The more completely the work in each division is divided into sections, the more completely the contractor will be able to review and compare the subcontractors' bid, and usually bid lower.

Many A/E offices are now writing their specifications using five-digit designators that match those used in the *Cost Accounting Guide* portion of the *Uniform System*. Let us take a look at what such a redivision means. Since we have referenced *Division 3—Concrete* earlier, let us use that division again as an example.

    Division 3—Concrete

       03050—Concrete Accessories

       03100—Concrete Formwork

       03105—Form Liners and Coatings

       03110—Wood Forms

03120—Prefabricated Forms

03150—Expansion and Contraction Joints

03200—Concrete Reinforcement

03210—Steel Bars and Welded Wire Fabric

03300—Cast-in-place Concrete

03350—Specially Finished Concrete

03400—Precast Concrete

03500—Cementitious Decks

     etc.

Then to make the same comparison between Division 3 and Division 9, let us look at the breakdown under the latter:

Division 9—Finishes

  09100—Lath and Plaster

  09110—Furring and Lathing

  09150—Gypsum Plaster

  09180—Cement Plaster

  09190—Acoustical Plaster

  09250—Gypsum Wallboard

  09260—Gypsum Wallboard Systems

  09280—Gypsum Wallboard Accessories

     etc.

The division 9 listing continues in like manner for Tile Work, Terrazzo, Veneer Stone, Acoustical Treatment, Wood Flooring, Resilient Flooring, Special Flooring, Special Coatings, Painting and Wall Coverings, and ending with *09990—Adhesives*. Other divisions are listed in a similar manner. Notice that these are narrowscope sections; thus, some materials or processes that might be specified together by the A/E are separated. Notice also that the extensive use of the accounting numbers for section numbers might increase the total number of sections beyond the point of reasonable use, since all the items listed above from 09100 through 09190 are normally done by one trade, namely the plastering trade. In some very large jobs the lathing and general base preparation work is done by crews who install metal studs, lath, and accessories, while the plastering work, including interior and exterior plaster (stucco), acoustical plaster, and any ornamental work, is done by a plastering crew. Although extensive subdividing of a section might be helpful in some cases, the specifications writer will be wise to avoid overdoing this practice. Contractors do not generally ask for subbids from different subcontractors on such completely divided items as metal lath and gypsum lath when both are required on the same project.

ACCEPTANCE

Soon after publication of the first draft of the CSI *FORMAT* it became apparent that this system had much merit. Upon the agreement among the various organizations for publication of the *Uniform System* its popularity quickly spread, first with A/E members of the CSI, and quickly followed by other offices and agencies. At this writing (1974) practically all agencies of the United States government (the United States Navy Public Works, the Army Corps of Engineers, the Indian Service, NASA), most state construction departments, many foreign government offices, and thousands of private and corporate offices of architects, engineers, developers, and industrial entrepreneurs are using the *Uniform System*. This acceptance is further extended by the hundreds of thousands of manufacturers, suppliers, contractors, and subcontractors using specifications based on the *Uniform System* to construct the work on which they are engaged.

In addition to its acceptance in the United States and Canada, there is a growing interest in other countries where a variety of systems, or sometimes no system at all, has been the custom. United States-based corporations engaged in constructing projects for their own use or for others, government agencies building foreign embassies or office structures, foreign architects, engineers, or builders visiting in the United States, and our own people visiting abroad have spread the use of the *Uniform System*. Although it is now published only in the English language, primarily for use in the United States, it may not be many years before it is published in other languages as the start of a worldwide system.

SUMMARY

The *Uniform System* is generally thought of as the arrangement of the *sixteen divisions* for writing of specifications but also includes a filing system, a *Cost Accounting Guide*, and an *Index of Key Words*. The divisions are always in the same sequence, grouped in the same order that construction proceeds; titles are easily memorized and may be expanded by as many sections as are necessary for a project. Slavishly following the suggested sections is not required, since these sections can vary with trade or local customs. Possibly with more time for development some rearrangement of Divisions 11 through 14 would have placed them after *Division 15—Mechanical* and *Division 16—Electrical* since many projects do not require sections covering *Equipment, Furnishings, Special Construction,* or *Conveying Systems.* However, this change is relatively unimportant if it is properly noted or if it is obvious from the construction documents. Despite differences of opinion, locale, type of material specified, or trade union jurisdictions, the *Uniform System* is now a tried and accepted method for writing specifications.

QUESTIONS

7.1. What organization originated *The Format for Construction Specifications*?

7.2. Name three of the national organizations that now sponsor and publish the *Uniform System*.

7.3. Name the four parts of the *Uniform System*.

7.4. List in proper order the divisions of the *Uniform System*.

7.5. Under which division would you specify wallpaper? hardwood strip flooring?

WRITING
A SPECIFICATION

This chapter tells "what it's all about," to use the current language. Previous chapters have given information on the various types of specifications, sources for information, specification language, *boilerplate*, and related material. Although these items are not the only knowledge necessary for the writing of specifications, they cover the basics. In this chapter we will try to show, step by step, the general procedure for writing a *privately-financed commercial project specification.* In following this process the reader must keep in mind that each project is different and each project will have variations that must be worked out by the specifications writer. Always remember that any specification should cover all of the materials and circumstances that are particular to the specific project; thus a thorough screening of the drawings and requirements is mandatory.

PRELIMINARY REVIEW

Preliminary drawings should be obtained from the designer or project manager when they are at a stage where they indicate shape, size, and general arrangement of the project. Conferences with the project manager should indicate most of the materials and any special conditions required in the project. The preliminary specifications should then be outlined. This is really the basis of the final specification, so extreme care should be exercised in tabulating all the obvious materials and conditions and an educated guess made for those that are not so obvious.

Start by numbering sheets of paper from one through sixteen to correspond with the sixteen divisions of the *Uniform System.* Now review the drawings and the various conference notes and, as each material is mentioned, write it on the proper sheet together with any identifying information that may be helpful later. To prevent overlooking an item, or noting it twice, use a colored pencil to make a check mark at each item as it is tabulated. To find some items again at a later date it is also helpful to indicate the page number and detail wherever possible. Where there is doubt about a material, mark the material in question on the drawing as the item is checked. When this review is completed the writer is ready to prepare the preliminary or *guide* specification.

THE PRELIMINARY SPECIFICATION

As mentioned earlier in this chapter, the *preliminary specification* is just that, a preliminary draft for use in developing the final specification. The *preliminary* may serve to indicate to the owner what materials will be used; it may also be a guide to the A/E. In some instances the preliminary may also be used, in connection with presentation drawings, to give a lending agency a better idea of the loan it is financing. It is not exact in every detail, nor is it complete in indicating installation, and it may or may not be changed as the working drawings and final specifications are processed.

The preliminary is more of an outline than anything else. After the various materials are listed on the sheets previously noted, the writer will need to rearrange them to fit his master list, the arrangement of the *Uniform System Index,* or some other logical system. Care should again be exercised because this early arrangement will usually be carried over into the final specification. A check list of possible items is often used and is recommended to avoid overlooking some category of the work. The format for a preliminary specification may be similar to the following example:

General Conditions: AIA form A201

Special Conditions:

    a.   Barricades required at each street in accordance with City Ordinance #1234A. Provide clearance and night illuminating lights at pedestrian walks.

    b.   Check underground gas line at SE corner and cooperate with utility company regarding rerouting.

Division 2: Site Work

Section 2A: Excavation and Grading

    a.   Excavate to undisturbed soil. Particular caution required at old fill at Center Street corner.

    b.   Backfill compacted to 90% for parking area and 95% beneath building. Laboratory tests required in accordance with state highway requirements.

    c.   Grade to 0.10 ft. maximum difference from finish elevation.

Section 2B: Landscape Work

    a.   Six in. minimum top soil in plant boxes. Soil mix per landscape architect.

    b.   Ground cover on all banks to be ornamental strawberry at 6 in. o.c. Approximately 50 junipers (one-gallon size) and ten ornamental white birch (10 ft. high specimen).

    c.   Maintain planting for six months after installation.

Division 3: Concrete Work

Setion 3A: Formwork

    a.   Plywood for all exposed work except *architectural concrete.*

    b.   *Architectural concrete* forms use type 102 checkerboard as mfgd. by XYZ Form Co. Samples required.

    c.   Forms not required for footings in stable soil.

Section 3B: Reinforcing

    a.   Deformed intermediate grade billet steel conforming to ASTM A615, grade 60.

    b.   Mesh, galvanized, conforming to ASTM A185.

    c.   Testing of reinforcing not required.

Section 3C: Cast-In-Place Concrete

    a.   Cement; domestic brand, natural grey, ASTM C150.

    b.   Aggregate; ASTM C33, washed, 2 in. maximum, not more than 1% schist, chert, feldspar, etc. Fine aggregate in accordance with state highway requirements.

    c.   Water shall be potable.

    d.   Mix; 2500 psi in accordance with ACI 613.

    e.   Testing; three cylinders each 50 cu yd or fraction. Test in accordance with ACI C33.

    f.   Ready-mix concrete acceptable if in accordance with ACI C94.

This example will give the writer an idea of the completeness or brevity of the preliminary draft. Each section is treated in a similar manner so that all conditions are included. If the mechanical or electrical preliminary is not written by the office specification writer, the engineering consultants should be fully advised of the format and the resulting work carefully reviewed. As must be readily apparent, the standards of the various testing or construction organizations are used wherever possible, rather than spelling out the requirements. In cases where no standards exist the requirements should be clearly but briefly defined. The reproduction and distribution of the preliminary specification is covered in another chapter.

BEGINNING FINAL SPECIFICATIONS

When should you actually begin to write the final specification? This is perhaps one of the most frequently asked questions regarding specifications — and the one most difficult to answer. In fact there is probably no absolute answer, since the starting time will be different for every project and will be greatly influenced by the type of project (whether it is normal or special), the availability of complete conference information, the progress of working drawings, the master specifications and the time available before deadline. Actually we start the final specification when we start the preliminary, since the specifications writer must organize his work by proper division and section; he must establish references for materials, testing, and installations; and he must have a good knowledge of the economics of the project. This latter is especially important since it is the economics that will, to a great degree, determine the quality of materials or installation. The quantity of these items will normally be determined by the drawings.

The specifications writer should keep in touch regularly with the project manager, the designer, or any other person in charge of the project. Whenever changes are made the writer should also make the corrections in his data file. At some point the working drawings reach a stage where the detailing of parts, rather than overall plans, elevations, sections, material lists and finish schedules, is the principal remaining work. This usually happens somewhere between 50 percent and 70 percent completion, and it is often at this time that final specifications can actually be started. In every project there are some items that can be established early and easily and for which the specification can be written first. Some of these items (sections) are ceramic tile, standard cabinet work, lathing and metal wall-framing (metal studs, lath), roofing, elevators, chalkboard and tackboard, and locker equipment. In most of these items there is usually little, if any, difference in quality or installation, and, whether there is one square foot or thousands of square feet, one unit or many, the specification will be the same.

Some writers claim to write from scratch and to write all sections in their final order. Except on very small jobs this would either be very time consuming, since all drawings and information would have to be 100 percent completed, or it would eliminate the use of master specifications or other reusable material. It is generally convenient for the specifications writer to use some sort of check-off list or tabulation. This list should be arranged by division and section and might very well have columns for first draft, typing, and reproduction. Each of these columns should allow space for a date, number of pages, a signature or initials, and other notations that will help in keeping track of both the progress and the size of the work. By using such a system the specifications writer can write any section at any time and can plug it into the whole specification where it belongs. It is rarely possible to wait until the working drawings are 100 percent completed before specifications are started.

THREE—PART SECTION

There are many ways in which a section can be arranged to provide the required information in the most understandable manner. Remember that the primary, perhaps the only, purpose of a section is to tell someone who is not familiar with the project exactly what is required. The Section can be roughly segregated into three parts: *the scope, the materials, and the installation.* The CSI has reviewed hundreds of specifications and a tabulation indicates that these three areas should be the major portions of a section, with as many or as few subportions as necessary. Each section should have a consistency of arrangement that provides both a uniform format and a uniform appearance.

Each of the three recommended parts has equal rank with the other two. All three are necessary. Next in rank is a paragraph, one or more of which occur in any one of the parts. The importance of the various paragraphs is indicated by their number or their order in the part. Subdivisions under each paragraph may be required to explain completely any additional information that is necessary. During the preparation of the CSI study much thought was given to selecting terms for the three parts. Finally the terms listed on the following page were chosen as being most comprehensive:

Part 1: General

Part 2: Products

Part 3: Execution

These parts are suggestions only and are somewhat flexible, but the recommended content of each part is as follows:[1]

Part 1: General

Scope
  Work Included
  Related Work
  Furnished by Others
  Installed by Others
  Supplied by Owner

All of these subparagraphs are part of the complete description of the work required. The requirements may be *loose* or *tight,* but they should be adequate to detail fully what is required, what is not required, and what will be supplied or installed by others.

Description of Systems
  Operating Instructions

This grouping is used mainly for mechanical or other engineering systems where a general description of what a system is or does is helpful or necessary.

Regulatory Agencies
  Permits
  Codes
  Regulations
  Agency Testing

Here are included requirements for compliance with various applicable codes or ordinances. Some agencies also require certain tests or presentation of proof of origin.

Qualifications

If qualifications are required they should be included here. These may be for manufacturer, contractors, welders, testing agencies, etc.

Submittals
  Time Schedules
  Shop Drawings
  Samples
  Manufacturers' Manuals
  Guarantees
  Bonds

Most specifications require samples or shop drawings in some sections. Manufacturers' parts lists, operating manuals, and similar literature is required also, especially for engineering work. Guarantees or bonds noted here may be limited to the material specified in this section.

Mock Up
  Models
  Sample Panels
  Assemblies

Where models or assemblies of wall systems, doors, windows, or similar items are required.

[1] Construction Specifications Institute, *Manual of Practice.*

Product Handling
Delivery
Storage
Special Handling

Delivery, handling, and storage of many materials is necessary. Special handling of certain materials, such as cement, requires special atmosheric considerations, which should be detailed here.

Environmental Conditions
Temperature
Humidity
Lighting
Ventilation

Climatic conditions may be very important to proper storage and handling of some materials. Temperatures are vitally important in the placing of concrete and roofing materials.

Protection
Paint Dropcloths
Fire Equipment
Rubbish Removal
Cleaning and Cleanup

Most of these subtitles explain themselves. *Cleanup* usually means the periodic cleaning up of trash and surplus material, while *cleaning* usually involves the polishing of glass, toilet fixtures, resilient floors, and work normally associated with final inspection.

Extra Stock
Maintenance Materials
Spare Parts

Included under this heading are extra stock of floor tile, acoustical ceiling material, and other units for·maintenance or repair. Some equipment may require spare parts.

There are a number of other minor items that might be covered in this first part. These are alternates, measurements, payments, and similar requirements. Some of these are used only in engineering works or are a part of the contract rather than the specifications. In general everything that is not materials or installation should be covered in this first part.

Part 2 of a section includes all factors that specify kind and quality of materials. It is a bit more difficult to limit titles for this part, since they could literally number in the hundreds. The major divisions can be listed as follows, most of which are self-explanatory:

Part 2: Products

Materials

Usually the various materials needed are covered here by listing each material separately.

Mixes

Many products require mixing, either at the job site or at the factory. With the materials specified in the subparagraph above, the mixing of plaster, concrete, asphalt paving, terrazzo, and similar materials is covered here.

Fabrication

Fabrication of door systems, window combinations, toilet partitions, structural steel work, and other work needing assembly are covered in this portion.

Quality Control

In general the factory-based tests or those to be made at source of materials should be covered here. One school of thought holds that job-site testing should be included in Part 3, but many writers include job-site testing along with factory testing.

The third part of a section includes all requirements for proper installation of the requisite materials. This part must be written with even more care and knowledge than either of the other two. The writer must be conversant with the proper methods used by the various trades to produce a satisfactory job and also should be aware of the nonapproved shortcuts that might be attempted if they were not prohibited. Included in Part 3 are the following:

Part 3: Execution

Condition of Surface

This portion is especially important where other work is dependent upon a subsurface. The work involved in painting, wall coverings, floor coverings, and acoustics usually is included in this catagory. There is often a statement included that the installer of a material "shall ascertain that subsurfaces are in proper condition and the unsatisfactory subsurfaces shall be reported to the general contractor for repair before surfacing material is installed."

Preparation of Surfaces
  Fine Grading of Paving
    Subgrade
  Concrete Formwork
  Galvanized Surfaces to
    Receive Paint
  Wood Surfaces for
    Applied Finishes

This unit may overlap the paragraphs for condition of subsurface, but it is primarily concerned with methods necessary for producing a desired surface. How to obtain these surfaces may require either a simple reference to some established standards or it may be a complete step by step description.

Installation
    Application
    Erection
    Placement
    Workmanship

The subtitle *Installation* may also be indicated by the terms listed below it. In general these all say the same thing: how to install the work properly. The selection of terms is sometimes dependent upon the material being used; for instance, *application* for roofing, *erection* for structural steel, *placement* for concrete, etc. Included in this part are requirements for tolerances and matching surfaces.

Field Quality Control

This position for job-site testing requirements is recommended by CSI on the theory that the tests are really a part of installation. Field testing includes soil compaction tests, various concrete tests, piling load tests, and the tests for plumbing and electrical work.

Adjusting
    Patching

These two items hardly need elaboration. Location at this point is consistent with the work process since this work of necessity must come after the original work has been installed.

Cleaning
    Cleanup

Cleaning and cleanup certainly should complete the requirements of any section. There is however a question of who or how this may best be done. In the past the requirement has been for each trade to clean its own work. Journeyman plumbers generally are not good cleaners, nor are glaziers good cleaners. This has suggested that all the requirements for periodic cleanup and final cleaning might better be combined in a special section related to professional cleaning personnel.

These three parts are applicable to almost any section, and a compliance with the recommendations will organize any specification. Some flexibility is allowed by combining or separating sections or by a slight variation in the content of the subparagraphs of the parts. A certain value of standardization will be obtained when the three-part system is voluntarily used time after time.

PARAGRAPH NUMBERING

Numbering of sections and paragraphs and subparagraphs within a section are very important. Although a few A/E firms do not hold with numbering paragraphs, and several go overboard with excessive numbering, data retrieval by contractors and others may be facilitated when a consistent and logical system is used. The system outlined herein, and used by a majority of A/E offices, is different from the decimal system used by the federal government and described in Chapter 9. Our system may also be different from specifications assembled by computer printout, where each line of each page is numbered. The primary idea behind the numbering of paragraphs is, of course, to allow easy and rapid reference to a line, subparagraph, or paragraph. This ease of reference is particularly important when contractors are discussing an item with the A/E, often by telephone. Unless there is easy identification of the discussed point in the documents, it is possible for the two parties to be considering completely different paragraphs on completely different pages.

There are those who hold that the subdivision of a paragraph beyond one subparagraph is excessive. In some cases this may be true and a new paragraph indicator, rather than another subparagraph may be required. The use of letters alone, or of numerals alone, also raises a problem when additional subparagraphs are required, and a decimal numeral system is cumbersome and requires considerable space if it is carried too far.

The most adaptable and usable system is a combination of letters and numerals. The difference between letters and numbers provides some visual contrast, and the use of capital letters, lowercase letters, and parentheses provides considerable flexibility. Illustrated below is a recommended outline for indicating portions of a section as well as for providing a guide for proper indentation, although all A/E firms do not accept the indentation method for quicker subject identification.

10A-01 Paragraph title
    a. Subparagraph
      1. Subparagraph
        (a) Subparagraph
          (1) Subparagraph

In the example above, *10A* indicates *Section A of Division 10,* and the subparagraphs simply means that *a* is a subparagraph of *01, 1* is a subparagraph of *a*, etc. Those A/E offices that use the *Uniform System Index* of section numbers will start with a five-digit number instead of *10A*, but the same system can be used or the order of letters and numbers reversed, if desired. Remember that this is an indication of subparagraphs. Whenever a new subject is needed a new first paragraph indicator is also needed, such as *10A-01, 10A-02, 10A-03*, etc. A new section would be indicated as *10B, 10C,* or a similar combination.

PROJECT—PAGE IDENTIFICATION

Every page of a specification should have the project, section, and page clearly indicated. Although it may be assumed that the master pages are in proper order and that all pages are for the same project, it is entirely possible to mix pages or projects, lose them, or collate them in the wrong order. When any form of master specification is used it is imperative that the same order for sections within a division be maintained; otherwise one of the principal values of a master is lost. One of the simplest systems for complete identification is shown below:

Upper right corner of each page.	Sunnyside Elementary School Project No. 12345
Lower right or center of each page.	Concrete Formwork Page 3A-6

These few items completely identify the project, the section title, section indicator (*3A*), and the page within that section (*6*). By using *3A-6* as a page indicator it is possible to start each section with a new series and thereby add or subtract pages or sections without disturbing the remainder of the work. This system also allows the writing or typing of specifications to proceed section by section but not in any consecutive order, since page numbering is complete within each section.

PAGE ARRANGEMENT

Habit and tradition have caused us to start reading a paragraph from the left. This same tradition has carried over to influence the physical location of titles, for most specifications. The title usually appears at the left side of the page with the author's suggestions for titles at the right. In books where the sheet is printed only on one side, and this covers a majority of specifications, it puts the titles down near the binding, the most inconvenient position for quick reference. Titles can be located anywhere so long as they clearly refer to the following subject matter. Specifications are not read as literary works but as references where a subject must be rapidly and easily identified. Why then not put the paragraph titles at the right of the page so that a quick riffle of pages can expose the titles without having to dig to the binding?

DRAFTING THE FINAL SPECIFICATION

Now the specifications writer should be able to get to the business of writing the final specification. Most of the suggestions outlined in the preceding paragraphs would probably be a matter of office preference and would not be established for each project in a different manner. Regardless of the master specification used, (computer, tape, or the writer's own) the process for the final drafting is comparable. In order not to be misleading, it might be well to repeat here that the process of writing the final specification is not one with a definite starting point, but one that starts with the first conference and continues until the final specification is distributed. If addenda and change orders are considered as a part of specification and substitutions during construction are included, the updating of the *final* continues until the notice of completion is recorded.

Roughly the same procedure is used to produce the final specification that is used for the preliminary. The drawings are reviewed with extreme accuracy, with special attention to items that appeared in the preliminary. Use colored chalk to check off all items. This is the point at which the writer may find that steel handrails have been changed to aluminum on the drawings, that formerly painted surfaces are now vinyl covered, or that some wood doors have now become steel. Actually, in the most efficient operations none of these things would come as a surprise, since the specification material would be collected and modified as the working drawings were produced.

Most specifications writers will write the specifications in order; this gives them the most freedom. For the sake of illustration let us select ceramic tile as a subject. The first thing to do is to check all possible locations where ceramic tile might be used: toilet rooms, showers, drinking fountains, kitchen units, laboratories, and similar areas. The preliminary specification will be a big help since it indicates whether ceramic tile is to be used and, if so, where. The various areas should be checked for tile sizes, type of base, corners, mortar-set, dry-set, adhesive, and type of grout. These different sizes or methods of installation should be listed, the master specifications checked, the required sizes and methods plugged into the master, and the extraneous material deleted. Presto! A specification for ceramic tile tailored to the project.

MATERIAL — METHODS RESEARCH

The tile illustration makes it seem child's play to produce a good specification. Look at a few drawings, make a few changes in a "canned" master specification, and you have it! Unfortunately it isn't quite that easy unless you have plenty of experience and complete, fully organized reference material. Someone must compile the references, and this is one of the most important functions of the specifications writer. Not that he does it from scratch, he uses literature from local or national manufacturers and associations, from contractors' groups, from government sources, from contacts with mechanics, and from his own experience. The younger man is at a disadvantage only to the extent of his inexperience and his ability (or lack of it) to use the work of others.

Let's look at the work required when no masters are available or when the writer is attempting to organize his own resources. In the case of ceramic tile, the writer should first check with the manufacturers of ceramic tile for the sizes and types available. Local suppliers and installers can tell him those that are distributed and used in his area. This should be a major consideration, since it is foolish to write specifications for materials that are not available or have high shipping costs that would limit competition. The writer must then select the sizes most used or list all of the sizes, indicate the different glazes available, and, if manufacturers are to be listed in the specifications, list the manufacturers and their addresses.

Exactly the same process, but in more detail, is necessary for proper installation specifications. Installation recommendations are published by trade associations. Local contractors or workmen can augment these printed instructions so that any local variations may be included. Different sets of installation paragraphs need to be written for mortar-set, dry-set, adhesive-set, and any other methods. In most master specifications the paragraph indicator is the same, so the writer usually selects the one that fits his particular project. The research for testing methods, guarantees, and all the other items included in a specification proceeds in the same manner.

In using the reference material, the specifications writer must have the experience or ability to put the proper materials items together with the appropriate installation items. Many specifications writers use a check list to be sure that the various parts fit together properly, but in most cases this is not necessary. One requirement that is often overlooked is the updating of information. Even with a "canned" master updating must be done continuously to maintain workable reference material.

CHECK AND RECHECK

On a major project, *check and recheck* is the name of the game. It should, and usually does, go on continuously. If the first set of working drawings is supplied to the specifications writer when it is approximately 75 percent finished, he should have another set at about 90 percent completion and a final set at 100 percent completion. Each set should have a review similar to the first to make sure that all changes in the drawings that affect the specifications are caught.

With good cooperation between the drafting force and the specifications department there should be a ready exchange whenever any major changes are made. Most changes are in the drawings, but the reverse may also occur if the specifications writer must substitute a product because of change of model or style, unavailability, discontinuance, or some other reason. Much of this updated information is available only from manufacturers' representatives, so close contact should be maintained with them.

How far should one go with the typing during this period? Of course the typist can wait until the specifications copy is 100 percent finished. This should eliminate any retyping, but it is not very practical when a deadline stares the writer in the face. The normal procedure would be to type each section as it is finished, at any time during the final writing. The greatest argument against this is that some work may have to be retyped as the check-and-recheck process goes on. The best argument for the early typing is that deadlines are more easily met; also, the retyping of several pages or even a complete section will not hold up completion as much as retyping an entire specification. The use of computer or magnetic tape masters can speed up this production period, so each writer will have to adjust his writing pace with that of his original-producing system.

THE LAST LOOK

As the completed construction documents go to bidding contractors and building permit departments there is usually a period during which the A/E office reviews those documents. This is a *last look* interval and changes may still be made or errors corrected. Often a *plan checker* is the reviewer. This person may never have seen either the drawings or the specifications before, and he will check coordination of these as well as compliance with codes. If the documents have not been distributed to contractors, the changes are easily made before issue of any drawings or specifications. If the documents have been released to bidders, the changes must go out as addenda, a bulletin, or a modification. Invariably there are errors or changes that might be overlooked in the reviewing program and any corrections after the bidding is over must be taken care of by Change Order.

SUMMARY

The drafting of final specifications is the provision of a written document that will supplement the drawings. After working drawings are partially completed the specifications writer may start his final draft and continue to add and revise as total completion approaches. The format of good specifications is reasonably well settled but the content is up to the writer. The use of masters of various kinds is designed to facilitate the final writing, but careful review of the drawings by the writer is the factor that determines what requirements are included in the three parts of each section. Specifications should be revised and re-revised as necessary to produce accurate bidding and working documents.

QUESTIONS

8.1. Name the three recommended parts of a section format.
8.2. Discuss paragraph numbering system. Can you devise a better approach?
8.3. Do you have any recommendations for better or easier identification of project, section, or page?
8.4. Compare possible arrangements of paragraph titles on specifications pages.
8.5. Have you any suggestions for compiling specifications materials to meet drawing conditions?

9

THE FEDERAL SPECIFICATION

The Federal specification is probably the most open specification of any. In fact this, together with the low bid usually accepted, prompted the now famous remark that space craft are the result of the low bid. Quality is difficult to demand or even anticipate when the requirements are such that almost any reasonably similar product is acceptable; this is the greatest drawback to this system. On the other hand the United States government has made hundreds of tests of products (as noted in Chapter 3), has established procedures for their selection, and has certain forms for their specification. These standard specifications for federal government work were authorized by an act of Congress in 1949, to be implemented by the General Services Administration. With very few exceptions they must be used for all federally funded projects, which include work done for the Corp of Engineers, the Navy Public Works, the Indian Service, the Forestry Service, various projects of the General Services Administration, the Federal Housing Administration, as well as other federal agencies and some state or local governments.

THE PDE

In the jargon of the United States Navy Facilities Command, *PDE* means *Project Design Engineer,* who is not necessarily an engineer or a designer per se, but the person in charge of the design phase of the project for the agency. This individual is the contact between the agency and the A/E. All information comes through the PDE to the A/E and all project submittals from the A/E go back to the PDE. In most cases the contact between these two groups is in the person of one official representative but the specifier, who is usually not the representative, should make the acquaintance of the PDE and the specifications department members at an early date.

The PDE often has information on the project that may not be apparent to the A/E or may not be included in any data supplied to the A/E. If at all possible the specifier should review the project with the PDE or sit in on initial conferences. At a later date direct contact with the specifications department may be warranted but most information supplied should be double checked with the PDE. The various project submittals will be reviewed by both the PDE and the specifications department of the agency and corrections noted as necessary.

Each agency has its own procedure. The contact man for an agency may have almost any title, but he is usually experienced in architecture or engineering and has administrative ability as well. In local work for school districts and similar organizations the contact man can be anyone from the superintendent of smaller districts to the superintendent of a sophisticated building or construction department much like that encountered in strictly federal work. In any case there are usually rules for the presentation and preparation of the working documents and these, together with any standards used by the client, should be closely followed.

PRELIMINARY SURVEY

Preliminary planning and general layout, a reasonably accurate construction cost estimate, and often some specification data on unusual materials or methods are usually supplied by the agency involved. Each agency has its own procedure, so the A/E should thoroughly check what will be supplied by the agency or required by it. As mentioned in Chapter 3, many agencies supply a manual of instruction to the selected A/E and perhaps the best advice to any A/E is to follow the instructions. *Don't use your own judgement*! If possible the specifications writer, as well as the project manager and engineers, should contact the agency engineer or agency specifier to clarify any possible questions.

The specification preliminary is essentially a list of materials with quality or installation indicated by proper Federal Specification designators. In the last few years almost all agencies of the federal government have required that construction specifications for any of their projects be organized in accordance with the sixteen divisions of the *Uniform System*. The initial effort on the part of the specifier should be toward listing all of the possible materials or methods that will be required on the project. When this list is completed a tabulation of available Federal Specifications (F.S.) or Military Specifications (MIL–) that best match these materials or methods should be made and obtained from the agency or government printing office.

The actual preliminary is then compiled from the list of materials and methods required by the project with proper references for Federal Specifications or Military Specifications and any others necessary. These later references can be any that are not *proprietary;* that is, they do not specify a material or method by manufacturer's name, trade name, or other limiting description. Such references as ASTM, lumber grading associations, tile institute recommendations, millwork associations, and mechanical and electrical standards are admissible so long as they do not restrict a material or method. Another source, as mentioned in Chapter 3, is the local type specification provided by the local agency office.

PRELIMINARY SUBMITTAL

Organize the various divisions in order and list the sections under each division. List the materials under each section. As the lead paragraph, copy the *scope* from the material provided by the agency. This is then followed by the standard paragraph, again copied, usually titled *Applicable Documents.* Under this lead paragraph are listed the various references, generally in the following order: Federal Specifications, Military Specifications, Bureau Specifications, Other Specifications. In each case these references are to be listed in alphabetical order or in succeeding numerical order. Be certain that the proper revision designator for each reference is up-to-date.

After all this initial plotting has been done, the rest is simply a matter of sorting out the proper paragraphs of the standards and referring to them in the submitted preliminary. This may take a little reading on the part of the specifier as some of the references for installation include several different kinds of a general item. A case in point is the United States Navy Bureau of Yards and Docks Specification 10Y titled *Metal Windows.* This document includes several types as well as several different materials for metal windows. Steel windows should have supplemental Federal Specifications covering any paint to be applied to the steel, whereas aluminum windows may need an ASTM specification for any anodic treatment required. The remainder of each section can simply be a notation of the types of materials, tests, accessories, or other items required.

Preliminary submittal is usually limited in quantity, so it may be typed on bond paper or a master for duplication by any method. This is not true of the final submittal, as will be discussed later. Again a conference with the PDE or agency specifications specialist will be valuable in determining the method to be used, copies required, and related information. A word of warning here may not be amiss. Although the agency requirements may call for a definite number of copies, for example six, experience will often dictate a duplication method that could produce ten to perhaps twenty copies, some immediately and some at a future date. For no apparent reason there never seems to be enough copies to distribute to each person or facility involved. A little advance planning in the reproduction of these submittals may ease the burden of retyping or expensive duplication.

WAITING PERIOD

Preliminary submittal is often followed by a period of waiting for agency review and comment. This can be a day or several months depending upon the size of the project, proximity of the agency and A/E offices, priority of the project, availability of reviewing personnel, and speed of distribution of the documents. None of these have any direct relationship with the A/E, so little can be done to speed the process. With this factor in mind it might be instructive to quickly review a possible *chain of approval* for a typical federal project of medium size, the remodeling of an existing building at a naval air station within a continental United States Navy Facilities Command district.

The project probably originated because base requirements for certain types of space were limited or not available. A review is made by base personnel of existing facilities and it is determined that an existing building is not being completely used, that it is in a suitable location on the base, and that it could be remodeled successfully. The base facilities office (public works) then surveys the building, makes some preliminary plans, a preliminary remodeling cost estimate, and a recommendation to proceed with the project or to drop it. This information is usually collected and organized by civilian personnel. The chief civilian in charge of the base office then confers with the service officer assigned as head of the office, and if the project is approved, the service officer confers with the base commanding officer and the district service officer. Upon approval, the project is given a priority and a date when funds might be available is projected. The project may then go to the district office, be assigned to a PDE for further processing, or it may be shelved, depending upon priority and funds available.

If priority is high and funds are immediately available, an A/E is selected through a series of conferences, and the project is processed further by direct contact between the PDE and the A/E representative. If priority is low, funds not available, or the project is deemed inadvisable, it is returned to the base office and is filed, which usually means it is a dead item. Often, however, there are *planning funds* available. This means that a project with a low immediate priority, but an ultimate higher priority, having no construction funds available may be processed to any point from preliminary studies to completed documents by an A/E. This point is usually determined by the amount of funds available and how soon construction money will be forthcoming. When preliminary or final documents are presented by the A/E, the chain of command is reversed and the path is from PDE to the district officer, district office to base officer, then to base civilian staff. If approved along this entire line, the process is again reversed with approval from base commander, then district office commander, and finally out for bidding.

All of this approval procedure and review takes time. During this waiting period the A/E office probably is continuing work on the project. The specifier should be double checking any references he expects to use, materials or methods included in the project that are not covered by acceptable nonproprietary specifications, special conditions that he will have to cover by writing from scratch, and the ability of prospective suppliers to provide the necessary materials on time. This last item is of particular importance, since some materials distributors do not like supplying federal projects because of the requirements of Federal Specifications. Other suppliers may be eliminated because of quality-price factors.

MANUFACTURER - DISTRIBUTOR

Here again we depend a great deal upon the representative of the manufacturer or local distributor for knowledgeable help. As mentioned in Chapter 3, many manufactured items have been checked out for compliance with ASTM, Federal Specifications, Military Specificaations, Underwriters Inc. standards, or other approved tests. This compliance is often listed in the literature of the manufacturer, but since the copy for this material may be more than a year old it is a wise precaution to check its current status with the local manufacturer's representative or distributor. In some fields the specifications writer just does not have enough exposure or knowledge to be able to indicate the proper item easily.

One of these semielusive fields is finishing hardware. The Federal Specification for *Hardware, Builders; Locks and Door-trim FF-H-106* illustrates, by the use of cuts, the general appearance of acceptable hardware but does not call out any trade name. In order to be sure that satisfactory hardware will be provided, the representative of a local hardware distributor can match FF-H-106 with obtainable lock-sets and other devices. This sounds easy, but again the matter of allowing almost everyone who manufactures hardware to bid comes into the picture. Some local distributors of high quality hardware might not be interested in bidding against a distributor whose product is lower in quality but still meets the minimum requirements. Unless the specifier has a good hardware contact, he must find a hardware consultant who, for a fee, will help him out. This same situation may be true for other portions of the work, so the specifier may have some research to do.

WRITING THE FINAL FEDERAL SPEC

The final specification for a federal project usually does not require more or different work than any other kind of project. If a master is used it should be rechecked for latest revisions. This is fairly simple since the batch of Federal Specifications and Military Specifications that were obtained at the very start of the project should be the latest. Occasionally, however, changes are made in the latest issue of a specification between the start of the project and the start of the final, so updating of references is important. A quick check with the PDE or the agency specifications department usually indicates this fact.

As with commercial projects, the specifications writer should check the drawings as they progress and prepare some sections of his work in advance if possible. While the working drawings are being completed, additional parts of the specifications may also be completed. One of the most difficult aspects of doing federal specifications is the tendency to overwrite. The printed guide specifications should be studied and only the portions that relate directly to the project should be considered. The portions that apply completely to the project should be copied, with the references to other documents corrected as necessary to meet the latest revisions. At the same time, it is expedient for the specifier to check the content of any references to be sure they meet project requirements. It could be very embarrasing to assume that crushed rock, for instance, be used for concrete aggregate if a referenced specification calls for steel slag, river gravel, *or* crushed rock. Variations may be authorized by local type specifications. These guides vary the national standards to bring them in accordance with local conditions. A similar review should be made to assure that they completely fit the project. In most cases these too are copied without change whenever they apply. One of the principal similarities between commercial and federal specifications is the primary arrangement of divisions, which is required by most agencies. The major differences are the use of a decimal system in federal specifications to indicate paragraphs in most cases, and the *cold copy* method for using most references.

FINAL FEDERAL SPECIFICATION

Before any typing is done, check the form that the masters must take. In the case of work for United States Navy Facilities Command offices, the final specifications must be typed on oversized sheets supplied by the agency, with a carbon copy. These sheets have nonprinting blue guide lines. Other agencies have similar regulations for proper submittal. Here again experience will probably teach that one carbon copy is never enough for the agency and that the A/E should probably have a copy for the inevitable future reference. Some offices have overcome this shortage by making the carbon a master for spirit duplication or electrostatic duplication. This method is well worth considering, since as many as a dozen or more copies are sometimes needed during the final checking.

The arrangement within each division is dictated by the number of materials or operations necessary to construct the project. This is the same process used for a commercial operation, but from that point on the systems differ. In federal specifications there is no three-part arrangement. The federal specification is arranged in accordance with the guide specifications, period. The specification is given an identification number that is somewhat similar to the commercial project number. It appears on each page of the specifications. The pages are numbered consecutively, which may or may not be similar to commercial specifications. Another major difference is the reference to *General Conditions.* These are usually preprinted, supplied by the agency, and in many cases are not a concern of the A/E except as a reference to *Section 1B, Division 1* or similar notation.

NONSTANDARD ITEMS

What happens when the Federal Specifications, Military Specifications, and other documents do not cover a material or method? This occasionally happens when the minimum is not good enough in quality, when existing work must be matched, or when only one material will actually do the job. This situation requires a complete description of the material and the installation in such terms that only one, or a very limited number, of products can be supplied in accordance with the specification. The description must be strictly nonproprietary to the extent that no trade names, manufacturers, or similar indication may be used. When such deviation from the normal procedure is necessary the writer must be certain that no standard specification covers the subject and that the PDE approves. Often this becomes a simple case of redesign using a standard product rather than a special one, although some argument may come from the design department of the A/E. Where a match of existing work is required, especially matching older, no-longer-manufactured items, the research may be extensive and the exact wording must be carefully considered.

FINAL SUBMITTAL

Upon completion of the A/E's work all of the required original documents are submitted to the PDE. This procedure is different from most commercial work, where the A/E retains possession of the original drawings and specifications. Unless the contract between the agency and the A/E indicates otherwise, the agency will usually print the working documents and supervise their distribution, as well as the ultimate construction of the project. The required number of copies is supplied by the A/E for final review by the agency. This ends the A/E's contract technically, but not practically. In many cases questions that arise during bidding or construction are relayed to the A/E project manager or specifier for clarification.

OTHER GOVERNMENT WORK

The foregoing is typical for a project under the direction of the United States Navy Facilities Command. It may be varied in many ways by other agencies. In the case of work for school districts, city, county, or state, the process is a combination of straight commercial procedure and federal procedure. Many of these semifederal or governmental agencies provide drafting standards as well as specifications material to project A/E's. The specifier should check the type of specifications references required: normal commercial, strictly Federal Specifications, the agencies own, or some combination of the three. Here the matching of existing equipment and the possibility of a variation from standards is greater than in a strictly federal project.

SUMMARY

Specifications for federal projects are considerably different from those of a commercial project. When commercial specifications are written, the material used may come from almost any source including trade names, named manufacturers, or the standards from many organizations. This is not so for a strictly federal project, where all reference is nonproprietary and linked to governmental standards. The federal type employs direct quotations and copied paragraphs from the printed material supplied to the A/E, as well as a reference by letter and numeral designator. Of particular importance is the continuous updating of the government standards, a primary research chore for the specifier. In between the strictly commercial project and one which is strictly federal are many projects that have specifications that are combinations of both. Probably one of the most important precautions that can be taken by those doing federal work is to follow the instructions provided by the agency. If the rules are diligently adhered to there should be very little difficulty in writing good federal specifications.

QUESTIONS

9.1. What is a PDE? How may this position be compared with a somewhat similar position in the A/E office?

9.2. Are federal specifications of the open or closed type? Explain.

9.3. Name the primary sources for information for writing federal specifications.

9.4. List the names of several organizations that you think might be using federal specifications for their construction projects.

9.5. Write a nonproprietary specification paragraph for an item you might want to include in a federal project and for which there is no standard.

10

ALTERNATES, ADDENDA, AND CHANGE ORDERS

In most building projects a continuous effort is made to provide the most construction within the predetermined budget. It is probably true that every architect or engineer at some time dreams about the "perfect" project where money is not important, but this ideal is not a common occurrence in real life. In order to try to balance the budget on a project, *alternates* are often included as a part of the construction documents. During the period allowed for bid surveys and estimating prior to actual bid time there may be answers to questions, clarifications, changes, or other information that should reach all bidders in the form of *addenda*. After the construction contract has been signed and during the entire course of construction there may be changes of various sorts that should be described and authorized by proper *change orders*. These documents have a direct influence on the specifications and the specifications writer.

Each of these documents occurs at a specific time and in most cases has a direct effect upon the construction budget. In addition, due to changes in materials involved, the specifications are altered in some fashion by these deviations. The references may be only a matter of indicating a different paragraph or section, or they may include an entirely new material or method for which a complete specification must be written. Quite often the required changes are difficult to show on the drawings; they must therefore be fully described in words with proper cross reference to some identifiable point in the drawings.

ALTERNATES

Alternates invariably come about because of budget problems. Once the dollar amount of the construction cost is agreed upon between the owner and the A/E, it becomes the problem of the A/E to provide the construction at or below that agreed-upon amount. Unfortunately, very few owners have definite enough ideas about their needs, or their wants, to keep them from injecting more area, quality, or detail into the proposal. It is true that the conscientious A/E will notify the owner of an estimated cost increase every time a major change is proposed, but somehow these increases are never cranked into the owners picture of ultimate cost. In some instances, due to actual or anticipated costs, the owner and A/E may mutually agree to add or delete portions of the work in order to more nearly match the budget. These are the reasons for the inclusion of alternates in the bid documents prior to bid time.

With good office operation, adequate liaison between specifications and project manager, and some agreed-upon possibilities, alternates are usually not too difficult to handle. When the proposed alternates are large, as in the possible deletion of a building wing or entire rooms, the alternate description can simply state that "all work from coordinates A-1 to A-6 shall be deleted etc." If the mechanical, electrical, and structural drawings have been detailed with this possibility in mind there will be pipe valves or plugs, electrical junction boxes, structural stubs of some nature, and various other details that allow the construction to proceed either as shown or with a portion deleted or added to more nearly fit the project budget. This method, of course, requires that drafting, cost estimating, engineering, and specifications work closely together so that alternates may be agreed upon at an early stage in the project. In some cases it is best to have alternate proposals drawn on separate sheets of paper, keeping in mind that these sheets may be retained as a part of the contract or deleted if certain deductive alternates are accepted. In most cases the specifications will not be affected very much since the general construction, roofing, wall construction, painting, hardware, and mechanical and electrical work as well as other sections will probably remain the same for the portion of work included under the contract.

The preceding paragraph outlines the alternate work when a complete segment of the construction is to be considered, with no great changes required for differences of quality or quantity, no design changes, and with items already specified to be used in other locations. This often occurs where there is a large budget adjustment, but more often there is a "nuts-and-bolts" type of alternate. This latter requires a careful review of the drawings and an equally careful review of the specifications. A common type of alternate is one in which quality is reduced or another product is substituted. This is particularly true in regard to floor coverings, wall finishes, and hardware. Where mechanical or electrical systems are the subject of alternates the entire system may be changed. Although a change in the quality of material is a most common alternate that usually requires a minimum of redrafting, it may, on the other hand, require a considerable specifications change.

Where an alternate is used to reduce costs through the reduction of quality, the basic product has usually already been specified. This is easily illustrated by assuming that we will lower the grade of asphalt tile in a particular area. The original specifications may have called for E grade tile. The alternate reduces the tile to C grade by a simple statement to that effect in the list of alternates. The method of installation, color selection, acceptable manufacturers, and other related data have already been given in the portion of the original specification and only the grade has been changed. This is one of the simplest methods for using alternates, and it works well so long as product or installation methods are not changed.

If the proposed alternate is not simply the complete deletion of a part of the construction or a reduction of quality, a different approach must be made. Quite often certain rooms or areas may be structurally completed but finish floors, wall surfaces, ceiling installations, mechanical or electrical work, and many other *finishing items* will be deleted. In the hope that the budget will cover their cost, these items have all been adequately specified in the original documents, so further specification is not needed. The major problem then is one of correctly and precisely stating what is to be left as is, deleted, or otherwise changed. With good drafting cooperation and adequate notes this can readily be done, but if the drawings are not clear and the alternates poorly written there may be considerable difference of opinion about what is expected.

The third method for alternates is the most difficult for the specifications writer. This method entails the complete change from one product or material to another that might be satisfactory but less expensive. To be properly effective a new specifications section, or at least a new materials portion, should be written for each new or different product used. This may sometimes be done as a part of the original specification if great care is taken to indicate which product is meant for the prime bid and which is to be used as an alternate. As an example, the original specification may call for asbestos-vinyl floor tiles installed in accordance with accepted standards. The alternate might be *C* grade asphalt tile. The differences in appearance, wearing qualities, maintenance, and other factors have been approved by the owner. This change is then called out as an alternate using asphalt tile as specified in the regular resilient flooring section. However, care must be taken to indicate clearly that the asphalt tile is an alternate. If no section on resilient flooring is available the entire requirement, scope, material, installation, etc., should be written for asphalt tile.

UNIT PRICES

Unit prices are sometimes used in lieu of alternates, especially when the extent of the work is not exact, when underground conditions cannot readily be determined, or when a basis for the cost of possible additional work is desired. Highway construction is often based almost completely upon unit prices. Unit prices may be required for the driving of piling in excess of a given length or for placing a number of cubic yards of concrete in foundations or roads. Drawings for this type of construction usually show typical design requirements, approximate cut-fill in excavation or grading, typical section of roadway and curb, minimum length and cluster of piling, and other typical requirements. This allows the contractor-bidder some leeway in bidding, since he is usually paid by calculating the amount of work done at the unit price quoted by him. This same sort of work may be encountered in building construction, especially when it is expected that the budget will not be exceeded by the bids and additional work is contemplated.

ADDENDA

Addenda to the contract documents add or delete requirements, answer questions, approve substitutions, change dates for bids or completion, and in general act as a catch-all to pass along information to the bidders. Time is the most important factor in the use of addenda, which must be clear and concise and reach all bidders well before the bid time. Distribution is usually by registered letter; the A/E then has a signed receipt for each letter, a precaution that should eliminate any disagreement about who received the addenda and when.

Upon the release of the working documents to prospective bidders, the project manager and specifications chief should carefully review the documents for errors or omissions. Each contractor, subcontractor, or material supplier will probably be doing the same. Most offices make it a policy to tabulate questions received from contractors and give no individual answers. After collecting several questions over a given period of time the A/E office then provides àll bidders with duplicate information. If individual answers are given to separate contractors it is possible to overlook one and have unhappy bidders or even a law suit as a result.

Addenda may cover any change or clarification necessary before bid time. Addenda are not used after bids are received. Addenda are issued to all who would be affected by any changes or clarifications. These three points are the basics necessary to an addendum. The format for good addenda varies with each office, but some fundamental items must be included regardless of the format used. Each addendum should be dated and given a consecutive number. The project name, location, and any other necessary identification should be clearly indicated. Some offices do not group items that are additions, deletions, changes or clarifications, but if all the items in each category are collected in a group it makes for easier reading and understanding. It is also helpful at the beginning of each item, to indicate adequately the subject, use one of the words *add, delete, or change,* and list any section or drawing reference. This practice allows a quick and easy check against the original documents. A typical addendum is shown in the following example:

John J. Jones Architect   Addendum No. 1
1030 Construction Ave.   2 January 19__
Anytown U. S. A
Phone 123-4567   Project: Villa Marina Hotel
                           Anytown U. S. A.
              Project No: 9876

The original drawings and specifications for this project, dated 1 December 1972, are amended as indicated herein. Receipt of this addendum shall be acknowledged by bidders by inclusion of number and date on their respective bid forms. All changes shall be reflected in proposed bids.

Item 1A—ADD—Drwg. 6—Spec. page 9A-2—Resilient Flooring. Add 9 x 9 x 1/8 asphalt tile, C grade, in storeroom 102.
Item 1B—ADD—Drwg. 19—Spec. page 15B-10—Boiler Room Piping. Paint all exposed steel pipes one coat primer plus one coat industrial enamel. Color to be selected by architect.

Item 1C—DELETE—Drwg. 1A—Spec. page 2C-2—Wire Fencing. Delete double gate at First St. parking entrance.

Item 1D—CHANGE—Instruction to Bidders—page 1, time of bid opening. Change from 2:30 P.M., 3 February, 19__ to 2:30 P.M., 6 February, 19__. Location for bid opening remains the same.

Item 1E—CLARIFICATION—Spec. page 6C-10—Cabinet Work. Blotted word par. 6C-5a, middle of 4th line after "CUSTOM grade" is OAK.

A variation of form might place all references to drawings in one group, all references to specifications in another, etc. The main problem with this method is that additions, deletions, changes, or clarifications are easily mixed together or may have a dual reference to both plans and specifications. In cases where entirely new specifications sections or new drawings are required, these are usually appended to the addendum form, with proper reference to them in the addendum items.

CHANGE ORDER

Change orders are often confused with Addenda but the principal difference is that addenda come into use before bid opening while *change orders are used after a contract is signed.* Change orders originate with the A/E as a simple request to the contractor for a cost estimate and also any time of completion variation for contemplated changes in the original concept of construction. These estimates are made by the contractor and returned to the A/E. If they are satisfactory to the A/E and the owner, they are then put in the form of a Change Order. When this change order form is properly completed and signed by both owner and contractor, it becomes part of the contract documents. In the process of constructing a major project there may be hundreds of change orders brought about by substitutions of materials, additions or deductions from the work, weather conditions, labor problems, or any other deviation from the requirements of the original documents. In almost every case the two items of time and money are of utmost importance.

The logical and consistent use of authorized and signed change orders will eliminate many of the arguments about costs of *extras* or credits for *deducts* throughout the life of a construction project. It is good basic business practice to allow the contractor to submit a cost prior to inclusion of the work and to allow the owner to accept or reject that cost prior to its accomplishment. There are several things however that the A/E, or his project manager or specifications chief, must keep in mind. Every change order should fully indicate the name of the project, its location, the date of the order, a complete description of the work involved, unit prices or the total cost of each item of work, the original contract amount, any credits or extras to date, credits or extras for current change order, new contract amount, and any revision of time for completion. This last item is of particular importance. Every change should indicate what will happen to the original completion date: extended, decreased, or unchanged.

Change orders should be made in triplicate at least, thereby allowing one copy to the owner, one to the contractor, and one to the A/E as a matter of record. On very large projects additional copies may be needed for the clerk-of-the-works, the contractor's field office, the A/E field office, and even for the financial backer or city building department. If the specifications writer is not involved in many of the changes, he certainly should be notified if materials are substituted or installation methods are changed. In addition, most specifications writers have gained, by osmosis, a fairly good knowledge of the cost of materials. This knowledge should be helpful in judging the validity of the proposed costs of changes.

SUMMARY

Alternates, addenda and change orders have one thing in common—they each in some manner change the original contract documents for a construction project. *Alternates and addenda are issued by the A/E prior to bid time* and, except for items covered as allowances, rarely include any price or cost information. Neither of these documents requires any signature other than that of the A/E and all parties holding sets of the original documents should also receive sets of the revisions to those documents. Bid forms should allow for verification of all addenda and should contain a statement that all cost factors due to such addenda have been incorporated in the bid.

Change orders are different. They are pure and simple *changes to a signed contract* after the fact and indicate mutual agreement for dollars and time between the parties to the contract: the owner and the contractor. The latest change order issued should show at a glance the latest agreed total cost of construction and the accepted final date of completion. Each item of each change order should be written as completely as possible to indicate accurately the work required, the cost for the change, and the time difference caused by the change.

Types of changes, both before and after bidding, stem from a number of sources. First, of course, are those originating from simple errors or omissions. Other reasons are: changes of requirements originating with the owner or required by a governmental agency, changes in time for bidding, known material shortages, and strikes or layoffs of various unions or producers. The specifier must be able to evaluate each item and spell out what is required in each document.

QUESTIONS

10.1. Give the time for processing of alternates, addenda and change orders in relation to bid time.
10.2. What is the basic reason for alternates?
10.3. What is the basic reason for addenda?
10.4. How are change orders originated and processed?
10.5. What two factors should each change order always include?

11

MECHANIZATION
OF SPECIFICATIONS

The word *mechanization* has been used in the title of this chapter rather than *automation* in an attempt to offset some of the poorly defined, misunderstood, misleading references to *data processing, computers,* and similar catch phrases now current and fashionable. An effort will be made to touch upon all phases of machine aids used in the production of specifications, keeping in mind that not every architectural or engineering office is equipped with all types of equipment but each uses one or more of the machines described, depending upon the size of the office and its specifications volume. Equipment manufacturers are usually glad to supply specialized information or demonstrations of their units if an inquiry is directed to them.

Machines cannot replace the specifications writer. Someone has to do the thinking and machines cannot do this—yet. On the other hand machines can help the specifications writer in producing his finished product by eliminating typing errors, speeding production, and improving final appearance. In the following pages we will review some of the many newer production tools available to both small and large offices. For the most part these mechanized assistants do not require operators with extensive, costly, or highly specialized training, and the few that do require such training are not in general use in A/E offices.

THE SYSTEMS APPROACH

Before we delve into the use or adaptability of various machines to help mechanize the production of specifications let us look at some of the earlier research that has been done on the subject. As mentioned in other parts of this book, the production of specifications has been brought about by the increasing number and kinds of building materials and their methods of installation. It follows logically that as the amount of description required to indicate fully the materials and methods increased so did the work load of the specifier, and he looked for help in many directions.

In order to better define the direction which could be recommended, the Construction Specifications Institute commissioned the Stanford Research Institute to make a study and report on the use and future of automated specifications writing. This report, titled *Automated Specifications, A Research Survey, STD-1* was published by CSI in 1967 and, among other things, proposed several levels of preparation with their attendant equipment. Although these levels may have some value in the future of specifications writing, they are not widely used now except in groups talking about the processes of specifications writing, and they may never be of paramount importance to most specifications writers. They are included here so that the system is known to exist and may be used as a reference basis if desired.

Primarily for purposes of classification the Stanford Research Institute, Palo Alto, California, proposed the following levels of preparation:

Level I   Manual system of cut-and-paste.

Level II   Automatic typing or printing.

Level III   Specifications storage, retrieval, and modification, using automated equipment.

Level IV   Advanced techniques for storage, retrieval, and modification of specifications by use of masters or computer.

Level V   Future integration of design, drafting, specifications, and related material by automatic equipment.

Level VI   Future systems, unidentified.

Although some smaller offices are still operating at Level I, the majority of A/E's in the United States are preparing their specifications, and many other office documents, at Level II or III, and an increasing number are at Level IV. There has been experimentation with the complete integration of design, working drawings, and specifications, but to date no system has been devised to provide Level V in reliable form at reasonable cost. Level VI of course is for the future; it allows for any new approach or development to be included.

CATALOG RETRIEVAL

Easy and rapid filing and retrieval of manufacturers' catalog information has been one of the industry's major problems for many years. Most offices are still dependent on a library of books, Sweet's volumes, loose-leaf binders or multiple-drawer filing for this vital information, and perhaps from a strictly financial standpoint this may be acceptable. The principal drawbacks of this elementary system are the time wasted in searching for appropriate catalogs and refiling them, as well as the cost of adequate storage space that will be readily available to the personnel using the material. To some extent the first of these objections can be overcome by employing a librarian to list, file, check out, and refile all reference material. This is not a complete answer, however, since many times a draftsman or spec writer will want to compare several catalogs before making a choice or will want to browse until the appropriate item is found.

With the ever-increasing number of products and the catalogs used to describe them the average office, even with help of a full time librarian, simply must find a better way. Some offices cut down on catalogs by deliberately refusing those which are not local or are not from manufacturers whose products appear repeatedly on their projects. This limits the scope of the office and often may inadvertently preclude the use of a newer or better product of which, because of the lack of a catalog, the office has no knowledge. Several mechanized systems have been proposed to overcome the need for the large amount of physical storage space for catalogs, to make product comparison easier, to update data periodically, and to provide some facility for the quick inspection or more leisurely reading of a *printout* copy. Of the several systems that have appeared in the past few years, none has survived on a continuing national basis. This is unfortunate, since there was every indication that these systems would solve a vexing problem; however, the problems of finances, updating, distribution of new data, as well as that of gaining widespread acceptance, were never really solved. Some units are still in use however, and more may be accepted; thus a brief survey of their operation will be helpful.

These resource and retrieval machines are sophisticated projectors operating from microfilm tape at high speed. The catalog pages are supplied by the various manufacturers, photographed in proper sequence on microfilm, and the film tapes combined with other tapes from manufacturers of similar products. The tapes are coded so that the specifier can either slowly scan the pages of each manufacturer's catalog in turn in order to compare products, or he can find a specific page of a specific manufacturer rapidly, simply by pressing the correct button. Tapes are indexed for content by *Uniform System* division and section. Then they are stored in a small cabinet for easy access and are updated at intervals of four to six months, together with an updated index list. The machine projects each page onto a viewing screen for on-site observation, but most machines have an additional feature providing a printout by an electrostatic process on 8½ by 11 paper so that the information can be taken back to the desk if desired.

Distributors of the retrieval equipment claim upwards of 4,000 current manufacturers' catalogs, with more becoming available soon. The actual size of the retrieval machine varies, but the average dimensions are 36 by 36 by 24 in. high for the table or stand mounting, plus space for film rolls adjacent. The product manufacturer generally is not charged a fee, but the machine user pays a monthly rental. This method practically guarantees the machine distributor an unlimited supply of catalog material and he need only "sell" the user on the value of having the machine in the office. What happened to discourage the use of such a seemingly effective system? Two of the many reasons for its failure lie in the system's introduction at an inopportune time and its high cost to the user.

AUTOMATIC TYPEWRITERS

Soon after the introduction and general acceptance of the electric typewriter we had the invention of the automatic typewriter. This device uses the electric typewriter as the heart of the machine, but it is activated by some sort of tape mechanism attached to it. Two basic types are available: the magnetic wire tape and the treated paper tape. The two leaders in this field use the same high-speed electric typewriter and produce similar finished typed products, claiming approximately the same savings in typing time and costs. The finished typed page may be standard bond paper, spirit masters, stencils, or paper offset plates, either in single sheets or multifold as desired. Several other manufacturers offer similar machines.

The automatic typewriter operates from the master tape or card system, previously typed with the specification data as a master. A typed or duplicated sheet is used to develop the new project specification by indicating portions to be retained or changed. This marked-up sheet is used by the typist to select the proper portions of the master and type in the changes or new material; the sheet can be used to change a letter, a word, a paragraph, or an entire page, with renumbering where necessary. In addition, some types of this machine will also simultaneously produce a project tape of the combined new material and changes, which may be retained as a record or reference for the particular project. If the magnetic wire tape is used, this record can be retained until the project is completed and then cleared and used for another project.

Typing speed for electric typewriters while operating automatically is 160-180 words per minute. An experienced typist cannot type more than about 15-20 words per minute when making changes or adding new material. The systems manufacturers claim a savings in typing time of about ½ to ⅔ over nonautomatic methods. Costs vary considerably. The best use-cost is on a lease basis where maintenance and new model improvements are included in the lease cost.

Automatic typewriters require trained operators. The machines, properly operated, are great time-savers when multiple copies are required, especially if the copies are to have a nonduplicated appearance. By the use of two tapes, a text can automatically be typed from one and addresses or other information from another. The typewriter can also be used as a conventional machine without using any of the automation features. Companies leasing these machines will train typists in the correct operation of the machines. This training is usually not longer than a day or two, and with the aid of an operating manual the typist can develop accuracy and speed in a very short time. One of the disadvantages of using automated typewriters is that it leads to greater personnel turnover; since the typist now has special training she can qualify for other, possibly more remunerative jobs, find one, and leave the office. New operators are trained as a part of the lease agreement, but sometimes this training gap is an inconvenience to the office.

This type of equipment (tape-operated electric typewriters) is, at this time (1974), probably the best choice for the average A/E office. The cost of leasing and operation is relatively low, the space required is only a little more than that of a normal typewriting desk, the machine may be used as a standard typewriter when not on automation, and the retention of proofread material, ready for immediate use, is invaluable. The cost difference between paper and magnetic tapes is considerable, but the prospective user should consider his selection in light of his particular office operation; the potential reuse or erasing frequency, the possible volume of material to be stored for specification masters, and the variety of projects the A/E is normally engaged in. In any case it is important to remember that any form of automatic typewriter still requires a manual compilation of a master before it can be automated.

COMPUTERS

The next step in automated hardware for the architect or engineering office is a big one, and in many cases it is unnecessary and expensive. This is the use of the computer to provide specifications output.

The first electronic computer was built at and for the University of Pennsylvania in 1946 as a result of the research into, and use of, electronic principles for war time equipment. From that start the computer industry has expanded to become a business of nearly 100 billion dollars per year. *Hardware*, the actual machinery that does the work, is produced by approximately twenty firms in the United States, with the International Business Machines Corporation leading the field. The operation of computer equipment requires special training in the programming of the system and in the actual operation of the machinery. This specially trained personnel is not usually available to the average architect or engineering office and the systems such as FORTRAN, COBOL, and ALGOL are essentially foreign languages. The net result of this need for special equipment and trained personnel is the *time sharing* of a central computer rather than *in-house* use by offices using computers to assist them.

Although the term *computer* is often synonymous with efficiency or sophisticated office operation, it may also be as expensive as other mechanized office methods. Computer use varies so much with individual interpretation that a survey taken several years ago by the American Institute of Architects indicated that a great proportion of architectural offices "used" computers. The survey was intended to show the number of offices whose major work in specifications, engineering, design, or similar architectural work was done by computer. It revealed that more than 80 percent of the offices surveyed used computers; however, this use was in the area of payroll through a bank, tax use through a consultant, or some similar usage, and *not* for architectural work. As time progresses we have more engineering data, specifications masters, and some design criteria available in computer banks or from commercial agencies that develop this material for others. In most cases it is not economical for an individual office to write and program its own specifications masters from scratch. The cost of a good specifications writer's time to produce a good master would be from $20,000 to $50,000, plus perhaps another $25,000 for programming and several thousands more for tapes, cards, and other *software*. Most offices simply do not have this kind of money to spend.

What then is the future use of computers for specifications? Accepting the fact that very few firms can afford in-house computers of their own and the personnel needed to operate them, there remain three principal ways that computers might be economically possible: by time sharing from a data-processing center; by time sharing with another A/E or association; and by time sharing with a master specification marketer. Computers operate at almost unbelievable speeds, so that, in addition to its prohibitive cost, an individual company cannot normally provide enough work to use the equipment on a full-time basis. The solution is *time-sharing*, which simply means that a number of users have work in process on one machine almost simultaneously. With the high operating speed possible, the work of several firms is switched in and out in a matter of microseconds; thus "dead time" is virtually eliminated. This of course reduces the cost and provides fast, accurate service to several subscribers.

How are specifications computerized? When the use of computers first appeared practical for specifications, a number of specifications writers voiced their misgivings that the machine would soon replace the man. This has not happened and probably never will. Good specifications information, in the desired format that designates the approved materials and is adaptable to the computer, must be composed originally by someone who has the brains to do it properly. With an original draft, we can assume that this is an accomplished fact. With masters prepared by others, it may be necessary to revise once or several times to make the master acceptable to the office using it. Unless they are changed or eliminated, errors in the purchased master, items not in normal use by the office, special requirements anticipated by the author of the master but not applicable to the user, and similar elements will be included in the computerized information. The common saying, "garbage in—garbage out" should be self-evident, since the computer can make no changes by itself.

The preparation of a master specification for an A/E office requires that the specifications writer consider the types of projects generally undertaken by that office. A firm specializing in schools or hospitals has a different requirement than one specializing in office buildings, housing, or industrial plants. Where a wide variety of projects is normal a number of different masters may be necessary. In addition, the types of material (concrete, masonry, steel) preferred may also determine the extent of specification material that will go into the master. The additional sections on roofing, floor covering, painting, miscellaneous metals, and other items regularly used on projects would have a high priority for review and revision.

For the past several years, masters for computerized specifications have been available; these will be discussed at greater length in Chapter 13. The principal advantage of the use of the computer for specifications is the speed at which the *smooth copy* can be produced once the changes required by the specific project have been made to the master in the memory bank of the computer. The computer may print 500 lines per minute as compared to 200 words per minute by electric typewriter.

SUMMARY

Each of the relatively few methods available to mechanize the production of specifications has many variations. The exact method depends to a great extent upon the volume of work by the office, the cost of the process, and the final appearance desired. The smaller office may not be in a position to use any of them economically, whereas the large office may use all or any combination of methods. Mechanization should allow an office to cut down expenses and provide more complete and uniform services; both results are desirable in any size operation. Unfortunately, the management of the smaller office often feels that modern mechanization is too expensive and the larger office sometimes does not keep up-to-date enough to change methods as the business changes.

QUESTIONS

11.1. Name the levels of the systems approach and briefly indicate what they signify.

11.2. In general how do mechanized catalog retrieval machines work?

11.3. How many major types of automatic typewriters are there? Describe their primary differences.

11.4. List three advantages offered by automatic typewriters.

11.5. Compare the advantages and disadvantages of using computers for specifications work.

12

REPRODUCTION
METHODS

At some point before the start of typing specifications the methods to be used for reproduction must be determined. This is necessary since different types of reproduction require different masters, stencils, plates, or other devices. Which method of reproduction will be used depends on such factors as the economics of each office, the personnel available, the equipment owned or obtainable, and to some extent the past experience of the office, although this last reason may not be valid if there has been no research on other methods. A small office may use inexpensive, minimum reproduction equipment, which may be operated with little knowledge and at low cost. As the office grows larger the same system is often retained, although it may no longer be the best system from the standpoint of economy, appearance, or speed. The following information covers the most common reproduction systems or processes now in general use.

Copies of specifications are subject to rough handling and must retain their usability not only during the bidding procedure but also during the entire time of construction of the project. With these requirements in mind the method of reproduction is an important problem. The usual distribution of specifications is made to qualified bidders during the bid period. Most A/E offices provide two or three sets of drawings and specifications upon receipt of a specified deposit. These sets, together with those that are often available through plan services, provide the general contractors, subcontractors, and material suppliers with the information necessary for their bidding.

Upon receipt and opening of general bids, the unsuccessful contractors return their sets of drawings and specifications *in complete and undamaged condition* to the A/E office, and their deposits are returned to them. The A/E office then reviews these returned documents, replaces any seriously damaged portions, checks to insure that sets are complete, and in general prepares them for use during construction of the project. The contractor who will do the work is then provided with an additional quantity of sets of these documents for construction purposes at no cost to him.

Specifications then, as well as the drawings, must be prepared to withstand considerable usage and abuse. Torn or otherwise damaged pages must be easily replaced, the duplicated material must not fade from exposure to the sun, the binding must be adequate to protect the enclosed pages, and the entire book must be of convenient size to be handled easily. This last requirement is particularly important when the total number of pages is great (the "break-point" is about 300 pages), or when the work seems to divide easily and naturally into two parts, *architectural* and *mechanical/electrical.* In some forms of civil engineering work the dividing point may be between *earth moving* and *architectural* work required.

CARBON PAPER

It is obvious that copies of specifications made using carbon paper have a rather limited future. About the most that can be expected is an original and perhaps six carbon copies. The use of carbons is probably the most economical of all methods; copies are made at the same time as the original, but they are subject to smearing and fuzziness. In addition, the paper used for the copies must of necessity be thin and not very durable. A limited edition of preliminary specifications may be made by this method but it is not practical for other uses. *Back-carboned* sheets, where the original has had a carbon reversed from its usual position to put the carbon on the back of the original, may be used as masters for duplication by blueprinting methods. An orange carbon rather than the usual blue or black reproduces better this way.

SPIRIT DUPLICATION

Spirit duplication possibly ranks first in use by the greatest number of architects' or engineers' offices. The method employs a heavy white paper master backed by a carbon sheet but separated from it by a lightweight blotter sheet. In use, the blotter sheet is removed (otherwise there will be no carbon on the back) and the information is typed on the front face of the white sheet. This picks up carbon from the carbon sheet and leaves it on the back of the white sheet. Errors may be corrected by scraping off the carbon or using tape to cover the error and retyping correctly, using new carbon. Drawings are easily made with a normal pencil in the same manner. Masters are available in grades that determine the average number of copies that can be made from each master. Masters cost about five cents each, and they may be stored until the carbon dies out and is unusable.

To make multiple copies of the typed work the master is installed on a drum. A wick, saturated in an alcohol solution, activates the carbon so that it prints on paper stock as it passes over this stock. Machines may be hand operated or electrically operated. Paper stock may be 16 lb or 20 lb, white or colored, 8½ by 11 or 8½ by 14 legal size. As the carbon deteriorates the print becomes lighter until it is unreadable; a master produces a maximum of about 400 copies.

This method has several disadvantages, even though it is economical. Typists do not like it since the carbon has a tendency to smear on hands, face, typewriter, and other surfaces unless plastic-coated masters are used. However, carbon smears are easily removed with a soft-soap lotion available from suppliers of the masters. Carbon is available in purple, a dark grey (called *black*), and in a limited number of other colors, usually red, green, or yellow. Purple, the most common color, disturbs some architects, while "black" doesn't print black. If other colors are to be used in conjunction with either purple or black, the proper colored carbon must be inserted where necessary and the base carbon sheet must either be removed or blocked out so it will not deposit upon the back of the master.

Prints from spirit masters have a tendency to fade rapidly when exposed to sunlight. The carbon on the backs of the masters, after being used once, often crystalizes, and an excess of liquid may be necessary to obtain additional prints. Too much liquid used during printing may cause blurred reproduction; too little liquid will produce barely legible results. Old, dried out masters usually require considerable liquid unless the carbon is completely used, in which case it may be possible to reproduce the typing on the face of the master by Xerox or photosensitive methods. The duplicating machines used have a tendency to throw several blank sheets along with the printed ones, which necessitates some hand sorting. Automatic sorters are not available for these duplicators.

MIMEOGRAPH DUPLICATION

This method of reproduction ranks a close second, if not in a tie, with the spirit duplication method. Stencils are supplied in both 8½ by 11 in. and 8½ by 14 in. size, in a special, thin, treated paper backed with a heavier backing sheet. The entire package of stencil and backer is loaded into the typewriter, the typing ribbon is removed, and the type allowed to actually cut letters through the stencil. Errors are corrected by resealing the master with collodian and retyping when dry. Drawings may be made with special metal-tipped "pencils" if care is exercised to prevent fallout of portions of the drawing. The cost for stencils is approximately the same as that for spirit masters.

In duplicating, the stencil is secured to a perforated drum, ink (many colors available) is poured inside the drum, and the drum rotated over the paper stock, allowing the ink to penetrate through the stencil and print on the paper. Printing may be done in several colors by cleaning the drum after each color is used and accurately registering the stencils and paper. The printed sheet usually does not fade and the stencil may be used for approximately 500 copies. Stencils may be cleaned of ink, dried, and stored with reasonable success.

The principal disadvantage of this system is the inadvertent spilling or leaking of ink, and the possibility of smearing if too much ink is used. The machines used have about the same kinds of mechanical difficulties of operation as spirit duplicators. The stencils are somewhat flimsy and require careful handling. If they are to be reused after one printing they are messy to clean, inconvenient to dry, and difficult to store properly. Stencils are hard to proofread.

ELECTROSTATIC DUPLICATING

This equipment, available in several sizes, is being installed in an increasing number of offices. Usually the machines are obtained on lease rather than through outright purchase; this procedure has definite advantages in maintenance, replacement, and operation. Although it is not one of the more economical methods for reproduction of specification, this process is convenient for duplicating letters, making copies of manufacturers' literature, and reproducing almost anything printed. No special masters or stencils are required and no ink or other liquid is used in duplication. Ordinary 8½ by 11 in. white bond paper and normal black typing or inked drawings make the best masters. Lead pencil drawings will also reproduce well if they are clear and sharp, but colored pencils will only reproduce shades of grey. Photographs may be reproduced if filter screens are used.

Electrostatic duplication is one of the simple reproduction methods. The machine is charged with paper stock and a carbon-black powder. The master is placed on a glass sheet and covered with a flexible blanket. The dials are adjusted for the required number of copies, and the *print button* is actuated. Automatically, the machine exposes the master and paper stock, carbon-black is picked up electrostatically on the paper and the copy is "printed." Multiple copies can be made by simply selecting the correct number on the machine. Sorters that will automatically distribute up to twenty copies are available for the larger machines. Costs for masters are of course negligible since bond paper is normally used. The cost of a copy is on a scale determined by the number of copies made; one to four copies are about five cents each; five to eight copies are about 3½ cents each, and over eight copies are about 1¾ cents each. Copies must be made from the same master at the same time. Each new original starts the cost-accounting mechanism over again from zero.

The newest series of machines has the capability of reduction-printing of the original. The copy can be the same size as the original or, by the adjustment of a simple selector, it can be any size down to a quarter of the original size. This reduction has definite advantages when paste-up systems for presentations or office work are involved and, although it is not so important in specifications work, it can be very advantageous in providing identical reduced-scale dummies for some types of architectural projects such as multiple apartments. Another advanced reproduction machine of similar nature reproduces photographs or printed illustrations.

Probably the greatest disadvantage of this process is the physical size of the machine. The smallest version requires approximately 48 in. by 48 in. with equal operating space, and the larger models require approximately 48 in. by 96 in. with equal operating space. Another, unexpected, "disadvantage" is the ease with which duplicates are made, since this invariably results in more duplication of less vital material and an increase in office operating expense. The cost is much too high for long runs of specifications, but runs of preliminary specifications of less than twenty copies are often comparable in cost to other methods and are certainly convenient. In addition to the production of copies the machine can be used to make paper plates for offset printing, and has several other uses.

PRINTING

In general, most printing methods are not readily usable in the average architect's or engineer's office. The equipment is costly and requires considerable space; in addition, trained operators must be employed, and for the equipment to be economically operated there must be a high use factor. The several processes briefly described here include offset printing, multilith, hot type, and hand-set type. Most are too expensive for specification duplicating except for long runs of considerable quantity.

Offset printing is the next most economical process after the several already described. In this method a heavy paper or light metal plate is made by photographic process from the bond paper original. This plate is installed in the machine and a solution of oil and water is used to carry ink over the plate. The ink is held only on the typed or lined work; then it is deposited, or off-set, onto a roller and deposited on the print paper. The reproduction is good, fast, and reasonable in cost and several hundred copies can be made from one plate. Where a specification runs from 250 to perhaps 500 pages with more than seventy-five copies required, the offset method, done outside the office, may be most economical and has an excellent appearance if the originals are good.

Offset reproduction gives a sharp black print that is an exact copy of the original. Until the plate actually wears out there is little deviation in quality, and there is negligible fading caused by exposure at the job site. Since no type is set, the reproduced letters have the same shape, size, style, and other characteristics as the typewriter upon which the master bond-paper original was made. Variations in headings made by rub-on letters, line drawings or hand lettering, and charts or graphs reproduce well as long as they are clearly made on the original. Shades of black reproduce exactly as in the original, but colors are not possible except by making several originals properly registered with each other and running them repeatedly, using different color inks in a manner similar to standard color printing.

Multilith printing requires an expensive metal plate, expensive equipment for printing, and trained operators. It is a printer's process, and because of the high cost is seldom used except by very large companies for very extensive specifications. Printing by typesetting is also too expensive. Material set by linotype using molten metal or handset type will give a clean, booklike appearance and any number of copies up to the thousands if needed, in black or in color. Drawings are difficult to print as they must be carefully made, cleanly lined, etched on metal plates and then printed. Color printing is also difficult, but it is sometimes used for brochures, covers, or letterheads. In color printing several plates are required, each printing only the color desired. *Four-color printing* means the use of four colors; red, yellow, blue, and black, properly registered and overlapped to create orange, green, purple, and shades of grey as well as the original primary colors.

COMPUTERS

The use of computers to provide the material for the specifications text is rapidly increasing. The computer produces a typed uniform printout when all required changes have been made. Some companies use the computer as a rapid and continuous printing machine to make duplicate copies of a specification, but this is not really what the computer is designed to do nor is it very economical. In addition, the normal printout is usually not in the most desirable physical form and the continuous folded pages require additional trimming and collating. For one or two copies of a section, a division, or perhaps even a small job, the computer might be used, but in most cases beyond these areas it just doesn't work to any advantage.

BLUEPRINTING

There are still quite a few architects and designers who find an interest and a living in residential or very small commercial work. They want to keep the specifications down to a minimum but not to the extent of a mere listing of materials or a stock-duplicated specification that is so general it only functions in theory. For years the specifications for this type work have been hand lettered on the drawing sheets and automatically reproduced by *blueprinting*. One of the more common ways to reduce the high cost of hand lettering has been to cut the drafting paper into 8½ in.-wide strips, type the required information on these strips on a standard typewriter, and then reassemble the strips into sheets that match the drafting sheets. The specs are then printed and bound with the drawings as a complete project without a separate book.

COLOR CODING

To make it easier for the contractor, mechanic, and architect to find certain portions of work in a specification, particularly if the spec is quite long, some offices have color coded certain parts. Generally they have adopted specific colors for the larger divisions but seldom go to the point of coding each section or division. Since most paper manufacturers produce at least white plus red, blue, green, and yellow, five colors of paper are available. It has been recommended that several national organizations adopt these five colors as standards, but as yet no definite action in that direction has been taken.

For many years paper manufacturers have been producing colored stock for duplicating paper. In addition to the five colors mentioned above, most firms also stock some additional shades such as pink, salmon, light green or light blue, orange or golden rod, and several shades of tan. These papers are supplied in exactly the same sizes, weights, and quantities as standard white, punched or not punched. Black, dark brown, dark green, and several other dark papers are available but normal print will not show up on them readily, so we need not consider them here. Black ink or even purple spirit-duplicator "ink" will usually show up well on the lighter colors.

Offices that color code specifications feel that it simplifies finding certain sections or divisions when questions arise. Several companies use green paper for everything until Division 2, white paper for Division 2 through Division 10, yellow paper for Division 11 through Division 14, red (pink, salmon) for Division 15, and blue for Division 16. Change Orders, Addenda, or other similar documents might be on some special color for differentiation. The cost of colored paper is a little more than for white since the paper is bleached and redyed, but is not really an expensive item. The use of more than the basic five or six colors is both expensive and inefficient since the variety of colors is as confusing as none at all.

BINDING

Although the various methods used for trimming and binding printed specifications may not seem to be a part of reproduction, they are necessary to provide a complete job. Many offices that use either spirit duplication or mimeograph also use a hand sorting method to assemble their book. This is about the simplest method that can be used. As the pages come from the machine they are laid crisscross in batches of the same numbered pages to keep them separated. A large table or similar surface is laid out with the number of copies required. Consecutive pages are placed on each pile, and the piles are straightened and then bound. This system requires considerable layout space, and often most of the office force is needed to lay out the sheets. It is also time consuming and allows for upside down placement, and the insertion of blank sheets if a close watch is not maintained; thus it is in no way a satisfactory binding method for a larger office. The slight irregularity of sheets after collating and binding makes the assembly look cheap, so many offices do not use this system.

Copying machines and most types of printer's equipment may be equipped with sorters that automatically distribute the printed pages into identical stacks. These stacks are then straightened by *joggers*, which lightly vibrate the pages into a smooth bundle. This semiautomatic printing and collating limits the blank sheets and upside down placement that are common when hand collating is done. The various bundles that will compose the book may then be bound and very often are again lightly trimmed at the edges to give a smooth, finished appearance.

The type of binding selected is dependent upon the attitude of the office regarding the separation of specifications by the contractor. There are two schools of thought regarding binding methods. If the architect or engineer assumes that the contractor will separate the specification into the various subcontract sections and has no objection to this method, binding may be accomplished with brass fasteners, *Chicago screws* or double-head sex-bolts, comb-type plastic binders or even three-ring binders. Almost anything that will keep the pages together will do, but most of the fasteners mentioned above allow easy separation of the specification into its several sections. It also follows that the equipment required by these methods is minimal, but the final appearance might leave something to be desired.

On the other hand, some offices feel that the contractor should not be able to separate the sections, so that each subcontractor may have the opportunity to read related sections, General Conditions, or more than one section if he is interested. This means that the specifications must then be bound *solid*. Sewing is the best method but is also usually the most expensive. Nailing, either from one side or from both front and back if the volume is thick, is the next best choice. Tape over nails or sewing and along the edge of the book covers the construction and helps bind the book. Professional binders who do this work also use presses and shears to trim the edges of the bound copies, providing a desirable finished look.

Several very large offices have their own departments to print and bind their specifications. Most offices however will at one time or another use different methods, depending upon the size of their projects, the number of copies required, and certainly to a large extent, their location. Smaller offices in smaller cities may find that some facilities are just not available or that shipping to another city for printing is not feasible. Unfortunately, the same factors that limit some offices may keep them in a rut when an occasional re-investigation might reveal new opportunities that could be beneficial.

PREPRINTED MATERIAL

Preprinted specification sheets are not very common in A/E offices unless the office has a considerable number of identical projects. For most projects there are enough minor differences to make the use of preprinted stock pages unworkable. There may be some sections such as *Supplemental Conditions, Testing,* or *Cleaning and Cleanup* that are the same on all projects, but even here the difficulty and cost of inserting preprinted pages may be a deterrent. The specifier may, however, be furnished with preprinted pages of specifications material from manufacturers of elevators and other equipment that are basically similar in many parts regardless of size or type. This material should be edited and retyped to match the remainder of the office specification.

SPECIFICATION COVERS

Every specification requires some sort of cover to contain and protect the pages and to distinguish it from other books and papers. With the spirit-duplicating or mimeograph processes this cover is usually simply another sheet run through the machine. More sophisticated specifications however usually have a hard cover, one that could not be printed by equipment that would roll or bend the paper stock. Here the economy lies in long-run printings, proper storage, and a design which will allow project names or other designation to be easily added whenever required. The preprinted covers can be supplied as needed for any project, and the cost of cuts, typesetting, and special stock is a one-time occurrence.

SUMMARY

The office just starting in business should select the most economical method for reproduction, namely spirit duplication or mimeograph. This should suffice until the office gains in project volume to the extent that perhaps one specification per month is produced. If this amount of work means that the typist, the office boy, and perhaps the draftsmen are required to print, collate, and bind the specification, the office has waited too long to investigate other systems. Blueprinting firms and commercial printers will usually be glad to give cost estimates on printing and binding, using offset or other methods. The wide-awake specifier should keep records of the cost involved in both the production of the specifications and the cost of reproduction so that he will be able to use the most economical means in the future.

QUESTIONS

12.1. What are the principal disadvantages of using carbon for multiple copies?

12.2. What is the principal ingredient of the spirit solution used in spirit duplication?

12.3. How does mimeograph reproduction differ from spirit duplication?

12.4. Can color be used in either spirit duplication or mimeograph reproduction? Explain.

12.5. How does xerography produce copies? What types of work or masters are reproduced by this system?

13

MASTER SPECIFICATIONS

The words *master specifications* keep cropping up in any text or conversation about specifications, and there are as many opinions of what a master specification is, what it can do for a specifier or an A/E office, how it works, its advantages and disadvantages, and its cost, as there are readers. Furthermore, it is not possible to answer accurately all of these questions satisfactorily, simply because each specifier or A/E office has different requirements, a different clientele, a different budget, and a different staff who will use, or not use, a master. One way or another nearly every specifications writer uses a master, whether he realizes it or not or whether it is called a master or not.

CUT — AND — PASTE MASTER

The *cut-and-paste* method of producing specifications is perhaps the oldest form of production and is not classed as a master system by many. To say that any material is a master, however, means that the construction or content of the various sentences, paragraphs, or sections may be used verbatim repeatedly or with minor changes. This is exactly what happens with most cut-and-paste assemblies of specifications. Someone, usually lost in obscurity, wrote the original documents. They served well and with a minimum of changes were used on the next project simply because they required few alterations. They may have been good, average, or even poor but so long as they did not develop any great amount of adverse feed-back they were used on the next construction, and the next, and so on until they became office masters. Quite often no changes were made at all.

The cut-and-paste method is exactly what it indicates: parts of older specifications are cut out and pasted together or pasted on new pages for a new project. Aside from the fact that this method is time consuming and rather old fashioned there is nothing basically wrong with it. It has some of the same faults as any other master in that it must be revised to fit the current project, it may be out of date for references of various kinds, and it is possibly subject to more misfiling than other masters. To a great extent the cut-and-paste method also depends upon the memory of an individual and, of course, the amount of work the A/E office is engaged in.

We can dispense with the master cut-and-paste system without further consideration, since its use is limited and it is rapidly being replaced by newer, better methods. Even the smallest office should never be too busy to investigate and consider a more modern procedure.

THE "TOPSY" MASTER

Any discussion of a master designed for the exclusive use of one A/E office or for a particular type of project should come at the end of this chapter, after other types have been considered.

Some office masters, like Topsy in *Uncle Tom's Cabin* "just grew." They evolved from early research that was written into a specification that worked well for a project and was reused on the next project. Any changes were incorporated in the specification for the second project. A succession of such incorporated changes resulted in what is considered a master specification. In many cases these selected portions of the specification were typed on filing cards or on reference sheets of some type. Almost without exception they did not start out being written for masters.

The specifications writer simply marked his work sheet with some designation for the paragraph or other portion he wanted to use, gave both the work sheet and the master card or page to the typist, and it was retyped for the new project. A number of printed masters, including the old *American Institute of Architects Work Sheets*, were designed to be used in this manner. The principal advantage is in the time saved in rewriting acceptable paragraphs or in designating approved products by specific names or other means. The primary disadvantages are the retyping and additional proofreading involved and the acceptance of a method arrived at by chance at the expense of research for the best installation method.

When masters are compiled by adequate research and development of a system, most of the disadvantages are eliminated. Even the problems of retyping and reproofing are eliminated almost totally when automatic typewriters are used, and such equipment should be considered a part of the package whenever a master is considered for development. Now, let us look into some procedures for writing master specifications. These same ideas may also be used to revise a purchased master to fit it for use in a particular office.

THE OFFICE MASTER

The office or specifier considering any type of master must first make some determination of the type of master that would be most useful. An office doing mostly residential work would have a different requirement than an office involved in commercial or government-financed work. Some offices doing a variety of work might best be served by using several masters, each designed to facilitate writing a particular type of specification. The first step then is to survey the most repeated project type and determine the extent to which the master applies.

Here we may revert to a cut-and-paste method to develop the master. Collect a number of good, older specifications and divide them into the respective sections. By comparing the various sections it is possible to sort out those portions that are repeated or have minor changes in content. These portions, usually lead sentences or paragraphs, should be studied, rewritten until they are clear and concise, and then used as a start for the master. It must be assumed at this point that the general format of a typical section has been determined by previous specifications and that this specification includes references to general and special conditions, the scope of the section, related work, material lead paragraph, guarantees, samples, and so on, all of which will be incorporated into the master. If the earlier specifications were not written with these portions included or were not in accord with the sixteen divisions of the *Uniform System*, the required revisions will be more complicated, or at least quite time consuming.

The *material* portion is one of the most important parts of a specification section and is treated in a number of different ways. Two approaches should be carefully considered; to some extent they will be influenced by the experience and ability of those who use the master. The two methods are nearly exact opposites, and may be classed as the *insert method* and the *delete method*. However, let us first consider exactly what a material portion should include. It should list a generic name for the material, followed by designations for grade or species, color classification, model number, testing designation, and acceptable manufacturer(s). Of course, all of these may not be used for every material, or there may be some additions that seem desirable.

Now let us look at a description of a material in the resilient flooring section (Division 9—Section 09650). Within this section we will ultimately consider all kinds of resilient flooring: asphalt tile, vinyl asbestos, cork, rubber, and sheet material or squares; for the present however, we will consider only asphalt tile. The following samples illustrate the obvious difference between the insert and delete methods.

> Asphalt tile shall be nominal _____ in. × _____ in. _____ in. thick, class
> _____ , _____ pattern, complying with _____ mfgd by _____ ;
> _____ ; _____ or approved equal.

This sample is the insert method. The experienced specifications writer fills in the blanks with the proper sizes, class, pattern, manufacturer, and so on. Notice the word *experienced*. The inexperienced writer probably will not know what is required in each blank space, or at best he will have considerable research to do in order to learn the various possibilities. A number of older approaches to a master specification used this method; it was useful where it was designed to act as a nationwide guide, but it has inherent disadvantages when used in a single office.

Eventually the user of an insert type of specification will find that many of the blanks are being filled in with the same information each time. For the inexperienced writer this is a definite advantage until some item is changed. The delete type of master doesn't eliminate all thinking or all faults, but it does reduce research time and it is easier for the inexperienced writer to use. Here is an example of a delete master for the same asphalt tile we looked at for an insert master.

> Asphalt tile shall be nominal (9″ × 9″) (12″ × 12″) ($\frac{1}{8}$″) ($\frac{3}{16}$″)
> thick, class (A) (B) (C) (D) (E), (woodtone, corktone, spatter, terrazzo)
> complying with Fed. Spec. SS-T-306, as mfgd. by ABC Co.; DEF Co.;
> GHJ Co. or approved equal.

146

This is an example of one kind of resilient flooring. In addition to asphalt tile there are those mentioned before plus special types, and this is only one section. Each type of flooring in a master, and each material in another section, needs similar treatment. By careful research all of the important features of each material can be properly listed. This means that a master for resilient flooring materials portion will have paragraphs similar to these examples for each material; the concrete section will have paragraphs for large aggregate, small (sand) aggregate, cement, water, admixtures of several types; the painting section will list the various types of paint, enamel or stain, and so forth.

A similar approach is necessary for the third portion of a section, the *installation*. Again, in the use of resilient flooring separate paragraphs must be written for installations over wood subfloors, concrete subfloors, for various adhesives, for coved base or top-set base, and other possibilities. For offices that operate in several different states or climatic conditions there may be different paragraphs required by these locations or by local building codes. The availability of materials in various locations may also determine to some extent the information included in any master specification. In short, the master specification ideally should include every material, every type of installation, every normal test, guarantee, or other requirement that could possibly be included in any building of the type for which the master might be used. This is certainly a big order; a master can probably never be complete and up-to-date, but even a good partial master of the most used sections is a time saver.

THE GOVERNMENT MASTER

This section title may be slightly misleading since a discussion of master specifications for the General Services Administration, the United States Navy Public Works, The United States Army Corps of Engineers, various states, cities, counties, and school districts is covered under this blanket title. You will remember that in earlier chapters we discussed the difference between the commercial specification, with the opportunity to call out manufacturer's names, and the federal specification, which does not normally allow any such identification. This fact, together with the many standards available, changes the picture for the production of a federal master. For example, consider a master designed for United States Navy Public Works (Facilities Command) use, since this type will illustrate the requirements of many similar agencies.

As this paragraph is read, refer to page 322 *Federal Specification.*

To begin with, the first line, titled *Scope* can be copied "cold." This sentence adequately, but not too specifically, covers the scope of the section in about 99 percent of all cases. The second paragraph also is standard and is rarely changed, even though it is quite long; it indicates the various government publications that might be used in the section. The third major portion is the list of government publications. These can again be listed for continuous reuse, with the possible omission of the various revision indicators. These indicators can be added as the masters are used. The materials listed can be treated in much the same manner as described for materials in a commercial master specification, with the exception that the requirements will probably be shorter due to reference to a Federal Specification standard. Here is a typical example, using our old friend, asphalt tile.

> Asphalt tile– $^1/_8''$ thick, 9″x 9″, group "C" terrazzo style, conforming to Fed. Spec. SS-T-306.

The installation methods are specifically set out in the various Federal Specifications, so they could be copied cold if desired. The copying of these standards is frowned upon by the agencies, but if any kind of automated equipment is used it is almost imperative that most of the material be taken verbatim.

THE CONSULTANT'S MASTER

Up to this point we have only discussed the master specification as it applies to the in-house specifications writer who works for one office and often on one general type of construction. The picture for the freelance professional specifications writer is similar in some ways but quite different in others. The consultant does work for a number of offices, many of which have their own form for specifications and personal preferences in the choice of product manufacturers. A consultant doing work for these A/E offices has two choices; he can use the format of the A/E office and any masters they may have or he can try to change their format to conform to his own. Both of these have problems.

The consultant will use his own masters in most cases and try to change them as little as possible to conform to the required format. This procedure is simply a version of the office master, with considerably more revision than might be required if it were used in only one A/E office. If he does much work for one office it will often be economical to convert information from his own masters and format to that of his client by use of tape-operated typewriters or computers. Of course if the various A/E clients have residential, commercial, school, industrial, federal, and other types of projects, the consultant must be able to adjust his own masters to satisfy the project.

PURCHASED MASTERS

In the past few years the development of commercially prepared masters has advanced in leaps and bounds. At first they were prepared by individuals who used their own ideas, format, preferred manu-facturers, and products. Most were provided to the buyer on cards or tapes and often were not usable in any other area than the one in which they were written. From this early start various organizations have developed masters that are now available to A/E offices.

MASTERSPEC

MASTERSPEC was authorized by the American Institute of Architects, Commission on Professional Practice in 1968, and by the A.I.A. Board in April, 1969 to sponsor a separate firm for its production. Production Systems for Architects and Engineers Inc. (PSAE) was chartered in Illinois to develop and operate automated production of this system. MASTERSPEC is a computer oriented master that is purchased by the prospective user, edited to suit his own use, and then fed into PSAE's computer system for printout. Three options for use are provided:

Level 1–A yearly updated set of Reference Catalogs for preparation of A/E specifications for their own system.
Level 2–Provides edited copy for retyping or automation by the individual A/E.
Level 3–Computer processes the A/E-edited text for a printout of the project.

The normal process for use of MASTERSPEC is to determine which of the various sections will be required for the project and request a copy of updated sections from PSAE. These masters are then properly edited by the A/E and sent to the nearest processing center where they will be computer-run and returned to the A/E. The A/E then proofreads the printout and proceeds with his own type of reproducing and distribution. If the master does not contain informa-tion that the A/E wants to use or if there are changes in the master, these are incorporated by a version of cut-and-paste. The computer does not provide good stencils or offset masters, so the A/E must make the appropriate originals for whatever reproduction method he chooses to use. Rules and suggestions for the editing process are supplied as part of the package from PSAE.

The sections provided by PSAE include *Related Documents, Description of the Work, General Requirements, Materials and Application Systems, Installation,* and *Submittals.* Each section specifies materials in a nonproprietary manner; it lists no specific manufacturers, but it does set up the material requirements by reference to industry standards, ASTM, or other recognized organizations. The printed text also has instructions regarding possible deletion of material that may not be needed. The general arrangement and editing procedure can be easily observed by inspection of the MASTERSPEC sample included in this book on page 293.

COMSPEC

COMSPEC is a "text-processing service for Architects and Engineers" authorized by the Construction Spectifications Institute and developed under contract with Pacific International Computing Corporation (PIC) in 1970. COMSPEC is part of an overall communications system called CONCOM (Construction Communications) that embraces other types of word processing. COMSPEC is designed to standardize communications in the building industry. In many respects COMSPEC is very similar to MASTERSPEC, so much so in fact that in 1973 the two were combined to provide the best of each system.

COMSPEC also is a computer-oriented system. Input is by way of any A/E office master or commercially available master, sorted in computer banks by PIC. COMSPEC also has three levels of operation as follows:

Level A—Immediate and direct connection via subscriber's in-house terminal.

Level B—Two-day turnaround service by use of PIC master computer without in-house terminal.

Level C—Three-day-plus turnaround service from A/E to PIC and return.

The process for use of COMSPEC is very similar to that of MASTERSPEC: the draft copy is edited by the A/E, then a printout is provided which may again be edited, and a final copy including changes is run, but identifying line count is erased. As originally constituted, COMSPEC was to be a storage and retrieval system, not supplying masters but holding the master of each A/E subscriber for his reuse. Actually, master sections have been provided for those who do not have a master of their own. One feature that COMSPEC has that is not now available in MASTERSPEC is the ultimate original for reproduction. As a part of COMSPEC service, the final copy may be made on bond paper or reproducable mats for printing by the A/E. Further printing from these originals is the responsibility of the A/E.

MISCELLANEOUS MASTERS

There are other master systems that have been developed since the computer has come into general use for rapid retrieval and printout. One of these systems, devised for the NASA program, uses the sixteen Division *Uniform System*, plus Division 17—Welding/Brazing/Soldering. These three items are of course vital in the space program, so they are minutely spelled out in this additional division. The master is very similar to many others and is called *speCSIntact*; "a computerized system for the effective utilization of standard construction specifications" (see page 305). Indications for material qualifications are by reference to ASTM or Federal Specifications, as might be expected since this is one type of federal specification where trade names or specific manufacturers may not be listed. The printout is difficult to read in the normal manner since each line has a designator, but headings or subheadings are not called out in any additional way.

At present (1974) there are approximately forty master specifications available to the A/E. Few are inexpensive enough to tempt the small office and all require considerable cut-and-paste remodeling to make them fit the requirements of the A/E who plans to use them. Many guide specifications are available from trade associations, some manufacturers, and professional organizations, and these, for the most part, have been thoroughly researched and carefully written so that they could be incorporated with minimum changes into an office master specification system.

SUMMARY

The primary reason for use of a master specification is to reduce the time required to provide a document that fits the particular project. Surveys by various professional organizations report that as much as a

60 percent savings in time and money is possible by the use of masters. Such use is not new, but at this stage use may become widespread, due partly to the availability of automated equipment for storing and reproduction of the information. Most specifications writers have a master that they use whether it is in some specific form or not, since it would be virtually impossible to start from scratch each time a new specification is required.

The master is not a cure-all for specifications writers. A great deal of judgement must be used in preparation of the material it should include or in the revisions necessary in a master provided by someone else. The master will be different for commercial work, schools, government-financed work, and other types, so one office may have several kinds of masters, each geared to a particular type of work. Because of the differences of opinion among writers and A/E offices, any master must be revised by those who will use it; this is true regardless of the origin of the so-called master. For this reason anyone contemplating the use of a master should carefully review what the master includes.

When masters first began to appear a great many specifications writers felt that their usefulness was threatened; with a master specification in the office, any A/E could simply have an office boy or secretary pick out the sections that were to be used and the spec would somehow materialize. Such a procedure is not possible, since every project has some differences from any other project. One of the most frequent criticisms of specifications is "they don't fit the project." This is exactly where the specifications writer comes in. His training and experience enable him to list the items of material or installation that are different or new, to professionally select from a master those parts he can use, and to write new material for circumstances not covered in the master. Regardless of the perfection of a master (and none are 100 percent perfect), no untrained person can put together an adequate specification. The master simply provides a vehicle for repetitive material and is a good timesaver.

QUESTIONS

13.1. What are the particular advantages of using a master specification?

13.2. How would you start an office master?

13.3. What are the two principal ways to describe materials in a master?

13.4. Compare MASTERSPEC and COMSPEC for use as a master.

13.5. What do you think a master should include to make your work as a specifications writer easier and quicker?

14

CONSULTANTS

For most of the years that architects and engineers have been doing business there have also been consultants of one sort or another working with them. For the most part these consultants have been structural, electrical, or mechanical engineers, who have done a special part of the work that the architect was not experienced in or had little interest in doing. In more recent years consultants for additional portions of the project have been required, and quite recently, in perhaps the last fifteen years, consultants for materials and specifications have come into the picture. These consultants also have consultants, who may also have consultants, and so on.

SPECIFICATIONS CONSULTANT

There was a time when the materials, their methods of installation, and similar details were relatively minor in number and importance, as we have noted in Chapter 1. Immediately after World War II a flood of new materials came on the market. One of the few side benefits of war is that technical ideas developed for military use are then available to the public after the war. With this rapid expansion, architects, and engineers, found themselves deluged with new products, new installation methods, and new ideas. As the pace continued instead of leveling off the architect/specifier felt the need for help in this field. Enter the specifications consultant.

Just what does a specifications consultant do? What training or experience should he have? Who are his clients? How does he operate his office? Is there much demand now or in the future for his services?

When an architectural office is first organized, often the owner/architect or one member of the partnership has the responsibility for preparing the specifications. This is done in the office, at home evenings and weekends, on vacations, and at other times out of the office. To many architects it is a chore rather than an enjoyable part of their work. To some it is an opportunity to act as plan-checker as they review the drawings while writing the specifications. To some it is work to be delegated to others. As the office grows and prospers the architect has less and less time available to do things himself, so little by little he employs consultants. For some reason, even though many architects do not enjoy writing specifications and may not be trained or able to write good ones, they continue to resist employing a specifications consultant until they begin to have trouble.

WHAT THE SPECIFICATIONS CONSULTANT DOES

Obviously all such consultants do not operate alike, but there are several functions that are customarily performed by all. The proper time for the specifications consultant to be called into the project is at an early stage in the design. At this point he will be able to help the designer and project manager in the selection of materials and will be available for questions or conferences as the drawings develop. When the drawings have reached a point of about 60 to 65 percent completion the consultant should be supplied with a complete set so that he may start listing materials or even start some specifications sections. At about this time or earlier he will provide the engineering consultants with a specification dummy as a guide to the proper format and arrangement of their sections, or he may confer with them regarding information he needs if he is to write their sections. Most architectural specifications consultants only write architectural specifications, leaving all mechanical or electrical work to be done by the respective engineers. Structural engineering work may or may not be written by the structural engineer. Landscape work is usually provided to the specifications consultant as notes to be incorporated into the proper section.

As the production of drawings progresses so does the production of the specifications. In reviewing the drawings the consultant will also probably act as a pseudochecker, marking up errors, mismatched sections, omissions, improper or impossible details, and violations of the building code. Also during this period he will provide the architect or job captain with preliminary runs or copies of some sections of specifications, contact manufacturers representatives, and consult with the contractor if he has been preselected. In offices where specifications consultants are used there is limited contact between office employees and manufacturers' representatives, the latter making their presentations primarily through the specifications writer/consultant.

Completion of the specifications varies possibly more than any other phase of the work. Some consultants provide finished typed originals on whatever master system the office uses, requiring only duplicating and binding to be done by the architect. The majority provide rough copy in one form or another for final typing by the architects office. There should be a good understanding of the extent of services and expectations prior to the start of work. Most often the specifications sections written by the engineering consultants are not a particular concern of the specifications consultant, but in some cases these too are collected from the engineers, typed or revised as necessary, and provided to the architect.

TRAINING AND EXPERIENCE

The training and experience of specifications consultants are so varied it is difficult to point to any single factor. When specifications consultants first appeared in the construction business they were mostly older men; not *old* men, but *older* men—older in experience primarily, with years of background in drafting, field inspection, cost estimating and writing of specifications in some architectural or engineering office, and interested in specifications in all of its ramifications. More recently younger men with perhaps better training but less experience have entered the field. Background formal education includes architecture, engineering, chemistry, construction technology, industrial management, business administration, and some training that is not even remotely connected with construction. A few are graduates of the "school of hard knocks" with a minimum formal education but a world of sound practical experience. Many are registered architects or engineers who have become specialized while working for someone else or have determined this course for themselves. Most are capable, but it would be foolish to say this of all specifications consultants, since there is the same difference of opinion as to the meaning of *capable* here as in other professions. The various abilities required are the same as those mentioned in earlier chapters, plus the ability to develop a clientele and operate an office profitably.

WHO ARE THE CLIENTS?

Who are the specifications consultant's clients? They are primarily architects or engineers who need periodic help for specifications, but there are others who may also need help from time to time. Clients are developed by "door-pounding" contacts with large offices where normal staff personnel cannot keep up, by contacts at meetings and similar places with architects or some of their employees, by judicious use of mailings or announcements, and by reputation passed along by satisfied clients. These are basically the requirements for any business. Surprisingly, it is the medium-to-large office that seems most interested in the consultant's services. Perhaps this is because they have already used consultants for engineering or because their principals realize that consultants are more specialized. The smaller offices seem generally reluctant to trust others with their work. Whether this is a matter of false economy, lack of knowledge, stubbornness, or what, it remains that many of these smaller offices could profit by the use of a specifications consultant.

In addition to architects or engineering offices there are others who employ specifications consultants. A great number of manufacturers have turned to consultants to put together meaningful information for their catalogs. Some firms have employed consultants to help put together volumes of drawings, manufacturing data, and specifications for architects or engineers. Engineers who do not write their own specifications will employ consultants to do it and coordinate it with those of the architect. Developers or owners may want *performance specifications* for new projects. All these possibilities are well worth investigating for supplemental work.

CONSULTANTS' OFFICE

The office of the specifications consultant is usually quite small as far as space and personnel are concerned. Due to the fact that in most cases there are not more than two or three writers, and usually only one, with a limited supporting staff, there is little need for a large area. Several work areas arranged with tables and desks suffice. A principal difference will be noted however in the amount of reference storage space required. The consultant will probably have 200 to 300 percent more reference material than any of the offices he does work for. This is necessary since he must be able to suggest comparable products, find specialized items, and be ready to specify materials that may be preferred by any of his clients. Copies of codes, testing methods, and many similar references must be available. If any of his clients do work outside of his immediate area, he must have reference material for that area also. In addition he needs space for typists, duplicating equipment, and some private office room. Reception space may be limited since few clients will come to him (he goes to them), but he does need adequate room for conferences with manufacturers' representatives or other consultants.

CONSULTANTS' FEES

This is another portion of the general consulting field that has so many facets that we can present here only a very general discussion. The average A/E office usually does not know the cost of producing its specifications, simply because the "boss" does them at home on week-ends, the in-office spec writer's salary is classed as overhead, reproduction machinery is not amortized, paper is purchased as office supplies, or a dozen similar reasons. A fairly recent survey however sets the cost of producing specifications at approximately 7 percent of the total technical cost. Many offices without adequate records would suggest that this estimate is rather high.

Consultants fees, for the most part, work out at lower than the 7 percent noted above. Why? The consultant has a smaller office with lower overhead, he does a considerable amount of repetitious work, thus allowing greater use of master or standard portions, he quite often employs typists on a part-time or piece-work basis, and most often he does not do any of the actual printing that is included in the 7 percent figure. Most fees are graduated, either by variations of a lump sum or by percentage, from perhaps 1.5 percent for a project of $50,000 to approximately 0.005 percent for a $10 million construction. Additions to or subtractions from fees may be made due to the nature of the project; generally more is asked for hospitals than warehouses, even though the total cost may be nearly the same. This difference is due to the more complex requirements of a hospital or similar project. Some other factors are: whether the consultant supplies finished typing or rough copy, whether he acts as a researcher beyond his ordinary scope, whether he writes, retypes, or coordinates the specifications of the consulting engineers, and whether any consultation during construction is included.

CONSULTANTS' CONSULTANTS

This is not double talk but a brief discussion of consultants or experts in certain fields who assist the specifications consultant. Let us first eliminate mechanical and electrical engineers since they usually produce their own specifications for their work; also, except for coordination of section designations, format and similar details have little direct relationship with the architectural specifications consultant. There are certain well established areas where he does need help.

Almost every building requires finishing hardware. This includes an array of butts, locksets, closers, pulls, cabinet hardware, and often bath or toilet room accessories. These products are not all made by one manufacturer, and there are many manufacturers turning out products of different qualities. In some localities a hardware consultant operates on a free-lance basis for a fee, and in others he is an employee of a hardware supply distributor and his services are essentially free. He will list all of the hardware items required for the project, in accordance with code requirements, by manufacturer's name, model, and size. If he represents a supply house he probably will also bid the job and the slight advantage he has by preparing the hardware schedule may get him the contract. Choosing the correct hardware item, specified to meet code requirements, coupled with other items from a different manufacturer, all combined to look and operate well together, is often too specialized for the specifications consultant. He must review the schedule, adapt it to the format, and provide the preamble and other data, but he seldom makes out the actual schedule.

Most multistory buildings have elevators, so here too is a product or system that may require a consultant to the consultant. The many kinds of elevators, escalators, lifts, dock ramps, and similar people-handling equipment have some characteristics in common, but each manufacturer has recommendations for size, speed, type, and control. Although the general features are similar, each manufacturer has special details that he feels are unique, necessary, and, of course, better than his competition. Elevator manufacturers' representatives will usually provide rough copy to the specifications in the form of preprinted pages setting forth all the general requirements for size, speed, and so forth, plus all of their company's own special features. These special features are carefully worded and innocent to casual reading but they may result in a closed specification of the section if they are not removed from the final copy.

In special cases additional experts may be required to complete a specification. The landscape architect has already been mentioned. He may write his own complete specification or provide material to the consultant. The interior designer, employed either within or outside of the architect's office, may have sections on furniture, drapes, carpet, or similar decorating work that will be provided, completed or as notes to be incorporated. And from time to time very special processing methods or equipment may require an expert to advise the specifications consultant.

THE RESEARCHER

With the continued development of present materials and the great number of new ones being invented or designed, most architectural or engineering offices face a continuing and growing question—what is the best material for appearance, strength, cost, obtainability, and installation? This same question has been with the specifier for years, but now it is multiplied a hundred- and even a thousand-fold. In addition most designers now are, or certainly should be, aware of the impossibility of knowing all the characteristics of the many products available. This combination has brought about the advent of the researcher for proper use of materials, especially for larger projects.

This researcher, trained as an architect, engineer, specifications writer, chemist, or in some related science, and fully aware of the economic aspects of construction, is being employed more and more to help assemble information in many offices. When a project is still in the schematic and preliminary stages the researcher works closely with the designers to help establish the materials that might be used. This entails many many conferences with representatives of the manufacturers who make the more standard materials such as concrete, steel, wood, glass, plastics, and paint. A good imagination is required to envision how some of these materials, or perhaps new ones still in limited production, can be used.

Experimental processes such as the explosion forming of metals, air or injection methods for plastics, plastic form-liners for concrete, post-tensioning of concrete, as well as production line assemblies for panels or even complete modular units must be considered. The researcher then steps out of his role as a specifications writer and becomes a very important decision-maker in regard to which materials and methods will be recommended. Even where a project is not particularly unusual there is need for the researcher. Food-handling establishments, processing plants, manufacturers, and even schools and office buildings have a continuing problem with maintenance or replacement of wall and floor coverings, exterior finishes, roofing installations, and equipment. A competent researcher can make valuable recommendations regarding cost, longevity, appearance, and availability.

Perhaps the field of the researcher is even broader and has a better future than does that of the general specifications consultant. With the great interest now being generated about the causes and effects of pollution the researcher may be in an ideal position to investigate and suggest materials not detrimentally affected by air pollutants such as sulphur oxide, nitrogen compounds, hydrocarbons, or other chemicals. With more concern being shown about water supplies and pollution a knowledge of marine biology is necessary, since this concern affects piling, metals, paints, plastics, and other underwater construction.

SUMMARY

What makes the specifications consultant so special and his services so unique? By training and experience he has a good general knowledge of the construction business, but by specialization he has a highly developed knowledge of one or more phases of the work. By virtue of this very specialization he becomes more expert each time he writes a new specification. Each time he develops a section for a new application, researches data for a new material, or makes contact with a new manufacturer he stores a little part of that work for possible future use. Since he is not engaged in the design or drafting phases he has more time for research in his field and can often provide new ideas or suggest new materials that could affect design. He is essentially an outsider so far as the architect's office is concerned, and so he reads the drawings as an outsider. If the drawings do not match or do not tell him what is to be constructed he can suggest corrections before the errors reach the construction stage. One of the most important aspects of the consultant services is that he can be the extra man needed to expedite a project without entering another employee on the office books for a short time. He has knowledge, ability, and availability. He must be responsible or he will not be in business very long.

QUESTIONS

14.1. What does an architectural specifications consultant do?

14.2. What size architectural office most often uses a consultant? Discuss this.

14.3. What possibilities for employment, in addition to that from architectural offices, does a specifications consultant have?

14.4. Name and discuss several types of consultants-to-consultants that may be necessary in a total concept.

14.5. Convince a friend that you could do a good job as a specifications consultant for his work.

15

THE FUTURE?

What future lies ahead for the specifications writer? This question certainly comes to the minds of specifiers now in the profession, and it must also be a factor in the choice of a field by students or by those considering a change of pace. From all indications, surveys, and other sources, it appears that as more materials and systems for installation are developed and as construction becomes more complicated, there will be a greater demand for trained and experienced specifications writers. Someone, someway, must provide the information necessary to define the materials and installation on every construction project. Not many schools include specifications writing as a major part of their curriculum; this tends to limit the number of trained writers.

The idea that specifications writing is a dull, uninteresting job, pushed off onto the oldest or least-resisting office member, still persists in many areas. Fortunately this idea is being slowly dispelled, and a better realization of the specifier's importance in helping to control construction costs as well as the specialization of personnel in the construction field assures that the specifier, or his successor, will be around for quite a while. One of the first college-level courses to be oriented toward specifications writing is provided at Pasadena (California) City College and has been operating for more than ten years. The course includes study in drafting, test methods, specifications writing, and related subjects. The graduates have been enthusiastically received into the construction industry. This is one indication of the change in feeling about the spec writer and may encourage more young people, with adequate training and interest, to think seriously about becoming specifications writers.

More manufacturers are also employing specifications writers to provide reliable information to their clients. This has been made necessary in part by the demand for more usable data than had previously been available from Madison Avenue type manufacturer's literature, which often has more advertising than product information. In the past few years this has become more important as manufacturers have changed some policies concerning manufacturer's representatives and have reduced the number of these people now contacting A/E offices in person. Literature such as SPEC DATA, which is distributed by various manufacturers, is normally written by experienced specifications writers. These writers must also know what the A/E wants in the specifications so that they can supply that material in a form most easily used in the A/E office.

The specifications consultant has been discussed in Chapter 14 but here again is an expanding field for those interested. Even the largest A/E firms, who may have an impressive staff of specifications personnel, often require a free-lance consultant to help them over a particular rush period and a deadline which cannot be met by the available office help. Another field closely related to the A/E office is that of the contractor/developer. The attitude of the professional architectural societies toward the developers has recently changed, and this has brought about some opportunity for interested specifications writers to do work, mostly of a preliminary or guide type, for some major developments. The topics discussed in Chapter 13 also provide an opportunity for specifications writers to write, edit, or otherwise process masters for commercial companies.

As more masters are produced and more new materials appear there is a greater need for research, and this too is a great field for those who would like to do this type of work and provide organized report data for others. Some new manufacturing processes have such complicated requirements for the plants in which they are produced that considerable investigation and comparison of existing items is required to select those of best value. This is especially true of many types of construction directly related to the various space programs and their test facilities. Some of the required items or products may not even be manufactured yet and the research will determine by performance-type specifications what is necessary.

Great changes in our present methods of construction will have to take place before the qualified specifications writer has his position jeopardized to any extent. Our nation is a vast conglomerate; climatic conditions, extreme differences in terrain, and differences between urban and suburban living all show important variations and are major factors in determining what may be constructed. Shipping distances may be considerable, and construction practices are different in different areas. The labor unions have rules that may be compatible in some areas and opposites in other parts of the country. All these contribute to create problems that, in part at least, affect the specifications writer, but the major item that will continue to plague the construction industry and, in turn, require the skills of the specifier are the building codes. Until the number of codes is reduced and standardized someone must be available to read them, evaluate their requirements, and devise specifications that will satisfy those requirements. Although some effort is being made to standardize building codes, and perhaps even to provide one national code, it seems very doubtful that the more than fifteen hundred codes now in use in the United States will be combined into one code very soon. In addition, many A/E firms and contractors are now working abroad, using different materials, different installation methods, local labor, and are complying with local codes of one kind or another. All of these new situations require some specifications to direct them.

In conclusion, even though we have unbelievable help from all sorts of automated typewriters, reproducing equipment, computers, vast resources of catalogs, standard tests, and hundreds of other aids, none of these can *think*. The specifications writer, or whatever he may ultimately be called, *can* think and this assures him a place in the future.

APPENDICES

APPENDICES

A

TYPICAL SPECIFICATIONS
OF THE CSI

The material presented in this section (see list below) is limited to typical publications of The Construction Specifications Institute and indicates some of the references which are available from that organization. Most of these items have been discussed earlier in the text; their appearance here should help in digesting the information and identifying each document.

Uniform System for Construction Specifications, Data Filing & Cost Accounting

The SPEC-DATA Sheet

Typical CSI Preliminary Series specification study

Typical CSI Final Specification Series study

Part One - SPECIFICATION OUTLINE

UNIFORM SYSTEM

for CONSTRUCTION SPECIFICATIONS, DATA FILING & COST ACCOUNTING

Title One - Buildings

UNIFORM SYSTEM FOR CONSTRUCTION SPECIFICATIONS, DATA FILING & COST ACCOUNTING

PART ONE
SPECIFICATION OUTLINE

NOTES

Many Section titles are shown in the plural in the Uniform System Specification Outline. These titles should be changed to the singular where project requirements indicate.

Specification Sections may be numbered by the specification writer in any way he prefers. He may choose to use the Uniform System Division number followed by a capital letter identifying each of the several Sections in that Division, "8A" for example. When a fixed numbering system is preferred, use of the four-digit system shown in the Cost Accounting Guide, Uniform System Part 3, is recommended.

The Specification Outline includes both BROADSCOPE and Narrowscope Sections in great variety and number, and the individual project specifications will rarely, if ever, follow Section titles and sequence in every detail. Typical specifications will use only a portion of the titles listed, and some will require the modification of Uniform System Section titles or the introduction of new titles. However, it is recommended that Section titles be selected whenever possible from the comprehensive set shown in Part 1.

Division 1 encompasses certain aspects of project requirements often included in the General Conditions. When the recommendations of Division 1 are followed, the Conditions of the Contract should include appropriate Supplementary Conditions to avoid duplication of material contained in such General Conditions as those published by the American Institute of Architects, the Consulting Engineers Council of the United States, and others.

1.2

UNIFORM SYSTEM FOR CONSTRUCTION SPECIFICATIONS, DATA FILING & COST ACCOUNTING

SPECIFICATION OUTLINE   **GENERAL REQUIREMENTS**

SUMMARY OF THE WORK

Encompasses summaries of work under this contract, work under other contracts related to the project, work & equipment to be provided by the owner, and work to be postponed to a date later than the designated completion date. It should be clearly stated here whether work is to be completed under a single contract or under several contracts.

SCHEDULES & REPORTS

Encompasses the certification of lines & levels, reference to applicable building standards of such organizations as American Society for Testing & Materials, American Standards Association, American Institute of Steel Construction, American Concrete Institute, and General Services Administration; required inspections; a schedule of required tests; a list of approved testing agencies or criteria for their selection & approval; subsurface soil reports; progress reports & photographs; work progress & critical path schedules; project master color schedule; a glossary of standard abbreviations & symbols; and similar items related to the project as a whole. See 2 EARTHWORK for testing related to soil compaction; 2 PILING for piling tests; 3 CAST-IN-PLACE CONCRETE & 3 PRECAST CONCRETE for testing & inspection of concrete.

SAMPLES & SHOP DRAWINGS

Encompasses procedures for submission of shop drawings & samples. Required shop drawings & samples are normally best specified here in scheduled or tabular form, but it is recommended that a reference to this portion of the Specifications be included in each of the various Sections covering work for which samples or shop drawings are required.

TEMPORARY FACILITIES

Encompasses access roads, barricades & lanterns, construction elevators & hoists, construction stairs, construction offices, storage of tools & equipment, first aid facilities, temporary fences & guardrails, moisture control, parking, runways, scaffolding, staging platforms, signs, site access restrictions, temporary telephone service, outdoor toilet facilities, watchman, and similar provisions necessary to the safe and expeditious progress of the work. This portion of the Specifications normally encompasses the *temporary* provision of electrical power, lighting, space heating, water, or indoor toilet facilities. It is recommended that a reference to this Section be included in each of the other Sections covering similar work of a permanent nature.

CLEANING UP

Encompasses the sweeping, brushing, and other general cleaning of completed work and the removal of debris, surplus material, tools not in active use, and scaffolding & other equipment no longer needed. See various Sections in other Divisions for removal of unwanted material, for initial cleandown of newly installed work, and for cleaning of existing work.

PROJECT CLOSEOUT

Encompasses procedures for delivering guarantees & bonds, for preparing the punchlist, and for final inspection of the project; as-built drawings & specifications required and procedure for their submission; scope & content of the maintenance manual and procedure for its submission; and similar items related to the project as a whole. It is recommended that a reference to this portion of the Specifications be included in each of the various Sections covering work for which as-built drawings & specifications, guarantees, bonds, or maintenance manual data are required.

ALLOWANCES

Tabulates and defines all cash allowances for specified portions of the work. It is recommended that dollar amounts appear only in a master list located here and that reference to this portion of the Specifications be included in each of the various Sections covering work similar to that for which cash allowance is to be made. Cash allowances may also be itemized on the Bid Form.

1.3

UNIFORM SYSTEM FOR CONSTRUCTION SPECIFICATIONS, DATA FILING & COST ACCOUNTING

GENERAL REQUIREMENTS   **SPECIFICATION OUTLINE**

ALTERNATES

Lists all Alternates, describing in complete detail those Alternates that affect the scope of the project and summarizing those Alternates that deal with materials & methods of construction. Further reference to Alternates of project scope normally is limited to the Bid Form, but Alternates of materials & methods must be specified in complete detail in each of the various Sections affected and in brief in the Bid Form. It is essential that the Bid Form list all Alternates, assign a number or other reference designation to each, describe each briefly, and provide space beside each for the bidders' insertion of consequent additions to or deductions from the base bid.

1.4

UNIFORM SYSTEM FOR CONSTRUCTION SPECIFICATIONS, DATA FILING & COST ACCOUNTING

SPECIFICATION OUTLINE

SITE WORK

2

CLEARING OF SITE

Broadscope Section encompasses work described below under Demolition, Structures Moving, Clearing & Grubbing.

Demolition

Narrowscope Section encompasses demolition of and materials salvage from designated buildings, sheds, towers, tanks, covered walkways, and other existing above-grade structures. Capping of existing utility lines is normally best specified here, but may in some instances be specified instead in appropriate Section or Sections of Divisions 15 and 16. See 2 EARTHWORK for demolition and removal of such on-grade or below-grade improvements as concrete slabs, foundation walls, footings, underground tanks, underground utility lines, paving, culverts, curbs, and gutters.

Structures Moving

Narrowscope Section encompasses the intact relocation, on the project site or elsewhere, of designated existing structures or portions thereof. Earthwork, foundations, utility lines, and other new work related to the relocated structures are normally best specified in other appropriate Sections.

Clearing & Grubbing

Narrowscope Section encompasses the felling of trees and shrubs and removal or other disposition of resulting trash and timber, stumps, and other vegetation. See 2 EARTHWORK for removal of rocks, boulders, and other on-grade or below-grade obstructions.

EARTHWORK

Broadscope Section encompasses work described below under Site Grading, Excavating & Backfilling, Dewatering, Subdrainage, Soil Poisoning, Soil Compaction Control, Soil Stabilization.

Site Grading

Narrowscope Section encompasses the movement of significant quantities of earth to alter the fundamental contours of the site. This Section normally includes large earth fills, particularly those requiring use of borrow pits off the site; relocation & compaction of earth in the general overlot grading; disposition of excess excavated material; and removal of natural rock formations by ripping, blasting, or other means. See Excavating & Backfilling below for the localized movement of earth for accommodating the various portions of the building and its equipment, for tunneling work, and for removal of various isolated obstructions on or below grade.

Excavating & Backfilling

Narrowscope Section encompasses the localized movement of earth for accommodating the various portions of the building and its equipment. This Section normally includes the digging of footing trenches, foundation pits, & basements and required working space around them; removal of rocks, boulders, & other obstructions encountered; shaping of footing & other pits & trenches; fine grading under slabs; tunneling under walks, roads, & other existing work; and required backfilling.

Dewatering

Narrowscope Section encompasses removal of subsurface water from the soil during the construction period by means of pitting & pumping, wellpointing, trenching below the water table, or other means. This Section normally includes control of subsurface water by use of cofferdams constructed of closely driven piles supporting impervious clay fill or wood lagging, of interlocking steel sheet piling, or of prefabricated assemblies of special design. See Subdrainage below for subsurface drainage provisions of a permanent nature. See 2 SITE DRAINAGE for storm drainage system external to the building. See 7 SHEET METAL WORK for gutters & downspouts.

1.5

UNIFORM SYSTEM FOR CONSTRUCTION SPECIFICATIONS, DATA FILING & COST ACCOUNTING

2 | SITE WORK

SPECIFICATION OUTLINE

Subdrainage

Narrowscope Section encompasses drainage fields below basement floor slabs and other concrete slabs on grade, footing tile drains, and drainage fields required to drain an underground spring or other subsurface water source. See Dewatering above for removal of subsurface water during the construction period. See 2 SITE DRAINAGE for storm drainage system external to the building. See 7 SHEET METAL WORK for gutters & downspouts.

Soil Poisoning

Narrowscope Section encompasses the introduction of poison into the soil around and under structures for control of termites, other vermin, and undesirable plant growth.

Soil Compaction Control

Narrowscope Section encompasses field sampling & laboratory testing for control of soil compaction. See 1 SCHEDULE & REPORTS for preliminary subsurface soil investigation.

Soil Stabilization

Narrowscope Section encompasses the pressure-injection or other introduction of portland cement or other substances into fissured or porous rock or soil in order to stabilize it, to increase its bearing capacity, to reduce its tendency to flow, or to make it more water-resistant. This Section normally includes rock bolting and vibratory methods of soil stabilization.

PILING

Broadscope Section encompasses treated wood piling, precast concrete piling, 'H'-section steel piling, drilled-&-poured concrete piling, concrete-filled steel pipe piling, and mandrel-driven thin-shell steel piling with concrete fill. This Section normally includes load-sustaining requirements and tests.

CAISSONS

Broadscope Section encompasses both drilled and excavated caissons. Furnishing and placement of attendant formwork, reinforcing, and concrete are normally best specified here, but may in some instances be specified instead in 3 CONCRETE FORMWORK, 3 CONCRETE REINFORCEMENT, & 3 CAST-IN-PLACE CONCRETE, respectively. When formwork, reinforcing, & concrete are specified here, it is recommended that a reference to this Section be included in these Sections of Division 3 as may be appropriate.

SHORING & BRACING

Broadscope Section encompasses work described below under Sheeting, Underpinning.

Sheeting

Narrowscope Section encompasses wood sheeting, interlocking steel sheeting, whalers & shores, cribbing, and piling with intermediate lagging serving as, or incorporated in, permanent retaining walls. Sheeting installed as temporary retaining walls is normally best specified in 1 TEMPORARY FACILITIES.

Underpinning

Narrowscope Section encompasses temporary or permanent support of portions of buildings being remodeled or of buildings adjacent to new construction by means of shoring, needling, or underpinning.

SITE DRAINAGE

Broadscope Section encompasses the storm drainage system external to project building or buildings and is distinguished from the subdrainage system by its collection of rain and other surface water rather than subsurface water. This Section normally includes drop inlets, side inlets, catchbasins, manholes, manhole covers & frames, headwalls, culverts, drainage ditches & related rip-rap, concrete raceways & flumes, downspout connections, and piping of terra cotta, concrete, steel, or other material suitable for the system. External downspouts, gutters, & leaders are normally specified in 7 SHEET METAL WORK, roof drains and internal rainwater piping in 15 ROOF DRAINAGE SYSTEM. When a Section on SITE UTILITIES is included as part of this Division, this Section may be combined with it as SITE UTILITIES & DRAINAGE.

1.6

UNIFORM SYSTEM FOR CONSTRUCTION SPECIFICATIONS, DATA FILING & COST ACCOUNTING

SPECIFICATION OUTLINE   SITE WORK

SITE UTILITIES

Broadscope Section encompasses site utilities systems to be constructed under separate contract as part of tract development work preceding construction of the buildings to which these systems are later to be connected or as part of a concurrent project for connection to the building service at some predetermined point, usually a specified distance outside the building. Systems that may be specified in this Section include electrical, gas, steam, sanitary sewer, telephone, and water distribution systems; sewage treatment systems; water treatment systems; water wells, pumps, & reservoirs; and similar facilities. Under normal circumstances, the systems encompassed by this Section are specified instead in various appropriate Sections of Divisions 15 & 16.

ROADS & WALKS

Broadscope Section encompasses work described below under Paving, Curbs & Gutters, Walks, Road & Parking Appurtenances.

Paving

Narrowscope Section encompasses paving for roadways, driveways, aircraft runways, parking areas, and malls. This Section normally includes the furnishing, placement, & finishing of gravel or crushed stone base courses, soil cement courses, macadam surfacing, bituminous concrete mats, & bituminous sealers; material & labor for construction of formwork; the placing & finishing of portland cement concrete; the placing of concrete reinforcement, and the setting of precast concrete, brick, or stone paving units. This Section may in some instances also include a complete specification of materials for the proportioning & mixing of portland cement concrete as well as materials for precast concrete, brick, or stone paving, but normally reference is made here to detailed specifications for these items in 3 CAST-IN-PLACE CONCRETE, 3 PRE-CAST CONCRETE, 4 UNIT MASONRY, & 4 STONE, respectively. This Section may sometimes be combined with the succeeding Section as Paving, Curbs, & Gutters, particularly if all are to be constructed of like material.

Curbs & Gutters

Narrowscope Section encompasses curbs & gutters of portland cement concrete, bituminous concrete, brick, or stone. This Section normally includes the furnishing, placement, & finishing of bituminous material; material & labor for construction of formwork; the placing & finishing of portland cement concrete; and the setting of brick or stone units. This Section may in some instances also include a complete specification of materials for, and the proportioning & mixing of, portland cement concrete as well as materials for brick or stone curbs & gutters, but normally reference is made here to detailed specifications for these items in 3 CAST-IN-PLACE CONCRETE, 4 UNIT MASONRY, & 4 STONE, respectively. This Section may sometimes be combined with the preceding Section as Paving, Curbs & Gutters, particularly if all are to be constructed of like material.

Walks

Narrowscope Section encompasses walks of cast-in-place or precast portland cement concrete, bituminous concrete, brick, stone slabs, or stone setts; and required base courses. This Section normally includes the furnishing, placement, & finishing of base courses, bituminous concrete mats, & bituminous sealers; material & labor for construction of formwork; the placing & finishing of portland cement concrete; and the setting of precast concrete, brick, or stone paving units. This Section in some instances also includes a complete specification of materials for and the proportioning & mixing of portland cement concrete as well as materials for precast concrete, brick, or stone walks, but normally reference is made here to detailed specifications for these items in 3 CAST-IN-PLACE CONCRETE, 3 PRECAST CONCRETE, 4 UNIT MASONRY, & 4 STONE, respectively.

1.7

UNIFORM SYSTEM FOR CONSTRUCTION SPECIFICATIONS, DATA FILING & COST ACCOUNTING

SITE WORK **SPECIFICATION OUTLINE**

Road & Parking Appurtenances

Narrowscope Section encompasses curb guards, guard rails, ice & dust control, parking & roadway striping, road barriers, road signs, wheel bumpers, and similar items. Parking gates, drive-up ticket dispensers, & other equipment for commercial parking garages or lots is normally best specified in 11 PARKING EQUIPMENT. Traffic control equipment is normally specified here, but if electrically operated, may sometimes be included instead in appropriate Section of Division 16.

SITE IMPROVEMENTS

Broadscope Section encompasses work described below under Fences, Playing Fields, Fountains, Irrigation System, Yard Improvements.

Fences

Narrowscope Section encompasses protective or decorative fences & gates of various types including those constructed of wood planks, wood stakes, split wood rails, barbed wire, chainlink or other metal mesh, or other suitable material and supported by wood, metal, or precast concrete posts, concrete or masonry piers, or other means. Electrified fences are normally specified in this Section, but may in some instances be included instead in appropriate Section of Division 16.

Playing Fields

Narrowscope Section encompasses the construction of outdoor sports and recreation facilities such as football, baseball, soccer, field hockey, & polo fields; tennis, squash, & jaialai courts; running tracks; and playgrounds. See 11 GYMNASIUM EQUIPMENT for sports & athletic equipment including gymnstands, 13 PREFABRICATED STRUCTURES for prefabricated grandstands, 13 SWIMMING POOLS for pool & natatorium construction & equipment.

Fountains

Narrowscope Section encompasses decorative fountains & fountain structures. Fountain equipment such as sprayheads, pumps, drains, & underwater lighting is normally furnished under this Section, but may in some instances be specified instead in appropriate Sections of Divisions 15 & 16. Installation of such items as sprayheads, piping, pumps, drains, waterproof junction boxes & connections, & underwater lighting is normally specified in appropriate Sections of Divisions 15 & 16, but may in some instances be included instead in this Section.

Irrigation System

Narrowscope Section encompasses irrigation ditching, irrigation piping, irrigation control system, fertilizing systems & equipment, and pesticide application equipment. This Section normally includes piping, valves, fittings, piping specialties, & labor for construction of underground or aboveground irrigation & spraying systems; the furnishing & installation of automatic gates, valves, timers, & other control or recording equipment; automatic equipment for metering & distributing soil chemicals, fertilizers, & pesticides; pump; and spray heads; but in some instances these may be specified instead in appropriate Sections of Division 15.

Yard Improvements

Narrowscope Section encompasses clothes posts, trashcan holders, bicycle racks, benches, and similar items normally not built into or attached to the building.

LAWNS & PLANTING

Broadscope Section encompasses work described below under Soil Preparation, Lawns, Ground Covers & Other Plants, Trees & Shrubs.

Soil Preparation

Narrowscope Section encompasses the preparation of soil for seeding, sodding, or planting of ground cover including furnishing & application of topsoil, elimination or control of undesirable seed or vegetable debris, soil aeration or scarification, incorporation in topsoil or specified neutralizers & fertilizers, tilling, & finish grading. Stripping & stockpiling of topsoil from the site are normally included in 2 EARTHWORK, but may in some instances be specified instead in this Section.

1.8

UNIFORM SYSTEM FOR CONSTRUCTION SPECIFICATIONS, DATA FILING & COST ACCOUNTING

SPECIFICATION OUTLINE

SITE WORK 2

Lawns

Narrowscope Section encompasses the furnishing & application of grass seed and sod, including the required relocation of existing sod, rolling, & temporary erosion control.

Ground Covers & Other Plants

Narrowscope Section encompasses the furnishing, planting, & mulching of vines, ground covers, flowers, & flower bulbs, including the required relocation of existing material.

Trees & Shrubs

Narrowscope Section encompasses the furnishing, planting, initial feeding, mulching, and protective pruning and spraying of trees and shrubs; the root excavation, balling & wrapping, moving, & replanting of designated existing trees & shrubs; and the furnishing & installation of protective trunk wrappings, guys, stakes, & root feeding pipes.

RAILROAD WORK

Broadscope Section encompasses construction on the project site of railroad trackage serving as an internal system for movement of heavy or bulky materials & equipment and of rail sidings extending & connecting to the main line and includes the furnishing & installation of ties, ballasting, rails, turnouts, crossings, switchstands, & car bumpers. See 2 EARTHWORK for roadbed grading, 3 CAST-IN-PLACE CONCRETE or 3 PRECAST CONCRETE for undertrack unloading pits of concrete, 5 STRUCTURAL METAL for incidental trestlework of metal, 6 ROUGH CARPENTRY for undertrack unloading bins & incidental trestlework of heavy timber, appropriate Section or Sections of Division 14 for car loading & unloading systems, and appropriate Section or Sections of Division 16 for overhead or underground power lines & related equipment for electrified trackage.

MARINE WORK

Broadscope Section encompasses work described below under Boat Facilities, Protective Marine Structures, Dredging.

Boat Facilities

Narrowscope Section encompasses docks, slips, boathouses, moorings, launching ramps, boat hoists, & marine accessories.

Protective Marine Structures

Narrowscope Section encompasses fender piles, seawalls, groins, & jetties.

Dredging

Narrowscope Section encompasses the underwater excavation of earth, sand, gravel or other substance and its subsequent disposition.

1.9

UNIFORM SYSTEM FOR CONSTRUCTION SPECIFICATIONS, DATA FILING & COST ACCOUNTING

CONCRETE **SPECIFICATION OUTLINE**

CONCRETE FORMWORK	Broadscope Section encompasses formwork of wood, plywood, fiber, metal, or plastics; patented formwork systems; form liners and coatings; form supports and shoring; and formwork accessories of every sort.
CONCRETE REINFORCEMENT	Broadscope Section encompasses steel reinforcing bars, welded wire fabric, bar supports, and miscellaneous reinforcement accessories. High-tensile steel wire & cable, anchorages for prestress tendons, and pre-stressing methods & equipment may be specified here but are normally best specified in 3 CAST-IN-PLACE CONCRETE or 3 PRECAST CONCRETE as may be appropriate.
CAST-IN-PLACE CONCRETE	Broadscope Section encompasses work described below under Heavyweight Aggregate Concrete, Lightweight Aggregate Concrete, Post-Tensioned Concrete, Nailable Concrete, Specially Finished Concrete, Specially Placed Concrete.
Heavyweight Aggregate Concrete	Narrowscope Section encompasses materials, proportioning, mixing, placement, curing, & finishing of concrete using aggregates of crushed stone or gravel.
Lightweight Aggregate Concrete	Narrowscope Section encompasses materials, proportioning, mixing, placement, curing, & finishing of concrete using lightweight aggregates, including insulating concrete. Insulating concrete roof decks may sometimes be specified here, but are normally best specified in 3 CEMENTITIOUS DECKS, particularly if part of a specialized system that includes formboards, supports, and reinforcing.
Post-Tensioned Concrete	Narrowscope Section encompasses materials and techniques of post-tensioning cast-in-place concrete structures. Tendons & anchorages may sometimes be specified in 3 CONCRETE REINFORCEMENT, but are usually best specified here.
Nailable Concrete	Narrowscope Section encompasses materials, proportioning, mixing, placement, curing, & finishing of concrete specially formulated to receive and retain hand-driven nails.
Specially Finished Concrete	Narrowscope Section encompasses concrete with finish requiring the use of special techniques such as aggregate transfer, use of set-retardant form coatings, acid or hydraulic etching, etc. Heavy-duty concrete floor toppings may sometimes be specified here, but are normally best specified in 9 SPECIAL FLOORING, particularly if they are to be installed by a specialty contractor or by use of specialized techniques.
Specially Placed Concrete	Narrowscope Section encompasses concrete placed by pump or spray.
PRECAST CONCRETE	Broadscope Section encompasses work described below under Precast Concrete Panels, Precast Structural Concrete, Precast Prestressed Concrete.
Precast Concrete Panels	Narrowscope Section encompasses conventionally reinforced precast concrete panels with as-cast or exposed aggregate finish.
Precast Structural Concrete	Narrowscope Section encompasses conventionally reinforced precast concrete structural elements, including lift slabs and tilt-up wall units.
Precast Prestressed Concrete	Narrowscope Section encompasses precast prestressed units of all types, including tendons, anchorages, & prestressing techniques.
CEMENTITIOUS DECKS	Broadscope Section encompasses work described below under Poured Gypsum Deck, Insulating Concrete Roof Decks, Cementitious Unit Decking.
Poured Gypsum Deck	Narrowscope Section encompasses materials for and installation of gypsum decks, including reinforcing, supports, and accessories. Formboards are sometimes specified in 3 CONCRETE FORMWORK, but are usually best specified here, particularly if especially designed for this use.
Insulating Concrete Roof Decks	Narrowscope Section encompasses materials for and installation of insulating concrete roof decks using perlite, vermiculite, or similar aggregates and including formboards, bulb-tees or other supports, reinforcing, and required accessories. Insulating concrete roof decks, particularly if used as fill over a separate structural deck, may sometimes be specified in 3 CAST-IN-PLACE CONCRETE.
Cementitious Unit Decking	Narrowscope Section encompasses decking units composed of organic or inorganic aggregates with cement binders in the shape of panels, planks, or channel slabs.

1.10

UNIFORM SYSTEM FOR CONSTRUCTION SPECIFICATIONS, DATA FILING & COST ACCOUNTING

SPECIFICATION OUTLINE

MASONRY

MORTAR	Broadscope Section encompasses materials, proportioning, mixing, and application of mortars and masonry cements, including epoxy and other special-duty mortars.
UNIT MASONRY	Broadscope Section encompasses work described below under Brick Masonry, Concrete Unit Masonry, Clay Backing Tile, Clay Facing Tile, Ceramic Veneer, Pavers, Glass Unit Masonry, Gypsum Unit Masonry, Reinforced Masonry.
Brick Masonry	Narrowscope Section encompasses pressed or fired clay bricks, of both common & facing type, and their installation.
Concrete Unit Masonry	Narrowscope Section encompasses solid, hollow, and pierced concrete masonry units and their installation.
Clay Backing Tile	Narrowscope Section encompasses loadbearing & non-loadbearing fired clay backing tile and its installation.
Clay Facing Tile	Narrowscope Section encompasses loadbearing & non-loadbearing fired clay facing tile, both glazed & unglazed, and its installation. Horizontally bedded units of terra cotta are normally specified here, but terra cotta facings composed of large units vertically bedded in cement or adhesive should be specified below under Ceramic Veneer.
Ceramic Veneer	Narrowscope Section encompasses terra cotta facing units installed in a vertical bed of organic or inorganic cement or adhesive, usually without the use of cramps or other mechanical fasteners.
Pavers	Narrowscope Section encompasses masonry units specially manufactured or specially installed as paving units, including paving bricks, heavy-duty fired clay units, & precast paving units of concrete or other material.
Glass Unit Masonry	Narrowscope Section encompasses glass blocks and their installation.
Gypsum Unit Masonry	Narrowscope Section encompasses gypsum partition & backup units & their installation.
Reinforced Masonry	Narrowscope Section encompasses the construction of masonry elements with joint reinforcement consisting of No. 3 or larger steel bars and with grout or mortar having bond strength sufficient to maintain complete continuity between masonry units & reinforcement under applied bending loads. Wall ties & other light wire reinforcement for masonry should be specified above in Brick Masonry, Concrete Unit Masonry, etc.
STONE	Broadscope Section encompasses work described below under Rough Stone, Cut Stone, Simulated Stone, Flagstone.
Rough Stone	Narrowscope Section encompasses as-quarried, rubble, or fieldstone units of any suitable natural stone, and their installation.
Cut Stone	Narrowscope Section encompasses natural stone units dressed to true surface & profiles, and their installation.
Simulated Stone	Narrowscope Section encompasses units manufactured under controlled plant conditions to precise shape, size, color, & texture simulating natural stone units.
Flagstone	Narrowscope Section encompasses natural flagstone and its installation.
MASONRY RESTORATION	Broadscope Section encompasses the removal, replacement, & repair of masonry units; the raking, filling, packing, and tuckpointing of masonry joints; and the cleaning of old masonry work.

1.11

UNIFORM SYSTEM FOR CONSTRUCTION SPECIFICATIONS, DATA FILING & COST ACCOUNTING

5 METALS

SPECIFICATION OUTLINE

STRUCTURAL METAL	Broadscope Section encompasses primary structural elements of steel or other metal, including fabrication & erection requirements. See also 2 PILING and 2 SHORTING & BRACING.
OPEN-WEB JOISTS	Broadscope Section encompasses short-span & long-span open-web joists, bridging, anchors, & accessories.
METAL DECKING	Broadscope Section encompasses ribbed, fluted, & cellular metal units for floor or roof decks. Metal roofing of the sort that does not require application of a separate weather surface should be specified in 7 PRE-FORMED ROOFING & SIDING or 7 SHEET METAL WORK.
LIGHTGAGE FRAMING	Broadscope Section encompasses metal stud & joist systems, metal tubing, and similar material, including fasteners & accessories.
MISCELLANEOUS METAL	Broadscope Section encompasses the various metal items customarily manufactured to more or less standard details in sizes conforming to specific project requirements. It may be desirable in some cases to specify certain miscellaneous metal items under one or more of the Narrowscope Sections described below under Metal Stairs, Floor Gratings, & Construction Castings or in other Sections established for the particular project. These may be used in place of or in addition to the MISCELLANEOUS METAL Section. Grilles & louvers of sheet metal may sometimes be specified in this Section, but are normally best specified in 7 SHEET METAL WORK. See also 5 ORNAMENTAL METAL & 5 SPECIAL FORMED METAL, as well as various Sections of Division 10.
Metal Stairs	Narrowscope Section encompasses metal stairs, stair landings, railings, ladders, & fire escapes. For preassembled metal stair forms, see CONCRETE FORMWORK.
Floor Gratings	Narrowscope Section encompasses metal gratings installed as heavy-duty floor surfacing, balconies, catwalks, stair treads, areaway covers, sidewalk vault covers, and in similar locations. Concrete-filled floor armoring grids may sometimes be specified in this Section, but are normally best specified in 9 SPECIAL FLOORING.
Construction Castings	Narrowscope Section encompasses construction castings of various sorts, including downspout boots, corner guards, foundation vents, & similar cast metal items of a utilitarian nature. See also 2 SITE DRAINAGE for downspout connections and various drainage castings. Manhole covers & frames not related to the drainage system are normally best specified here.
ORNAMENTAL METAL	Broadscope Section encompasses nonferrous metalwork of a custom & more or less highly finished nature. Decorative grilles & louvers should be specified here if wrought, cast, or die-cast. Decorative sheet metal grilles & louvers may sometimes be specified in this Section, but are normally best specified in 7 SHEET METAL WORK. See also various Sections of Division 10, 12 ARTWORK, & 12 ECCLESIASTICAL EQUIPMENT.
SPECIAL FORMED METAL	Broadscope Section encompasses ferrous metalwork of a semi-custom or custom nature, particularly that requiring the use of die-forming or progressive-roll-forming processes.

1.12

UNIFORM SYSTEM FOR CONSTRUCTION SPECIFICATIONS, DATA FILING & COST ACCOUNTING

SPECIFICATION OUTLINE
CARPENTRY

6

ROUGH CARPENTRY
Broadscope Section encompasses work described below under Framing & Sheathing, Heavy Timber Work.

Framing & Sheathing
Narrowscope Section encompasses the framing of light wooden structures, including the use of preassembled components; and their sheathing with wood, plywood, or other materials.

Heavy Timber Work
Narrowscope Section encompasses timber trusses, mill-framed structures, and pole construction.

FINISH CARPENTRY
Broadscope Section encompasses work described below under Wood Trim, Millwork, Wood Siding.

Wood Trim
Narrowscope Section encompasses running & standing trim, moldings, & stock ornaments.

Millwork
Narrowscope Section encompasses wood stairs & railings, wood door frames, mantelpieces, entrances, high-pressure plastic laminates, lumber, plywood, veneer of various species, hardboard, particleboard, & various sorts of prefinished panels. Custom wood window frames are usually specified in this Section, but stock wood windows are normally best specified in 8 WOOD WINDOWS. Cabinetry & countertops of a utilitarian nature intended for on-site assembly are usually specified here, but cabinetry using veneers, finishes, and joinery usually associated with fine furniture is best specified in 6 CUSTOM WOODWORK, particularly when it is to match adjacent custom panelwork. For wood doors, see 8 WOOD DOORS.

Wood Siding
Narrowscope Section covers various sidings of wood, plywood, & hardboard. For wood shingles & shakes, see 7 SHINGLES & ROOFING TILES.

GLUE-LAMINATED WOOD
Broadscope Section encompasses structural elements & deckings of glue-laminated wood, including shoes, hangers, splines, and other accessories.

CUSTOM WOODWORK
Broadscope Section encompasses work described below under Custom Cabinetwork, Custom Panelwork.

Custom Cabinetwork
Narrowscope Section encompasses cabinetry using veneers, finishes, & joinery usually associated with fine furniture, particularly where it is to match adjacent custom panelwork.

Custom Panelwork
Narrowscope Section encompasses panelwork surfaced with specially selected and matched hardwood veneers joined and finished in much the same manner as fine furniture. Wood doors that are to match the paneling are usually best specified in this Section rather than in 8 WOOD DOORS as they would otherwise be.

1.13

UNIFORM SYSTEM FOR CONSTRUCTION SPECIFICATIONS, DATA FILING & COST ACCOUNTING

7 MOISTURE PROTECTION   SPECIFICATION OUTLINE

WATERPROOFING	Broadscope Section encompasses work described below under Membrane Waterproofing, Hydrolithic Waterproofing, Liquid Waterproofing, Metallic Oxide Waterproofing. Materials & methods specified in this Section are those capable of resisting moisture under hydrostatic pressure. They are distinct from materials & methods specified in 7 DAMP-PROOFING.
Membrane Waterproofing	Narrowscope Section encompasses waterproofing composed of one or more layers of felt, fabric, or any of various preformed elastic sheets set in bituminous or other waterproofing compounds.
Hydrolithic Waterproofing	Narrowscope Section encompasses cement or other toppings with liquid, powder, or paste waterproofing substances added.
Liquid Waterproofing	Narrowscope Section encompasses waterproofing compounds of elastomeric or other substances applied in liquid form and curing to an impervious membrane.
Metallic Oxide Waterproofing	Narrowscope Section encompasses waterproofing composed of cement, sand, finely divided particles of iron or other metal, an oxidizing agent, and water.
DAMPPROOFING	Broadscope Section encompasses work described below under Bituminous Dampproofing, Silicone Dampproofing, Cementitious Dampproofing, Preformed Vapor Barrier.
Bituminous Dampproofing	Narrowscope Section encompasses bituminous dampproofing compounds and their application with brush, mop, spray, or trowel.
Silicone Dampproofing	Narrowscope Section encompasses silicone dampproofing compounds and their application with brush or spray.
Cementitious Dampproofing	Narrowscope Section encompasses dampproofing compounds based on portland cement or other cements, and their application with brush, spray, or trowel.
Preformed Vapor Barrier	Narrowscope Section encompasses preformed vapor barriers of asphalt, polyethylene, elastomers, synthetic & natural rubber, metal, & other substances. Vapor barriers to be installed as part of a membrane roofing assembly are normally best specified in 7 MEMBRANE ROOFING; those installed under concrete slabs on grade in 3 CAST-IN-PLACE CONCRETE.
BUILDING INSULATION	Broadscope Section encompasses thermal insulation for buildings, including both organic and inorganic material in the form of batts, blankets, rolls, pellets, granules, foils, planks, panels, & foams. Installation of perimeter insulation is normally best specified in 3 CAST-IN-PLACE CONCRETE, of insulation placed in masonry wall cavities in 4 UNIT MASONRY, of insulation forming part of a buildup roof system in 7 MEMBRANE ROOFING, and of mechanical equipment insulation in 15 BASIC MATERIALS & METHODS.
SHINGLES & ROOFING TILES	Broadscope Section encompasses work described below under Asphalt Shingles, Asbestos-Cement Shingles, Wood Shingles, Slate Shingles, Clay Roofing Tiles, Concrete Roofing Tiles, Porcelain Enamel Shingles, Metal Shingles.
Asphalt Shingles	Narrowscope Section encompasses asphalt shingles of all types.
Asbestos-Cement Shingles	Narrowscope Section encompasses asbestos-cement shingles of types designed for roof or wall application.
Wood Shingles	Narrowscope Section encompasses both wood shingles & handsplit wood shakes and their application to roof or wall.

1.14

UNIFORM SYSTEM FOR CONSTRUCTION SPECIFICATIONS, DATA FILING & COST ACCOUNTING

SPECIFICATION OUTLINE   **MOISTURE PROTECTION**   7

Slate Shingles	Narrowscope Section encompasses natural slate shingles and their application.
Clay Roofing Tiles	Narrowscope Section encompasses fired clay roofing tiles of various types and flat fired clay units simulating various kinds of shingles.
Concrete Roofing Tiles	Narrowscope Section encompasses precast concrete roofing tiles of both overlapping & interlocking types.
Porcelain Enamel Shingles	Narrowscope Section encompasses metal shingles with porcelain enamel finish.
Metal Shingles	Narrowscope Section encompasses metal shingles with painted or metallic finishes.
PREFORMED ROOFING & SIDING	Broadscope Section encompasses work described below under Preformed Metal Roofing, Preformed Metal Siding, Asbestos-Cement Panels, Preformed Plastic Panels, Custom Panel Roofing.
Preformed Metal Roofing	Narrowscope Section encompasses preformed metal roofing units with interlocking or overlapping joints that do not require application of a separate weather surface. Fasteners, grommets, sealants, filler strips, batten caps, & other accessories should be specified in this Section.
Preformed Metal Siding	Narrowscope Section encompasses preformed metal siding units & systems including fasteners, trim, insulation, sealants, & installation.
Asbestos-Cement Panels	Narrowscope Section encompasses asbestos-cement panels of flat, corrugated, or other profile and their installation as siding or as overlapping roof units not requiring application of a separate weather surface.
Preformed Plastic Panels	Narrowscope Section encompasses preformed rigid panels of various plastics in flat, corrugated, and other profiles, and their application as siding or as overlapping roof units not requiring application of a separate weather surface.
Custom Panel Roofing	Narrowscope Section encompasses large roofing panels custom fabricated to serve as the weather surface of domes, vaults, & other curved or folded roof structures.
MEMBRANE ROOFING	Broadscope Section encompasses work described below under Builtup Bituminous Roofing, Prepared Roll Roofing, Elastic Sheet Roofing, Elastic Liquid Roofing.
Builtup Bituminous Roofing	Narrowscope Section encompasses roofing with continuous weather surfaces of alternating layers of bitumen & felt or other fabric, including bituminous base flashing, special base sheets, cants & edge strips, & embedded toppings of gravel, crushed stone or other suitable aggregates. Rigid roof insulation & vapor barriers are usually best specified here, but may sometimes be specified in 7 BUILDING INSULATION & 7 DAMPPROOFING respectively.
Prepared Roll Roofing	Narrowscope Section encompasses mineral-surfaced asphalt & other roll roofing.
Elastic Sheet Roofing	Narrowscope Section encompasses elastic roofing sheets of chlorosulfonated polyethylene, polyvinyl fluoride, butyl rubber, silicone rubber, & other similar substances.
Elastic Liquid Roofing	Narrowscope Section encompasses elastic roofing compounds applied in liquid form, including chlorosulfonated polyethylene, butyl & silicone rubbers, & other similar substances.

1.15

UNIFORM SYSTEM FOR CONSTRUCTION SPECIFICATIONS, DATA FILING & COST ACCOUNTING

7 | **MOISTURE PROTECTION** | SPECIFICATION OUTLINE

SHEET METAL WORK	Broadscope Section encompasses work described below under Sheet Metal Roofing, Metal Roof Flashing & Trim, Gutters & Downspouts, Grilles & Louvers, Decorative Sheet Metal Work. For air distribution ductwork of sheet metal, see 15 AIR TEMPERING SYSTEM.
Sheet Metal Roofing	Narrowscope Section encompasses roofing of steel, terne metal, galvanized steel, or other suitable metal, and its installation with flat seams, standing seams, batten seams, or other weathertight joints. Preformed metal roofing not requiring a continuous structural deck for its support is specified in 7 PREFORMED ROOFING & SIDING.
Metal Roof Flashing & Trim	Narrowscope Section encompasses gravel stops; roof expansion joint covers of metal; metal counterflashing of cants & curbs and machinery supports, pipes, ducts, column stubs, and other elements penetrating the roof; and other metal flashings in or above the roof. Metal through-wall flashing may sometimes be specified in 7 WALL FLASHING, but is normally best specified in this Section, particularly if it is to include an integral receiver for bituminous base or parapet flashing.
Gutters & Downspouts	Narrowscope Section encompasses builtin & hung gutters, leaders, downspouts, & scuppers of galvanized steel, copper, aluminum, or other metals.
Grilles & Louvers	Narrowscope Section encompasses decorative & functional grilles & louvers of sheet metal. For wrought or cast metal grilles & louvers, see 5 ORNAMENTAL METAL; for wood grilles & louvers, 6 FINISH CARPENTRY.
Decorative Sheet Metal Work	Narrowscope Section encompasses decorative facia covers, spandrel covers, facings, & trim of sheet metal.
WALL FLASHING	Broadscope Section encompasses wall flashing of sheet metal, sheet plastic, impregnated fabric or felt, metallic-faced paper, & other flexible sheet materials installed in masonry walls at foundations, spandrels, sills, heads, & other locations. Metal through-wall flashing may sometimes be specified here, but is normally best specified in 7 SHEET METAL WORK.
ROOF ACCESSORIES	Broadscope Section encompasses work described below under Plastic Skylights, Metal-Framed Skylights, Roof Hatches, Gravity Ventilators.
Plastic Skylights	Narrowscope Section encompasses plastic skylights, curbs, ceiling domes, and other accessories.
Metal-Framed Skylights	Narrowscope Section encompasses fabrication & erection of metal-framed skylights. Curbs may sometimes be specified in other appropriate Section, glass in 8 GLASS & GLAZING, and counterflashing in 7 WALL FLASHING, but these are normally best specified here.
Roof Hatches	Narrowscope Section encompasses hatches of various sorts and their installation in the roof to provide access, smoke venting, or pressure relief.
Gravity Ventilators	Narrowscope Section encompasses roof-mounted gravity ventilators of various sorts. They may, in some instances, be specified in 15 AIR-TEMPERING SYSTEM when designed as an integral part of that system.
CALKING & SEALANTS	Broadscope Section encompasses fibrous & resilient packing, oil-base & elastic-base calking compounds, narrow-joint sealants, gaskets, & tapes. Glazing compounds are normally best specified in 8 GLASS & GLAZING, curtainwall sealants in 8 CURTAINWALL SYSTEM, & storefront sealants in 8 STOREFRONT SYSTEM.

1.16

UNIFORM SYSTEM FOR CONSTRUCTION SPECIFICATIONS, DATA FILING & COST ACCOUNTING

SPECIFICATION OUTLINE   **DOORS, WINDOWS, & GLASS**

METAL DOORS & FRAMES

Broadscope Section encompasses work described below under Hollow Metal Doors & Frames, Aluminum Doors & Frames, Stainless Steel Doors & Frames, Bronze Doors & Frames, Metal Storm & Screen Doors. Section title may be altered as required to 8 METAL DOORS or 8 METAL FRAMES. Doors & frames to be installed as part of a correlated system of storefront components are normally best specified in 8 STOREFRONT SYSTEM.

Hollow Metal Doors & Frames

Narrowscope Section encompasses formed steel doors, including labeled doors, and formed steel frames for doors, sidelights, transoms, borrowed-light partitions, & similar installations. Section title may be altered as required to 8 Hollow Metal Doors or 8 Hollow Metal Frames.

Aluminum Doors & Frames

Narrowscope Section encompasses formed & extruded aluminum doors and frames for doors, sidelights, transoms, borrowed-light partitions, & similar installations. Section title may be altered as required to 8 Aluminum Doors or 8 Aluminum Frames.

Stainless Steel Doors & Frames

Narrowscope Section encompasses stainless steel doors and frames for doors, sidelights, transoms, borrowed-light partitions, & similar installations. Section title may be altered as required to 8 Stainless Steel Doors or 8 Stainless Steel Frames.

Bronze Doors & Frames

Narrowscope Section encompasses bronze doors & frames for doors, sidelights, transoms, borrowed-light partitions, & similar installations. Section title may be altered as required to 8 Bronze Doors or 8 Bronze Frames.

Metal Storm & Screen Doors

Narrowscope Section encompasses storm doors, screen doors, & combination doors of aluminum, stainless steel, & painted or galvanized steel.

WOOD DOORS

Broadscope Section encompasses panel doors with solid stiles & rails & solid or veneered panels; hollow-core flush doors of various core constructions; and solid-core flush doors, including labeled doors. Wood doors that are to match custom panelwork in grain & finish are normally best specified in 6 CUSTOM WOODWORK. For wood door frames & entrances, see 6 FINISH CARPENTRY. For hardware, see 8 FINISH HARDWARE. Wooden storm & screen doors should be specified in this Section.

SPECIAL DOORS

Broadscope Section encompasses work described below under Sliding Metal Firedoors, Metal-Covered Doors, Coiling Doors & Grilles, Plastic-Faced Doors, Folding Doors, Overhead Doors, Sliding Glass Doors, Tempered Glass Doors, Revolving Doors, Flexible Doors, Hangar Doors. Many door types included in this Section are normally supplied with special hardware or operators, which should be specified here. For other door hardware, see 8 FINISH HARDWARE; for roof hatches, 7 ROOF ACCESSORIES; for compartment & cubicle doors, 10 COMPARTMENTS & CUBICLES; for doors forming part of a demountable partition system, 10 DEMOUNTABLE PARTITIONS; for prison doors, 11 PRISON EQUIPMENT; for sound-retarding doors, 13 AUDIOMETRIC ROOMS & 13 BROADCASTING STUDIOS; for lead-lined doors, 13 RADIATION PROTECTION; and for vault doors, 13 STORAGE VAULTS.

Sliding Metal Firedoors

Narrowscope Section encompasses sliding firedoors of metal and attendant hardware. For other firedoors, see also 8 METAL DOORS & FRAMES, 8 WOOD DOORS, 8 Metal-Covered Doors, 8 Coiling Doors & Grilles, 8 Plastic-Faced Doors.

1.17

UNIFORM SYSTEM FOR CONSTRUCTION SPECIFICATIONS, DATA FILING & COST ACCOUNTING

DOORS, WINDOWS. & GLASS   SPECIFICATION OUTLINE

Metal-Covered Doors	Narrowscope Section encompasses doors composed of metal facings of relatively light gage wrapped around a core of wood or other material and serving a decorative or protective, rather than a structural, function. Kalamein doors & other metal-covered swinging firedoors are included in this Section.
Coiling Doors & Grilles	Narrowscope Section encompasses horizontally & vertically coiling doors composed of formed or extruded interlocking sections and coiling grilles composed of metal links hinged together in an open mesh pattern. Coiling firedoors & fire shutters should be specified here. Housings, tracks, & other hardware normally supplied by the door or grille manufacturer should be specified in this Section.
Plastic-Faced Doors	Narrowscope Section encompasses doors constructed of various materials and faced with melamine plastic sheets, vinyl sheets, polyvinyl fluoride films, or other special-duty or decorative plastics.
Folding Doors	Narrowscope Section encompasses folding doors of various types with leaves of various widths & thicknesses.
Overhead Doors	Narrowscope Section encompasses overhead doors of sectional vertical-lift, and canopy types, including hardware & operators if supplied by the door manufacturer. For other hardware see 8 FINISH HARDWARE.
Sliding Glass Doors	Narrowscope Section encompasses narrow-stile sliding doors of steel, aluminum, wood, or other material, including hardware, screens, & accessories if supplied by the door manufacturer.
Tempered Glass Doors	Narrowscope Section encompasses interior & exterior doors of tempered glass, both figured & polished. Hardware is normally supplied with the door and specified in this Section.
Revolving Doors	Narrowscope Section encompasses revolving doors & vestibules, including all revolving door hardware & accessories.
Flexible Doors	Narrowscope Section encompasses flexible doors of rubber or plastic, including all flexible door hardware & accessories.
Hangar Doors	Narrowscope Section encompasses specially fabricated doors for aircraft hangars, including all hardware for their installation & operation.
METAL WINDOWS	Broadscope Section encompasses work described below under Steel Windows, Aluminum Windows, Stainless Steel Windows, Bronze Windows. Window hardware supplied with the windows should be specified in this Section, other window hardware in 8 FINISH HARDWARE.
Steel Windows	Narrowscope Section encompasses steel windows of all types, including hardware supplied with the windows.
Aluminum Windows	Narrowscope Section encompasses aluminum windows of all types, including hardware supplied with the windows.
Stainless Steel Windows	Narrowscope Section encompasses stainless steel windows of all types, including hardware supplied with the windows.
Bronze Windows	Narrowscope Section encompasses bronze windows of all types, including hardware supplied with the windows.
WOOD WINDOWS	Broadscope Section encompasses wood windows of all types, including plastic-faced wood windows. Custom wood window frames are normally best specified in 6 FINISH CARPENTRY. Window hardware supplied with the windows should be specified in this Section, other window hardware in 8 FINISH HARDWARE. Glass & glazing should be specified in 8 GLASS & GLAZING unless windows are to be factory glazed, in which case they are normally best specified here.

1.18

UNIFORM SYSTEM FOR CONSTRUCTION SPECIFICATIONS, DATA FILING & COST ACCOUNTING

SPECIFICATION OUTLINE

DOORS, WINDOWS, & GLASS

FINISH HARDWARE

Broadscope Section encompasses finish hardware for doors, windows, & cabinets, including locksets, latchsets, hinges, exit devices, closers, checks, push and pull units, kick and mop plates, bolts, casement openers, doorstops, doorholders, sash balances, window cleaners' hooks, sash lifts and latches, thresholds, weatherstripping, special knobs and trim, cabinet hardware, key cabinets, and the like, should be specified here. Hardware furnished by the door or window manufacturer as part of his product should be specified in 8 SPECIAL DOORS, 8 METAL WINDOWS, or 8 WOOD WINDOWS, as may be appropriate. Cabinet hardware may sometimes be specified in 6 FINISH CARPENTRY or 6 CUSTOM WOODWORK, but is normally best specified here.

OPERATORS

Broadscope Section encompasses those operators for doors & windows that are not supplied as part of a package by door or window manufacturer, including both self-contained mechanisms and those with remote pumps or power units, as well as mats, photocells, transmitters, and other actuating devices.

WEATHERSTRIPPING

Broadscope Section encompasses all types of weatherstripping in the form of spring bronze or other metallic inserts; pile fabric strips of natural or synthetic fiber; gaskets of neoprene, polyvinyl chloride, silicone or butyl rubber, or other flexible substance; or other suitable form.

GLASS & GLAZING

Broadscope Section encompasses glazing materials of all types, including sheet glass, plate glass, heat- & glare-reducing glass, insulating glass, tempered glass, laminated glass, & various transparent or translucent plastics; ceramic-coated, corrugated, figured, silvered, & other decorative glass; and glaziers' points, setting pads, glazing compounds, & other installation materials. For glass masonry units, see 4 UNIT MASONRY; for tempered glass doors & sliding glass doors, see 8 SPECIAL DOORS. See also 8 STOREFRONT SYSTEM & 8 CURTAINWALL SYSTEM.

CURTAINWALL SYSTEMS

Broadscope Section encompasses curtainwall systems, including framing sections, fixed & operable sash, wall panels, glass, fasteners, & sealants when these are to be installed as a correlated system.

STOREFRONT SYSTEMS

Broadscope Section encompasses storefront systems, including die-formed & extruded metal facing, bulkheads, sills, mullions, moldings, & miscellaneous trim. Doors, entrances, & glass should be specified in this Section when they are to be installed as part of a correlated system.

1.19

UNIFORM SYSTEM FOR CONSTRUCTION SPECIFICATIONS, DATA FILING & COST ACCOUNTING

9 FINISHES

SPECIFICATION OUTLINE

LATH & PLASTER	Broadscope Section encompasses work described below under Metal Furring, Metal Lath, Gypsum Lath, Plaster Partition Systems, Plastering Accessories, Plaster, Stucco, Acoustical Plaster, Plaster Moldings & Ornaments.
Metal Furring	Narrowscope Section encompasses metal furring sections of various shapes, including hangars, tie wires, & joint fittings.
Metal Lath	Narrowscope Section encompasses expanded metal lath of plain, ribbed, & self-furring types, and various sorts of woven wire lath, including lath backed with paper or other flexible sheet materials. Metal lath forming part of a proprietary plaster partition system is normally best specified in 9 Plaster Partition Systems if Narrowscope titles are used.
Gypsum Lath	Narrowscope Section encompasses plain, perforated, & foil-backed gypsum lath, including backer board & fire-rated gypsum lath. Gypsum lath forming part of a proprietary plaster partition system is normally best specified in 9 Plaster Partition System if Narrowscope titles are used.
Plaster Partition Systems	Narrowscope Section encompasses correlated proprietary systems of studs, furring channels, runners, grounds, metal or gypsum lath, & required fasteners designed to receive a plaster finish. Plaster may sometimes be specified in this Section, but if Narrowscope titles are used it is normally best specified in 9 Plaster, 9 Stucco, or 9 Acoustical Plaster, as may be appropriate.
Plastering Accessories	Narrowscope Section encompasses casings, grounds, screeds, corner beads, partition caps, & other plastering accessories not specified as part of a proprietary plaster partition system.
Plaster	Narrowscope Section encompasses plasters formulated for interior application, including mixing water, gypsum plaster, gauging plaster, Keene's cement, lime putty, fibrous & granular plaster aggregates, binders, coloring agents, & various admixtures. Portland cement plaster may be specified in this Section if used in interior locations, but is normally specified in 9 Stucco. See also 9 ACOUSTICAL PLASTER.
Stucco	Narrowscope Section encompasses stucco & portland cement plaster for exterior application. When Narrowscope titles are used, it may sometimes be desirable to combine this Section with 9 Plaster as Plaster & Stucco.
Acoustical Plaster	Narrowscope Section encompasses proportioning, mixing, & application of acoustical plaster, including stippling or other surface treatment required.
Plaster Moldings & Ornaments	Narrowscope Section encompasses running moldings of plaster, cast plaster ornaments, & other decorative plaster work. See 12 ARTWORK for plaster sculpture & sgraffito.
GYPSUM DRYWALL	Broadscope Section encompasses work described below under Gypsum Drywall System, Gypsum Drywall Finishing.
Gypsum Drywall System	Narrowscope Section encompasses gypsum drywall material and its application with nails, screws, or adhesives, including predecorated gypsum drywall panels & trim.

1.20

UNIFORM SYSTEM FOR CONSTRUCTION SPECIFICATIONS, DATA FILING & COST ACCOUNTING

SPECIFICATION OUTLINE **FINISHES**

9

Gypsum Drywall Finishing	Narrowscope Section encompasses the taping of gypsum drywall joints, application & filling of corner beads, & filling of depressions around nailheads & screwheads, including intermediate & final cementing & sanding operations. This Section also encompasses the hand or machine application of thin coats of specially formulated plasters or other coatings to all exposed drywall surfaces in lieu of joint filling & sanding operations.
TILE WORK	Broadscope Section encompasses work described below under Ceramic Tile, Ceramic Mosaics, Glass Mosaics, Conductive Ceramic Tile.
Ceramic Tile	Narrowscope Section encompasses the application of glazed & unglazed ceramic tile to floor, steps, base, wainscot, wall, countertop, or ceiling with organic or inorganic cements or adhesives, including furnishing of all materials, preparation of the setting bed or surface, grouting of joints, and cleaning down. Tile units having face areas less than four square inches are normally best specified in 9 Ceramic Mosaics when Narrowscope titles are used, but in some instances it may be desirable to specify both tiles & mosaics in a single Section entitled 9 Ceramic Tile & Mosaics.
Ceramic Mosaics	Narrowscope Section encompasses the application of glazed & unglazed ceramic mosaics to floor, steps, base, wainscot, wall, countertop, or ceiling with organic or inorganic cements or adhesives, including furnishing of all materials, preparation of the setting bed or surface, grouting of joints, & cleaning down. Tile units having face areas greater than four square inches are normally best specified in 9 Ceramic Tile when Narrowscope titles are used, but in some instances it may be desirable to specify both tiles & mosaics in a single section entitled 9 Ceramic Tile & Mosaics. Ceramic mosaic murals custom designed of nonstandard units by an artist and installed by him or under his direct supervision are normally best specified in 12 ARTWORK.
Quarry Tile	Narrowscope Section encompasses the application of quarry tile to floor, steps, base, wainscot, wall, countertop, or ceiling with organic or inorganic cements or adhesives, including furnishing of all material, preparation of the setting bed or surface, grouting of joints, & cleaning down.
Glass Mosaics	Narrowscope Section encompasses the application of glass mosaics with inorganic or organic cements or adhesives, including furnishing of all materials, preparation of the setting bed or surface, grouting of joints, and cleaning down. Glass mosaic murals custom designed by an atirst and installed by him or under his direct supervision are normally best specified in 12 ARTWORK.
Conductive Ceramic Tile	Narrowscope Section encompasses conductive ceramic tile & mosaics & their installation, including installation of electrostatic grounds, preparation of the setting bed, grouting of joints, & cleaning down.
TERRAZZO	Broadscope Section encompasses work described below under Cast-In-Place Terrazzo, Precast Terrazzo, Conductive Terrazzo.
Cast-In-Place Terrazzo	Narrowscope Section encompasses cast-in-place terrazzo floors, base, stairs, & wainscots composed of portland cement, coloring agents, & marble chips of various sizes, including divider strips and initial cleaning & sealing. Sand bed materials & their installation should be specified here if terrazzo is to be of the unbonded type; grinding, application of bonding agents, or other required treatment of the substrate should be specified here if terrazzo is to be of the bonded type. Installations using organic binders in place of portland cement are normally best specified in 9 SPECIAL FLOORING.

1.21

UNIFORM SYSTEM FOR CONSTRUCTION SPECIFICATIONS, DATA FILING & COST ACCOUNTING

9 FINISHES

SPECIFICATION OUTLINE

Precast Terrazzo	Narrowscope Section encompasses precast units of portland cement, coloring agents, & marble chips of various sizes; their installation with organic or inorganic cements or adhesives; grouting or packing of joints; & cleaning down. Installations using tiles composed of marble chips in resinous or other plastic matrix are normally best specified in 9 RESILIENT FLOORING.
Conductive Terrazzo	Narrowscope Section encompasses conductive terrazzo and its installation, including installation of electrostatic grounds, preparation of the setting bed, provision & installation of dividing strips, grinding, cleaning, & sealing.
VENEER STONE	Broadscope Section encompasses furnishing & installation of natural stone cut in panels or tiles usually 1¼" or less in thickness and used for wainscots, wall covering, floor tile, countertops, window stools, thresholds, base, or stair treads. Stone countertops, window stools, thresholds, base, & stair treads may sometimes be specified in 9 TILE WORK. Window stools of stone may sometimes be specified in 4 UNIT MASONRY.
ACOUSTICAL TREATMENT	Broadscope Section encompasses acoustical panels & tiles of glass, mineral, wood, cane, or other fiber held together with cementitious, resinous, or other binders; perforated panels of metal, hardboard, or other material backed with sound-absorbing elements; suspension systems; adhesives; & accessories. Perforated hollow masonry units with sound-absorbing inserts should be specified in 4 UNIT MASONRY; perforated cellular metal decking with sound-absorbing inserts in 5 METAL DECKING; acoustical plaster in 9 LATH & PLASTER.
WOOD FLOORING	Broadscope Section encompasses work described below under Wood Strip Flooring, Wood Parquet Flooring, Plywood Block Flooring, Resilient Wood Floor System, Wood Block Industrial Floor.
Wood Strip Flooring	Narrowscope Section encompasses hardwood strip & plank floors, both unfinished & prefinished, & softwood strip floors. Wood strip flooring forming part of a resilient wood floor system is normally best specified in 9 Resilient Wood Floor System when Narrowscope titles are used.
Wood Parquet Flooring	Narrowscope Section encompasses flooring composed of short hardwood strips installed in a predetermined decorative pattern.
Plywood Block Flooring	Narrowscope Section encompasses flooring made up of hardwood-faced plywood units, usually with splined or interlocking edges, and including those simulating parquet floors.
Resilient Wood Floor System	Narrowscope Section encompasses wood strip floor installations utilizing resilient pads or spring metal units for mounting sleepers to which the flooring surface is fastened.
Wood Block Industrial Floor	Narrowscope Section encompasses heavy-duty wood floors composed of end-grain wood blocks, usually treated with bituminous or other preservative material, and installed with mechanical fasteners or mastics.
RESILIENT FLOORING	Broadscope Section encompasses work described below under Resilient Tile Flooring, Resilient Sheet Flooring, Conductive Resilient Floors.
Resilient Tile Flooring	Narrowscope Section encompasses the furnishing & installation of resilient tile of all types, including asphalt, vinyl-asbestos, vinyl, linoleum, epoxy, cork, & leather tiles & tile adhesives.
Resilient Sheet Flooring	Narrowscope Section encompasses the furnishing & installation of resilient flooring in sheet or roll form, including vinyl, linoleum, cork, & other materials & the necessary adhesives.

1.22

UNIFORM SYSTEM FOR CONSTRUCTION SPECIFICATIONS, DATA FILING & COST ACCOUNTING

SPECIFICATION OUTLINE

FINISHES

9

Conductive Resilient Floors	Narrowscope Section encompasses conductive resilient floor materials & their installation, including installation of electrostatic grounds.
SPECIAL FLOORING	Broadscope Section encompasses work described below under Magnesium Oxychloride Floors, Epoxy-Marble-Chip Flooring, Elastomeric Liquid Flooring, Heavy-Duty Concrete Toppings.
Magnesium Oxychloride Floors	Narrowscope Section encompasses cast-in-place floors composed of magnesium oxychloride cement, coloring agents, marble chips, & metal or plastic dividing strips, and includes preparation of the substrate.
Epoxy-Marble-Chip Flooring	Narrowscope Section encompasses cast-in-place flooring of marble chips in an epoxy matrix, including preparation of the substrate.
Elastomeric Liquid Flooring	Narrowscope Section encompasses various elastomeric flooring materials applied in liquid form and curing to form a decorative or special-duty surface.
Heavy-Duty Concrete Toppings	Narrowscope Section encompasses heavy-duty concrete toppings of various types, including those utilizing special hardners, densifiers, or other additives or special techniques for finishing or curing. Heavy-duty concrete toppings may sometimes be specified in 3 CAST-IN-PLACE CONCRETE, but are normally best specified here, particularly if they are to be installed by a specialty contractor. Metal floor armoring grids to be filled with concrete may sometimes be specified in 5 MISCELLANEOUS METAL, but are normally best specified here.
SPECIAL COATINGS	Broadscope Section encompasses work described below under Cementitious Coatings, Elastomeric Coatings, Fire-Resistant Coatings. Materials specified in this Section normally include those products that cannot, because of specific performance, intended use, chemical composition, or method of application, be readily specified as part of 9 PAINTING. See also 7 WATERPROOFING, 7 DAMPPROOFING.
Cementitious Coatings	Narrowscope Section encompasses special-duty coatings of cementitious materials fortified with resins or other additives and their application by spray, brush, or trowel.
Elastomeric Coatings	Narrowscope Section encompasses decorative & special-duty coatings of elastomeric or other plastic materials, including epoxy, polyester, and polyvinyl fluoride.
Fire-Resistant Coatings	Narrowscope Section encompasses fire-resistant coatings of incombustible or intumescent material applied with spray, brush, trowel, mop, or roller. Fire-retardant treatment of wood is normally best specified in 6 ROUGH CARPENTRY or 6 FINISH CARPENTRY, concrete fireproofing in 3 CAST-IN-PLACE CONCRETE, plaster fireproofing in 9 LATH & PLASTER.
PAINTING	Broadscope Section encompasses paint, enamel, varnish, shellac, lacquer, wood filler, crack filler, colored wax, & stain and their application, including surface preparation.
WALL COVERING	Broadscope Section encompasses wallpaper, wall fabrics, plastic wall tile, plastic wall films, flexible wood sheets, and their application.

1.23

UNIFORM SYSTEM FOR CONSTRUCTION SPECIFICATIONS, DATA FILING & COST ACCOUNTING

SPECIALTIES

SPECIFICATION OUTLINE

CHALKBOARD & TACKBOARD	Broadscope Section encompasses slate, composition, porcelain enameled steel, & glass chalkboards; natural cork, fabricated cork, & composition tackboards; & wood or metal chalkrails, map rails, & trim, including miscellaneous fittings.
CHUTES	Broadscope Section encompasses chutes of a largely prefabricated nature for depositing laundry, packages, dry bulk materials, and other items, including terminal fittings & closures. See also 14 MATERIALS HANDLING SYSTEMS.
COMPARTMENTS & CUBICLES	Broadscope Section encompasses work described below under Hospital Cubicles, Office Cubicles, Toilet & Shower Compartments.
Hospital Cubicles	Narrowscope Section encompasses hospital cubicles & privacy screens of all sorts made of metal, plastic, wood, & glass in various combinations, as well as those consisting of fabric curtains, tracks, & hangers.
Office Cubicles	Narrowscope Section encompasses office cubicles of an essentially free standing nature composed of panels, gates, doors, posts, & attendant hardware constructed of painted steel, aluminum, stainless steel, wood, high-pressure plastic laminates, glass, & other materials in various combination. Material to be specified in this Section is distinct from that used to form a full-height partitioning system as included under 10 DEMOUNTABLE PARTITIONS.
Toilet & Shower Compartments	Narrowscope Section encompasses toilet & shower compartments of painted steel, porcelain enameled steel, stainless steel, marble, & other materials, including doors & hardware. Section title may be altered as required to 10 Toilet Compartments or 10 Shower Compartments.
DEMOUNTABLE PARTITIONS	Broadscope Section encompasses full-height partitioning systems of painted steel, aluminum, stainless steel, wood, high-pressure plastic laminates, glass, & other materials in various combination, including doors & hardware. Material to be specified in this Section is distinct from that used to construct office cubicles of an essentially free-standing nature as included under 10 COMPARTMENTS & CUBICLES.
DISAPPEARING STAIRS	Broadscope Section encompasses pull-down stairs of wood or metal providing access to attic, storage room, or penthouse. For fire escapes, see 5 MISCELLANEOUS METAL.
FIREFIGHTING DEVICES	Broadscope Section encompasses fire extinguishers & extinguisher cabinets & related items. For automatic sprinklers & other central fire extinguishing systems, see 15 FIRE EXTINGUISHING SYSTEM.
FIREPLACE EQUIPMENT	Broadscope Section encompasses work described below under Fireplace Accessories, Fireplace Dampers, Prefabricated Fireplace.
Fireplace Accessories	Narrowscope Section encompasses built-in & portable fireplace screens, andirons, log baskets, grates, fireplace tools, & other related items.
Fireplace Dampers	Narrowscope Section encompasses fireplace dampers of all types.
Prefabricated Fireplace	Narrowscope Section encompasses prefabricated fireplaces of metal or other material and prefabricated fireplace forms, including prefabricated fireplace flues & chimneys.
FLAGPOLES	Broadscope Section encompasses flagpoles of metal or wood, including installation, hardware, & lines.
FOLDING GATES	Broadscope Section encompasses folding gates of all types, including tracks, recess frames & doors, and other specialized hardware.
IDENTIFYING DEVICES	Broadscope Section encompasses work described below under Directory & Bulletin Boards, Painted Signs, Plaques, Three-Dimensional Signs.

1.24

UNIFORM SYSTEM FOR CONSTRUCTION SPECIFICATIONS, DATA FILING & COST ACCOUNTING

SPECIFICATION OUTLINE   **SPECIALTIES** 10

Directory & Bulletin Boards	Narrowscope Section encompasses indoor & outdoor directory & bulletin boards of all sorts. Section title may be altered as required to 10 Directory Boards or 10 Bulletin Boards. For tackboards, see 10 CHALKBOARD & TACKBOARD.
Painted Signs	Narrowscope Section encompasses flat signs fabricated & painted in the shop. Site-painted lettering is normally best specified in 9 PAINTING.
Plaques	Narrowscope Section encompasses fabricated, cast, & carved plaques & tablets of metal, stone, wood, or plastic.
Three-Dimensional Signs	Narrowscope Section encompasses fabricated signs of metal, plastic, glass, wood, or other material and cast & fabricated metal, plastic, or other letters. Electrified signs are normally best specified in this Section, but in some instances may be specified instead in 16 LIGHTING FIXTURES.
LOCKERS	Broadscope Section encompasses wardrobe & box lockers of wood or metal, including basket systems for temporary storage of clothing or other goods.
MESH PARTITIONS	Broadscope Section encompasses woven wire partitions, expanded metal partitions, and other partitions of a utilitarian nature, including doors, wickets, and hardware normally furnished as part of a correlated package.
POSTAL SPECIALTIES	Broadscope Section encompasses letter slots, mail boxes, mail chutes, & other similar items.
RETRACTABLE PARTITIONS	Broadscope Section encompasses work described below under Coiling Partitions, Folding Partitions.
Coiling Partitions	Narrowscope Section encompasses partitions composed of metal, wood, or other units with articulated joints that permit their withdrawal by coiling about a vertical drum or spindle. Tracks, hangers, guides, operators, & miscellaneous fittings furnished with the partition and necessary to its proper installation should be specified here.
Folding Partitions	Narrowscope Section encompasses partitions composed of metal, wood, or other panels fitted to floor or ceiling tracks and hinged together for folding and stacking. Tracks, hangers, guides, & miscellaneous fittings furnished with the partition and necessary to its proper installation should be specified here.
SCALES	Broadscope Section encompasses bathroom scales, vendors' scales, grain scales, truck scales, & other scales, particularly if built in.
STORAGE SHELVING	Broadscope Section encompasses utility shelving of wood, metal, or plastic. For bookshelving & bookstacks, see 11 LIBRARY EQUIPMENT.
SUN CONTROL DEVICES	Broadscope Section encompasses awnings, canopies, fixed and movable fins, marquees, portable walkway covers, sunshades, truck vestibules, & other devices providing protection from solar heat & glare and the other elements. For solar-shielding screens of unit masonry, see 4 UNIT MASONRY.
TELEPHONE BOOTHS	Broadscope Section encompasses indoor & outdoor telephone booths of various sorts.

1.25

UNIFORM SYSTEM FOR CONSTRUCTION SPECIFICATIONS, DATA FILING & COST ACCOUNTING

SPECIALTIES

SPECIFICATION OUTLINE

TOILET & BATH ACCESSORIES	Broadscope Section encompasses robe hooks, towel bars & rings, medicine cabinets, magazine racks, paper holders, shelves, soap dishes, grab bars, toothbrush holders, tumbler holders, waste receptacles, towel dispensers, sanitary napkin dispensers, soap dispensers, and other similar items. Mounted mirrors to be installed in bath, lavatory, or washroom are normally best specified in this Section, but may on occasion be specified instead in 8 GLASS & GLAZING. Hooks, paper holders, & other hardware furnished with toilet compartments or shower compartments are normally best specified in 10 COMPARTMENTS & CUBICLES.
VENDING MACHINES	Broadscope Section encompasses vending machines of all sorts, particularly if built in.
WARDROBE SPECIALTIES	Broadscope Section encompasses coat checking equipment, hat & coat racks, & other items for temporary storing of clothing. See also 10 LOCKERS.
WASTE DISPOSAL UNITS	Broadscope Section encompasses work described below under Packaged Incinerators, Waste Compactors.
Packaged Incinerators	Narrowscope Section encompasses metal & precast concrete incinerators largely or wholly prefabricated. For site-constructed incinerators, see 13 INCINERATORS.
Waste Compactors	Narrowscope Section encompasses waste compaction equipment & systems. Bottle crushers may, in some instances, be specified in 11 FOOD SERVICE EQUIPMENT, but they are normally best specified here.

1.26

UNIFORM SYSTEM FOR CONSTRUCTION SPECIFICATIONS, DATA FILING & COST ACCOUNTING

| SPECIFICATION OUTLINE | EQUIPMENT | 11 |

BANK EQUIPMENT

Broadscope Section encompasses work described below under Depository Units, Outdoor Tellers' Windows, Safes, Tellers' Counter. For vault construction, see 13 STORAGE VAULT.

Depository Units

Narrowscope Section encompasses bulk depositories & after-hours cash depositories of various types.

Outdoor Tellers' Windows

Narrowscope Section encompasses prefabricated drive-up or walk-up tellers' windows and their installation.

Safes

Narrowscope Section encompasses unit safes of all types for installation in wall or cabinet or as freestanding units.

Tellers' Counters

Narrowscope Section encompasses tellers' counters constructed as a specialized unit or series of units utilizing wood, plywood, stone, metal, plastic, or other materials and including cash drawers & other tellers' storage units.

COMMERCIAL EQUIPMENT

Broadscope Section encompasses equipment for barber shops, beauty salons, retail stores, automobile service stations, and other commercial enterprises, including turnstiles, cash registers, & display fixtures of all types.

DARKROOM EQUIPMENT

Broadscope Section encompasses cassette boxes, film & print storage cabinets, developing tanks, print driers, illuminators, and other specialized equipment including countertops & worktables.

ECCLESIASTICAL EQUIPMENT

Broadscope Section encompasses work described below under Baptismal Tanks, Bells, Carillons, Chancel Fittings, Organs, Pews. For stained glass work, see 12 ARTWORK.

Baptismal Tank

Narrowscope Section encompasses baptismal tanks constructed of metal, reinforced plastic, or other material and partially or wholly prefabricated. Baptismal tanks to be constructed on the site should be specified in other Section appropriate to the materials and methods used, with reference to that Section included here.

Bells

Narrowscope Section encompasses cast tower bells, manual & automatic tolling equipment, and electronic bell simulators.

Carillons

Narrowscope Section encompasses carillons and their installation complete with manual console or automatic ringing equipment.

Chancel Fittings

Narrowscope Section encompasses altars, lecterns, pulpits, confessionals, fonts, & communion rails. Altar vestments may sometimes be specified in this Section but are normally best specified in 12 ARTWORK, particularly if hand crafted by a skilled artisan to his own design.

Organ

Narrowscope Section encompasses pipe organs, electronic organs, electronically amplified reed organs, other musical instruments of similar nature, and their installation complete with console, blowers, motors, electrical equipment, volume control shutters, and ductwork.

Pews

Narrowscope Section encompasses pews, pew pads, kneelers, and fittings necessary for their installation.

EDUCATIONAL EQUIPMENT

Broadscope Section encompasses work described below under Art & Craft Equipment, Audio-Visual Aids, Language Laboratory, Prefabricated Astro-Observatory, Vocational Shop Equipment. See also 11 LABORATORY EQUIPMENT.

Art & Craft Equipment

Narrowscope Section encompasses easels, potters' wheels, kilns, clay storage bins, looms, and other equipment of a related nature.

1.27

UNIFORM SYSTEM FOR CONSTRUCTION SPECIFICATIONS, DATA FILING & COST ACCOUNTING

EQUIPMENT   **SPECIFICATION OUTLINE**

Audio-Visual Aids

Narrowscope Section encompasses equipment for audio-visual projection, including filmstrip projectors, slide projectors, sound film projectors, opaque projectors, & projection screens. See also 16 COMMUNICATION SYSTEM.

Language Laboratory

Narrowscope Section encompasses various language laboratory devices for recording, reproducing, & monitoring the spoken word, including related cabinets & cubicles.

Prefabricated Astro-Observatory

Narrowscope Section encompasses prefabricated domes & related equipment for astronomical observations.

Vocational Shop Equipment

Narrowscope Section encompasses workbenches, hand tools, tool racks, and those units of fixed equipment for woodworking or metalworking intended primarily for the amateur craftsman or vocational trainee rather than for high-volume commercial production work. Heavy-duty power equipment is normally best specified in 11 INDUSTRIAL EQUIPMENT.

FOOD SERVICE EQUIPMENT

Broadscope Section encompasses work described below under Bar Units, Cooking Equipment, Dishwashing Equipment, Food Preparation Machines, Food Preparation Tables, Food Serving Units, Refrigerated Cases, Sinks & Drainboards, Soda Fountains. For residential kitchen equipment, see 11 RESIDENTIAL EQUIPMENT. For bottle crushers, see 10 WASTE DISPOSAL UNITS.

Bar Units

Narrowscope Section encompasses bar & back-bar units & equipment for serving food & liquor, including barstools. For residential bar units, see 11 RESIDENTIAL EQUIPMENT.

Cooking Equipment

Narrowscope Section encompasses ranges, ovens, cooktops, griddles, grills, kettles, & other cooking units heated by gas, electricity, or steam.

Dishwashing Equipment

Narrowscope Section encompasses commercial dishwashers and clean & soiled dish counters including garbage scuppers. Garbage grinders to be installed in soiled dish counters may, in some instances, be specified in 11 Food Preparation Machines, but are normally best specified in this Section. Tray conveyors are sometimes specified in 14 MATERIALS HANDLING SYSTEMS, but are normally best specified here.

Food Preparation Machines

Narrowscope Section encompasses commercial & institutional kitchen machines of all sorts, including mixers, peelers, slicers, meat saws, grinders, juicers, blenders, bread toasters, & knife sharpeners. Garbage grinders may, in some instances, be specified in this Section but are normally best specified in 11 Sinks & Drainboards &/or 11 Dishwashing Equipment.

Food Preparation Tables

Narrowscope Section encompasses food preparation tables with laminated hardwood, stainless steel, galvanized steel, or other tops for use as bakers' tables, salad preparation tables, meat preparation tables, butchers' blocks & utility tables in commercial & institutional kitchens. Overhead pot racks may, in some instances, be specified in 5 MISCELLANEOUS METAL but are normally best specified here.

Food Serving Units

Narrowscope Section encompasses fixed & portable serving line units of all types including hot dish tables, cold dish tables, salad tables, bain-maries, dish carts, dish dispensers, tray slides, sneeze guards, & coffee urns. Glass fillers & automatic ice-cube makers may sometimes be specified in 15 PLUMBING FIXTURES & TRIM, but are normally best specified here if part of a food serving line.

1.28

UNIFORM SYSTEM FOR CONSTRUCTION SPECIFICATIONS, DATA FILING & COST ACCOUNTING

SPECIFICATION OUTLINE   EQUIPMENT

Refrigerated Cases	Narrowscope Section encompasses refrigerators, freezers, refrigerator-freezer combinations, ice cream cases, & other refrigerated cases of commercial size & quality, including those with remote refrigerating units. Prefabricated walk-in coolers & freezers may, in some instances, be specified in this Section but are normally best specified in 13 INSULATED ROOMS.
Sinks & Drainboards	Narrowscope Section encompasses scullery sinks and food preparation sinks & related drainboards, backsplashes, aprons, & leg assemblies of stainless steel, galvanized steel, or other suitable material. Soiled & clean dish counters should be specified as part of the dishwashing line in 11 Dishwashing Equipment. Garbage grinders to be installed in food preparation sinks may, in some instances, be specified in 11 Food Preparation Machines, but are normally best specified in this Section. For water supply piping, waste piping, faucets & trim see 15 WATER SUPPLY SYSTEMS, 15 SOIL & WASTE SYSTEM, & 15 PLUMBING FIXTURES & TRIM, respectively.
Soda Fountains	Narrowscope Section encompasses soda fountain equipment & related counterwork of a specialized nature.
GYMNASIUM EQUIPMENT	Broadscope Section encompasses indoor sports equipment, scoreboards, scoring desks, gymnasts' equipment, and gymstands of all types. See 2 SITE IMPROVEMENTS for playing fields & playgrounds; 12 SEATING for fixed seating for stadium, fieldhouse, or gymnasium; 13 SWIMMING POOLS for pool & natatorium construction & equipment.
INDUSTRIAL EQUIPMENT	Broadscope Section encompasses industrial equipment of a largely pre-engineered & pre-assembled nature, including industrial belting, canning & bottling equipment, cyclones, drop forges, flamecutters, grinders, heat treaters, measuring devices, milling machines, pallets, presses, protective equipment, sawmills, shears, shafting & pulleys. For hoists & cranes, see 14 HOISTS & CRANES; for dock levellers & other lifts, 14 LIFTS; for conveyors & other materials handling equipment, 14 MATERIALS HANDLING SYSTEMS; and for motors & motor controls, 16 ELECTRICAL POWER EQUIPMENT. Industrial equipment involving significant amounts of special design work and on-site or other custom fabrication should be specified in appropriate Sections of Divisions 15 & 16.
LABORATORY EQUIPMENT	Broadscope Section encompasses specialized laboratory casework, sinks, tables, fume hoods, reagent racks, experimental apparatus, & laboratory instruments. For specialized laboratory piping, see 15 SPECIAL PIPING SYSTEMS. See also 13 AUDIOMETRIC ROOMS & 13 CLEAN ROOMS.
LAUNDRY EQUIPMENT	Broadscope Section encompasses commercial laundry equipment such as washers, tumblers, extractors, driers, ironers, pressers, & linen trucks, including coin-operated laundry & drycleaning equipment. For residential laundry equipment, see 11 RESIDENTIAL EQUIPMENT.
LIBRARY EQUIPMENT	Broadscope Section encompasses work described below under Bookshelving, Bookstacks, Charging Counters, Chairs, tables, & study carrels may be specified here if part of library furnishings, but are normally best specified in 12 FURNITURE.
Bookshelving	Narrowscope Section encompasses units of wood or metal for storage & display of books, magazines, newspapers, phonograph records, or other material filed for reference or circulation. For multilevel, self-supporting systems of shelves for book or records storage, see 11 Bookstacks. Decorative bookcases for home or executive office use are normally best specified in 12 FURNITURE.

1.29

UNIFORM SYSTEM FOR CONSTRUCTION SPECIFICATIONS, DATA FILING & COST ACCOUNTING

EQUIPMENT

SPECIFICATION OUTLINE

Bookstacks	Narrowscope Section encompasses multilevel, self-supporting systems of shelving for book or records storage, including stairs, railings, & catwalks furnished as correlated components.
Charging Counters	Narrowscope Section encompasses librarians' charging desk, card catalog units, and related counterwork.
MEDICAL EQUIPMENT	Broadscope Section encompasses work described below under Dental Equipment, Examination Room Equipment, Hospital Casework, Incubators, Patient Care Equipment, Radiology Equipment, Sterilizers, Surgery Equipment, Therapy Equipment. For hyperbaric rooms, see 13 HYPERBARIC ROOMS.
Dental Equipment	Narrowscope Section encompasses dental chairs and equipment of all sorts for dentistry, orthodontia, & dental surgery.
Examination Room Equipment	Narrowscope Section encompasses examination tables, chairs, & devices of various types. For dental chairs, see 11 Dental Equipment.
Hospital Casework	Narrowscope Section encompasses specialized casework for installation in nurses' stations, pharmacies, examination rooms, and other locations in hospital, clinic, or physician's office.
Incubators	Narrowscope Section encompasses infant incubators, including installation, controls, & completion of required service connections.
Patient Care Equipment	Narrowscope Section encompasses hospital beds, bedding, & accessories; special bedside units; & portable privacy screens.
Radiology Equipment	Narrowscope Section encompasses equipment for radiological examination & treatment, including X-ray machines, fluoroscopes, radioistopic treatment devices, & prefabricated radiation screens. On-site construction for radiation shielding, including radiation-retardant doors, should be specified in 13 RADIATION PROTECTION. Film storage & processing equipment for the radiological suite may sometimes be specified in 11 DARKROOM EQUIPMENT, but is normally best specified in this Section.
Sterilizers	Narrowscope Section encompasses autoclaves and other devices of both cabinet & built-in types for sterilizing instruments, clothing, & other equipment.
Surgery Equipment	Narrowscope Section encompasses operating tables, autopsy tables, instrument tables, anaesthetic machines, resuscitators, and other specialized surgery equipment. Special surgery lighting fixtures are normally best specified in this Section for installation under 16 LIGHTING FIXTURES but may sometimes be specified completely within that section. For conductive floors, see 9 TILE WORK, 9 TERRAZZO, or 9 RESILIENT FLOORING as may be appropriate.
Therapy Equipment	Narrowscope Section encompasses correctional exercise equipment, whirlpool baths, Hubbard tubs, occupational therapy equipment, diatherapy equipment, & saunas.
MORTUARY EQUIPMENT	Broadscope Section encompasses embalming tables, mortuary refrigerators, and other mortuary & crematorium equipment.
PARKING EQUIPMENT	Broadscope Section encompasses parking gates, drive-up ticket dispensers, & other equipment for commercial parking garages or lots. See also 2 ROADS & WALKS.
PRISON EQUIPMENT	Broadscope Section encompasses prison cells, cell doors, and other specialized prison equipment.

1.30

UNIFORM SYSTEM FOR CONSTRUCTION SPECIFICATIONS, DATA FILING & COST ACCOUNTING

SPECIFICATION OUTLINE

EQUIPMENT

RESIDENTAL EQUIPMENT

Broadscope Section encompasses work described below under Central Vacuum Cleaner, Kitchen & Lavatory Cabinets, Residential Kitchen Equipment, Residential Laundry Equipment, Unit Kitchens.

Central Vacuum Cleaner

Narrowscope Section encompasses central vacuum cleaner composed of exhauster with motor & related controls, piping or ducts, outlets, flexible hose, & various cleaning attachments.

Kitchen & Lavatory Cabinets

Narrowscope Section encompasses kitchen wall & base cabinets of metal, wood, or other material; cabinets of similar construction to be installed as lavatory or vanity units; and countertops, backsplashes, & endsplashes of high-pressure plastic laminates, plastic sheet material, laminated hardwood, stainless steel, or other suitable material. Medicine cabinets, normally specified in 10 TOILET & BATH ACCESSORIES, should be specified in this Section if fabricated & finished to match lavatory cabinets. Kitchen sinks & their fittings may in some instances be specified in this Section, but are normally best specified in 15 PLUMBING FIXTURES & TRIM. Section title may be altered as required to 11 Kitchen Cabinets or 11 Lavatory Cabinets.

Residential Kitchen Equipment

Narrowscope Section encompasses cabinet ranges, cooktops, ovens, refrigerators & freezers, residential dishwashers, residential food waste disposers, packaged exhaust fans & hoods, and built-in kitchen machines. For commercial & institutional kitchen equipment, see 11 FOOD SERVICE EQUIPMENT.

Residental Laundry Equipment

Narrowscope Section encompasses residential washers, driers, washer-drier combinations, and ironers. Laundry trays & their fittings may in some instances be specified in this Section, but are normally best specified in 15 PLUMBING FIXTURES & TRIM.

Unit Kitchens

Narrowscope Section encompasses prefabricated kitchen units and freestanding or built-in bar units for installation in homes or executive offices.

STAGE EQUIPMENT

Broadscope Section encompasses proscenium draperies & curtains, cycloramas, tormenters, flats, demountable risers & platforms, orchestra shells, flyloft rigging & equipment, and other equipment necessary to the live presentation of theatrical or musical programs. Stage gridirons may in some instances be specified in 5 MISCELLANEOUS METAL, but are normally best specified in this Section. For public address or commercial projection systems, see 16 COMMUNICATION SYSTEM; for stage lighting, see 16 LIGHTING FIXTURES & 16 ELECTRICAL DISTRIBUTION SYSTEM. Powered lifts for installation in stage or orchestra pit may sometimes be specified in this Section, but are normally best specified in 14 LIFTS.

1.31

UNIFORM SYSTEM FOR CONSTRUCTION SPECIFICATIONS, DATA FILING & COST ACCOUNTING

 FURNISHINGS   **SPECIFICATION OUTLINE**

ARTWORK

Broadscope Section encompasses easel paintings; mural work in oil, fresco, sgraffito, glass or stone mosaic, & other media; photomurals; carved or cast statuary & relief work of wood, metal, stone, concrete, or other material; and glass work using rolled, blown, slab, or faceted glass set in lead cames, concrete, or other matrix. Altar vestments & other chancel fittings are normally best specified in this Section if created especially for the project by a skilled artisan to his own design. Chancel fittings of more or less standard design & construction should be specified in 11 ECCLESIASTICAL EQUIPMENT.

BLINDS & SHADES

Broadscope Section encompasses venetian blinds, vertical blinds, roller blinds, roll-up shades, interior shutters, fretwork panels, shojis, & other window treatments. For drapery & curtains and related accessories, see 12 DRAPERY & CURTAINS.

CABINETS & FIXTURES

Broadscope Section encompasses work described below under Classroom Cabinets, Dormitory Units.

Classroom Cabinets

Narrowscope Section encompasses specialized classroom storage units of stock design and largely preassembled for installation as movable, fixed, or built-in elements. See also 6 FINISH CARPENTRY, 11 EDUCATIONAL EQUIPMENT, 11 LABORATORY EQUIPMENT.

Dormitory Units

Narrowscope Section encompasses coordinated dormitory units including wardrobes, beds, & study units.

CARPETS & MATS

Broadscope Section encompasses rugs, wall-to-wall carpeting, carpet cushions, mats, & matting, including carpetlaying accessories & installation. For tumbling mats, see 11 GYMNASIUM EQUIPMENT.

DRAPERY & CURTAINS

Broadscope Section encompasses work described below under Drapery Tracks, Fabrics. For stage curtains & draperies, see 11 STAGE EQUIPMENT.

Drapery Tracks

Narrowscope Section encompasses drapery tracks of all types; related cornices, valances, & other fittings; & their installation.

Fabrics

Narrowscope Section encompasses drapery & curtain fabrics, linings, accessories, & trim and their fabrication & installation. Upholstery fabrics should be specified in 12 FURNITURE.

FURNITURE

Broadscope Section encompasses freestanding, movable furnishings including portable lighting, chairs, sofas, tables, desks, cabinets, chests, and other units appropriate for installation in residential, commercial, & institutional buildings.

SEATING

Broadscope Section encompasses work described below under Auditorium Seating, Classroom Seating, Stadium Seating.

Auditorium Seating

Narrowscope Section encompasses fixed seating units of wood, metal, molded plastic, or upholstered construction for indoor installation.

Classroom Seating

Narrowscope Section encompasses student desks, desk-chair units, chairs with or without tablet arms, & teachers' desks of wood, metal, or plastic.

Stadium Seating

Narrowscope Section encompasses fixed seating units with or without backs or arms, constructed of wood, metal, or molded plastic for outdoor installation.

1.32

UNIFORM SYSTEM FOR CONSTRUCTION SPECIFICATIONS, DATA FILING & COST ACCOUNTING

SPECIFICATION OUTLINE   **SPECIAL CONSTRUCTION**   13

AUDIOMETRIC ROOMS

Broadscope Section encompasses materials & techniques for construction of anechoic chambers and other soundproof rooms for calibration of instruments, testing, & research in the field of sound, including structural vibration isolators, sound-absorbing material, sound baffles, and sound-retarding doors. Vibration isolating mounts for specific pieces of building equipment should be specified in 15 BASIC MATERIALS & METHODS, 11 INDUSTRIAL EQUIPMENT, 16 ELECTRICAL POWER EQUIPMENT, or appropriate Section of Division 14.

BOWLING ALLEYS

Broadscope Section encompasses the construction of tenpin or duckpin lanes & installation of pinsetting equipment, gutters, ball returns, ball racks, & other specialized bowling equipment.

BROADCASTING STUDIOS

Broadscope Section encompasses the construction of radio, television, and recording studios & transmitting facilities.

CLEAN ROOMS

Broadscope Section encompasses the construction of permanent or demountable rooms designed to establish & maintain a controlled environment free of airborne & other debris of any kind for research & for manufacture of electronic, chemical, pharmaceutical, & other products involving critical tolerances.

CONSERVATORIES

Broadscope Section encompasses the construction of conservatories & similar enclosures of special design for propagation or display of botanical specimens & gardens. For prefabricated greenhouses, see 13 PREFABRICATED STRUCTURES.

HYPERBARIC ROOMS

Broadscope Section encompasses rooms constructed as large pressure vessels for surgical treatment and bed care of the critically ill, including attendant equipment & protective devices.

INCINERATORS

Broadscope Section encompasses incinerators to be constructed on the site. For packaged incinerators, see 10 WASTE DISPOSAL UNITS.

INSULATED ROOMS

Broadscope Section encompasses on-site construction of rooms for cold or frozen storage & for sharp-freezing, including insulation, insulated structural panels, insulated doors, floors, shelving, & other equipment and accessories required for a complete installation. Refrigeration equipment may in some instances be specified in this Section, but is normally best specified in 15 REFRIGERATION.

INTEGRATED CEILINGS

Broadscope Section encompasses coördinated ceiling systems incorporating acoustical, lighting, air distirbution, & partition supporting elements in various combination. It is usually more desirable to specify integrated ceiling systems in 15 AIR-TEMPERING SYSTEM when the air-tempering function predominates or in 16 LIGHTING FIXTURES when lighting predominates.

OBSERVATORIES

Broadscope Section encompasses the construction of observatory structures for housing astronomical telescopes & related activities. For prefabricated astro-observatories, see 11 EDUCATIONAL EQUIPMENT.

PEDESTAL FLOORS

Broadscope Section encompasses pedestal floors of the sort that provide a plenum below for free access to wiring & other mechanical equipment, including steps, ramps, closures, & other fittings required for a complete installation. If resilient or other floor covering is to be provided by the pedestal floor supplier, it should be specified in this Section; if by others, it should be specified in 9 RESILIENT FLOORING or other appropriate Section.

PREFABRICATED STRUCTURES

Broadscope Section encompasses prefabricated structures of various types, including grandstands, greenhouses, livestock buildings, storage structures, and others requiring a minimum of on-site work.

1.33

UNIFORM SYSTEM FOR CONSTRUCTION SPECIFICATIONS, DATA FILING & COST ACCOUNTING

SPECIAL CONSTRUCTION   **SPECIFICATION OUTLINE**

RADIATION PROTECTION

Broadscope Section encompasses radiation shielding materials and their application to or incorporation in walls, ceilings, & floors of x-ray & fluoroscopy rooms, radiological treatment rooms, nuclear accelerator buildings, nuclear reactor installations, and fallout shelters, including radiation-retardant doors. Prefabricated radiation screens may sometimes be specified in this Section, but are normally best specified in 11 MEDICAL EQUIPMENT.

SPECIAL CHIMNEY CONSTRUCTION

Broadscope Section encompasses the construction of large chimneys & stacks of radial brick, metal, asbestos-cement, or other material installed as part of institutional, industrial, power-generation, or other such facility.

STORAGE VAULTS

Broadscope Section encompasses the construction of various types of maximum-security vaults, including vault doors & other specialized equipment, for protection of records, securities, cash, jewelry, furs, & other valuables against theft, fire, or other loss.

SWIMMING POOLS

Broadscope Section encompasses on-site construction of swimming pools & natatoria, the installation of prefabricated swimming pools, and the furnishing & installation of such pool equipment as diving boards, diving towers, guard's chairs, ladders, lines & floats, pool covers, & pool maintenance equipment. Underwater & overhead lighting may sometimes be specified in this Section, but are normally best specified in 16 LIGHTING FIXTURES. Filters, pumps, & other mechanical equipment are normally best specified in 15 WATER SUPPLY SYSTEM.

ZOO STRUCTURES

Broadscope Section encompasses aviaries, aquariums, barred & barless cages & other structures for housing zoological specimens.

1.34

UNIFORM SYSTEM FOR CONSTRUCTION SPECIFICATIONS, DATA FILING & COST ACCOUNTING

SPECIFICATION OUTLINE   **CONVEYING SYSTEM** 14

DUMBWAITERS

Broadscope Section encompasses both manual & power-operated dumbwaiters, including hoistway doors & other related equipment.

ELEVATORS

Broadscope Section encompasses freight & passenger elevators of all types, including cabs, entrances, controls, safety equipment, tracks & hoistway fittings, & elevator machinery.

HOISTS & CRANES

Broadscope Section encompasses mobile cranes, monorail hoists, window cleaners' hoists, stationary cranes, travelling hoists, and other similar equipment. Ash hoists may sometimes be specified in this Section, but are normally best specified in 15 FUEL HANDLING SYSTEM.

LIFTS

Broadscope Section encompasses automobile lifts, man lifts, dock levellers, sidewalk lifts, and related shafts, pits, pumps, motors, controls, and other items required for a complete installation. Platform lifts & stage lifts may sometimes be specified in 11 STAGE EQUIPMENT, but are normally best specified in this Section.

MATERIALS HANDLING SYSTEMS

Broadscope Section encompasses endless bucket conveyors, gravity rollers, powered rollers, powered belts, turntables, and other devices for transfer of bulk or packaged materials. Tray conveyors installed as part of a dishwashing line may sometimes be specified in this Section, but are normally best specified in 11 FOOD SERVICE EQUIPMENT. For chutes of various sorts, see 10 CHUTES.

MOVING STAIRS & WALKS

Broadscope Section encompasses passenger conveying systems composed of moving belts or treads installed in horizontal or inclined position complete with handrails, balustrades, tracks, slider plates, motors, controls, safety equipment, and other related items necessary for a complete installation.

PNEUMATIC TUBE SYSTEMS

Broadscope Section encompasses pneumatic tube systems, including tubes, fittings, carriers, switching devices, terminal cabinets, air exhausters, controls, & other related equipment.

1.35

UNIFORM SYSTEM FOR CONSTRUCTION SPECIFICATIONS, DATA FILING & COST ACCOUNTING

MECHANICAL   **SPECIFICATION OUTLINE**

GENERAL PROVISIONS | Broadscape Section encompasses items of a general nature as described below under Codes & Standards, Mechanical Systems Schedule, Mechanical Reference Symbols. If separate contracts are to be executed for work of this Division, it is recommended that this Section include a reference to the Conditions of the Contract and requirements of Division 1 noting their applicability to all project contracts.

Codes & Standards | Narrowscope Section establishes & describes required standards of quality and performance for products, systems, & methods encompassed by Division 15, including appropriate ASA, ASTM, or other established codes & standards by reference.

Mechanical Systems Schedule | Narrowscope Section summarizes the various systems to be installed under Division 15, outlining interrelationships, subsystems, & components in tabular or other convenient form.

Mechanical Reference Symbols | Narrowscope Section lists & defines symbols & abbreviations used on the Drawings or in the Project Manual to identify or describe work encompassed by Division 15.

BASIC MATERIALS & METHODS | Broadscape Section encompasses products, assemblies, & methods of fabrication described below under Pipe & Pipefittings, Valves, Piping Specialties, Mechanical Supporting Devices, Vibration Isolation, Mechanical Systems Insulation. Items specified in this Section are normally limited to those products & assemblies required by more than one of the project systems encompassed by Division 15; installation is usually specified in the Section encompassing the particular system.

Pipe & Pipefittings | Narrowscope Section encompasses pipe & pipefittings of cast iron, wrought iron, steel, galvanized steel, copper, brass, bronze, lead, aluminum, asbestos-cement, fired clay, tempered glass, rubber, various fiber-resin compounds, polyvinyl chloride & other plastics, ceramic materials, & other suitable substances. Flexible hose & tubing, including hose clamps & other fittings, may also be specified here.

Valves | Narrowscope Section encompasses globe valves, check valves, gate valves, relief & safety valves, motor-operated valves, pneumatic valves, self-operated, valves, expansion valves, quick-opening valves, pressure & temperature control valves, & other valves of various types.

Piping Specialties | Narrowscope Section encompasses pipeline strainers, porous ceramic or plastic filters, absorption separators for removal of vapor or liquid, magnetic separators, traps, escutcheons, expansion joints, packing, gaskets, pressure joint connectors, pulsation absorbers, pipe identification systems, and other piping specialties.

Mechanical Supporting Devices | Narrowscope Section encompasses hangers and other supporting devices for piping, ductwork, and various items of mechanical equipment. For vibration isolating techniques & devices, see 15 Vibration isolation. For electrical supporting devices, see 16 BASIC MATERIALS & METHODS. For plumbing fixture carriers, see 15 PLUMBING FIXTURES & TRIM.

Vibration Isolation | Narrowscope Section encompasses mounting devices & techniques for isolation of vibrations generated by mechanical equipment. For pulsation absorbers, see 15 Piping Specialties; for sound-absorbent duct linings, fabric duct connectors, & sound-absorbing baffles for duct installation, see 15 AIR-TEMPERING SYSTEM.

1.36

UNIFORM SYSTEM FOR CONSTRUCTION SPECIFICATIONS, DATA FILING & COST ACCOUNTING

SPECIFICATION OUTLINE

MECHANICAL

Mechanical Systems Insulation

Narrowscope Section encompasses thermal insulation & vapor barriers of various sorts, including preformed casings, and their application to hot piping, chilled piping, domestic water piping, interior rainwater piping, surfaces of heated or chilled equipment, underground conduit, & other mechanical equipment. Canvas, paint, plastic, & other protective finishes for mechanical systems insulation are normally best specified in this Section, but may in some instances be specified in 9 PAINTING or 9 SPECIAL COATINGS, as appropriate. For insulated ductwork, see 15 AIR-TEMPERING SYSTEM.

WATER SUPPLY SYSTEM

Broadscope Section encompasses work described below under Water Supply Piping System, Domestic Hot Water System, Domestic Iced Water System, Water Well & Wellpump. See also 2 SITE UTILITIES.

Water Supply Piping System

Narrowscope Section encompasses water supply piping system including such water treatment equipment as domestic water softeners, ion exchange or other demineralization equipment, & filtration units. Filters, pumps, & piping for swimming pools may sometimes be specified in 13 SWIMMING POOLS, but are normally best specified in this Section. For boiler feedwater treatment equipment, see 15 STEAM HEATING SYSTEM, or 15 HOT WATER HEATING SYSTEM.

Domestic Hot Water System

Narrowscope Section encompasses water heaters, hot water storage tanks, heating coils, and their installation with attendant piping and fittings.

Domestic Iced Water System

Narrowscope Section encompasses chilled water piping installed as a separate system to provide iced drinking water in hotels, motels, and other buildings, or in some cases to provide chilled water for medical or laboratory use. For water chillers, see 15 REFRIGERATION.

Water Well & Wellpump

Narrowscope Section encompasses the drilling of water wells & installation of well casing, piping, wellpump, and other related equipment.

SOIL & WASTE SYSTEM

Broadscope Section encompasses work described below under Soil & Waste Piping, Waste Treatment Equipment, Sanitary Sewers. See also 2 SITE UTILITIES.

Soil & Waste Piping

Narrowscope Section encompasses the installation of soil & waste piping, including vents, traps, floor drains, interceptors, cleanouts, & other soil & waste fittings. For P-traps & fixture drains, see 15 PLUMBING FIXTURES & TRIM.

Waste Treatment Equipment

Narrowscope Section encompasses equipment for treatment of sanitary & industrial waste including septic tanks, aeration tanks, holding basins, equipment for treatment of various liquid industrial wastes, catalytic gas treatment equipment, and other such equipment.

Sanitary Sewers

Narrowscope Section encompasses sanitary sewers & sewage disposal fields.

ROOF DRAINAGE SYSTEM

Broadscope Section encompasses roof drains & interior rainwater piping, including connection to the storm drainage system. The storm drainage system external to the building may sometimes be specified in this Section, but is normally best specified in 2 SITE DRAINAGE.

PLUMBING FIXTURES & TRIM

Broadside Section encompasses water closets, lavatories, tubs, urinals, bidets, mop sinks, mop receptors, shower receptors, wash fountains, drinking fountains, fixture carriers, toilet seats, and such plumbing specialties as sill cocks, hose bibbs, hydrants, faucets, stops, P-traps, & fixture drains. Kitchen sinks & laundry trays may sometimes be specified in 11 RESIDENTIAL EQUIPMENT, but are normally best specified in this Section.

1.37

UNIFORM SYSTEM FOR CONSTRUCTION SPECIFICATIONS, DATA FILING & COST ACCOUNTING

15 MECHANICAL   **SPECIFICATION OUTLINE**

GAS PIPING SYSTEM	Broadscope Section encompasses installation of the piping system for supplying natural or manufactured gas to furnaces, ranges, water heaters, & other gas-burning equipment, and includes all fittings, pressure-reducers, stops, and other required accessories. See also 2 SITE UTILITIES.
SPECIAL PIPING SYSTEMS	Broadscope Section encompasses work described below under Compressed Air System, Vacuum Piping System, Oxygen Piping System, Nitrous Oxide Piping System, Process Piping System. If piping systems for other fluids are to be installed in the project and Narrowscope titles used, Section titles should be added properly identifying such systems.
Compressed Air System	Narrowscope Section encompasses piping, valves, compressors, and other equipment for supplying compressed air for laboratory, industrial, or other use.
Vacuum Piping System	Narrowscope Section encompasses piping, valves, air exhausters, and other equipment for providing partial vacuum required in medical, laboratory, industrial, & other installations.
Oxygen Piping System	Narrowscope System encompasses piping, valves, manifolds, & other equipment for supplying oxygen to laboratories, hospital rooms, surgeries, treatment rooms, & other locations from a central source.
Nitrous Oxide Piping System	Narrowscope Section encompasses piping, valves, manifolds, & other equipment for supplying nitrous oxide to laboratories, treatment rooms, & other locations from a central source.
Process Piping System	Narrowscope Section encompasses specialized piping systems & valves for metering, mixing, sampling, & otherwise controlling the flow of fluids in industrial processes for manufacturing petroleum products, drugs, paints, plastics, & various other substances.
FIRE EXTINGUISHING SYSTEM	Broadscope Section encompasses work described below under Automatic Sprinkler System, Carbon Dioxide System, Elevated Water Reservoir, Standpipe & Firehose Stations, Underground Fire Lines. See also 10 FIREFIGHTING DEVICES.
Automatic Sprinkler System	Narrowscope Section encompasses installation of both wet-pipe & dry-pipe sprinkler systems, including piping, hangers, sprinkler heads, and other related equipment.
Carbon Dioxide System	Narrowscope Section encompasses piping systems for production & automatic distribution of carbon dioxide fog or foam.
Elevated Water Reservoir	Narrowscope Section encompasses water reservoirs of wood, metal, or other material providing a gravity supply of water for fire protection.
Standpipe & Firehose Stations	Narrowscope Section encompasses standpipes, siamese & other firehose connections, firehose cabinets & reels, and other related equipment.
Underground Fire Lines	Narrowscope Section encompasses underground piping installed as part of the fire extinguishing system for a building or a group of buildings.
FUEL HANDLING SYSTEM	Broadscope Section encompasses automatic & semi-automatic systems for weighing, metering, storing, & transfering coal, coke, oil, or other solid or liquid fuels and equipment for ash & cinder removal, including on-site storage bins & tanks, stokers, ash hoists, etc.
STEAM HEATING SYSTEM	Broadscope Section encompasses work described below under Steam Boiler & Equipment, Steam Circulating System, Steam Terminal Units. See also 2 SITE UTILITIES.
Steam Boiler & Equipment	Narrowscope Section encompasses package steam boilers, site-constructed steam boilers, combustion chamber equipment & construction, forced draft equipment, boiler feedwater treatment equipment, gauges, safety equipment, breeching pipe, and steam boiler accessories of various sorts.

1.38

UNIFORM SYSTEM FOR CONSTRUCTION SPECIFICATIONS, DATA FILING & COST ACCOUNTING

SPECIFICATION OUTLINE · **MECHANICAL** · 15

Steam Circulating System	Narrowscope Section encompasses the steam circulating system connecting steam boilers to steam terminal units, and its installation complete with pipe & pipefittings, expansion fittings & loops, condensate-return & other pumps, insulation, & other required fittings & accessories.
Steam Terminal Units	Narrowscope Section encompasses radiators, convectors, finned tubes, unit ventilators, unit heaters, & other terminal units heated by steam. Enclosures furnished with the units should be specified in this Section; enclosures of special design or construction are normally best specified in 5 SPECIAL FORMED METAL or 5 ORNAMENTAL METAL as may be appropriate.
HOT WATER HEATING SYSTEM	Broadscope Section encompasses work described below under Hot Water Boiler & Equipment, Hot Water Circulating System, Hot Water Terminal Units, Hot Water Snow-Melting System.
Hot Water Boiler & Equipment	Narrowscope Section encompasses package hot water boilers, site-constructed hot water boilers, combustion chamber equipment & construction, forced draft equipment, boiler feedwater treatment equipment, gauges, safety equipment, breeching pipe, and hot water boiler accessories of various sorts.
Hot Water Circulating System	Narrowscope Section encompasses the hot water circulating system connecting hot water boilers to hot water terminal units and its installation complete with pipe & pipefittings, expansion fittings & loops, modulating valves, circulating pumps, insulation, & other required fittings & accessories.
Hot Water Terminal Units	Narrowscope Section encompasses radiators, convectors, finned tubes, unit ventilators, unit heaters, & other terminal units heated by hot water. Enclosures furnished with the units should be specified in this Section; enclosures of special design or construction are normally best specified in 5 SPECIAL FORMED METAL or 5 ORNAMENTAL METAL as may be appropriate.
Hot Water Snow-Melting System	Narrowscope Section encompasses hot water coils embedded in or below walks, drives, terraces, & other exterior surfaces for melting snow & ice.
CHILLED WATER CIRCULATING SYSTEM	Broadscope Section encompasses the chilled water piping & such chilled water terminal units as cooling coils & fan-coil units, comprising a separate system for space cooling. Water chillers & related equipment are sometimes specified in this Section, but are normally best specified in 15 REFRIGERATION. For domestic iced water system, see 15 WATER SUPPLY SYSTEM.
DUAL-TEMPERATURE SYSTEM	Broadscope Section encompasses dual-temperature piping, & such dual-temperature terminal units as coils & fan-coil units comprising a separate system for maintaining building temperatures at levels required for human comfort or proper operation of mechanical instruments & equipment. See 15 HOT WATER HEATING SYSTEM for hot water boilers & 15 REFRIGERATION for water chillers to be connected to the dual-temperature piping. Heat pumps may sometimes be specified in this Section, but are normally best specified in 16 ELECTRICAL COMFORT SYSTEM.
AIR-TEMPERING SYSTEM	Broadscope Section encompasses work described below under Warm Air Furnaces, Air-Handling Equipment, Air Filtration Equipment, Humidity Control Equipment, Packaged Air-Tempering Units, Air Distribution Duct System, Tempered Air Terminal Units, Air Curtains. See also 16 ELECTRICAL COMFORT SYSTEM.

1.39

UNIFORM SYSTEM FOR CONSTRUCTION SPECIFICATIONS, DATA FILING & COST ACCOUNTING

MECHANICAL   **SPECIFICATION OUTLINE**

Warm Air Furnaces	Narrowscope Section encompasses warm air furnaces of all types and gas-fired & oil-fired unit heaters.
Air-Handling Equipment	Narrowscope Section encompasses air-handling units & related equipment of all sorts, including fans, blowers, face & by-pass dampers, & control devices.
Air Filtration Equipment	Narrowscope Section encompasses air filtration units & filters, including coated filters, electrostatic filters, disposable fibrous filters, and filters of various other materials & types.
Humidity Control Equipment	Narrowscope Section encompasses humidifiers & dehumidifiers and related controls & accessories.
Packaged Air-Tempering Units	Narrowscope Section encompasses packaged air-conditioners for window, through-the-wall, or other installation, including summer-winter units. It may sometimes be desirable to specify unducted units in 16 ELECTRICAL COMFORT SYSTEM. See also 15 CHILLED WATER CIRCULATING SYSTEM, 15 DUAL-TEMPERATURE SYSTEM, & 15 REFRIGERATION.
Air Distribution Duct System	Narrowscope Section encompasses ductwork of sheet metal or other material for the distribution of air at normal or high pressures or velocities, including flexible ductwork, fabric connectors, regulating dampers, fire dampers, turning vanes, duct access panels & doors, noise attenuators & baffles, grilles, diffusers, registers, & duct specialties. Packaged kitchen exhaust fans & hoods are normally best specified in 11 RESIDENTIAL EQUIPMENT & laboratory fume hoods in 11 LABORATORY EQUIPMENT, but in some instances these may be specified here. Integrated ceilings should be specified here when the air-tempering function predominates, but may be specified in 13 INTEGRATED CEILINGS or 16 LIGHTING FIXTURES.
Tempered Air Terminal Units	Narrowscope Section encompasses indirect-fired unit heaters & unit ventilators supplied with air warmed or cooled at a central source.
Air Curtains	Narrowscope Section encompasses mechanical equipment providing tempered air in a pattern and at a velocity that minimize air infiltration through open entrances to shops, restaurants, cold storage rooms, or other spaces.
REFRIGERATION	Broadscope Section encompasses work described below under Water Chillers, Commercial Refrigeration Units, Cooling Towers.
Water Chillers	Narrowscope Section encompasses water chillers & related equipment serving the domestic iced water system & the chilled water circulating system.
Commercial Refrigeration Units	Narrowscope Section encompasses refrigerant compressors, evaporative condensers, absorption units, steam vacuum units, and other refrigeration units serving central air-cooling installations and refrigerated rooms; including rooftop units & ice-making equipment. See also 11 FOOD SERVICE EQUIPMENT & 13 INSULATED ROOMS.
Cooling Towers	Narrowscope Section encompasses cooling towers of various materials & types.
HVC CONTROLS & INSTRUMENTS	Broadscope Section encompasses controls & instruments related to the operation of heating, ventilating, & cooling systems & equipment specified in Division 15, including electric, electronic, pneumatic, hydraulic, & mechanical devices serving as sensing, actuating, or recording elements. Section title may be altered to 15 HVC CONTROLS as required. Electrical system controls & instruments should be specified in 16 ELECTRICAL SYSTEM CONTROLS & INSTRUMENTS.

1.40

UNIFORM SYSTEM FOR CONSTRUCTION SPECIFICATIONS, DATA FILING & COST ACCOUNTING

SPECIFICATION OUTLINE

ELECTRICAL

GENERAL PROVISIONS

Broadscope Section encompasses items of a general nature as described below under Codes & Standards, Electrical Systems Schedule, Electrical Reference Symbols. If separate contracts are to be executed for work of this Division, it is recommended that this Section include a reference to the Conditions of the Contract and requirements of Division 1 noting their applicability to all project contracts.

Codes & Standards

Narrowscope Section establishes & describes required standards of quality and performance for products, systems, & methods encompassed by Division 16, including appropriate ASA, ASTM, or other established codes & standards by reference.

Electrical Systems Schedule

Narrowscope Section summarizes the various systems to be installed under Division 16, outlining interrelationships, subsystems, & components in tabular or other convenient form.

Electrical Reference Symbols

Narrowscope Section lists & defines symbols & abbreviations used on the Drawings or in the Project Manual to identify or describe work encompassed by Division 16.

BASIC MATERIALS & METHODS

Broadscope Section encompasses products, assemblies, & methods of fabrication described below under Raceways & Fittings, Busways, Conductors, Electrical Supporting Devices. Items specified in this Section are normally limited to those products, assemblies, & methods required by more than one of the project systems encompassed by Division 16; installation is usually specified in the Section encompassing the particular system.

Raceways & Fittings

Narrowscope Section encompasses electrical metallic tubing, rigid metallic or other conduit, flexible conduit, wireways, wiremolds, pull boxes, junction boxes, outlet boxes, connectors, covers, & other related fittings.

Busways

Narrowscope Section encompasses bus ducts, feeder ducts, trolley ducts, high-voltage ducts, high-frequency ducts, plug-ins, & various related fittings.

Conductors

Narrowscope Section encompasses conductors of various types for communications, low-voltage, high-voltage, control, & other circuits; including wire insulated with rubber, plastic, or other material; mineral-sheathed cable; shielded cable; fixture cords; splicing materials; and electrical insulation.

Electrical Supporting Devices

Narrowscope Section encompasses cable trays, conduit racks, hangers, & other supporting devices for electrical equipment. For mechanical supporting devices, see 15 BASIC MATERIALS & METHODS. For outdoor lighting standards & poles, see 16 LIGHTING FIXTURES.

ELECTRICAL SERVICE SYSTEM

Broadscope Section encompasses work described below under Overhead Electrical Service, Underground Electrical Service, Electrical Substations, Electrical Entrance Equipment, Grounding System, Standby Electrical System. See also 2 SITE UTILITIES.

Overhead Electrical Service

Narrowscope Section encompasses power poles, insulators, guys, service conductors, weatherheads, & other items required for bringing the building electrical service to the electrical entrance equipment. Portions of the electrical service not part of the Contract by virtue of their installation by the electric utility company should be so noted.

Underground Electrical Service

Narrowscope Section encompasses installation of underground electrical service cable in conduit of concrete, fiber, or other material or by direct burial techniques. Portions of the electrical service not part of the Contract by virtue of their installation by the electric utility company should be so noted.

1.41

UNIFORM SYSTEM FOR CONSTRUCTION SPECIFICATIONS, DATA FILING & COST ACCOUNTING

ELECTRICAL   **SPECIFICATION OUTLINE**

Electrical Substations

Narrowscope Section encompasses substations, switchyards, high-voltage transformers, rectifiers & converters, related protective devices & other accessories. Transformer vaults may in some instances be specified in this Section but are usually best specified in 3 CAST-IN-PLACE CONCRETE or other Section appropriate to the type of construction to be used.

Electrical Entrance Equipment

Narrowscope Section encompasses meter sockets, main panels, service disconnects & protective devices, & related switchgear & accessories.

Grounding System

Narrowscope Section encompasses grounding stakes, ground connections, and interconnecting conductors for equalizing electrical potentials between building equipment & ground at all points.

Standby Electrical System

Narrowscope Section encompasses motor-generator sets, batteries & battery chargers, and other equipment for providing emergency electric power & light.

ELECTRICAL DISTRIBUTION SYSTEM

Broadscope Section encompasses work described below under Feeder Circuits, Branch Circuits, Panelboards, Wiring Devices, Underfloor Electrical System.

Feeder Circuits

Narrowscope Section encompasses the installation of conductors, raceways, and attendant fittings for feeder circuits connecting the electrical service to various load centers, panelboards, & other locations for connection, switching, & electrical protection of branch circuits.

Branch Circuits

Narrowscope Section encompasses the installation of conductors, raceways, and attendant fittings for branch circuits connecting load centers & panelboards to lighting fixtures, motors, & other electrical or mechanical equipment.

Panelboards

Narrowscope Section encompasses panels & panelboards, switchboards, & load centers for powering & controlling lighting, machines of various sorts, convenience & appliance circuits, & other equipment requiring electricity. Dimming equipment of resistance, reactance, & electronic types are normally best specified in this Section, but may in some instances be specified in 11 STAGE EQUIPMENT. Miniature dimmers for outlet box mounting should be specified in 16 Wiring Devices.

Wiring Devices

Narrowscope Section encompasses wiring devices of all sorts for operation at low, medium, or high voltage; including switches, convenience outlets, & special-purpose outlets of various types.

Underfloor Electrical System

Narrowscope Section encompasses underfloor electrical systems utilizing cellular metal decking, cellular concrete decking, header ducts above or below the structural floor, and other materials & techniques for underfloor distribution of electrical power, as well as cables for telephone or intercommunication systems. Floor-mounted outlets of various types are included here.

LIGHTING FIXTURES

Broadscope Section encompasses work described below under Indoor Lighting Fixtures, Outdoor Lighting Fixtures.

Indoor Lighting Fixtures

Narrowscope Section encompasses fluorescent, incandescent, metallic vapor, & other indoor lighting fixtures, including luminous-ceilings and their installation complete with lamps, ballasts, starters, reflectors, diffusers, lenses, shielding, and various fittings & accessories. For portable lighting units, see 12 FURNITURE; for dimming equipment, see 16 ELECTRICAL DISTRIBUTION SYSTEM. Integrated ceilings should be specified here when the lighting function predominates, but may be specified in 13 INTEGRATED CEILINGS or 15 AIR-TEMPERING SYSTEM.

1.42

UNIFORM SYSTEM FOR CONSTRUCTION SPECIFICATIONS, DATA FILING & COST ACCOUNTING

SPECIFICATION OUTLINE

ELECTRICAL

16

Outdoor Lighting Fixtures	Narrowscope Section encompasses incandescent, fluorescent, metallic vapor, & other outdoor lighting fixtures and their installation complete with lamps, ballasts, starters, reflectors, diffusers, lenses, shielding, mounting standards, brackets, pole bases, and various fittings & accessories. General-purpose & special-purpose fixtures for building flood-lighting, sports lighting, street lighting, & other such installations are included here. Electrified signs may sometimes be specified in this Section, but are normally best specified in 10 IDENTIFYING DEVICES.
COMMUNICATION SYSTEMS	Broadscope Section encompasses work described below under Telephone Equipment, Intercommunication System, Public Address System, Paging System, Nurses' Call System, Alarm & Detection System, Clock & Program System, Audio-Video Reproducers, Closed-Circuit Television, Radiotelephone System, Commercial Projection System. See also 2 SITE UTILITIES.
Telephone Equipment	Narrowscope Section encompasses the installation of telephone conduit systems, switchboards, terminal & switching equipment, conductors, & handsets. Portions of the work not part of the Contract by virtue of their installation by the telephone utility company should be so noted.
Intercommunication System	Narrowscope Section encompasses intercommunication equipment & its installation, including master & remote transceiving units, wires & cables, conduit system, & required service connections. See also 16 Paging System & 16 Radiotelephone System.
Public Address System	Narrowscope Section encompasses speakers, amplifiers, microphones, playback equipment, & interconnecting cables required for auditorium, fieldhouse, stadium, & other public address systems.
Paging System	Narrowscope Section encompasses annunciators, callboards, wireless paging units, and other such equipment, including conductors, fittings, & other items required for a complete installation.
Nurses' Call System	Narrowscope Section encompasses equipment for visual signaling by the bed patient.
Alarm & Detection Systems	Narrowscope Section encompasses automatic alarm systems, automatic detection systems, & combined alarm & detection systems for protection against burglary, fire, smoke, or other loss. Section title may be altered to 16 Alarm System or 16 Detection System as required.
Clock & Program System	Narrowscope Section encompasses central clock control equipment & automatic sequencing equipment for producing audible or other signals noting classroom instruction periods or other time intervals; including classroom clocks, bells, & required wiring & outlets. Section title may be altered to 16 Clock System or 16 Program System as required.
Audio-Video Reproducers	Narrowscope Section encompasses radio & television receivers, phonographs, high-fidelity components, tape recorders, and other equipment for receiving, recording, & reproducing audio or video signals of all sorts. This Section encompasses both built-in & cabinet type equipment.
Closed-Circuit Television	Narrowscope Section encompasses pickup & reproduction equipment, controls, wiring, & related accessories for closed circuit television systems.
Radiotelephone System	Narrowscope Section encompasses radiotelephone transceivers, transmitter towers, antennae, & related citizens' band, police, or other short-wave equipment.
Commercial Projection System	Narrowscope Section encompasses commercial soundfilm projectors, screens, amplifiers, & other projection booth & cinema equipment. For portable projectors, see 11 EDUCATIONAL EQUIPMENT.

1.43

16 | **ELECTRICAL** | **SPECIFICATION OUTLINE**

ELECTRICAL POWER EQUIPMENT	Broadscope Section encompasses work described below under Motors & Motor Controls, Special Transformers, Frequency Converters, Rectifiers. See also 11 INDUSTRIAL EQUIPMENT & various Sections of Division 15. For motor-generator sets, see 16 ELECTRICAL SERVICE SYSTEM.
Motors & Motor Controls	Narrowscope Section encompasses AC, DC, & universal motors and motor controls furnished as separate items for on-site installation & connection to various pieces of mechanical equipment, including manual, magnetic, or other starting devices & various protective devices. Motors & related devices furnished as integral parts of other equipment are normally best specified with the equipment in other appropriate Sections, but final connection is normally best specified here, in which case cross-references should be included in all Sections affected.
Special Transformers	Narrowscope Section encompasses special transformers of all types serving individual pieces of equipment or systems. For other transformers, see 16 ELECTRICAL SERVICE SYSTEM.
Frequency Converters	Narrowscope Section encompasses electrical frequency converters of various types & related equipment required for their installation.
Rectifiers	Narrowscope Section encompasses rectifiers of various types & related equipment required for their installation.
ELECTRICAL COMFORT SYSTEM	Broadscope Section encompasses work described below under Electrical Heating System, Packaged Air-Tempering Units, Electrical Snow-Melting System, Heat Pumps.
Electrical Heating System	Narrowscope Section encompasses electrical resistance heating equipment, including convectors, radiant heaters, baseboard units, in-duct units, & embedded coils of various sorts for installation in ceiling or other surfaces.
Packaged Air-Tempering Units	Narrowscope Section encompasses packaged air-conditioners for window, through-the-wall, or other installation, particularly if unducted, including summer-winter units. See also 15 AIR-TEMPERING SYSTEM.
Electrical Snow-Melting System	Narrowscope Section encompasses electrical resistance equipment for melting snow & ice including built-in radiant units, flexible cables, & portable mats.
Heat Pumps	Narrowscope Section encompasses heat pumps & their installation, including controls & service connections. Heat pumps to be installed as part of a dual-temperature piping system are sometimes specified in 15 DUAL-TEMPERATURE SYSTEM, but are normally best specified here.
ELECTRICAL SYSTEM CONTROLS & INSTRUMENTS	Broadscope Section encompasses controls & instruments related to the operation of electrical heating systems, electrical snow-melting systems, and other electrical systems. Controls & instruments related to heating, ventilating, & cooling systems should be specified in 15 HVC CONTROLS & INSTRUMENTS. Section title may be altered to 16 ELECTRICAL SYSTEM CONTROLS as required.
LIGHTNING PROTECTION SYSTEM	Broadscope Section encompasses lightning rods, conductors, insulators, ground stakes, and their installation including all required fittings & accessories.

1.44

SPEC-DATA

This Spec-Data Sheet conforms to editorial style prescribed by The Construction Specifications Institute. The manufacturer is responsible for technical accuracy.

1. PRODUCT NAME

2. MANUFACTURER

3. PRODUCT DESCRIPTION
Basic Use:

Limitations:

4. TECHNICAL DATA
Test

Viscosity:

Sheen:

Spread Rate:

5. INSTALLATION
Surface Preparation:

Priming:

Method of Application:

Equipment Clean - Up:

6. AVAILABILITY AND COST
Availability:

Cost:

7. GUARANTEES

8. MAINTENANCE

9. TECHNICAL SERVICE

10. FILING SYSTEMS
Uniform System.

July 1970

9

SPECIAL COATINGS
decorative and protective

The ten-point Spec-Data® format has been reproduced from publications copyrighted by CSI, 1964, 1965, 1966, 1967, and used by permission of The Construction Specifications Institute, Inc., Washington, D. C. 20036

09800

FOR REVIEW AND COMMENT

SPECIFYING:

SUBDRAINAGE SYSTEMS

DEADLINE FOR COMMENTS

NOVEMBER 15, 1972

CSI
PRELIMINARY
SERIES

By: North central Pennsylvania Chapter, CSI

Chapter Committee:

J. Carl Crouse, Chm.
Frank A. Wagner
Mikel E. Tompkin
Joseph Teplica

Published by The Construction
Specifications Institute, Inc.
1150 Seventeenth Street, N.W.
Washington, D. C. 20036

Please follow instructions on
the back of this sheet.

02510

THIS STUDY

This study provides a guide for specifying construction of sub-drainage systems for site roads, parking areas, retaining walls, basement footings, and floors.

Subdrainage systems are required when the ground water level, at any time of the year, rises to within one foot from the bottom of the base course, within three feet of the pavement surface of roads and parking areas, or within one foot of the underside of slab of basement floors.

Subsurface water, due to hydrostatic head, may lift sections of slabs, pavements, parking areas, and dislodge sections of retaining walls.

This study does not include storm and surface drainage.

This study has been prepared by a committee of the Northcentral Pennsylvania Chapter, CSI.

DRAWINGS AND SPECIFICATIONS

Drawings:

Drawings should show correct method of bedding and jointing pipe to suit various loading conditions. Such conditions are vehicular loads, deeply laid pipes, heavily loaded basement and slabs, under which such pipes, by necessity, must be placed.

The pipe size, slope, spacing, depth of subgrade drains, clean-outs, manholes, sediment traps, sumps, and drainage pattern to suit local engineering conditions, should be shown on the drawings. Show pipe stubs, as applicable, for future expansion, on the drawings.

Drawings should also define depth of porous backfill, thickness of filter mat, and depth of compacted backfill as well as intercepts, discharge lines, and location of weepholes, as appropriate.

Specifications:

The specifications should include requirements of regulatory agencies, qualification of installer, and submittals required. Material requirements, applicable AASHO, Federal or ASTM standards, inspection requirements, preparatory work, installation, and field quality control should also be defined.

02510-2

GUIDE SPECIFICATIONS

This Guide Specification is intended to be used as a basis for the development of an office master specification or in the preparation of specifications for a particular project. In either case, this Guide Specification must be edited to fit the conditions of use. Particular attention should be given to the deletion of inapplicable provisions. Include necessary items related to a particular project and include appropriate requirement where blank spaces have been provided.

	Notes to the Specifier
SECTION 02_____	
SUBDRAINAGE	
PART 1 - GENERAL	
1.01 RELATED WORK SPECIFIED ELSEWHERE:	
A. Subsurface Exploration: Section 02_____.	1.01.A May also require coordination with General Conditions based upon original site investigations to determine ground water conditions.
B. Earthwork: Section 02_____.	
C. Site Drainage: Section 02_____.	1.01.C Coordinate with Surface Drainage.
D. Paving: Section 02_____.	
E. Landscaping: Section 02_____.	
F. Cast-In-Place Concrete: Section 03_____.	
G. Unit Masonry: Section 04_____.	
1.02 QUALITY ASSURANCE:	
A. Installer to have not less than two years experience installing subdrain systems.	

02510-3

B. Testing Requirements: Culvert pipe and
    drain tile: AASHO T33-_____.

        ** OR **

B. Testing Requirements:

    1. Clay tile pipe: ASTM C 301-_____.

    2. Concrete pipe or tile:
        ASTM C 497-_____.

    3. Bituminous-fiber pipe:
        ASTM D 2314-_____.

    4. Laminated-wall bituminous-fiber pipe:
        ASTM D 2315-_____.

        ** ** **

C. Qualifications of Testing Agencies:

    1. Independent testing laboratory

    2. Minimum experience in conducting
        specified tests: two years.

        ** OR **

C. Manufacturer's Qualifications:

    1. Regularly engaged for past five years
        in the manufacture of products
        specified.

    2. Manufacturer's products certified to
        meet or exceed minimum requirements
        as specified.

        ** ** **

1.03 REQUIREMENTS OF REGULATORY AGENCIES: Material
and workmanship in conformance with _____
Sanitary and Drainage Codes.

1.04 SUBMITTALS:

    A. Samples: Submit _____ samples of the
        following:

        1. Drain pipe or tile and couplings.

1.03 Identify appropriate
federal state or local codes
applicable. When more than
one jurisdiction applies
specify most stringent.

02510-4

    2.   Perforated drain pipe or tile and couplings.

    3.   Cleanouts.

    4.   Each type of compression joint.

    5.   Discharge pipe.

    6.   Insect screen.

B.   Certificates:

    1.   Submit notarized certification of installer's experience, identifying previous projects with names of Owner and Architect/Engineer.

    2.   Submit notarized certification that materials meet or exceed specification requirement.

1.05 PRODUCT DELIVERY, STORAGE, AND HANDLING:

A.   Deliver materials on manufacturers original skids or in original unopened protective packaging.

B.   Store materials to prevent physical damage.

C.   Protect materials during transportation and installation to avoid physical damage.

PART 2 - PRODUCTS

2.01 MATERIALS:

2.01 Pipe and tile should be selected to resist concentrated loads and other engineering conditions of the project.

A.   Perforated Underdrains: Clay pipe AASHO M65-_____, Class _____.

       ** OR **

2.01.A (Standard Strength), (Extra Strong Strength).

02510-5

A. Perforated Underdrains: Clay Pipe, ASTM C 211-_____, Class _____.

    ** OR **

A. Perforated Underdrains: Clay Pipe, ASTM C 498-_____, Class _____.

    ** OR **

A. Perforated Underdrains: Concrete Pipe, _____, Type _____.

    ** OR **

A. Perforated Underdrains: Asbestos-cement Pipe _____, Type _____.

    ** OR **

A. Perforated Underdrains: Galvanized Iron or Steel: AASHO M36-_____, Type III, Class _____.

    ** OR **

A. Perforated Underdrains: Aluminum Alloy: AASHO M197-_____, Type _____.

2.01.A (I, Standard Strength); (II, Extra Strength).

2.01.A (Standard Strength); (Heavy Duty), (Extra Strength), (Extra Quality).

2.01.A (AASHO M175-_____), (ASTM C 444-_____), (1, circular perforations); (2, slotted perforations).

2.01.A (AASHO M189-_____), (ASTM C 508-_____). Type (I), for use where moderately aggressive water and soil of moderate sulfate content are expected to come in contact with the pipe. Type (II), for use where highly aggressive water or water and soil of high sulfate content, or both, are expected to come in contact with pipe. Type (III), for use where contact with aggressive water or soil is not expected.

2.01.A Class (I) is helically corrugated pipe with a helical corrugated pipe with a welded longitudinal scam. Class (III) is circumferentially corrugated pipe with riveted lap joints.

2.01.A Type (I) is helically corrugated pipe with a helical lock scam. Type (II) is helically corrugated pipe with a welded longitudinal scam.

02510-**6**

	Type (III) is circumferentially corrugated pipe with a welded longitudinal scam. Type (IV) is circumferentially corrugated pipe with riveted lap joints.
** OR **	
A. Perforated Underdrains: Aluminum Alloy FS WW-P-402-_____:	
1. Class: _____.	2.01.A.1 Class (I) is annular corrugated pipe; Class (II) is helically corrugated pipe; and Class (III) is fabricated of structural steel plate and has annular corrugations.
2. Shape: _____.	2.01.A.2 Shape No. 1-full circular; shape No. 2-factory elongated; Shape No. 3-pipe arch cross-section; and shape No. 4-arches of circular cross-section.
3. Coating: _____.	2.01.A.3 A. Fully bituminous coated. B. Half bituminous coating with paved invert. C. Full bituminous coating with paved invert. D. Paved invert only. E. Full bituminous coating and fully paved.
** OR **	
A. Perforated Underdrains: Bituminous Fiber: AASHO M177-_____, Type _____.	2.01.A Type (I) pipe has tapered joints both ends. Type (III) pipe has tapered male joint one end and tapered female joint one end.
** OR **	
A. Perforated Underdrains: Bituminous Fiber: ASTM D 2311-_____, Type _____ Joint.	2.01.A (TJ), (BJ). Type TJ pipe has molded tapered joints and tapered couplings; Type BJ pipe has square cut ends and split collar couplings.
** OR **	

02510-7

A. Perforated Underdrains: Laminated-wall Bituminous Fiber, ASTM _____, Type _____ joint.	2.01.A (D2417-_____), (D2418-_____), (TJ), (BJ). Joint types are same as described above.
** ** **	
B. Porous Underdrains: Concrete, AASHO M176-_____, _____ Class.	2.01.B (Standard Strength), (Extra Strength).
C. Cradle-invert Underdrains: Clay, AASHO M65-_____, Class _____.	2.01.C (Standard Strength), (Extra Strength).
** OR **	
C. Cradle-invert Underdrains: Galvanized Steel, AASHO M36-_____, Type III, Class IV.	
** OR **	
C. Cradle-invert Underdrains: Bituminous Coated Steel, FS WW-P-405_____.	
D. Drain Tile:	
1. Clay: AASHO M179-_____, Type _____.	2.01.D.1 Type I, Standard; Type II, Extra-Quality; Type III, Heavy-Duty.
** OR **	
1. Clay: ASTM C 4-_____, Class _____.	2.01.D.1 (Standard), (Extra Quality), (Heavy-Duty).
** ** **	
2. Concrete: AASHO M178-_____, Class _____.	2.01.D.2 (Standard), (Extra Quality), (Special Quality). ASTM C 412 is identical.
E. Run-off Pipe: Clay, AASHO M65-_____, Class _____.	2.01.E · (Discharge Pipe), (Standard), (Extra Strength).
** OR **	
E. Run-off Pipe: Clay, ASTM C 13-_____, Standard Strength.	
** OR **	
E. Run-off Pipe: Clay, ASTM C 200-_____, Extra Strength.	
** OR **	

02510-8

E. Run-off Pipe: Nonreinforced Concrete: AASHO M86-_____, _____.	2.01.E (Standard Strength), (Extra Strength). ASTM C 14 is identical.
** OR **	
E. Run-off Pipe: Reinforced Concrete: AASHO M170-_____, Class _____.	2.01.E Class I=D load 800 lbs. Class II=D load 1000 lbs. Class III=D load 1350 lbs. Class IV=D load 2000 lbs. Class V=D load 3000 lbs. ASTM C 76 is identical.
** OR **	
E. Run-off Pipe: Reinforced Concrete: AASHO M206-_____, Class _____.	2.01.E Class A-II=D load 1000 lbs. Class A-III=D load 1350 lbs. Class A-IV=D load 2000 lbs. ASTM C 506 is identical.
** OR **	
E. Run-off Pipe: Laminated-wall Bituminous Fiber: ASTM D 1862-_____.	
** OR **	
E. Run-off Pipe: Cast Iron: AASHO M64-_____, Class _____.	2.01.E (Standard), (Heavy), (Extra Heavy). ASTM A 142 is identical.
** ** **	
F. Clay Bell and Spigot Pipe Compression Joints: ASTM C 425-_____.	
** OR **	
F. Concrete Pipe Compression Joints: AASHO M198-_____.	2.01.F ASTM C 443 is identical.
** OR **	
F. Mortar Joints:	
1. Cement: AASHO M85-_____, type I.	2.01.F.1 ASTM C 150-71, type I is identical.
2. Mortar sand: AASHO M45-_____.	2.01.F.2 ASTM C 144 is identical.

02510-9

3.   Packing: Oakum: FS T-0-56_____.

. ** ** **

G.   Insect Cloth: Copper Wire Cloth
FS RR-W-360_____.

    1.   Mesh: 18 x 18.

    2.   Wire size: 0.02 in. diameter.

    ** OR **

G.   Copper Wire Screen: FS L-S-125_____.

    1.   Mesh: 18 x 18.

    2.   Wire size: 0.011 in. diameter.

    ** OR **

G.   Nonmetallic: FS L-S-125_____.

    1.   Mesh: 18 x 18.

    2.   Filament size: 0.012 in. diamater.

    ** ** **

H.   Clean Out Pipes and Fittings:
FS WW-P-401_____, Class XH.

I.   Fill Box: Galvanized steel with brass
caps, complete with gasket and wrench.

J.   Joint Covers: Paper: FS UU-B-790_____,
Type I, Grade D, Style 4.

    ** OR **

J.   Joint Covers: Duck: AASHO M166-_____.

    ** ** **

K.   Crushed Stone, Washed:

    1.   Graded: 3/4 to 3/16 in. (19 to 5 mm).   2.01.K (Porous bed for nonperforated pipe).

    2.   Graded: 3/4 to 1/2 in. (19 to 13 mm).   2.01.K.2 (Porous bed for perforated pipe).

    3.   Graded: AASHO M43-_____, size No. 2.   2.01.K.3 (Porous backfill).

02510-10

L.   Filter Mat: Clean, Dry straw.

PART 3 - EXECUTION

3.01 INSTALLATION:

A.   General:

1.   Verify that trench bottoms are dry when laying _____.

    3.01.A.1 (pipe), (tile).

2.   Lay drain pipe/tile to elevations and grades indicated.

3.   Thickness of stone bedding: Minimum 4 in. (100 mm), and not less than 1/4 of the pipe diameter.

4.   After bedding is placed, carefully tamp stone below haunches and around sides of pipe barrel.

5.   Place crushed stone backfill above tamped bedding to a height of 12 in. (300 mm) above maximum ground water level.

6.   Construct a filter mat on top of backfill using straw, compacted to 4 in. (100 mm).

7.   Place compacted earth backfill over filter mat to within _____ of finish grade elevation.

    3.01.A.7 Usually 3 to 4 in. (75 to 100 mm).

8.   Place compacted top soil over backfill to grade.

9.   Install cast iron soil pipe and fittings where they pass through walls.

10. Set invert of _____ for foundation wall drainage not lower than 4 in. (100 mm) below top of footing.

    3.01.A.10 (pipe), (tile).

** OR **

10. Lay footing drains to level grade on top of foundation footings around perimeter of foundation.

** ** **

02510-11

11. Where foundation footings change grade or elevation, step _____ down by means of vertical standpipe.

      3.01.A.11 (pipe), (tile).

12. Extend vertical standpipe to, or above grade, and cap with removable cap.

B. Clay Pipe In Pervious Trench:

1. Joint spacing not to exceed 1/4 in.

2. Cover pipe joints with _____ wired on with copper wire.

      3.01.B.2 (screening), (duck), (paper), (burlap).

3. Bed nonperforated _____ with crushed stone.

      3.01.B.3 (pipe), (tile).

4. Bed perforated _____ with crushed stone.

      3.01.B.4 (pipe), (tile).

5. Place pipe perforation downward.

      3.01.B.5 Perforations may be placed down or up. Normally placed down.

C. Clay Pipe In Impervious Trench:

1. Install nonperforated bell and spigot pipe.

2. Install in compliance with ASTM C 12-_____.

D. Perforated Bituminized Pipe in Pervious Trenches:

1. Connect pipes by means of couplings.

2. Place pipe with perforations down.

3. Bed with crushed stone.

E. Bituminized Fiber Drain and Sewer Pipe In Impervious Trench: Install in compliance with ASTM D 2316.

F. Cover rear opening of clay tile weepholes in retaining walls, with nonmetallic insect screening, wired on with copper wire.

* END OF SECTION *

02510-22

FS WW-P-401D, <u>Cast Iron Soil Pipe and Pipe Fittings.</u> This specification describes two classes of cast iron soil pipe. Class SV describes service weight soil pipe. Class XH describes extra heavy soil pipe.

FS WW-P-405A(1), <u>Corrugated Zinc Coated Iron or Steel Pipe.</u> This specification defines three classes, four shapes, and nine supplemental coatings available for corrugated zinc coated iron or steel pipe. The supplemental coatings are used to provide additional protection over that provided by the basic zinc coating.

INSPECTION

At time of delivery of material, verify that all items are specified and are free of visible indications of physical damage.

At Time of Installation:

Verify that trenches are dry.

Confirm that pipe beds are properly prepared and to grades and elevations required.

Verify that material showing interior bulges, damaged ends, or split or cracked pipe is not installed.

Observe that proper installation procedures are practiced and installed pipe and tile is free from blockage of flow.

Confirm that joints are properly assembled and pipe is in correct alignment.

Observe that bedding material is properly tamped into place without damaging pipe or placement.

Verify that porous backfill, filter mat, and earth backfill are properly placed and compacted as specified.

REFERENCES

<u>Clay Pipe Engineering Manual,</u> Pittsburgh, Pennsylvania: National Clay Pipe Institute.

<u>Civil Engineering Design Manual,</u> Washington, D. C.: Navdocks DM-5, Department of the Navy.

02510-23

Soil Mechanics, Foundations, and Earth Structures, Washington, D. C.: Navdocks DM-7, Department of the Navy.

Drainage of Asphalt Pavement Structures, (MS-15), College Park, Maryland: Asphalt Institute.

Blenderman, Louis, Design of Plumbing and Drainage Systems, New York, New York: Industrial Press.

Luthin, James, Drainage Engineering, New York, New York: John Wiley & Sons.

GLOSSARY

D-load - Test load expressed in pounds per linear foot per foot diameter to produce a 0.01 in. (0.25 mm) crack in reinforced concrete pipe.

Drainage - Facilities for collecting and removing water.

Filter - A material which readily permits the flow-through of water, but restricts the passage of soil particles.

Ground Water - Water below the surface of the ground, such water being free to move.

Hydraulic Head - The energy possessed by a quantity of water, due to its elevation above a base line, its velocity, and its pressure.

Intercepting Drainage - The system of subdrains used for the collection and removal of water flowing in pervious strata or springs.

Pervious Strata - A porous layer of thickness of earth or rock which readily permits passage or transmission of water.

Run-off Pipe - The discharge pipe utilized to carry collected water away from the drainage collection system.

Subdrain - Any construction below the surface of the ground used to collect and carry away water that is below the surface of the ground.

Subgrade Drainage - The method of collection and removal of ground water.

Specifying: Perlite Insulating
Concrete Roof Decks

CSI
SPECIFICATION
SERIES

03521
January 1973

Table of Contents

Page

THIS DOCUMENT 2

DRAWINGS AND SPECIFICATIONS 3

GUIDE SPECIFICATION 4

REFERENCE STANDARDS 9

INSPECTION 10

REFERENCES 10

GLOSSARY 11

This Document

This document covers specifications for cast-in-place lightweight insulating perlite concrete roof decks used over forming systems and on structural or precast concrete roof slabs. This document is limited to insulating concrete made with perlite aggregate listed under Group 1 of ASTM C 332 and with a density of 50 pcf or less. The forming systems are not included in this document.

Perlite insulating concrete roof deck systems should be vented. Perimeter or edge venting of the insulating concrete should be provided. This is accomplished by use of an open, metal gravel guard or facia, or vented cap flashing systems. A vented type insulation board can also be used in insulating concrete installations. Nailing the base sheet is the preferred method of attachment and should be used on perlite concrete applied over structural concrete. The materials and methods of venting are not included in this document.

This document has been prepared by the Perlite Institute, Inc. in cooperation with CSI.

Drawings and Specifications

Drawings:

The drawings must show thickness of perlite insulating concrete including specific details on slope to drain. Thickness indicated on the drawings should be selected to provide design "U" value. Minimum recommended thickness is 2 in. (51 mm).

Size, location, and width of control joints should be well defined. If all joints are typical, only one detail is necessary. However, any variation or special treatment should be clearly identified. Control joints should be installed through the thickness of the perlite concrete at the juncture of all roof projections and parapet walls. These joints should be 1 in. (25 mm) wide and should be increased to a width of 1½ in. (38 mm) at the perimeter of roofing areas over 100 ft. (30 m) in length. Control joints within the areas of insulating concrete should occur in the location of the joints in structural slabs. Decks of galvanized, corrugated metal forms and perlite insulating concrete, designed as a diaphragm, to resist horizontal forces, do not require control joints.

In roof systems where a reinforcing mesh is required, such as a form board system, or where mesh is needed to meet specific fire rating requirements, the size and type of mesh should be noted on the drawings.

Specifications:

The specifications should define the specific materials and physical properties of the various components of the roof deck system. Specifications should indicate the types of materials to be used and referenced to the appropriate standards. The physical properties of materials should also be specified.

Coordination:

The forming materials and systems or substrate materials used as the support for the perlite insulating concrete are not included in this specification but would require coordination with these requirements. Roofing requirements should also be coordinated with this section as to surface preparation conditions necessary for roofing installation.

Guide Specification

This Guide Specification is intended to be used as a basis for the development of an office master specification or in the preparation of specifications for a particular project. In either case, this Guide Specification must be edited to fit the conditions of use. Particular attention should be given to the deletion of inapplicable provisions. Include necessary items related to a particular project. Include appropriate requirements where blank spaces have been provided.

SECTION 03521

PERLITE INSULATING CONCRETE ROOF DECKS

PART 1 - GENERAL

1.01 RELATED WORK SPECIFIED ELSEWHERE:

    A. Cast-In-Place Concrete: Section 03300.

    B. Metal Decking: Section 05300.

    C. Flashing and Sheet Metal: Section 07600.

    D. Rigid Insulation: Section 07212.

    E. Membrane Roofing: Section 07500.

1.02 QUALITY ASSURANCE:

    A. Acceptable Manufacturers:

        1. Perlite aggregate produced by manufacturer regularly engaged in production of heat expanded aggregate.

        2. Perlite insulating concrete product of acceptable concrete supplier regularly engaged in production of lightweight insulating concrete.

    B. Applicator Qualifications:

        1. Insulating concrete placed by applicator certified by aggregate manufacturer.

        2. Experienced in special techniques required for placing perlite insulating concrete during freezing weather.

Notes to the Specifier

1.01.A Would include coordination of control joints and structural slabs.

1.01.C Would include vented metal gravel stops, facias, and flashing systems.

1.02.A.2 Include when mix is to be provided by qualified ready-mix plant.

1.02.B.2 Delete except for work to be performed in cold weather.

4/03521 January 1973

C. Methods of Test:

    1. Compressive strength of insulating concrete: ASTM C 495-_____.

    2. Oven dry density of perlite concrete: ASTM C 495.

    3. Wet density of perlite concrete: ASTM C 138-_____.

1.03 SUBMITTALS: Submit certified test reports stating that concrete physical properties meet specification requirements.

1.04 PRODUCT DELIVERY, STORAGE, AND HANDLING:

    A. Deliver materials in manufacturer's original undamaged packages or acceptable bulk handling equipment.

    B. Store packaged materials off ground in manner to protect them from elements, especially moisture damage.

    C. Remove cement showing indications of moisture damage, caking, or other signs of deterioration from project site and replace with undamaged material.

** OR **

1.04 PRODUCT DELIVERY:

    A. Deliver mixed perlite insulating concrete materials to project site in quantities permitting immediate placement.

    B. Do not rotate drums during transit.

    C. Upon arrival at site mix materials for approximately five minutes.

** ** **

1.04 Include this article if materials will be job-mixed.

1.04 Include if ready-mix materials are to be used.

235

1.05 WEATHER CONDITIONS:

    A. All concrete materials, reinforcement and forms with which perlite concrete may come in contact should be free of frost.

    B. No frozen material or materials containing ice should be used.

    C. When it is anticipated outside temperature will be below 40°F 24 hours after placing concrete, mixing water should be heated to maximum of 120°F.

    D. Extreme Dry Weather Curing: Sprinkle insulating concrete with water for three days to allow hydration of cement and to minimize shrinkage cracking.

> 1.05.D Under severe drying conditions take precautions for proper curing.

PART 2 - PRODUCTS

2.01 MATERIALS:

    A. Portland Cement: ASTM C 150-_____, Type ____ _____.

> 2.01.A (Type I); (Type III). Use of Type III is recommended during cold weather conditions.

    B. Perlite Aggregate: ASTM C 332-_____, Group 1.

              ** OR **

    B. Perlite Aggregate: Type _____, manufactured by _____.

> 2.01.B Use this paragraph only when proprietary brands are desired. Indicate type or trade name and manufacturer. Coordinate with paragraph 1.02.A.

              ** ** **

    C. Water: Clean and free from deleterious substances.

    D. Air Entraining Admixture: recommended by aggregate manufacturer.

> 2.01.D Do not use admixtures containing calcium chloride when insulating concrete is placed over galvanized metal or when galvanized metal is used within the deck structure.

    E. Control Joint Filler: Glass fiber, compressible to ½ original thickness under load of 25 psi (0.02 kgf/mm²).

> 2.01.E Delete paragraph when utilizing galvanized metal form units if roof is designed as diaphragm to resist horizontal forces.

    F. Welded Wire Fabric: ASTM A 185-_____, 4 x 8-12/14, galvanized.

> 2.01.F Include welded wire fabric for form board system, when structural concrete slope exceeds 30 degrees, or when required for fire or insurance ratings.

              ** OR **

F. Unwelded wire fabric, Type _____,

manufactured by _____.

2.02 CONCRETE PHYSICAL PROPERTIES:

A. Maximum Oven Dry Density: _____ pcf.

B. Minimum Compressive Strength: _____ psi.

C. Wet Density at Point of Placement: _____ pcf.

PART 3 - EXECUTION

3.01 INSPECTION:

A. Examine top surfaces of structural concrete scheduled to receive perlite insulating concrete to assure that it has not been treated or sealed.

B. Do not proceed until conditions are satisfactory.

3.02 PREPARATION:

A. Layout control joint locations before starting placement of materials.

B. Set screeds to assure insulating concrete is minimum of 2 in.

C. Cover drains before installing insulating concrete.

3.03 INSTALLATION:

A. Wire Fabric:

1. Install with minimum end lap of 6 in. (152 mm) with sides lapped minimum of 2 in., or tied.

2. Cut to fit at walls, curbs, and openings.

3. Do not run fabric through control joints.

B. Insulating Concrete:

1. During placement, exercise care to avoid segregation of materials and convey from

---

2.01.F Refer to CSI Manual of Practice "Proprietary Specifications," MP-3D.

2.02 Refer to Reference Standards for range of physical properties.

3.01.A Sealing prevents required movement of moisture from perlite insulating concrete through the structural deck.

mixer to place of final deposit by methods
that will produce specified physical properties at points of placement.

2. Do not vibrate.

3. Provide minimum 1 in. (25 mm) wide control
joint through thickness of insulating concrete at building expansion joints in structural roof deck, at roof projections, and
parapet walls.

3.03.B.3 Does not apply when roof deck is designed as diaphragm to resist horizontal forces. Delete condition not included.

4. Provide minimum 1½ in. (38 mm) wide control joint through thickness of insulating
concrete at roof projections, and parapet
walls.

3.03.B.4 Include when roof exceeds 100 ft. (30 m) in length. Delete condition not included.

5. Place insulating concrete to screed depth.

6. Do not tamp or vibrate concrete.

3.03.B.6 Vibrating or tamping will segregate aggregates from concrete mixture.

7. Screed or float to even surface.

C. Curing:

1. Air cure minimum of three days.

3.03.C.1 Insulating concrete mixture normally has adequate mixing water for curing without additional precautions or methods.

2. Protect concrete from damage due to impact,
overloading, or marring of surfaces during
curing period.

3.04 FIELD QUALITY CONTROL:

A. Perform wet density samplings conforming to
ASTM C 138-_____.

B. Adjust mixture and mixing procedures according
to field sampling information.

3.05 PROTECTION:

A. Do not proceed with roof application until perlite concrete has been cured minimum of three
days.

B. Do not allow traffic over insulating concrete
surface until thoroughly cured for minimum
period.

* END OF SECTION *

Reference Standards

The information provided below is intended only as an aid in understanding the reference standards contained in the Guide Specification part of this document. Guidance on the use of reference standards is contained in Chapter MP-3C, CSI Manual of Practice.

American Society for Testing and Materials (ASTM)

ASTM A 185-70, *Specifications for Welded Steel Wire Fabric for Concrete Reinforcement*, covers welded wire fabric cold drawn steel wires fabricated into sheets for the reinforcement of concrete. The finished material consists essentially of a series of longitudinal and transverse wires arranged at right angles to each other and welded together at all points of intersection.

ASTM C 136-71, *Test for Sieve or Screen Analysis of Fine and Coarse Aggregates*, covers determination of particle size distribution of fine and coarse aggregates by sieving or screening. The fine aggregates with at least 95% passing a No. 8 (2.3 mm) sieve shall weigh approximately 100 grams and with 90% passing a No. 4 (4.76 mm) sieve and more than 5% retained by No. 8 (2.38 mm) sieve shall weigh approximately 500 grams.

ASTM C 138-71, *Test for Unit Weight, Yield, and Air Content (Gravimetric) of Concrete*, covers procedures for determining unit weight of freshly mixed concrete and gives formula for calculating volume of concrete produced from a mixture of known quantities of component materials; volume of concrete per unit volume of cement; actual cement factor.

ASTM C 150-71, *Specification for Portland Cement*, describes physical requirements of five types of portland cement, their general uses, methods of packaging, marking, inspecting, and testing. Type I and Type III are recommended for use in insulating concrete. Type III is recommended for cold weather conditions.

ASTM C 332-66 (1971), *Specifications for Lightweight Aggregates for Insulating Concrete*, describes general types of lightweight aggregates. Group 1 as used in this document includes aggregates prepared by expanding products such as perlite or vermiculite. Grading requirements and unit weight requirements are included.

ASTM C 495-69, *Test for Compressive Strength of Lightweight Insulating Concrete*, describes preparation of specimens and determination of compressive strength of lightweight insulating concrete having an oven-dry weight not exceeding 50 lbs./cu. ft. (800 kg/m^3).

The Perlite Institute, Inc., 45 West 45th Street, New York, New York 10036. The Perlite Institute has established specification recommendations for specifying perlite lightweight insulating concrete. Current Catalog 30 includes technical data on the installation of perlite insulating concrete over galvanized steel form units, over form boards, and over structural or precast concrete roof slabs. The following table includes the typical physical properties of perlite insulating concrete which should be included in the specifications according to particular project requirements:

Dry Density Range pcf	Thermal Conductivity Range "K"	Compressive Strength Range psi	Minimum Compressive Strength psi	Wet Density When Placed pcf
33.5 to 40.0 (36)	0.72 to 0.85	350 to 500	300	50.5 ± 2.0
29.3 to 32.5 (30½)	0.62 to 0.69	230 to 340	230	45.5 ± 2.0
24.0 to 28.0 (27)	0.54 to 0.61	140 to 200	140	40.5 ± 2.0
20.0 to 24.0 (22)	0.47 to 0.54	80 to 125	80	36.5 ± 2.0

The materials per cu. yd. based on 100 percent yield are:

Oven Dry Density pcf	Cement Bags	Perlite cu. ft.	Water gallons	Air Entraining Agent pints
36	6.75	27	61	6¾
30½	5.40	27	59½	6¾
27	4.50	27	54	6¾
22	3.38	27	54	6¾

B

"MASTER"
SPECIFICATIONS

Appendix B contains material directly concerned with the production of a specification. Included are various forms of reference or "master" specifications as well as other lists or forms commonly applicable which may be used by the specifications writer (see contents below). The specifier must keep in mind that any "master" must be reviewed and revised to fit a new project. The "masters" included in this Appendix are some of the most used and available, and although incomplete here as space is limited, the sets provided represent the typical arrangement.

Specification Check List
Short Residential specification—Concrete Work
Authors' Master Specification (Commercial)—Cast-In-Place Concrete
Authors' Master Specification (Federal)—Cast-In-Place Concrete
COMSPEC Master section—Pacific International Computer Corporation
MASTERSPEC section—Production Systems for Architects & Engineers Inc.
Computerized Master Section—anonymous
Manufacturer's Association master guide specification—Woodwork Institute of
   California

JANUARY, 1971

PRELIMINARY
SPECIFICATION CHECK LIST

Project: Title and Number: _____

_____

Time due or to complete Contract Documents: _____

DIVISION NO. 1:

01100 Proposed Alternates: _____

_____

_____

01800 Allowances: _____

Special Conditions: _____

Time to Complete Project: _____

Liquidated Damages: $_____ per day

Federal Finance: _____   Agency: _____

DIVISION NO. 2 - SITE WORK:

02100 Clearing of Site: _____

02110 Demolition: Building(s) to be removed or demolished -

(__) Remove trees, (__) fences, (__) paving, (__) poles, (__) founda-

tions, etc. _____

Items to be saved or salvaged: _____

_____

SPECIFICATION CHECK LIST
Page 1 of 13

02200   Earthwork: (__) Clear site, (__) Compaction Control,
(__) Pilings, (__) Caissons. Special Conditions: _____

_____

02250   Soil Poisoning, Termite Control: _____

_____

02612   Bituminous Paving: (__) Asphalt Paving (_____) thickness
2 (____) inches. Rock Base Course 4 (____) inches, (__) Poured-in-
Place Concrete Curbs, (__) Redwood Curbs, (__) Painted lines, (__)Pre-
cast manufactured curbs, (__) Heavy Duty Paving, etc. _____

_____

02700   Site Improvements: _____

02710   Masonry Wall Fences: _____

02711   Chain Link Fencing: _____

02714   Wood Fencing: _____

02740   Irrigation System: _____

02743   Lawn Sprinkler System: _____

02800   Landscaping: (__)Lawn, (__) Trees, (__)Plants, etc. _____

Civil Engineering: _____

_____

DIVISION 3 - CONCRETE:

03100   Concrete Formwork: (__) Fiberglass Forms, (__) Metal Forms,
(__) Coffer Dome (__) Steel (__) Fiberglass (__) Fiber Round
Tube Forms   (__) Waffle-Slab Pans, (__) Architectural (H.D.)
Plywood Forms, (__) Redwood Walk Dividers _____

_____, etc., _____

_____

SPECIFICATION CHECK LIST
Page 2 of 13

243

03300 Cast-in-Place Concrete: Strengths _____ P.S.I.,
(__) Slumps _____ inches, (__) Colored Concrete Floors,
(__) Exposed Aggregate, (__) Non-Shrink Dry Pack Grout, (__) Floor
Hardener, (__) Concrete Pipe or Tile, (__) Water Barrier Membrane,
(__) Architectural Concrete, (__) Waterstops, (__) Concrete Tilt-Up
Panels, _____ finish.

Air-Entrained _____
Tests by (__) Allowance (__) Owner
Metal Formed Construction Joints (__) Exposed Joints (__)

03302 Lightweight Aggregate Concrete: (__) Perlite (__) Vermiculite
Compressive Strengths (__) 300-500 (__) 140-225 (__) 90-125

03400 Precast Architectural Concrete: (__) Exposed Colored Aggregate
Quartz, (__) Smooth Surface, Other Requirements: _____

_____

03420 Structural Prestressed Concrete: (__) Double Tees (__) Single
Tees, (__) Prestressed Slabs, (__) Joists; Other - _____

DIVISION 4 - MASONRY

04100 Mortar and Grout: Strength or type _____
(__) Colored Mortar, Interior Joints (__) Concave Rodded (__) Struck
Flush (__) Weathered (__) Raked (__) Sacked (__) Weeping, Exterior
Joints (__) Concave Rodded (__) Struck Flush (__) Weathered (__) Raked
(__) Sacked (__) Weeping

04210 Brick Masonry: Size _____, (__)Common Brick
(__) Faced Brick (__) Used Brick (__) Glazed Brick

04220 Concrete Masonry Units: (__) Gray Block (__) Slump Block
(__) Split Face Block (__) Colored Block

04400 Stone Work: Type _____, Laying Method _____

_____

04840 Fireclays: _____ Fire Brick
_____ Flue Liners _____

Reinforcing, Horizontal_____Spacing _____
Joint Requirements: _____
(Specify Joints Spacing:) 3/8 inches (_____ inches)
(__) Running Bond (__) Stacked Bond (__) Flemish - Other _____
Masonry Vermiculite Insulation _____

Decorative Screen Block _____

Rubber Control Joints _____

DIVISION 5 - METALS

05100 Structural Steel: ASTM (__) A-36 (__) A-440 - Other _____

05200 Steel Joists: SJI Type _____

05300 Metal Decking: Type _____ (__) Galvanized
(__) Black

05330 Composite Cellular Deck: _____

05500 Miscellaneous Metals: Handrailing (__)Steel (__) Aluminum
(__) Pipe Handrailing (__) Pedestrian Grating (__) Vehicular Grating

Wrought Iron and Ornamental Work _____

Metal Stair Tread Nosings _____

Fasteners, Hangers & Supports _____

_____

05505 Reinforcing Steel: ASTM A-615, (__) Grade 40, (__) Grade 60,
(__) Welded Wire Fabric

05700 Ornamental Metal: _____

Other - _____

DIVISION 6 - WOOD AND PLASTICS:

06100 Carpentry: (__) Post and Beams Rough Sawn (__) Plywood Rough Sawn

Beams Grade: _____ Finish S4S _____ Rough Sawn

Framing Horizontal: Grade _____

Framing Vertical: Grade _____

Columns: Grade _____

06175 Glued Laminated Wood: Finish - (__) Stained (__) Natural
(__) Painted (__) Rough Sawn (__) S4S, (__) Water-resistant Glue
(__) Waterproof Glue , Grade - (__) Industrial (__) Architectural
(__) Premium

06180 Heavy Wood Decking: Species _____, Finish -
(__) S4S (__) Rough Sawn - Other _____

Wood Fascia: Species _____, Grade _____

SPECIFICATION CHECK LIST
Page 4 of 13

Plywood (__) Subflooring (__) Underlayment _____

Plywood Sheathing _____

Medium Density Plywood _____

Specialty Plywood: (__) Texture 1-11 (__) Rough Sawn, Etc. _____
_____

Particle Board _____

Redwood _____

Hardboard _____

Treated Lumber: (__) Non-pressure Treated (__) Pressure Treated
(__) Fire Retardant

06400 Architectural Millwork - As based on "Architectural Woodwork
Institute" (AWI): (__) Paneling (__) Railings (__) Prefinished
Paneling (__) Plastic Laminated Faced Casework (__) Natural Hardwood
(__) Paint Grade Wood

Casework: AWI (__) Premium (__) Custom (__) Economy Grade. Casework
Construction Types: (__) Exposed Face Frame - Flush (__) Exposed
Face Frame - Lipped (__) Flush Overlay (__) Reveal Overlay

Plastic Laminated Types and Grades: _____

DIVISION 7 - THERMAL AND MOISTURE CONTROL

07100 Waterproofing and Dampproofing: (__) Membranes (__) Emulsions

Locations: _____

07170 Silicone Dampproofing: _____

07180 Cementious Dampproofing: _____

07200 Insulation, Fibrous: (__) Ceiling R-19 (__) Walls R-11
(__) Blown (__) Unfaced (__) Foil (__) Kraft Faced

07230 Roof Rigid Insulation: (__) Fiberglass (__) Perlite Board
(__) Urethane (__) Fiber Board, Thickness _____, R Value

_____, C Value _____, (__) Vapor Barrier

07310 Asphalt Shingles: Class (__) A (__) C, Weight _____,
(__) Roof Pitch _____, (__) Self Sealing, Color _____

SPECIFICATION CHECK LIST
Page 5 of 13

07330 Wood Cedar Shakes: Grade _____

07350 Clay Roofing Tiles: Type _____

07360 Concrete Roofing Tiles: _____

07500 Membrane Roofing: Neoprene _____

07510 Built-Up Bituminous Roofing: (__) Organic (__) Inorganic (__) Fiberglass (__) Coal-tar Pitch (__) Asbestos Felts (__) Asphalt Rag Felts (__) Mineral Cap-sheet (__) Gravel (__) Coated (__) Slag,

Roof Pitch _____

Bond(able)_____ years, Other - _____

07600 Sheet Metal Work: Metal Types - (__) Aluminum (__) Stainless Steel (__) Copper Clad Stainless Steel (__) Copper (__) Galvanized, Items - (__) Fascias (__) Downspouts (__) Gutters (__) Louvers

Manufactured Counterflashing _____

07800 Roof Accessories: _____

07810 Plastic Skylights: ( ) Double Glazed (__) Single Glazed; Other -
_____

07830 Roof Hatches: _____

07900 Calking and Sealants: (__) Polysulfide (__) Hypalon (__) Butyl (__) Silicone (__) Polyurethane, Special Treatment _____
_____

DIVISION 8 - DOORS, WINDOWS AND GLASS

08100 Metal Doors and Frames: (__) Fire Rated Doors (__) Hollow Metal Window Frames (__) Metal Frames

08200 Wood Doors: (__) Flush Doors (__) Panel Doors, (__) Paint Grade (__) Natural (__) Medium Density Overlay Faced (__) Plastic Laminated (__) Solid Core (__) Hollow Core (__) Carved Decorative - Pine or Mahogany (__)With Lites (__) Sound Retardant Doors; Wood Fire Rated Doors (__) 3/4F (__) 1F (__) 1-1/2F

08300 Special Doors: _____

08310 Sliding Metal Firedoors: _____

08325 Roll-Up Pass-Thru Windows: _____

SPECIFICATION CHECK LIST
Page 6 of 13

247

08326 Aluminum Pass-Thru Windows: (__) Glazed; _____

_____

08327 Metal Roll-Up Doors: (__) Hand (__) Chain (__) Power Operated, (__) Steel (__) Aluminum

08361 Overhead Doors: _____

08370 Aluminum Sliding Glass Doors: _____

08371 Metal Framed Sliding Glass Doors: _____

08500 Metal Windows: (__) Aluminum (__) Steel, Type _____

08520 Aluminum Projected Windows: _____

08525 Aluminum Sliding Windows: _____

08550 Solar Shade Screens: (__) Aluminum (__) Bronze; Finish _____

_____

08600 Wood and Plastic Cover Windows: _____

08700 Finish Hardware: Series _____ ,Finishes _____

Keying _____ , Allowance _____

08750 Door Operators: _____

08770 Weatherstripping: _____

08850 Glass and Glazing: (__) Plate (__) Double Strength Sheet Glass (__) Single Strength Sheet Glass (__)Bronze (__) Gray (__) Tempered (__) Mirrors (__) Obscure; Insulated Double Glass Type _____
Other Remarks: _____
Heat Reflective _____; (__) Acoustical (__) Acrylic Plastic; Glazing - (__) Glazing Tape (__) Sealants, Other _____

08855 Porcelain Enamel Panels: Type _____

08900 Curtainwall System: _____

08950 Storefront Systems: (__) Hard Anodic Color (__) Clear Anodic Color; Design Type _____; Hardware _____

_____

DIVISION 9 - FINISHES

09105 Lathing: (__) Metal Studs, (__) Suspended Ceilings, (__) Metal Lath (__) Gypsum Lath (__) Stucco Lath

09160 Plastering: Finishes - (__) Acoustical Plaster (__) Keene's Cement Plaster (__) Marblecrete; Fire Rated Plaster Systems - _____

_____; Ceramic Tile Backing Plaster - _____

_____; Portland Cement Plaster & Stucco - _____

_____

09250 Gypsum Drywall Wallboard: (__) Metal Framing (__) Wood Framing (__) Single Layer (__) Double Layer (__) Suspended Ceilings (__) Metal Studs (__) Texturers (__) Sound Boards _____; Thickness - (__) 1/2 (__) 5/8, Other - _____; (__) Unfinished backing board (__) Sound Insulation Batts (__) Fire-Retardant Type ____ _____; (__) Water-Resistant (__) Foil Backed Insulating (__) Sound Walls

09310 Ceramic Tile: Setting Beds - (__) Water-Resistant Organic Adhesive (__) Latex Portland Cement (__) Portland Cement Mortar (__) Dry-Set Portland Cement Mortar (__) Epoxy Grout and Mortar (__) Colored Grout.

Floor Tile: (a) Unglazed (__) Porcelain (__) Natural Clay (__) Mosaic Tile; (b) Unglazed Paver Tile; (c) Quarry Tile (__) Non-Slip (__) Colored (__) Shadowflashed

Wall Tile: Glazed Finish - (__) Matt (__) Bright (__) Crystalline Size - (__) 4-1/4 x 4-1/4 (__) 6 x 4-1/4 (__) 6 x 6 (__) 6 x 3 (__) 1 x 1,

Other: _____

Glazed Mosaic: Size and Type - _____

Decorative Glazed: Size and Type - _____

Unglazed Mosaic: _____

Glass Mosaic: _____

Porcelain Bath Accessories: _____

Expansion Joints: (__) Polysulfide Sealants (__) Silicone Sealants

SPECIFICATION CHECK LIST
Page 8 of 13

249

09400 Terrazzo (Gray or White NTMA Color Patterns): Types - (__) NTMA "Bonded to Concrete Terrazzo" (__) NTMA "Monolithic Terrazzo" (__) NTMA "Venetian Terrazzo" (__) Thermosetting Polyester Terrazzo (__) Oxychloride Cement Terrazzo; Divider Strips - (__) Brass (__) White alloy Zinc (__) Plastic

09460 Marble Panels: _____

09520 Acoustic Tile: (__) Cellulose Fiber (__) Mineral Cast Tile; Thickness - (__) 1/2 (__) 5/8 (__) 3/4 (__) Other - _____; Pattern - (__) Random Pin Perforated (__) Fissured (__) Other - _____

_____; (__) AIMA No. 1 Adhesive Mounting (__) AIMA No. 2 Nail or Staple Mounting (__) Other - _____

09530 Acoustical Suspended Ceiling Systems: (__) Mineral Fissured 24 x 48 x 5/8 inch Lay-In Panels (__) Other - _____

_____; AIMA No. 7 Mounting (__) Exposed Grid (__) Semi-exposed Grid (__) Concealed Grid (__) Fire-Rated System

_____

09550 Wood Flooring: (__) Parquet (__) Strip (__) Maple Gym. (__) Fir

09650 Resilient Flooring: Vinyl Asbestos Tile - Thickness (__) 1/16" (__) 3/32" (__) 1/8", Size - (__) 9" x 9" (__) 12" x 12"

Homogeneous Solid Vinyl Tile: _____

Rubber Base: (__) Coved (__) Straight Carpet Type (__) 2-1/2" (__) 4" (__) 6", (__) Stair Tread (__) Abrasive Type _____

09680 Carpeting: Nylon, Acrylic, Wool - Other - _____; Pad - Factory bonded to back (__) Sponge Rubber (__) High Density Foam (__) Vinyl (__) Durogan Rubber (__) Hair Pad - Other - _____; Adhesive - Release Reinstallation Type. Carpet Tack Strip Installation, Other - _____

09810 Cementious Acrylic Coating: Texture - On (__) Masonry (__) Plaster - _____

09811 Glazed Vitreous Finish: On (__) Masonry (__) Plaster (__) Gypsum Wallboard, _____

09900 Field Painting:

Special Finishes - _____

_____

Special Conditions: (__) Parking Lot Striping (__) Light Standards
in Parking Lots (__) Walls and Fences (__) Silicone Treating (__) Patina
Copper Treatment (__) Antique Finishes, Other - _____

_____

Color Systems: (__) Plochere (__) Federal Standard No. 595 (__) Pipe
Identification and Marking

Workmanship Standard: PDCA (__) Type I "Standard" (__) Type II "Premium"

Materials: (__) Vinyls (__) Stains (__) Clear Sealers (__) Alkyd
Enamels (__) Colored Concrete Floor Wax (__) Oil Rubbed (__) Varnish
(__) Epoxy (__) Polyurethane , And _____

_____

09950 Wallcovering: (__) Wallpaper (__) Vinyl Coated Fabrics (__) Burlap

DIVISION 10 - SPECIALTIES

10100 Chalkboards and Tackboards: (__) Hardboard Backed (__) Asbestos
Backed (__) Steel with Porcelain Finish; Other _____

10130 Chutes: _____

10170 Hospital or Office Cubicles: _____

10180 Toilet Room Compartments: Type - (__) Headrail-Overhead Braced
(__) Floor Braced (__) Ceiling-Hung Design Type; Finish - (__) Baked
Enamel (__) Porcelain (__) Plastic Laminated (__) Marble; Other - ____

_____

10180 Shower Compartments: _____

10240 Dock Facilities: (__) Bumpers (__) Dock Leveling Platforms

_____

10252 Fire Extinguishers and Cabinets: _____

10350 Flagpoles: (__) Steel (__) Aluminum; Type - _____

10400 Identifying Devices: (__) Directory and Bulletin Boards
(__) Signs (__) Plaques (__) Metal Letters

10500 Lockers: _____

SPECIFICATION CHECK LIST
Page 10 of 13

251

10545 Metal Access Doors: Types - ( ) For Acoustical Tile ( ) Plaster
( ) Masonry ( ) Gypsum Wallboard ( ) Fire Rated; _____

10600 Partitions: ( ) Coiling ( ) Demountable ( ) Folding ( ) Wire
Mesh Partitions ( ) Operable Walls

10670 Storage Shelving: ( ) Wood ( ) Metal

10800 Toilet, Bath & Custodial Accessories: ( ) Mirrors ( ) Soap Dispen-
sers ( ) Paper Towel Dispenser ( ) Waste Receptacle ( ) Toilet Tissue
Dispenser ( ) Seat Cover Dispenser ( ) Napkin Vendor ( ) Napkin Disposal
( ) Mirror-Purse-Book Shelves ( ) Ashtrays-Wall Urns ( ) Hand-Hair Dryer
( ) Grab Bars ( ) Safety Railing ( ) Anchors ( ) Shower Curtain Rod
( ) Soap Dish ( ) Medicine Cabinet ( ) Towel Bars ( ) Robe Hook ( ) Mop-
Broom Holder ( ) Vacuum Hose Holder ( ) Pail-Ladder Hook
DIVISION 11 - EQUIPMENT
11100 Bank Equipment: ( ) Depository Units ( ) Outdoor Tellers'
Units ( ) Safes ( ) Vanet Doors

11150 Commercial Equipment: _____

11180 Darkroom Equipment: _____

11200 Eccelsiastical Equipment: ( ) Baptismal Tanks ( ) Pews _____

11300 Education Equipment: _____

11400 Food Service Equipment: ( ) Bar Units ( ) Cooking Equipment
( ) Dishwashing Equipment ( ) Food Preparation Machines ( ) Food
Preparation Tables ( ) Food Serving Units ( ) Refrigerated Cases
( ) Sinks and Drainboards; ( ) Galvanized ( ) Stainless Steel

11495 Kitchenette Units: _____

11500 Athletic, Industrial, or Laboratory Equipment: _____

11650 Library Equipment: ( ) Bookshelving ( ) Bookstacks ( ) Charging Counters ( ) Carrels

11700 Medical Equipment: ( ) Incubators ( ) Mortuary Equipment

11830 Musical Equipment: _____

11850 Parking Equipment: _____

11970 Theatre or Stage Equipment: _____

DIVISION 12 - FURNISHINGS

12200 Blinds and Shades: _____

12300 Cabinets and Fixtures: (__) Classroom Cabinets (__) Dormitory
Units (__) Metal Casework (__) Educational Casework (__) Hospital
Casework (__) Industrial Casework (__) Laboratory Casework

12500 Drapery and Tracks: _____

12600 Furniture: _____

12670 Rugs and Mats: _____

12700 Seating: (__) Auditorium Seating (__) Classroom Seating

DIVISION 13 - SPECIAL CONSTRUCTION

13050 Access (Computer) Flooring: _____

13100 Audiometric Room: (__) Clean Room (__) Greenhouse (__) Hyperbaric
Room (__) Sound Isolation (__) Storage Vaults

13400 Incinerators: _____

13450 Walk-In Refrigerator and Freezer: _____

13500 Integrated Ceiling: _____

13650 Prefabricated Structures (Carports): _____

13661 Steel Prefabricated Buildings: _____

13700 Radiation Protection: _____

13720 Sauna Rooms: _____

13820 Tennis Courts: _____

13850 Swimming Pools: _____

DIVISION 14 - CONVEYING SYSTEMS

14100 Dumbwaiters: _____

14200 Elevators: (__) Passenger (__) Freight; _____

14400 Lifts: (__) Hydraulic (__) Dock Levelers; _____

14500 Material Handling Systems: (__) Conveyors; _____

14600 Moving Stairs and Walks: _____

14610 Escalators: _____

SPECIFICATION CHECK LIST
Page 12 of 13

14700 Pneumatic Tube Systems: _____

DIVISION 15 - MECHANICAL

15180 Insulation: (__) Pipe (__) Ductwork; _____

15200 Water Supply and Treatment: _____

15300 Waste Water Disposal and Treatment: _____

15400 Plumbing: _____

15550 Fire Protection: (__) Hose Cabinets (__) Chemical Fire Sprinklers; (__) Sprinklers - Dry or Wet System: _____

15600 Power or Heat Generation: _____

15650 Air Conditioning, Heating and Ventilating: _____

_____

15900 Controls and Instrumentation: _____

_____

DIVISION 16 - ELECTRICAL

16200 Power Generation: (__) Emergency (__) Temporary (__) Permanent

16400 Service and Distribution: _____

16500 Lighting: Types - _____

_____

16600 Special Systems: ( ) Lightning Protection; _____

16700 Communications: (__) Telephone (__) Television Antenna System
(__) Intercommunication (__) Alarm and Detection (__) Clock and Program

16900 Controls and Instrumentations: _____

_____

* * * * *

SPECIFICATION CHECK LIST
Page 13 of 13

SECTION 3A

CONCRETE WORK

Scope: General and Supplemental Conditions apply the
            same as though written herein in full. The work
            includes all forms; mixing, placing, finishing
            and curing of concrete; reinforcing as required;
            and stripping of forms.

Material: a. Forms may be made from plywood or dressed
                lumber at the option of the contractor.

            b. Concrete shall be transit-mixed, meeting the
                requirements of ASTM-C94, 2500 lb. strength,
                3/4" max. coarse aggregate.

            c. Reinforcing shall be sizes noted, intermediate
                grade deformed steel, conforming to ASTM A-315,
                free of grease or other surface film.

Installation: Forms shall be true to shape and size required and
            shall be strong enough and adequately braced to
            withstand the use to which they will be subjected.
            All exposed surfaces shall be smooth. Forms will
            not be required for footings or walls which may be
            cast against firm earth surfaces.

            Concrete reinforcing, including dowels for masonry
            work, shall be accurately shaped, properly placed
            and securely held in place. Concrete shall be
            placed in accordance with applicable ACI standards
            with no drop of mixed concrete more than four feet.
            Transit-mix trucks shall mix at least three minutes
            at the job site just prior to releasing batch of
            concrete. Test cylinders will not be required but
            each truck load or portion of a load shall have a
            batch ticket indicating proportions of all ingre-
            dients. Batch tickets shall be delivered to the
            Architect.

            Concrete shall be vibrated in all walls. Footings
            need not be vibrated but shall be thoroughly com-
            pacted and free of rock-pockets or similar defects.
            All reinforcing steel shall be enclosed with not
            less than 2" of concrete on all sides. Finished
            surfaces to be covered need have only a screed or
            wood-trowel finish. All concrete shall be kept
            damp continuously for a period of not less than
            three days after placing. Forms may be loosened
            after two days, removed after three days except as
            otherwise directed by the Architect for beams or
            similar construction.

Page 3A-1

REMINDER NOTES

SECTION 3A

CAST-IN-PLACE CONCRETE

1. Change the following work sheets to fit the requirements of the job by deleting paragraphs which do not apply, or in some cases by the addition of paragraphs or a limited amount of editing of the standard paragraphs.

2. Par. 03 - Related Work - Be sure that this work IS SPECIFIED ELSEWHERE. If formwork or reinforcement is to be included as a part of the CONCRETE work, copy appropriate paragraphs from the section used.

3. Par. 05 - Materials - In smaller jobs where aggregate is not to be specified for separation requirements, use only the first portion of 05-b. Delete 05-c if "lightweight" concrete is not included. Delete 05-d if no ADMIXTURE is used or allowed.

4. Par. 07 - Concrete Mix Designs - Note that there are two par. "c". Use the first if the Contractor is to arrange for and pay for mix design. Second designed for payment by the Owner and controlled by the Architect or Engineer.

5. Par. 10 - Finishing - Check these sections carefully to insure that the finish is the one YOU need.

6. Par. 12 - Curing - Delete the paragraphs which relate to walls or columns if your job has only concrete floor slabs.

7. Par. 13 and 14 - Special Weather Conditions - "Hot Weather" and "Cold Weather" mixing, placement, and finishing as well as general protection is not necessary UNLESS your job is in the desert during summer or in cold locations during winter. Desert MAY be a "cold" location at times during the winter.

8. Par. 15 - Structural Lightweight Concrete - Note that this is for STRUCTURAL lightweight concrete, NOT lightweight fill or lightweight cover for metal decking.

9. Par. 16 - Abrasive Finish - Select reflective Silicon Carbide Crystals (CARBORUNDUM or CARBOLON) OR aluminum oxide (ALOXITE or EXOLON). Aluminum oxide is light brown color, non-reflective, and slightly cheaper than silicon carbide.

CAST-IN-PLACE CONCRETE
Page   3A-0

SECTION 3A

CAST IN PLACE CONCRETE

01 GENERAL

The applicable provisions of the A.I.A. General Conditions, the Supplemental General Conditions, and the Special Requirements shall govern the work of this section the same as though written herein in full.

02 SCOPE

Furnish all material, labor, transportation and equipment and properly install all work specified herein, shown on the drawings, or reasonably implied to complete the construction. Included as a part of the work of this section, but not necessarily limited by it, are the following items:

a. Mixing, placing and curing of cast-in-place concrete.

b. Placement of inserts supplied by others.

c. Joint sealers and waterstops.

03 RELATED WORK

Not included as a part of the work of this section, but specified elsewhere, are the following items of related work:

a. Formwork, Section 3C.

b. Concrete reinforcement, Section 3E.

c. Pre-cast or pre-stressed concrete work Sections 3D and 3E.

d. Waterproofing except as noted above, Section 7F.

e. Excavation and backfill, Section 2C.

04 GENERAL
      REQUIREMENTS

a. The following conditions shall govern use and placement of forms, shoring, cast-in-place concrete, reinforcement where applicable, and related work shall be done in compliance with applicable sections of Uniform Building Code (Calif. Title 21) or other references sited.

CAST-IN-PLACE CONCRETE
Page   3A-1

b. <u>Joints</u> - All control joints or construction joints shall be made as detailed. The contractor shall submit a plan of proposed locations for pour joints and shall have prior approval of such plan by the Architect before installation of concrete. Construction joints in slabs, beams or girders shall be made at mid-point in general. Construction joints in walls and columns shall be at the underside at floor slabs, beams or girders; 2-5/8" above wall footings for walls; and at least 2" above footings for columns. Reinforcement shall be continuous through all control or construction joints.

c. <u>Slabs and beams</u> resting upon walls or columns shall not be poured until at least two (2) hours after pours of such walls or columns.

d. <u>Imposed Loads</u> - Beams and girders supporting walls above shall have adequate shoring to sustain such work in proper position until at least 28 days after the upper wall pour or until directed otherwise by the Architect.

05 MATERIALS

a. <u>Portland Cement</u> shall conform to A.S.T.M. Standard Specifications for Portland Cement C150, Type I or II. Cement shall be stored in moisture proof silos or sheds.

b. <u>Concrete Aggregates</u> shall conform to A.S.T.M. Standard Specifications for Concrete Aggregate C33. Limits for combined grading of fine and coarse aggregates to be as follows:

Percentage of Weight

Sieve number or size in inches	1-1/2 inch maximum	1-inch maximum	3/4 inch maximum
Passing a 2 inch	----	----	----
Passing a 1-1/2 inch	95-100	----	----
Passing a 1 inch	75-90	80-100	----
Passing a 3/4 inch	55-77	70-90	90-100
Passing a 3/8 inch	40-55	45-65	60-80
Passing a No. 4	30-40	31-47	40-60

<u>CAST-IN-PLACE CONCRETE</u>
Page   3A-2

Passing a No. 8	22-35	23-40	30-45
Passing a No. 16	16-30	17-35	20-35
Passing a No. 30	10-20	10-23	13-23
Passing a No. 50	2-8	2-10	2-15
Passing a No. 100	0-3	0-3	0-5

c. Lightweight Concrete Aggregate: (for floor fill) shall conform to A.S.T.M. C-330 and shall be natural or expanded shale weighing approximately 110 lb./cu. ft. and satisfactory to the Architect. (For roof fill) Expanded vermiculate weighing approximately 30 lb. per cu. ft.

d. Admixture shall be a lignosulfonic base type conforming to A.S.T.M. C-494. Admixture shall increase the workability of the concrete and reduce the water demand of the concrete. Admixture shall be used only if required or permitted.

e. Curing membrane shall be non-staining paper (Orange label Sisalkraft or equal) or polyethylene film (Visqueen or equal). Sprayed parafine or asphalt base liquids will NOT BE ALLOWED for use in areas where resilient flooring is to be installed but may be used in other areas upon approval of the Architect.

f. Concrete Hardener. Sika Hardener, Aquabar or Hornstone, 2 impregnations, applied as per manufacturer's published directions.

g. Concrete Sealer. Sika No. 2, Cem-Seal or Horntraz applied as per manufacturer's published directions.

h. Bonding Agent. Weld-Crete as manufactured by Larsen Products Corp.

i. Air Entraining Agent shall meet requirements of A.S.T.M. C-260 and shall have the prior approval of the Architect.

j. Water shall be fit to drink, free of sulphur, alkali or other detrimental materials.

06 TESTS AND INSPECTION

For testing requirements see Section 1F - Testing and Inspections.

CAST-IN-PLACE CONCRETE
Page   3A-3

07   CONCRETE MIX DESIGNS

a. Mix designs shall be made in accordance with the procedure given in the Appendix to "Recommended Practice
for Selecting Proportions of Concrete", A.C.I. 613.
The mixes selected to be used for the work shall be
determined by using the water-cement ratio shown by
the trial mixes to produce a strength 15% greater than
that specified. Each combination of strength and
workability required to be used for different portions
of the work shall be evaluated separately.

b. Mix designs shall be established by a registered
testing laboratory, satisfactory to the Architect,
and operating under the direction of a registered
Civil Engineer.

c. Contractor shall arrange for design of trial mixes
and shall pay all costs entailed for design and
testing of trial mixes. Contractor shall submit test
data, test results, and mix designs to the Architect
for verification of compliance with the specified
procedure.

(c) Costs of mix designs shall be paid for by the Owner,
except that costs for additional designs required by
change of material, change of Source of material, or
failure of material to meet specifications shall be
paid for by the Contractor.

d. If transit-mix concrete is used, the transit mix
company's designs will be accepted providing:

1. They meet the specifications.

2. Past performance data is available on each mix.

3. They are guaranteed by the Contractor.

4. A copy of each design mix is furnished to the
Architect.

e. If transit-mix company design mix is used, the
minimum concrete and maximum water content shall be
4-1/2 - (94#) sacks of cement minimum and 8 gal. of
water maximum per cubic yard.

f. Concrete mixes shall be designed to meet the requirements shown on the drawings for the various classes
of concrete.

CAST-IN-PLACE CONCRETE
Page   3A-4

<u>08   TRANSIT MIXED</u>
<u>CONCRETE</u>

Obtain approval of equipment, etc., before use, and meet
requirements of A.S.T.M. Designation C-94. The Ready-Mix
Plant Operator must guarantee not over 60 minutes interval
between trucks during any pouring operation. In event of
violation of this requirement during a pour, the Architect
or his representative may direct concrete to be ordered
immediately from other sources at Contractor's expense.
Plant must furnish job Inspector with Weigh Master Certificate for each batch delivered stating exact amount of
each ingredient therein.

<u>09   CONVEYING AND</u>
<u>PLACING</u>

a. <u>Preparation</u> - Before placing of any concrete, all
forms shall be thoroughly cleaned, washed out with
water, and made tight by wetting. Before reinforcing
steel is placed on top of and/or adjacent to forms
which have been oiled, the surface oil shall be wiped
off so that none may be tracked over, or in any other
way come in contact with the reinforcing steel or the
tie wire.

b. <u>Incrustations</u> - All incrustations shall be removed
from forms and reinforcing steel at construction
joints. Concrete which has been previously placed
shall be prepared for following placing by one of the
following methods:

1. Concrete which has been placed longer than 3-1/2
hours but less than 6-1/2 hours may be prepared by
removing all laitance from concrete and thoroughly
washing surfaces of concrete and forms with water.
Concrete which has taken its initial set may be
prepared by wire brushing and thoroughly washing
surfaces of concrete and forms.

2. Concrete which has been placed longer than 6-1/2
hours shall be prepared by sand blasting to
roughen surface. Clean thoroughly with water.

c. Transit-mix trucks shall be clean and capable of
thorough mixing of material. Not more than 3/4 of
total water shall be added to batch at the plant.
Additional water shall be added at job-site under
direction of the Inspector. Material shall be job-
mixed for approximately three minutes prior to placing.
Concrete in transit for more than 90 minutes or 300
revolutions of mixing drum shall not be accepted for
this work.

<u>CAST-IN-PLACE CONCRETE</u>
Page   3A-5

d. <u>Conveying</u> - Concrete shall be conveyed from the mixer to the place of final deposit by chuting, hoppers, tremmies, or other conveyances that will prevent segregation of materials. Concrete from its point of release at mixer shall not be permitted to drop more than four feet. When conveying has once started, it shall be carried on as a continuous operation until the placing of a panel or section is completed.

e. <u>Placing</u> - No structural concrete shall be placed without the continuous presence of the Inspector. Placing of concrete shall be done with a workable, non-segregating mixture, tamped and vibrated in such a manner as to produce a dense, smooth job, free from rock pockets and voids. Contractor shall at all times have sufficient manpower available to properly accomplish same. Concrete shall be deposited in the forms as nearly as practicable in its final position to avoid flowing. It shall be so deposited as to maintain, until the completion of the unit, approximately horizontal plastic surfaces. In columns, walls or thin sections of considerable height, openings in forms, elephant trunks, tremmies or other approved devices shall be used that will permit the concrete to be placed in a manner which will prevent segregation and accumulations of hardened concrete on forms or metal reinforcement above the level of the concrete. Such devices shall be so installed that the concrete will be dropped vertically, with a free fall of four feet maximum. When concrete placing is once started, it shall be carried on as a continuous operation until the section is completed between predetermined construction joints. Horizontal joints shall be properly prepared before new material is added. Before new concrete is added on top of a horizontal wall joint, thoroughly hose clean and soak with water. A heavy grout composed of the regular concrete less 1/2 the large aggregate shall be deposited on the joint surface in a layer approximately 2" deep.

f. <u>Compacting and Screeding</u> - After placing concrete flatwork, the concrete shall be compacted throughout its depth by tamping or rolling. The surface shall then be screeded to the true finish grades or elevations. All concrete in walls, footings, columns, beams, etc., shall be compacted using mechanical vibrators approved by the Architect. Care shall be exercised that concrete is not over-vibrated to separation of ingredients. Form-mounted vibrators will not be allowed.

g. Stoppage - The Architect or his representative shall approve when and where any pouring shall stop or start. The flow surfaces to the fresh poured concrete shall be level wherever any pour is stopped and tight dams shall be built as necessary. See details on drawings for construction joints.

10 FINISHING

a. Floating - Soon after screeding and while the concrete is still plastic the surface of all flatwork shall be floated with wood floats or a power float. The surface shall be tested and variations shall not exceed 1/8 inch under a ten-foot straight edge.

b. Troweling (smooth finished areas)

1. Floating shall be followed by steel troweling either by machine or hand. Before starting this operation, the floating finish shall stand until surface water sheen has disappeared. In no case shall cement, cement and sand, or water be applied to the surface to facilitate troweling.

2. Both power and hand troweling shall be required as soon as little or no cement paste clings to the blades. Troweling shall be continued until the surface is dense, smooth, and free from all minor blemishes.

3. Final hand troweling shall be required to remove slight imperfections left by troweling machines and to bring the surface to a dense, smooth, polished finish. Final hand troweling shall be continued until a ringing sound is heard as the trowel passes over the surface.

c. Special Finishes. The following general schedule shall be used as a guide for the surface finishing of all concrete work.

1. Screed and float - no troweling required:
   Surfaces covered with ceramic tile, terazzo asphaltic concrete or similar material.

2. Screed, float and trowel smooth:
   Exposed concrete surfaces for no other surfacing.
   Roof surfaces.
   Surfaces to receive resilient flooring.

3. Screed, float and lightly broom:
   Walks, steps, concrete exposed in garage floors.

CAST-IN-PLACE CONCRETE
Page   3A-7

    4. Patch and sack:
         Walls, columns, and similar surface not
         covered with other materials.

11 PATCHING CONCRETE

a. Any concrete which is not formed as shown on the plans,
or for any reason is out of alignment or level, or
shows a defective surface shall be considered as not
conforming with the intent of these specifications and
shall be removed from the job by the Contractor at his
expense unless the Architect grants permission to patch
the defective area, which shall be done in accordance
with the following procedure. Permission to patch any
such area shall not be considered a waiver of the
Architect's right to require complete removal of the
defective work if the patching does not, in his
opinion, satisfactorily restore the quality and
appearance of the surface.

b. Immediately after removing forms, all tie holes shall
be patched, and all concrete surfaces shall be inspected and any poor joints, voids, stone pockets or
other defective areas (if permitted by the Architect to
be patched) shall be patched. Where necessary, defective areas shall be chipped away to a depth of not less
than 1 inch with the edges perpendicular to the surface.
The area to be patched and a space at least 6 inches
wide entirely surrounding it shall be wetted to prevent
absorption of water from the patching mortar. A grout
of equal parts Portland Cement and sand, with sufficient water to produce a brushing consistency, shall
then be well brushed into the surface, followed immediately by the patching mortar. The patch shall be
made of the same material and of approximately the
same proportions as used for the concrete except that
the coarse aggregate shall be omitted. The mortar
shall not be richer than one part cement to 2-1/2
parts sand. The amount of mixing water shall be as
little as consistent with the requirements of handling
and placing. The mortar shall be retempered without
the addition of water by allowing it to stand for a
period during which time it will be mixed with a trowel
to prevent setting; this period shall be directed by
the Architect to suit the various conditions.

c. The mortar shall be thoroughly compacted into place
and screeded off so as to leave the patch slightly
higher than the surrounding surface. It shall then be
left undisturbed for a period of one to two hours to
permit initial shrinkage before being finally finished.
The patch shall be finished in such a manner as to

match the adjoining surface. On exposed surface where unlined forms have been used, the final finish shall be obtained by striking off the surface with a straight-edge spanning the patch and held parallel to the direction of form marks.

d. Surfaces of concrete exposed to view shall receive a finish known to the concrete trade as "Grinding and Sacking," unless otherwise directed. Parts to be plastered over and concrete cast against Fibreglas forms or plastic-coated wood forms do not require the "sacking" treatment. "Sacking" shall be accomplished as follows:

First: Patch all defects as specified above;

Second: Any projections of concrete caused by improper joining of forms shall be toned down with a carborundum stone;

Third: Wet the surface of the concrete sufficiently to prevent absorption of water from the grout and apply the grout with brushes or a spray gun uniformly, completely filling air bubbles and holes. Immediately after applying the grout, float the surface with a cork or other suitable float, scouring the wall vigorously. While the grout is still plastic, the surface shall be finished with a sponge rubber float removing all excess grout. This finishing shall be done at the time when grout will not be pulled from holes or depressions. Next allow surface to dry thoroughly, then rub it vigorously with dry burlap to completely remove any dried grout. There shall be no visible film or grout remaining after this rubbing. The entire cleaning operation for any area must be completed the day it is started. No grout shall be left on the wall over night.

12 CURING

a. General. Maintain all forms containing concrete in a thoroughly wet condition until forms are removed. Maintain all concrete in a moist condition for not less than 7 days after placing; maintain floor slabs on grade in moist condition for 14 days, except as provided for elsewhere in these specifications. Freshly placed concrete shall be protected from injurious action by the sun, rain, flames, water, wind, temperature, and mechanical injury and shall not be permitted

CAST-IN-PLACE CONCRETE
Page   3A-9

to dry out from the time the concrete is placed until the expiration of the minimum curing period specified.

b. <u>Floors</u>. As soon as practicable after the floor slabs have been finished, curing shall be started. All concrete shall be maintained in a continuously moist condition not less than 7 days after placing. Floor slabs shall be covered with reinforced building paper for curing and to protect the floor during construction. After curing paper has been removed, floors shall be allowed to air dry for at least 48 hours prior to allowing traffic on the floor. Surfaces shall be protected during curing period from all forms of abrasion.

c. Surfaces not to be covered with resilient flooring may be protected with a sprayed coat of approved curing compound. Such compound shall be non-staining and of a type which will disintegrate gradually during the life of the job. All portions of such curing film remaining at the end of the job shall be removed by the Contractor before acceptance of the work.

d. <u>Walls, columns</u> and similar surfaces shall be kept <u>continuously moist</u> with a fog spray of water for not less than two days before forms are stripped and for an additional five days including Saturdays, Sundays and holidays. The surfaces shall be sprayed at least three times per day.

13 "HOT WEATHER"
<u>CONCRETE WORK</u>

a. Design mix, mixing procedures, placing, finishing and curing of concrete when the concrete temperature is more than 90 degrees F. shall be deemed "hot weather" concrete work, and shall require additional and special procedures for such work.

b. Mix design, proportioning of mix, and actual mixing shall require a design containing more water as well as maintaining the desirable water-cement ratio in order to reduce the temperature of the concrete both in mixing and in place after discharge from the mixer. This additional requirement shall be included as a part of the mix design by the laboratory and shall be presented to the Architect for approval prior to actual mixing.

c. Special efforts shall be made to provide placement of concrete under "hot weather" conditions in the cooler parts of the day or at night in order to reduce the

effects of the sun and wind. Mixers, pipe lines,
chutes and similar equipment shall be insulated,
painted white, water sprayed, or covered as much as
possible. Earth surfaces, forms, reinforcing steel
and similar parts shall be sprayed with water at least
one day before pours are scheduled and at intervals
until actual placement is in process in order to
reduce surface temperatures. No standing water shall
be allowed on surfaces which will receive concrete.

d. Placement of concrete shall be well planned in advance
and enough workmen shall be employed to place the
concrete quickly. Prolonged mixing shall be avoided.
If transit-mixed concrete is used it shall be discharged from the mixer truck in not more than 45
minutes after all ingredients are added and shall be
mixed at not more than 250 RPM.

e. Finishing of concrete shall be done as rapidly as
possible and shall be protected with temporary sun-
shades and wind brakes as necessary. Plastic shrinkage cracks in fresh concrete shall be troweled over
and every effort made to consolidate them into the
concrete surface. Finishing shall not be started
before the water sheen has disappeared or before the
concrete can support the weight of a man.

f. Curing of concrete shall be especially important under
"hot weather" conditions and shall require special
care. Wood forms shall be kept moist at all times
until removal. Exposed concrete surfaces shall have
curing started as soon as possible after finishing and
shall be continuously fog-sprayed with clean water for
at least three days after finishing, after which time
the concrete shall be protected with curing paper or
plastic sheets until removal is directed by the
Architect. Upon the prior approval of the Architect,
moist curing may be stopped at the end of 24 hours
after finishing and a curing compound providing a
white or aluminum reflective surface may be installed
and made watertight.

g. Admixtures may be used to delay setting time of the
concrete or to lessen the amount of mixing water
required, but such measures shall be used only upon
the written approval of the Architect and shall in no
way interfere with the compressive strength requirements for the concrete. Admixtures shall meet all
requirements of A.S.T.M. for such use and shall be
tested with trial mixes of the actual aggregate,
cement and admixture proposed.

CAST-IN-PLACE CONCRETE
Page   3A-11

14 "COLD WEATHER"
CONCRETE WORK

a. Design mix, mixing procedures, placing, finishing
and curing of concrete when the concrete temperature
is lower than 55 degrees F. or when the temperature of
the air is lower than 40 degrees F. shall be deemed
"cold weather" concrete work and shall require additional and special procedures for such work.

b. Concrete aggregates shall be warmed, water shall be
warmed, and all equipment shall be kept as near concrete temperature as possible. Water-cement ratio
shall be carefully adjusted to prevent excessive
cooling or possible freezing. In excessively low
temperature conditions all areas to receive concrete
shall be protected with enclosures and the temperature
maintained above the allowed minimum with space
heaters, salamanders or similar equipment.

c. After concrete is placed and compacted the finishing
shall be done as quickly as possible and the concrete
retained at a temperature of not less than 65 degrees
F. for at least three days, after which time the
temperature may be reduced at the rate of not more
than one degree per hour for the first 24 hours.
Salts, admixtures with chemicals detrimental to the
required strength for the concrete, or foreign matter
of any kind shall not be used in concrete to prevent
freezing.

d. Curing shall be provided by waterproof paper, plastic
sheets or similar methods. If layers of sand, hay or
other material is to be used it shall be free of
moisture and shall have the prior approval of the
Architect before it is used. Freezing of concrete
shall be prevented in any case, and any concrete
frozen before completely cured shall be removed and
replaced at no additional cost to the job.

15 STRUCTURAL LIGHT-
WEIGHT CONCRETE

a. "Structural" lightweight concrete is defined as
concrete which has a 28 day compressive strength as
shown and an air-dry weight of less than 115 lb. per
cubic foot. Requirements for "structural" lightweight
concrete shall meet the requirements of A.S.T.M. C-330
and aggregate shall be expanded shale, clay or similar
approved material. Design mix for "structural" lightweight concrete shall be submitted to the Architect
for approval prior to any mixing or placing.

CAST-IN-PLACE CONCRETE
Page   3A-12

b. Mixing, placing and curing of "structural" lightweight
concrete shall follow the general procedures for
regular weight concrete insofar as possible. Concrete
slump shall not exceed 4 inches and vibration shall
not exceed 7000 RPM.

c. Job placed stationary mixers shall be charged with
approximately two-thirds of the total water requirement, and all of the predampened aggregate. This
batch shall be mixed for 30 seconds, after which time
the cement admixture and withheld portions of the
water shall be added and the mixing continued for at
least 1 minute plus 15 seconds for each additional
yard capacity beyond one yard.

d. Transit mixed materials shall not generally be mixed
on the way to the job site. At the job site two-
thirds of the water and all of the aggregate shall be
mixed for approximately 30 seconds or until the initial
water demand is satisfied, then cement and withheld
water shall be added and the batch mixed for 60 or 70
drum revolutions. After such mixing the drum shall be
revolved at high speed for a minimum of five revolutions before the batch is discharged.

16 ABRASIVE FINISH

While the concrete is still soft and un-set, lightly trowel
in a uniform covering of abrasive crystals over the exposed
surfaces to have abrasive finish. Crystals shall be 14/36
size, reflective silicon carbide (aluminum oxide) as manufactured by the Carborundum Co. (CARBORUNDUM or ALOXITE);
The Exolon Co. (CARBOLON or EXOLON) or approved equal, and
shall be distributed in the amount of approximately 25
pounds per 100 sq. ft. of surface.

FEDERAL SPECIFICATION

REMINDER NOTES

CAST-IN-PLACE CONCRETE

SECTION 3A

1. Change the text of the following work sheets to
    fit the requirements of the job by deleting
    paragraphs or lines which do not apply, or in
    some special cases by the addition of paragraphs
    or a limited amount of editing of the standard
    paragraphs.

2. Par. 3A-.1 - Scope - Notice that this section does
    NOT include reinforcing steel or concrete formwork.
    These are specified in other sections of Division 3.

3. Par. 3A-.2.3 - Other Specifications - If air-
    entrained concrete or lightweight concrete are NOT
    included be sure to delete the references in this
    section that pertain to these items.

4. Par. 3A-.4 - Materials - Select only the items of
    materials which will be used for this job. Delete
    all others.

5. Par. 3A-.7 - Concrete Construction - Delete
    paragraphs which specify items NOT on this job
    such as "splash blocks", etc.

6. Par. 3A-.10 - Concrete Finishes - Fill in the
    appropriate areas that require finishes as noted.
    Be sure to READ Specification 13Yg to determine
    exactly what the various finishes are to be.

DIVISION 3

SECTION 3A - CAST-IN-PLACE CONCRETE

3A-.1 Scope - The work includes proportioning, mixing, placing and finishing of all cast-in-place concrete.

3A-.2 Applicable Documents: The following specifications and standards of the issue listed in this section (including the amendments, addenda, and errata designated) but referred to hereinafter by basic designation only, form a part of this specification to the extent required by the references thereto. (See paragraph entitled "Specifications and Standards", in Section 1B, Division 1 for additional information.)

3A-.2.1 Federal Specifications:

SS-A-281b(1)	Aggregate, for portland cement concrete.
SS-C-192g	Cement, portland.
SS-S-158a	Sealing compound, cold application, for joints in concrete.
SS-S-171	Sealer, mineral-filled asphalt, for joints in concrete.

3A-.2.2 Bureau of Yards and Docks Specifications:

13Yg	April 1963 Concrete construction.

3A-.2.3 Other Specifications:

American Society for Testing and Materials

ASTM C-31-62T	Making and curing Concrete Compression and Flexure Test Specimens in the Field.
ASTM C-260-63T	Air-entraining Admixtures for Concrete.
ASTM C-309-58	Liquid Membrane-forming Compounds for Curing Concrete.
ASTM C-330-64T	Lightweight Aggregates for Structural Concrete.

Spec. No.   Page 3A-1

3A-.3 General Requirements: The work in this section includes all proportioning, mixing, placing, compacting, finishing and curing of all cast-in-place concrete, and shall be in accordance with Specification 13Yg unless specified otherwise herein.

3A-.3.1 Concrete formwork is specified in another section of Division 3 in this specification. Reinforcing steel supply, fabrication and installation is specified in another section of Division 3 of this specification.

3A-.3.2 Pre-cast and pre-stressed concrete are specified in another section of Division 3 of this specification.

3A-.4 Materials: Materials shall be new, of quality and sizes specified or shown on the drawings, stored in separate bins or piles and kept free of dampness.

3A-.4.1 Cement shall be domestic brand conforming to Fed. Spec. SS-C-192g, type I or II. Where air-entraining is used cement may be type IA or IIA.

3A-.4.2 Aggregate shall conform to the requirements of Fed. Spec. SS-A-281b(1) and paragraphs .2.3 and 2.4 of Specification 13Yg.

3A-.4.3 Aggregate for lightweight concrete shall conform to requirements of ASTM C-330 and as noted on the structural drawings.

3A-.4.4 Air-entraining admixtures shall be in accordance with Specification 13Yg, paragraph 2.7.2.

3A-.4.5 Admixtures for control of water-cement ratio, acceleration of concrete setting, retarders, or other use shall be commercial products manufactured for the use intended and approved by the Officer-in-Charge before their use.

3A-.4.6 Mixing water shall be free of alkali, oil, acid, or other organic or vegetable matter and fit to drink.

3A-.4.7 Reinforcement of concrete shall be as specified under another section of Division 3.

3A-.4.8 Elastomer waterstops shall be shapes and sizes shown on the drawings and conforming to the requirements of Specification 13Yg paragraph 2.9.2.

3A-.4.9   Curing compounds or sheet polyethylene films shall be in accordance with Specification 13Yg, paragraphs 2.10.3, 2.10.4, 2.10.6 and/or 2.10.7. Reference to Fed. Spec. UU-P-264 is deleted.

3A-.4.10   Expansion joint material shall be nominal 1/2" thick, width of the concrete where used, asphalt saturated fibreboard made for this use, commercial quality.

3A-.4.11   Joint-sealer shall be polysulphide compound for exterior use, two-part type job-mixed in accordance with the manufacturers recommendations, non-sagging, gray color unless noted otherwise.

3A-.5   <u>Proportioning and Mixing Concrete</u>: Proportioning of concrete shall be in accordance with Modification No. 1 to Specification 13Yg. Delete references to Table I, Normal Concrete, and Table II, Air-Entrained Concrete under paragraph 3.1 of 13Yg.

3A-.5.1   References to Fed. Spec. SS-R-406 regarding testing of concrete for compression or other testing shall be deleted.

3A-.6   <u>Preparations for Placing Concrete</u>: Forms for concrete shall be inspected for proper shape, bracing and other details. All waterstops, dams, inserts, anchors and similar work shall be in place and securely fastened. Earth beneath slabs shall be level and compacted as necessary.

3A-.6.1   <u>Vapor barrier</u> of .004" polyethylene film shall be provided beneath the entire concrete floor slab of the building over the compacted fill that is specified under another section. The material shall be placed in the greatest widths and lengths practicable so as to eliminate joints wherever possible; where joints are necessary, the material shall be lapped not less than 6 inches for the side and end laps and sealed with approved adhesive. Torn, punctured, or damaged vapor barrier material shall be removed and replaced as directed, prior to the placing of concrete. Concrete shall be placed in a manner to preclude damage to the vapor barrier material.

3A-.7   <u>Concrete Construction</u>: Concrete shall be conveyed, placed, and compacted in accordance with Specification 13Yg. Finishes of various surfaces shall be as specified hereinafter.

Spec. No.   Page 3A-3

3A-.7.1 <u>Pits and trenches</u> shall have the bottom slabs and walls keyed and bonded together properly and in an approved manner. Where practicable, the bottom slabs and walls shall be placed integrally. Slabs forming covers for pits and trenches shall have openings formed to suit the installation of equipment and apparatus.

3A-.7.2 <u>Concrete lintels, copings, and sills</u> shall be either cast-in-place or precast concrete. All exposed surfaces shall be smooth and true, with sharp edges. If precast concrete is used, it shall be damp-cured for not less than seven days and allowed to dry out before being moved. Steel reinforcement of two no. _ _ rods or of zinc-coated welded wire fabric of equivalent cross-sectional area shall be provided in copings and sills. If precast concrete is used, suitable provision shall be made for anchoring the sections to the walls and each section shall be set in a full bed of portland cement mortar. If cast-in-place concrete is used for copings, expansion joints 1/2 inch wide shall be provided near the corners of the building and at intermediate intervals not to exceed 50 feet apart. All vertical joints shall be grouted solidly except for a 3/4-inch depth at front, back, and top surfaces; the front and back shall be tuck-pointed, and the top surface shall be filled with a non-staining and non-shrinking calking compound. Copings and sills shall be provided with seats, washes, lugs, and drips, where indicated and/or necessary to provide proper drainage.

3A-.7.3 <u>Splash blocks</u> shall be provided at outlets of downspouts emptying at grade; they shall be of precast concrete, 24 inches long, 12 inches wide, and 6 inches thick, with counter-sunk dishes finished smooth and sloped to drain away from the building. The earth shall be compacted to provide firm bases for the blocks.

3A-.7.4 <u>Setting miscellaneous material</u>: Anchors and bolts including those for machine and equipment bases, frames or edgings, hangers and inserts, door bucks, pipe supports, pipe sleeves, pipes passing through walls, metal ties, conduits, flashing reglets, drains, and all other materials in connection with concrete construction shall, where practicable, be placed and secured in position when the concrete is placed. Anchor bolts for machines shall be set to templates, shall be plumbed carefully and checked for location and elevation with an instrument, and shall be held in position rigidly to prevent displacement while concrete is being placed.

Spec. No.   Page 3A-4

3A-.7.5 <u>Inserts</u> may be provided in lieu of the dovetail anchor slots. The wood core shall be nailed to the forms at the time the concrete is placed and removed when the forms are stripped, exposing wire to which brick ties or anchors will be fastened.

3A-.7.6 <u>Roof slab top surfaces, fill, cants, and crickets</u> shall be finished to smooth straight surfaces suitable for the proper application of the materials to be installed thereon.

3A-.8 <u>Concrete sidewalks</u> shall be Class D-1 concrete, not less than 3-5/8 inches in thickness. Concrete sidewalks shall have contraction joints every __ linear feet, cut within two to three hours after the concrete is placed to a depth of 3/4 inch with a jointing tool. Transverse expansion joints shall be installed at all returns, driveways, and opposite expansion joints in curbs. Where curbs are not adjacent, transverse expansion joints shall be installed at intervals of approximately __ feet. Expansion joints shall be made with preformed joint material. Edges of the sidewalks and joints shall be edged with a tool having a radius not greater than 1/8 inch. Sidewalks adjacent to curbs shall have a slope of 1/4 inch per foot toward the curb. Sidewalks not adjacent to curbs shall have a transverse slope of 1/4 inch per foot or shall be crowned as directed with transverse slope of 1/4 inch per foot. The surface of the concrete shall show no variation in cross section in excess of 1/4 inch in 5 feet.

3A-.9 <u>Concrete curbs and/or curb-and-gutter</u> shall be constructed as indicated using Class D-1 concrete in accordance with Specification 13Yg. At the option of the contractor, the curbs and curb-and-gutter may be precast or cast in place. If cast in place, contraction joints similar to those specified for concrete sidewalks shall be provided at intervals of from 8 to 10 feet. If precast, the curbs and curb-and-gutter shall be precast in lengths of from 4 to 5 feet. The curbs and/or curbs-and-gutter shall be given a steel trowel finish.

3A-.10 <u>Concrete Finishes:</u> Concrete work shall be finished as specified hereinafter. Work not specifically itemized shall be finished in a manner most closely associated with similar surfaces or as directed by the Officer-in-Charge.

3A-.10.1 <u>Grout finish</u> shall be provided for _ _ _
— —.

3A-.10.2 <u>Rubbed finish</u> shall be provided for _ _
_ _.

3A-.10.3 <u>Float finish</u> shall be provided for _ _ _
_ _ _ _ _ _ _ _ _ _ _ _ _ _ _ _ _ _ _ _.

3A-.10.4 <u>Sealer-hardener finish</u> (dust-inhibitor
treatment) shall be provided for _ _ _ _ _ _ _ _ _
_ _ _ _.

3A-.10.5 <u>Vacuum finish</u> shall be provided for _ _
_ _ _ _ _ _ _ _ _ _ _ _ _ _ _ _ _.

3A-.10.6 <u>Dusted-on finish</u> shall be provided for
_ _ _ _ _ _ _ _ _ _ _ _ _ _ _ _ _ _.

3A-.10.7 <u>Standard topping finish</u> shall be
provided for _ _ _ _ _ _ _ _ _ _ _ _ _ _ _ _ _.

3A-.10.8 <u>Emery aggregate finish</u> shall be provided
for _ _ _ _ _ _ _ _ _ _ _ _ _ _ _ _.

3A-.10.9 <u>Non-slip finish</u> shall be provided for
_ _ _ _ _ _ _ _ _ _ _ _ _ _ _ _ _ _.

SPECIFIER'S NOTES

SECTION 05200

STEEL JOISTS

INSTRUCTIONS FOR USING THESE NOTES:

Some of the items covered in the Draft Copy (accompanying these notes) may not apply to your project. The Specifier should check each paragraph carefully and modify the specification as required. Fill in appropriate blank spaces to meet the needs of the project; add or delete portions of the specification as necessary. Correlate the specification with the contract drawings.

Where you make changes in the text of the Draft Copy to meet the requirements of the project, please circle the line numbers on the margin alongside these modifications to direct attention to them at the computer service center.

Strike out the portions of specification that do not apply.

Material to be added should be typed or legibly hand-printed in the space provided in the wide margin to the right of the line numbers on the Draft Copy.

Specifier's notes are keyed to the text of the complete master section of the specifications as a guide to assist in making modifications. If the project specifications require data on products, methods or systems not covered in the Draft Copy or herein, obtain this information from a qualified technical consultant. The computer service center will provide a print-out of the section incorporating the modifications made on the Draft Copy. Please retain these notes for future reference as needed. Updated notes will be sent to you for each draft copy ordered.

1. Paragraph 1.01-A, add the items required and/or delete the items not required for the project.

2. Paragraph 1.01-B, add related items specified and/or delete the items not specified in other sections.

3. Paragraph 1.01-C, if "Not In Contract" (NIC) items are indicated on the drawings and/or mentioned in the specifications, such NIC items should be listed in the paragraph; otherwise the paragraph should be deleted.

4. Paragraph 1.02, modify or delete as desired to meet project requirements.

BSN05200-1

277

5. Paragraph 1.03, note exception to Uniform Building Code.
    Where a city building code or other local code takes
    precedence over the Uniform Building Code, then such
    a code and proper reference paragraph sould be inserted
    in place of the Uniform Building Code. Other codes and
    Standards specified are usually considered applicable
    for most projects and should normally be left in the
    specifications. This determination must be made by the
    Specifier and modificaitons completed accordingly.

6. Paragraph 1.04, modify or delete as desired to meet
    project requirements.

7. Paragraph 1.05, modify as desired to meet project
    requirements.

8. Paragraph 1.06, modify as desired or delete to meet
    project requirements.

9. Paragraph 1.07, list appropriate section, and alternatives
    that apply to the project requirements.

10. Paragraph 2.01, modify or delete as desired to meet
     project requirements.

11. Paragraph 2.02, modify or delete as desired to meet
     project requirements.

12. Paragraph 2.03, modify or delete as desired to meet
     project requirements.

13. Paragraph 2.04, modify as desired to meet project
     requirements.

14. Paragraph 2.05, modify or delete as required. Fill in
     blank spaces where indicated.

15. Paragraph 3.01, modify or delete as desired to meet
     project requirements.

16. Paragraph 3.02, modify or delete as desired to meet
     project requirements.

17. Paragraph 3.03, modify or delete as desired to meet
     project requirements.

18. Paragraph 3.04, add applicable work schedule if required
     or desired; otherwise delete the heading.

19. Paragraph 3.05, add applicable work schedule if required
     or desired; otherwise delete the heading.

20. Paragraph 3.06, add acceptance requirements if applicable
     or desired; otherwise delete the heading.

BSN05200-2

SPECIAL NOTES:

OPEN WEB STEEL JOISTS - SPAN RANGES AND BASIC DATA BY TYPES
DESIGNATED BY THE STEEL JOIST INSTITUTE AND THE AMERICAN
INSTITUTE OF STEEL CONSTRUCTION.

General Information:

1. Open web (shortspan) steel joists: J & H series

2. Intermediate span steel joists: BJ & BH series

3. Longspan steel joists: LJ & LH series

4. Deep longspan steel joists: BLJ & BLH series

Design Information and Load Tables:

Consult catalogs and literature provided by manufacturers listed
as members of the Steel Joist Institute. Where intermediate
span steel joists can be used on a project, they are frequently
more economical than either shortspan or longspan joists. All
accessories, outriggers, and extended top chords available with
J and H series joists are usually available with the BJ and
BH series from most manufacturers. Most manufacturers provide
a protective coating for joists prior to shipping. Paints
conform in performance to requirements established by the Steel
Structure Painting Council (Specification 15-67T). Paint systems
vary according to the manufacturer but usually include black
asphalt, red oxide, and gray metal primer.

Type	Series	Design Stress (psi)	Span (feet)	Depth (inches)
Open Web (Shortspan)	J	22,000	16 to 48	8 to 24
	H	30,000	16 to 48	8 to 24
Intermediate Span	BJ	22,000	24 to 60	24 to 30
	BH	30,000	24 to 60	24 to 30
Longspan	LJ	22,000	25 to 96	18 to 48
	LH	30,000	25 to 96	18 to 48
Deep Longspan	BLJ	22,000	89 to 120	52 to 60
	BLH	30,000	89 to 120	52 to 60

Camber: The camber provided for joists will vary according
to the manufacturer, consult the literature and tables provided.
A representative table is provided as an example (Bethlehem's
BJ and BH series of intermediate span joists):

BSN05200-3

279

Top Chord Length ft-in.	Approximate Camber in.
30-0	3/8
40-0	5/8
50-0	1-1/8
60-0	1-1/2

MANUFACTURERS OF OPEN WEB STEEL JOISTS BY TYPES AND GEOGRAPHIC LOCATION OF MAIN OFFICE:

Members of the Steel Joist Institute, Dupont Circle Building, Washington, D.C. 20036 as listed January 1969. Contact the manufacturer for technical data concerning products, plant or warehouse locations availability. (*Denotes manufacturers with plants or outlets in most areas of the U.S.)

Area:	Manufacturer:	J	H	LJ	LH
Eastern:	*Bethlehem Steel Corp.; Bethlehem, Pa.	X	X	X	X
	Guille Steel Products Co., Inc.; Norfolk, Va.	X	X	X	X
	J. W. Hancock, Jr., Inc.,; Roanoke, Va.	X	X		
	Northern Virginia Steel Corp.; Springfield, Va.	X	X		
	*Republic Steel Corp., Mfg. Div.; Youngstown, Pa.	X	X		X
	Structures, Inc.; Johnstown, Pa.	X	X		X
	Todd Steel Division of Std. Int. Corp.; Frederick, Md.				X
	Trebor-Filk; Croydon, Pa.				X
	Raychord Corporation; Apollo, Pa.		(Not Listed)		
Southern:	American Longspans; Columbia, S. C.			X	X
	Central Texas Iron Works, Inc.; Waco, Texas	X			
	Costal Steel Construction Co., Inc.; St. Petersburg, Fla.	X			
	Congaree Iron & Steel; Columbia, S. C.	X	X	X	X
	Florida Steel Corporation; Tampa, Florida	X	X		
	Joists, Ind.; Houston, Texas		X		X
	Nuclear Corp. of America; Charlotte, N. C.	X	X	X	X
	Owen Joist Corporation; Cayce, S. C.	X	X	X	X
	Owen Joist Corp. of Florida; Jacksonville, Florida			X	X
	Robberson Steel Company;				

BSN05200-4

280

```
              Oklahoma City, Okla.              X  X        X
              Socar, Inc.; Florence, S. C.                  X
              Tucker Steel Div. of U.S.
              Industries Inc.;
              Knoxville, Tenn.                  X  X
              Valley Steel, Inc.;
              Fort Payne, Alabama               X  X

Mid-West: *Armco Steel Corporation;
              Kansas City, Mo.                  X  X  X  X
          *The Ceco Corporation;
              Bethlehem, Pa.                    X  X  X  X
           Delongs, Inc.;
              Jefferson City, Mo.                     X  X
           Laclede Steel; St. Louis, Mo.        X  X
           Macomber, Inc.; Canton, Ohio         X

West:      Colorado Builders Supply Co.;
              Denver, Colorado                  X  X
         **Inland-Ryderson Const. Products
           Co.; Milwaukee, Wis., and
           San Francisco, Calif.                   X        X
```

  **Not a member of the Steel Joist Institute. Produces steel
    joists conforming to requirements of the American Institute
    of Steel Construciton and Steel Joist Institute.

Note: Several manufacturers operate plants in a number of
areas. The listing shown above denotes the firm's headquarters.
For complete information, contact the manufacturer to obtain
data regarding the types of steel joists marketed, the service
area covered and availability of products.

BSN05200-5

SECTION 05200   7

STEEL JOISTS   9

The General Conditions, any Supplementary General Conditions   13
and Division 1, General Requirements are hereby made a part   14
of this section as fully as if repeated herein.   16

1   GENERAL   18

   1.01   SCOPE   20

      A   Work Included: Perform all work necessary and   23
        required for the construction of the project as   24
        indicated. Such work includes but is not limited 25
        to the following:

        1.   Furnishing and installing of all open-web and   28
           longspan steel joists.

        2.   Furnishing and installing of all specially   30
           fabricated steel joists.   31

        3.   Furnishing and installing of steel fasteners   34
           and bolts.

        4.   Welding of steel.   36

        5.   Bases, bearing plates, and anchors.   38

        6.   Grouting.   40

        7.   Shop paint primers.   42

      B   Related Work in Other Sections: The following items   45
        of associated work are included in other sections   46
        of these specifications:

        1.   Structural steel work; shapes, bars, tubing,   49
           connectors, and plates.   50

        2.   Reinforcing steel for concrete.   52

        3.   Reinforcing steel for masonry.   54

        4.   Steel decking.   56

        5.   Light gauge steel structural framing.   58

        6.   Anchors, bolts, fastenings, and other   61
           miscellaneous metal items.

        7.   Finish painting of metal.   63

BM05200-1

<u>8</u>. Steel bar gratings, casting, and forgings.   65

<u>9</u>. Loose lintels.   67

<u>10</u>. Steel crane rails, elevator guide rails, and   70
structural supports.

<u>C</u> By Others: The following items of work will be   72
performed by others and are not included in the   73
contract:

     <u>1</u>.   75

     <u>2</u>.   77
                               (

<u>1.02</u> SUBMITTALS   80

<u>A</u> Shop Drawings and Catalog Cuts: Submit fully   83
detailed shop drawings of all open-web and longspan   85
steel joists, along with a complete schedule of   86)
all steel joists, to the Architect/Engineer for
approval. Shop drawings shall include all shop   87
and erection details, including catalog cuts, copes,   88
connections, holes, and welds. All welds, both   89
shop and field, shall be indicated by standard
welding symbols in accordance with the "Standard   90
Code for Arc and Gas Welding in Building   91
Construction" of the American Welding Society.
Drawings will show the size, length, and type of   92
each weld. Contractor shall be responsible for   93
all errors of fabrication and for correct fitting   94
of structural members shown on shop drawings.

<u>B</u> Submittals shall be made in accordance with Section   96
01200, "Shop Drawings and Submittals", which   97
describes the number and manner of submittals.   98

<u>C</u> Contractor shall furnish for information three (3)   101
copies of a detailed erection procedure, including
a sequence of erection and temporary staying and   102
bracing. This procedure will not be returned.   103

<u>D</u> No joists shall be fabricated or delivered to the   106
job site until the shop drawings, catalog cuts,   107
and erection procedure have been approved and   108
returned to the Contractor.

<u>E</u> Mill Reports and Certification: Contractor shall   111
furnish three (3) copies of all mill reports covering   112
the chemical and physical properties of the steel   113
used. Contractor shall also furnish three (3)   114
copies of manufacturer's certification that materials   115
and fabrication conform to the requirements of this
specification.

BM05200-2

1.03 CODES AND STANDARDS   118

    A Except as modified by the requirements specified   121
       herein and/or the details on the Drawings, all work   123
       included in this section shall conform to the   124)
       applicable provisions of the following codes and
       standards:

       1. International Conference of Building Officials   127
           (ICBO): "Uniform Building Code", Volume I,   128
           Chapter 27, "Steel and Iron".

       2. American Institute of Steel Construction (AISC): 131

           a. "Manual of Steel Construction".   133

           b. "Specifications for the Design, Fabrication 136
              and Erection of Structural Steel for   137
              Buildings".

       3. Steel Joist Institute (SJI):   139

           a. "Standard Specifications for Open-Web Steel   142
              Joists, H-Series". Also "J-Series" if   143
              applicable.

           b. "Standard Specifications for Intermediate   146
              Span Steel Joists, BJ and BH-Series".   147

           c. "Standard Specifications for Longspan Steel   149
              Joists, LJ, LH-Series".   150

           d. "Standard Specifications for Deep Longspan   152
              Steel Joists, BLJ and BLH-Series".   153

       4. American Welding Society (AWS): "Code for Arc   156
           and Gas Welding in Building Construction", AWS   157
           Standard Code D1.0.

       5. American Society for Testing and Materials   160
           (ASTM): The specifications and standards   161
           hereinafter referred to, latest editions.

       6. Steel Structure Painting Council (SSPC);   164
           Specification 15.   165

    B Codes and Standards of local regulatory agencies   167
       having jurisdiction, latest edition.   168
                                                (

1.04 WORKMANSHIP AND QUALIFICATIONS   171

    A Design of members and connections for any portion   174
       of the structures not indicated on the contract   176
       drawings shall be completed by the fabricator and   )
       indicated on the shop drawings. All steel joists   178

                            BM05200-3

exposed within any one enclosed space shall have 178
architecturally similar components, panel point 179
spacing, and overall depth.

B Substitutions of sections or modifications of 182
details, or both, and the reasons therefor shall
be submitted with the shop drawings for approval. 183
Approved substitutions, modifications, and necessary 184
changes in related portions of the work shall be 185
coordinated by the Contractor and shall be 186
accomplished at no additional cost to the Owner. 187

C Responsibility for Errors: Contractor shall be 190
responsible for all errors of detailing, fabrication,
and for the correct fitting of the structural 191
members. Coordinate all connection details to 192
concrete. Report any discrepancies to the 193
Architect/Engineer immediately.

D Welding and qualification of welders shall conform 196
to the applicable requirements of Section 05100, 197
"Structural Metal", and the Drawings.

E Load tests shall be conducted in accordance with 200
the paragraph, "Inspection and Tests", as hereinafter 201
specified.

F Coordination: Coordinate the work of this section 204
with work specified under other sections so that 205
all related work shall accurately and properly join.

G Field Measurements and Templates: Contractor shall 208
obtain all field measurements required for proper 209
and adequate fabrication and installation of the
work covered by this section. Exact measurements 210
are the Contractor's responsibility. Furnish 211
templates for exact location of items to be embedded
in concrete and any setting instructions required 212
for all installation work.

H Qualification of Manufacturer: To be considered 215
for approval by the Architect/Engineer, a 216
manufacturer's products shall have been checked
by the Steel Joist Institute and found to conform 217
to the Institute's Standard Specifications and Load
Tables for types of joists that are required for 218
project.

1.05 STORAGE AND HANDLING OF MATERIALS. Steel joists shall 221
be stored above the ground upon platforms, pallets, 222
skids, or other supports. Material shall be kept free 223
from dirt, grease, and other foreign matter, and shall
be protected from corrosion. 224

BM05200-4

1.06   INSPECTION AND TESTS   227

       A   Inspection and Tests: Materials are subject to   230
           inspection and tests in the mill, shop, and field, 232
           and will be conducted by a qualified person or   233
           Testing Laboratory paid for by the Owner. Such   234
           inspection and tests, however, shall not relieve
           the Contractor of responsibility for furnishing   235
           satisfactory materials. The right is reserved to   236
           reject any material at any time before final
           acceptance, if the Architect/Engineer finds material 237
           and/or workmanship that do not conform to   238
           specification requirements. The   239
           Architect's/Engineer's acceptance of any materials
           shall not prevent its rejection later if defects   240
           are discovered. Contractor shall remove and replace 241
           any installed materials which are rejected by the   242
           Architect/Engineer at no additional cost to the
           Owner, and to the satisfaction of the   243
           Architect/Engineer. Standards for tests will be   244
           as set forth in the applicable ASTM specifications
           and SJI specifications.   245

       B   Load tests of steel joists will be required and   248
           shall be performed in accordance with applicable   249
           SJI specifications. Load tests will be paid for   250
           by the Owner and then deducted from the contract   251
           price.

       C   Costs of Tests: Costs of materials tests will be   254
           paid for by the Owner, except that when additional 255
           tests are required due to failure of material, the 256
           costs of such additional tests will be at the expense 257
           of the Contractor and will be deducted from the
           contract price. Costs of load tests will be paid   259
           for by the Owner as hereinbefore specified and then 260
           deducted from the contract price.

       D   Mill Reports and Certification: Contractor shall   263
           furnish three (3) copies of all mill reports, and   264
           manufacturer's certification of materials and
           fabrication conformance to the requirements of this 265
           specification as stipulated in the paragraph, "Mill 266
           Reports and Certification", hereinbefore specified.

   1.07   ALTERNATES. See "Alternatives", Section _____ for   270
          requirements that affect work specified herein.

2 PRODUCTS   273

   2.01   MATERIALS   275

       A   Steel for steel joists shall conform to ASTM A36,   278
           with minimum design stress of 22,000 psi and 30,000 279
           psi as hereinafter specified.   280

                                          BM05200-5

286

B   Steel joists shall conform to the Steel Joists   283
    Institute's Standard Specifications hereinbefore   284
    referenced under the paragraph, "Codes and
    Standards", of the types as shown and noted on the   285
    Drawings, and shall conform to the following   286
    requirements:

    1. J-Series joists. Cold-formed or hot-rolled   289
        open-web steel joists with minimum allowable   290
        design stress of 22,000 psi.   291

    2. H-Series joists. Cold-formed or hot-rolled   294
        open-web steel joists with minimum allowable   295
        design stress of 30,000 psi.   296

    3. BJ-Series joists. Intermediate span steel   299
        joists with minimum allowable design stress   300
        of 22,000 psi.

    4. BH-Series joists. Intermediate span steel   303
        joists with minimum allowable design stress   304
        of 30,000 psi.

    5. LJ-Series joists. Longspan steel joists with   307
        minimum allowable design stress of 22,000 psi.   308

    6. LH-Series joists. Longspan steel joists with   311
        minimum allowable design stress of 30,000 psi.   312

    7. BLJ-Series joists. Deep longspan steel joists   315
        with minimum allowable design stress of 22,000   316
        psi.

    8. BLH-Series joists. Deep longspan steel joists   319
        with minimum allowable design stress of 30,000   320
        psi.

    9. Specially fabricated joists. Steel joists   323
        fabricated as shown on the Drawings with minimum   324
        allowable design stress of _____ psi.

C   Anchors, bolts, and fastenings shall conform to   327
    ASTM A307 and ASTM A563.

D   Grout: Master Builders' "Embeco" pre-mixed grout,   331
    Conrad Sovig's "Metal-Mix Grout", or an approved
    equal, or approved Portland cement and aluminum   332
    powder pre-mixed grout.

E   Electrodes: All arc-welding electrodes shall conform   335
    to ASTM A233 for Steel Arc Welding Electrodes, and   336
    shall be coated rods of size and classification
    number as recommended by their manufacturers for   337
    the positions and other conditions of actual use.

                              BM05200-6

F   Shop paint primers shall be a Red Lead Primer   340
conforming to Federal Specification TT-P-86, type   341
II, or a rust-inhibitive metal primer formulated
of red lead, metallic oxide, black asphalt, gray   342
pigmented, or other suitable type to receive the   343
specified type of paint for field coats, if any.
All shop primers used shall conform in performance   344
to Steel Structure Painting Council Specification
15.

                                               (

2.02   FABRICATION   347

A   Shop Fabrication and Assembly: Steel joists shall   350
be fabricated and assembled in the shop to the   351
greatest extent possible. Shearing, flame cutting,   353)
and chipping shall be done carefully and accurately.

B   Connections shall be welded as indicated.   355
Connections not indicated shall be made to conform   357
with the SJI "Standard Specifications" hereinbefore
referenced under "Codes and Standards". One-sided   359
or other types of eccentric connections will not
be permitted unless shown in detail and approved   360
on the shop drawings.

C   Welding shall conform to the applicable requirements 363
of Section 05100 "Structural Metal", and the
drawings.

D   Bolting: Bolt holes shall be punched or drilled   366
1/16 inch oversize. Torch burning of bolt holes   367
will not be permitted.

)

E   Gas Cutting: 370

  1.   A gas cutting torch may be used to make   373
unimportant shear cuts provided that stress   375
will not be transmitted into the metal through
the burned surface. Cuts shall be true to line   376
with a maximum deviation of 1/16 inch. Burned   377
edge shall be finished by grinding whenever
the above deviation is exceeded or where it   378
is exposed to view when in the judgment of the
Architect/Engineer the burned edge will be   379
unsightly.

  2.   The metal adjacent to a burned surface for a   382
distance equal to the thickness of the material
shall not be considered a part of the net section   383
for tension members.

  3.   Burning shall be done only by mechanics skilled   386
in this work and after the Architect/Engineer   387
has been notified where cuts are to be made.

BM05200-7

F Finished surfaces of all exposed members shall be   390
  smooth and free of any markings, burrs, or other   391
  defects.

G Extended Ends: Provide extended ends for top chords   394
  of joists where indicated or noted on the Drawings.   395
  Extension members shall be designed as cantilever   396
  beams with their reactions carried back at least   397
  to the first point of the joist.

H Ceiling Extensions: Where Drawings show contact   400
  ceilings occur directly below underslung type joists,   401
  ceiling extensions shall be provided, or the lower
  chord member extended.   402

2.03 ANCHOR BOLTS AND BEARING PLATES. Furnish all anchors   405
     and bearing plates in ample time so that no delay will   406
     be caused to other work. Contractor shall assume full   407
     responsibility for correct placement of embedded items. 408

2.04 EQUIPMENT. Contractor shall furnish all material and   411
     equipment necessary for the erection of the specified   412
     work and shall remove same from the premises when the   413
     work is completed.
                                                               (
2.05 SOURCE QUALITY CONTROL   416

     A Testing Agency will perform the following _____.   419
)
        1. Inspection of the source of base material (the   423
            steel plant).

        2. Determine chemical composition of all steel.   425

        3. Determine physical and mechanical properties   428
            in accordance with ASTM A370, of the following   429
            materials:

            a. Steel joists.   431

            b. Steel fasteners, bolts, bases, bearing plates, 434
               and anchors.

            c. Filler materials for welding.   436

        4. Qualifications of shop _____ procedure and   439
            personnel.

        5. Inspection of shop fabricated steel members   441
            and assemblies for conformance with the   442
            requirements specified.   443

        6. Inspection shop welds shall comply with Section   446
            6 of AWS Building Code and as follows:

                        BM05200-8

      a. Visual inspection of all shop welds in   449
         accordance with Article 605.

      b. Liquid inspection of the shop welds in   452
         accordance with ASTM E165, Procedure B.

  7. Inspection of shop painting.   455

      a. Surface preparation prior to painting will 458
         be visually evaluated for degree of cleaning 459
         by comparison with SSPC pictorial standards.

      b. Measurement of dry film thickness of each 463
         coat of shop applied paint will be in   464
         accordance with ASTM D1005.

3 EXECUTION   467

3.01 ERECTION AND INSTALLATION   469

  A General: Splices and field connections shall be 472
     welded as indicated. Bridging and connections to 474
     bearing plates shall be field welded. Erecting 476
     equipment shall be suitable and safe for the workmen.
     Errors in shop fabrication or deformation resulting 477
     from handling and transportation that prevent the 478
     proper assembly and fitting of parts shall be
     reported immediately to the Architect/Engineer, 479
     and approval of the method of correction shall be 480
     obtained. Approved corrections shall be made at 481
     no additional cost to the Owner.

  B Speed of Erection: Steel joists shall be erected 484
     as rapidly as the progress of other work will permit. 485
     A sufficient number of skilled mechanics shall be 486
     furnished to handle the work expeditiously and all 487
     shall be erected at such time and in such a manner 488
     as to be completed within as short a time period
     as possible.

  C Field Assembly: After assembly, the joists shall 491
     be aligned and adjusted accurately before being 492
     fastened. Tolerances shall conform to AISC "Code 493
     of Standard Practice". Fastening of splices of 494
     compression members shall be done after the abutting 495
     surfaces have been brought completely into contact.
     Bearing surfaces and surfaces that will be in   496
     permanent contact shall be cleaned before the members 497
     are assembled. As erection progresses, the work 498
     shall be securely fastened to take care of all dead 499
     load, wind, and erection stresses. Splices will 500
     be permitted only where indicated.

  D Bolting and Temporary Bracing: Steel joist work 503
     shall be set accurately at the established lines 504

BM05200-9

and levels. Joists must be plumb and level before 505
bolting is commenced. Temporary bracing shall be 506
provided as required and must be kept in position 507
until final completion.

E Bases and Bearing Plates: Bases, bearing plates, 510
and the ends of beams which require grouting shall 511
be supported exactly at the proper level by means 512
of steel wedges and by means of adjustment nuts 513
on anchor bolts.

F Gas Cutting: The use of a gas cutting torch in 516
the field for correcting fabrication errors will 517
not be permitted on any major member. The use of 519
a gas cutting torch will be permitted only on minor
members, when the member is not under stress, and 520
then only after the approval of the 521
Architect/Engineer has been obtained in writing.

G When so required to receive other materials, as 524
indicated on the Drawings, joists shall be designed 525
with a factory-formed nailing groove in the chord, 526
or shall have continuous wood nailer strip applied 527
to the chord with adequate size lag screws or bolts
spaced not more than 36 inches apart. Where special 529
type nails are required for nailing groove. provide 530
an adequate supply with the joists.

H Bridging, minimum bearings, and anchorage shall 533
conform to SJI Specifications and/or project drawings 534
as related to particular type of support.

I Execute general handling and erection in accordance 537
with SJI Specifications. Joists shall be permanently 538
fastened to supports and all bridging and anchors 539
completely installed before any construction loads,
other than workmen, are placed on joists. 540

J Execute welding in accordance with AWS "Code for 543
Arc and Gas Welding in Building Construction", and 544
only by welding operators who have been previously
qualified to perform type of work required and 545
approved.

3.02 GROUTING. Approved pre-mixed grout shall be prepared 548
and installed in accordance with the manufacturer's 549
written recommendations. Contractor shall assume full 550
responsibility for all grouting and its proper
performance.

BM05200-10

3.03   FIELD QUALITY CONTROL   553 (

   A   Testing Agency will perform the following: 556

      1.   Qualification of field _____ procedures and   559
           personnel.   560
)
      2.   Inspection of erected steel work for conformation   563
           with the requirements specified.

      3.   Inspection of field assembled construction in.   566
           accordance with applicable provisions of AISC   567
           Specifications.

      4.   Inspection of field welds will be in accordance   570
           with Section 6 of AWS Building Code and   571
           applicable ASTM requirements.

3.04   CLEANING AND PAINTING   574 (

   A   Cleaning: All surfaces shall be thoroughly cleaned   577
       of rust, mill scale, grease, dirt, and foreign   579
       matter. All welds shall be wire brushed to   580)
       completely remove all oxidized material.   581

   B   Shop coat all surfaces thoroughly with Red Lead   584
       Primer conforming to Federal Specification TT-P-   585
       86, Type II, or a rust-inhibitive metal primer   586
       standard with the manufacturer conforming to SSPC
       15.

   C   After erection, spot paint all field bolts, field   589
       welds, and abrasions to shop coat. Steel to be   590
       embedded in concrete shall not be painted.

   D   Finish painting of exposed joists is specified in   593
       Section 09900, "Painting".

3.05   SCHEDULES   595

3.06   ACCEPTANCE   596

                              BM05200-11

PSAE MASTERSPEC   11-1-70

SECTION 3E1 - CAST-IN-PLACE CONCRETE

RELATED DOCUMENTS:

The general provisions of the contract, including General
Conditions and General Requirements (if any), apply to the work
specified in this section.

DESCRIPTION OF WORK:

The extent of cast-in-place concrete work is shown on the
drawings.

The work includes providing cast-in-place concrete consisting of
portland cement, fine aggregate, coarse aggregate, water,
admixtures; designed, proportioned, mixed, placed, finished and
cured as herein specified.

The following types of cast-in-place concrete are specified in
this section:

                         REVISE BELOW TO SUIT PROJECT.

    Standard weight concrete.

    Lightweight structural concrete.

    Lightweight concrete fill.

    Lightweight insulating concrete.

GENERAL:

Codes and Standards:

Comply with the provisions of the following codes, specifications
and standards, except as otherwise shown or specified:

    ACI 301 "Specifications for Structural Concrete for
    Buildings".

    ACI 318 "Building Code Requirements for Reinforced Concrete".

    ACI 614 "Recommended Practice for Measuring, Mixing and
    Placing Concrete".

    ACI 311 "Recommended Practice for Concrete Inspection".

                    DELETE BELOW IF NOT REQUIRED.

Where provisions of the above codes and standards are in conflict
with the building code in force for this project, the building
code shall govern.

                    CAST-IN-PLACE CONCRETE   3E1 - 1

PSAE MASTERSPEC   11-1-70

Workmanship:

All concrete work which does not conform to the specified
requirements, including strength, tolerances, and finishes, shall
be corrected as directed by the Architect at the Contractor's
expense, without extension of time therefor. The Contractor
shall also be responsible for the cost of corrections to any
other work affected by or resulting from corrections to the
concrete work.

                    DELETE BELOW IF NOT REQUIRED.

Qualifications of Contractor's Testing Laboratory:

Contractor's selection of a testing laboratory is subject to the
Architect's acceptance.

Select a testing laboratory thoroughly experienced in design and
testing of concrete materials and mixes. Submit a written
description of the proposed concrete testing laboratory giving
qualifications of personnel, laboratory facilities and equipment,
and other information as may be requested by the Architect.

CONCRETE MATERIALS:

                    DELETE MATERIAL TYPES NOT REQUIRED.
                    REVISE ITEMS TO SUIT PROJECT.

Portland Cement:

Comply with the requirements of ASTM C 150.

                    SELECT CEMENT TYPE (S) TO SUIT PROJECT.
                    DELETE TYPES NOT REQUIRED.

   Provide Type I cement, except as otherwise indicated. Type
   III cement may be used in lieu of Type I at Contractor's
   option, when acceptable to the Architect.

   Provide Type II cement for mass concrete foundation systems,
   and elsewhere as noted on the drawings.

   Provide Type III cement for High-Early Strength concrete where
   shown or scheduled.

   Provide White cement where shown or scheduled.

Only one brand of cement may be used for each required type
throughout the project, unless otherwise accepted by the
Architect.

Shrinkage Compensating Cement:

Provide "ChemComp" as manufactured by a licensee of the

                    CAST-IN-PLACE CONCRETE   3E1 - 2

PSAE MASTERSPEC   11-1-70

Chemically Prestressed Concrete Corporation.

Manufacturers offering products to comply with the "non-shrinkage" requirements include the following:

Kaiser Cement & Gypsum Corp.
Medusa Portland Cement Co.
Penn Dixie Cement Corp.
Texas Industries, Inc.
Southwestern Portland Cement Co.

Aggregates, Normal Weight Concrete:

Comply with the requirements of ASTM C 33 and as herein specified.

REVISE OR DELETE TO SUIT PROJECT AND AVAILABLE AGGREGATES.

Do not use aggregates containing soluble salts or other substances such as iron sulphides, pyrite, marcasite or ochre which can cause strains on exposed concrete surfaces.

DELETE BELOW IF NOT REQUIRED.

Provide aggregates from a single source for all exposed aggregate finish and architectural concrete.

Fine Aggregate: Clean, sharp, natural sand free from loam, clay, lumps or other deleterious substances.

DELETE BELOW IF OTHER SAND PERMITTED.

Dune sand, bank run sand, and manufactured sand are not acceptable.

Coarse Aggregate: Clean, uncoated, processed aggregate containing no clay, mud, loam, or foreign matter, as follows:

DELETE TYPE(S) OR COARSE AGGREGATE NOT APPLICABLE TO PROJECT. ADD ANY SPECIAL AGGREGATES OR MORE STRINGENT REQUIREMENTS.

Crushed stone, processed from natural rock or stone.

Washed gravel, either natural or crushed. Use of pit or bank run gravel is not permitted.

Blast-furnace slag, crushed and processed from air cooled, iron blast-furnace slag weighing not less than 70 lbs. per cu. ft. in the dry, compacted state when determined in compliance with ASTM C 29.

CAST-IN-PLACE CONCRETE   3E1 - 3

PSAE MASTERSPEC   11-1-70

> SELECT AGGREGATE SIZES, OR REVISE TO SUIT
> PROJECT.   COORDINATE   WITH STRUCTURAL
> DESIGN   REQUIREMENTS.   ADD   OTHER
> GRADATIONS FOR SPECIAL AGGREGATES, AS
> REQUIRED.

Use Size 467 (maximum aggregate size 1-1/2") for footings,
foundations, walls, slabs on ground, and reinforced slabs
6" or greater in thickness, except as otherwise specified.

Use Size 57 (maximum aggregate size 1") for columns, beams
and all other concrete, except as otherwise specified.

Use Size 7 (maximum aggregate size 1/2") for columns, beams
and other members where reinforcing steel clearances are
too small to permit use of Size 57, except as otherwise
specified.

Use Size 8 (maximum aggregate size 3/8") for nonreinforced
slabs and other flatwork having a depth of less than 2-
1/2".

> DELETE BELOW IF NONE.

Aggregates, Lightweight Insulating Concrete:

Comply with the requirements of ASTM C 332.

> SELECT "GROUP" TO SUIT PROJECT. GROUP I
> WILL PRODUCE CONCRETE WEIGHING FROM 15 TO
> 50 PCF WITH THERMAL CONDUCTIVITY OF 0.45
> TO 1.50 (VERMICULITE, PERLITE). VERY LOW
> STRENGTH CHARACTERISTIC OF THIS GROUP.

Use Group I aggregates only.

> GROUP II AGGREGATES PRODUCE CONCRETE
> WEIGHING FROM 40 TO 95 PCF WITH THERMAL
> CONDUCTIVITY OF 1.05 TO 3.00 (EXPANDED
> SHALE,   SLATE, BLAST-FURNACE SLAG, FLY
> ASH, CLAY, ETC.). MUCH HIGHER STRENGTH
> THAN GROUP I.

Use Group II aggregates only.

> RETAIN   BELOW IF STRENGTH, WEIGHT OR
> THERMAL CONDUCTIVITY NOT CRUCIAL.

Use either Group I or Group II aggregates, at Contractor's
option.

> DELETE BELOW IF NONE.   THESE ARE
> BASICALLY THE SAME AS GROUP II OF ASTM C
> 332, WITH MORE RESTRICTIVE REQUIREMENTS.

                CAST-IN-PLACE CONCRETE   3E1 - 4

PSAE MASTERSPEC   11-1-70

Aggregates, Lightweight Fill or Structural Concrete:

Comply with the requirements of ASTM C 330.

                DELETE BELOW IF ANY OF ASTM C 330
                AGGREGATES ACCEPTABLE. RETAIN IF ONLY
                SLAG DESIRED.

Use expanded blast-furnace slag, unless otherwise accepted by
the Architect.

                DELETE BELOW IF NOT APPLICABLE. RETAIN
                FOR EXPOSED AGGREGATE AND BLASTED
                FINISHES.

Supply of Aggregates:

Provide aggregates from one source of supply to ensure uniformity
in color, size and shape.

Water for Washing Aggregates, Mixing and Curing:

Clean, fresh, free from oil, acid, organic matter or other
deleterious substances. Provide water for curing that does not
contain impurities in sufficient amount to etch concrete
surfaces, or cause discoloration to concrete indicated to remain
exposed and unpainted.

CONCRETE ADMIXTURES:

                ADMIXTURES MUST BE COORDINATED WITH
                STRUCTURAL ENGINEER FOR TYPES AND
                QUANTITIES.

Provide admixtures produced by recognized admixture manufacturers
and use im compliance with the manufacturer's printed directions.
Do not use admixtures which have not been incorporated and tested
in the accepted design mixes, unless otherwise authorized in
writing by the Architect.

                SELECT ADMIXTURES FROM BELOW, DELETE
                OTHERS, OR REVISE TO SUIT PROJECT.

Air-Entraining Admixture:

Comply with the requirements of ASTM C 260.

Products offered by manufacturers to comply with the
requirements include the following:

                REVISE OR DELETE BELOW TO SUIT PROJECT.

Darex AEA; Dewey and Almy Chemical Div./W.R. Grace.
Sika AER; Sika Chemical Corp.

CAST-IN-PLACE CONCRETE   3E1 - 5

PSAE MASTERSPEC   11-1-70

MB-VR; Master Builder's Co.

Water Reducing Admixture:

> TYPE A SPECIFIED BELOW IS WATER-REDUCING
> TYPE ONLY.   OTHER   TYPES   ARE   SET-
> ACCELERATING AND SET-RETARDING. REVISE
> IF REQUIRED.

Comply with the requirements of ASTM C 494, Type A, and contain
no set-accelerating, or set-retarding compounds, chlorides,
fluorides, or nitrates.

> REVISE OR DELETE BELOW TO SUIT PROJECT,
> OR IF OTHER THAN TYPE A.

   Products offered by manufacturers to comply with the
   requirements include the following:

   WRDA; Dewey and Almy Chemical Div./W.R. Grace.
   Pozzolith; Master Builder's Co.
   Placewel-R; Johns-Manville Corp.

Integral Waterproofing:

Provide a manufactured product consisting of a balanced blend of
water repellant stearates and non-air-entraining water-reducing
agent, in powder, paste, or liquid form.

   Products offered by manufacturers to comply with the
   requirements include the following:

   Toxement IW; Toch Bros.
   Anti-Hydro; Anti-Hydro Waterproofing Co.
   Hydratite; A.C. Horn/W.R. Grace.

Fly Ash:

Comply with the requirements of ASTM C 618, Class F.

> RETAIN BELOW IF CALCIUM CHLORIDE NOT
> PERMITTED.

Calcium Chloride:

Do not use calcium chloride in concrete, except as otherwise
authorized in writing by the Architect. Do not use any
admixtures containing calcium chloride where concrete is placed
against any galvanized steel, or in any mix using high-early
strength cement.

> RETAIN BELOW IF CALCIUM CHLORIDE WILL BE
> CONSIDERED. DO NOT ALLOW FOR EXPANSIVE
> CEMENTS.

                CAST-IN-PLACE CONCRETE   3E1 - 6

RETAIN BELOW (AND DELETE ABOVE) IF OWNER
TO CONTROL SITE TESTING SERVICES.

The Owner will employ a separate testing laboratory to perform
all other tests and to submit test reports to the Architect.

Materials and installed work may require testing and retesting as
directed by the Architect at anytime during the progress of the
work. Allow free access to material stockpiles and facilities at
all times. Tests, not specifically indicated to be done at the
Owner's expense, including the retesting of rejected materials
and installed work, shall be done at the Contractor's expense.

DELETE BELOW WHEN (IF) CERTIFICATES OF
COMPLIANCE WILL BE PERMITTED IN LIEU OF
LABORATORY TESTS. TESTS ARE RECOMMENDED
FOR PROJECTS WHEN THE QUANTITY OF
CONCRETE EXCEEDS 1,000 CU. YDS. AND
WHEN CONCRETE QUALITY IS CRUCIAL.

Tests for Concrete Materials:

Sample and test proposed concrete materials for design concrete
mixes as listed below:

DELETE TESTS NOT REQUIRED.

Test fine aggregate from each material source and report the
following:

Sieve Analysis: ASTM C 136.
Fineness Modulus: ASTM C 125.
Material Passing No. 200 Sieve: ASTM C 117.
Amount Of Friable Particles: ASTM C 142.
Amount Of Organic Impurities: ASTM C 40.
Amount Of Coal And Lignite: ASTM C 123.
Magnesium Sulphate Soundness Test: ASTM C 88.
Specific Gravity And Absorption: ASTM C 128.

Test coarse aggregate from each material source and each grading,
and report the following:

Sieve Analysis: ASTM C 136.
Fineness Modulus: ASTM C 125.
Amount of Friable Particles: ASTM C 142.
Amount of Soft Particles: ASTM C 235.
Amount of Chert, as an Impurity: ASTM C 235.
Material Passing No. 200 Sieve: ASTM C 117.
Amount of Coal and Lignite: ASTM C 123.
Magnesium Sulfate Soundness Test: ASTM C 88.
Compacted Unit Weight: ASTM C 29.
Los Angeles Abrasion Test: ASTM C 131 or C 535.
Specific Gravity and Absorption: ASTM C 127.

<u>Test portland cement</u> from each material source, type and color, and report the following:

<u>Chemical Analysis:</u> ASTM C 114.
<u>Fineness of Grind:</u> ASTM C 115 or C 204.
<u>Autoclave Expansion:</u> ASTM C 151.
<u>Time of Setting:</u> ASTM C 266.
<u>Air Content of Mortar:</u> ASTM C 185.
<u>Compressive Strength:</u> ASTM C 109.
<u>Heat of Hydration:</u> ASTM C 186.
<u>False Set:</u> ASTM C 451.

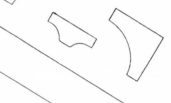

ADD OTHER TESTS AS REQUIRED.

<u>Submit written reports</u> to the Architect for each material sampled and tested prior to the start of work. Provide the project identification name and number, date of report, name of contractor, name of concrete testing service, source of concrete aggregates, material manufacturer and brand name for manufactured materials, values specified in the referenced specification for each material, and test results.

RETAIN BELOW EVEN IF OWNER'S LABORATORY DOES QUALITY CONTROL TESTING. MODIFY TO SUIT PROJECT, OR DELETE IF NOT REQUIRED FOR SMALLER WORK.

<u>Quality Control Testing During Construction:</u>

Concrete shall be sampled and tested for quality control during the placement of concrete as follows:

<u>Sampling Fresh Concrete:</u> ASTM C 172, except modified for slump to comply with ASTM C 94.

<u>Slump:</u> ASTM C 143; one test for each concrete load at point of discharge; and one for each set of compressive strength test specimens.

<u>Air Content:</u> ASTM C 231, pressure method; one for each set of compressive strength test specimens.

<u>Compression Test Specimens:</u> ASTM C 31; one set of 6 standard cylinders for each compressive strength test.

<u>Concrete Temperature:</u> Test hourly when air temperature is 40° F. and below, and when 80° F. and above; and each time a set of compression test specimens made.

<u>Compressive Strength Tests:</u> ASTM C 39; one set for each 100 cu. yds. or fraction thereof, of each concrete class placed in any one day; 2 specimens tested at 7 days, 3 specimens tested at 28 days, and one specimen retained in reserve for later testing if required.

CAST-IN-PLACE CONCRETE   3E1 -16

PSAE MASTERSPEC   11-1-70

    Hohmann & Bernard, Inc.
    Gateway Engineering Co.
    National Construction Specialties.

                    DELETE OR REVISE BELOW TO SUIT PROJECT.

Provide threaded inserts of malleable cast iron, furnished
complete with full-depth bolts; 3/4" bolt size, unless otherwise
shown.

Provide flashing reglets formed of sheet metal of the same type
and gauge as the flashing metal to be built into the reglet,
unless otherwise shown. Where resilient or elastomeric sheet
flashing or bituminous membranes are terminated in reglets,
provide reglets of not less than 20 gauge galvanized sheet steel.
Size, shape and install reglets as detailed. Fill reglet or
cover face opening to prevent intrusion of concrete or debris.

CONCRETE MIXING:

General:

Concrete may be mixed at batch plants or it may be transit-mixed
as   specified   herein.   Batch plants must comply with the
requirements of ACI 614, with sufficient capacity to produce
concrete of the qualities specified in quantities required to
meet the construction schedule. All plant facilities are subject
to the acceptance of the Architect.

Job Site Mixing:

Mix all materials for concrete in an acceptable drum type batch
machine mixer. For mixers of one cu. yd., or smaller capacity,
continue mixing at least 1-1/2 minutes, but not more than 5
minutes after all ingredients are in the mixer, before any part
of the batch is released. For mixers of capacity larger than one
cu. yd., increase the minimum 1-1/2 minutes of mixing time by 15
seconds for each additional cu. yd., or fraction thereof. Do
not exceed the catalog rating or name-plate capacity for the
total volume of materials used per batch. Equip the mixer with
automatic controls, or semi-automatic controls if acceptable, for
proportioning materials and the proper measured quantities. Do
not exceed 30 minutes total elapsed time between intermingling of
damp aggregates and cement to the discharge of the completed mix.

Provide a batch ticket for each batch discharged and used in the
work, indicating the project identification name and number,
date, mix type, mix time, quantity and amount of water
introduced.

Ready-mix Concrete:

Comply with the requirements of ASTM C 94, and as herein
specified, provided the quantity and rate of delivery will permit

                    CAST-IN-PLACE CONCRETE   3E1 -25

PSAE MASTERSPEC   11-1-70

unrestricted   progress   of   the   work   in   accordance   with   the
placement   schedule.   During   hot   weather,   or   under   conditions
contributing   to rapid setting of concrete, a shorter mixing time
than specified in ASTM C 94 may be required, as specified   below.
Proposed   changes   in   mixing   procedures,   other   than   herein
specified,   must   be   accepted   by   the   Architect   before
implementation.

> THE FOLLOWING MODIFICATIONS TO ASTM C 94
> PROVIDE   MORE   STRINGENT   REQUIREMENTS TO
> READY-MIXED CONCRETE.   DELETE   IF   NOT
> DESIRED.   COORDINATE   WITH   STRUCTURAL
> ENGINEER.

Modifications to ASTM C 94 are as follows:

Quality of Concrete: Provide concrete materials, proportions,
and properties as herein specified, in lieu of ASTM Section 4.

Tolerances in Slump: Provide slump of not more than the values
as herein specified, in lieu of ASTM Section 5.1. Comply with
other criteria of ASTM Section 5.

Mixing and Delivery: Delete the references for allowing
additional   water   to   be added to the batch for material with
insufficient slump.   Addition of water to the batch will   not
be permitted as specified in ASTM Section 9.7.   In addition to
the requirements of ASTM Section 9.7, when the air temperature
is   between 85° F.   and 90° F., reduce the mixing and delivery
time from   1-1/2 hours to 75 minutes,   and   when   the   air
temperature   is   above   90° F., reduce the mixing and delivery
time to 60 minutes. When a truck mixer is used for the
complete mixing of the concrete, begin the mixing operation
within 30 minutes after the cement has been intermingled   with
the aggregates.

Certification: Furnish duplicate delivery tickets with each
load of concrete delivered to the site, one for the   Architect
and   one   for the Contractor. In addition to the requirements
of ASTM Section 14.1, provide the following information   on
delivery tickets:

   Type and brand of cement.

   Cement content (in 94-lb. sacks) per cu yd.   of
   concrete.

   Maximum size of aggregate.

   Amount and brand name of each admixture.

   Total water content expressed as water/cement ratio.

Strength: Delete ASTM Section 15; comply with concrete testing

CAST-IN-PLACE CONCRETE   3E1 -26

requirements as herein specified.

Maintain equipment in proper operating condition, with drums cleaned before charging each batch. Schedule rates of delivery in order to prevent delay of placing the concrete after mixing, or holding drymixed materials too long in the mixer before the addition of water and admixtures.

CONCRETE PLACEMENT:

General: Place concrete in compliance with the practices and recommendations of ACI 614, and as herein specified.

Deposit concrete continuously or in layers of such thickness that no concrete will be placed on concrete which has hardened sufficiently to cause the formation of seams or planes of weakness within the section. If a section cannot be placed continuously, provide construction joints as herein specified. Perform concrete placing at such a rate that concrete which is being integrated with fresh concrete is still plastic. Deposit concrete as nearly as practicable to its final location to avoid segregation due to rehandling or flowing. Do not subject concrete to any procedure which will cause segregation.

Screed concrete which is to receive other construction to the proper level to avoid excessive skimming or grouting.

Do not use concrete which becomes non-plastic and unworkable, or does not meet the required quality control limits, or which has been conta inated by foreign materials. Do not use retempered concrete. Remove rejected concrete from the project site and dispose of in an acceptable location.

                         DELETE BELOW IF NOT REQUIRED.

Placement Schedule:

Prepare a placement schedule and submit to the Architect for acceptance before starting concrete placement operations, indicating an even distribution of loads throughout the entire structure. Rigidly follow placement sequence or schedule (if any) shown on the drawings, unless otherwise directed.

Pre-Placement Inspection:

Before placing concrete, inspect and complete the formwork installation, reinforcing steel, and items to be embedded or cast-in. Notify other crafts involved in ample time to permit the installation of their work; cooperate with other trades in setting such work, as required. Thoroughly wet wood forms immediately before placing concrete, as required where form coatings are not used.

Soil at bottom of foundation systems are subject to testing for

PSAE MASTERSPEC   11-1-70

soil bearing value by the testing laboratory, as directed by the
Architect.   Place   concrete   immediately   after   approval   of
foundation excavations.

Concrete Conveying:

Handle concrete from the point of delivery and transfer to the
concrete conveying equipment and to the locations of final
deposit as rapidly as practicable by methods which will prevent
segregation and loss of concrete mix materials.

Provide   mechanical   equipment   of   such   size   and   design   for
conveying concrete to ensure a continuous flow of concrete at the
delivery end.   Provide runways for wheeled concrete conveying
equipment from the concrete delivery point to the locations of
final deposit.   Keep interior surfaces of conveying equipment,
including chutes, free of hardened concrete, debris, water, snow,
ice, and other deleterious materials.

Placing Concrete in Forms:

Deposit concrete in forms in horizontal layers not deeper than
18" and in a manner to avoid inclined construction joints.

Remove temporary spreaders in forms when concrete placing has
reached the elevation of such spreaders.

Consolidate all concrete placed in forms by mechanical vibrating
equipment supplemented by hand-spading, rodding or tamping.   Use
vibrators designed to operate with vibratory element submerged in
concrete, maintaining a speed of not less than 6000 impulses per
minute when submerged in the concrete.   Vibration of forms and
reinforcing will not be permitted, unless otherwise accepted by
the Architect.

Do not use vibrators to transport concrete inside of forms.
Insert and withdraw vibrators vertically at uniformly spaced
locations not farther than the visible effectiveness of the
machine. Do not insert vibrators into lower layers of concrete
that have begun to set. At each insertion, limit the duration of
vibration to the time necessary to consolidate the concrete and
complete embedment of reinforcement and other embedded items
without causing segregation of the mix.

Do not place concrete in supporting elements until the concrete
previously placed in colums and walls is no longer plastic.

Placing Concrete Slabs:

Deposit and consolidate concrete slabs in a continuous operation,
within the limits of construction joints, until the placing of a
panel or section is completed.

Consolidate concrete during placing operations using mechanical

CAST-IN-PLACE CONCRETE   3E1 -28

SECTION 3A

CAST-IN-PLACE CONCRETE

NOTE: CAST-IN-PLACE CONCRETE ENCOMPASSES NORMAL-
WEIGHT PORTLAND CEMENT CONCRETE, INCLUDING
FORMWORK, REINFORCEMENT, FINISHING, AND CONCRETE
FLOOR TOPPINGS, FOR BUILDING AND CONSTRUCTION.

DRAWINGS SHOULD INCLUDE A COMPLETE DESIGN INDICAT-
ING THE CHARACTER OF THE WORK TO BE PERFORMED AND
GIVING THE FOLLOWING:

LOADING ASSUMPTIONS, AND UNIT STRESSES USED IN
THE DESIGN.

DETAILS OF REINFORCEMENT, SHOWING REINFORC-
ING BAR NUMBER, SIZES, BENDS, AND STOPPING
POINTS; DETAILS OF STIRRUPS; AND LOCATION
AND SIZE OF WELDED WIRE FABRIC.

SPECIFIC LOCATIONS FOR USE OF THE VARIOUS
CLASSES OF CONCRETE WHEN REQUIRED.

DETAILS OF ALL CONCRETE SECTIONS, SHOWING
DIMENSIONS AND COVER OVER REINFORCEMENT.

DETAILS AND LOCATIONS OF EXPANSION AND
CONSTRUCTION JOINTS, INCLUDING WATERSTOPS
WHEN REQUIRED.

DETAILS AND LOCATIONS OF ISOLATION JOINTS.

LOCATIONS AND DETAILS WHICH REQUIRE A DEPRES-
SED STRUCTURAL SLAB OR OTHER CONDITIONS IN
ORDER TO PROVIDE FINISHED SURFACES AT THE
SAME ELEVATIONS.

LOCATIONS AND DETAILS FOR ARCHITECTURAL
CONCRETE WHEN REQUIRED.

LOCATION OF FINISHES FOR FORMED SURFACES,
MONOLITHIC SLABS, AND FLOOR TOPPING WHEN
REQUIRED.

CAST-IN-PLACE CONCRETE FOR SITE WORK IS SPECIFIED
IN DIVISION 2 "SITE WORK", SECTION 15A "PLUMBING
SYSTEM", AND SECTION 16A, "ELECTRICAL SITE WORK".

EARTH FILLS UNDER CONCRETE SLABS ON GROUND ARE
SPECIFIED IN SECTION 2D "EXCAVATION, FILL AND
BACKFILL FOR STRUCTURES".

CAST-IN-PLACE LIGHWEIGHT NONINSULATING CONCRETE
FLOOR AND ROOF FILLS ARE SPECIFIED IN SECTION 3D
"LIGHWEIGHT CONCRETE FILL".

SETTING BEARING PLATES, INCLUDING BEDDING MORTAR,
IS SPECIFIED IN SECTION 5A "STRUCTURAL STEEL"
AND SECTION 5C "STEEL JOISTS".

METAL FLOOR DECKING AND METAL FORMS TO RECEIVE
CONCRETE FILLS ARE SPECIFIED IN SECTION 5F
"METAL FLOOR DECKING" AND SECTION 5G "PERMANENT
METAL FORMS FOR CONCRETE".

CAST-IN-PLACE CONCRETE FOR COOLING TOWERS IS
SPECIFIED IN SECITON 15J "PROCESS COOLING
TOWER WATER SYSTEM".

FIRE-RESISTANCE-RATED CONSTRUCTION USING CAST-
IN-PLACE CONCRETE IS DESCRIBED IN UNDERWRITERS'
LABORATORIES INC., GUIDE NO. 40 U18, "FIRE
RESISTANCE CLASSIFICATION" (INCLUDED IN UL'S
"BUILDING MATERIAL LIST") AND AMERICAN INSURANCE
ASSOCIATION "FIRE RESISTANCE RATINGS". FIRE-
RESISTANCE-RATED CONSTRUCTION LIMITS AGGREGATE
MATERIALS AND CONCRETE COVER OVER REINFORCEMENT.

---GENERAL REQUIREMENTS---

---REFERENCE STANDARD: ABBREVIATIONS

```
1
2
3
4
5
6 AA
6 AB
6 AC
6 AD
6 AE
6 AF
6 AG
6 AH
6 AI
6 AJ
6 AK
6 AL
6 AM
6 AN
6 AO
6 AP
6 AQ
6 AR
6 AS
6 AT
6 AU
6 AV
6 AW
6 AX
6 AY
6 AZ
6 BA
6 BB
6 BC
6 BD
6 BE
6 BF
6 BG
6 BH
6 BI
6 BJ
6 BK
6 BL
6 BM
6 BN
6 BO
6 BP
6 BQ
6 BR
6 BS
6 BT
6 BU
6 BV
6 BW
6 BX
6 BY
6 BZ
6 CA
6 CB
6 CC
6 CD
6 CE
6 CF
6 CG
6 CH
6 CI
6 CJ
6 CK
6 CL
6 CM
6 CN
6 CO
6 CP
6 CQ
6 CR
6 CS
6 CT
6 CU
6 CV
6 CW
6
7
8
9
10
```

3A-   1

REFERENCE STANDARDS ARE REFERRED TO HEREINAFTER IN ACCORDANCE WITH THE FOLLOWING
ABBREVIATIONS:

AASHO	AMERICAN ASSOCIATION OF STATE AND HIGHWAY OFFICIALS
ACI	AMERICAN CONCRETE INSTITUTE
ASTM	AMERICAN SOCIETY FOR TESTING AND MATERIALS
AWS	AMERICAN WELDING SOCIETY
FS	FEDERAL SPECIFICATION
USDC	UNITED STATES DEPARTMENT OF COMMERCE

---DEFINITION OF ACI BUILDING CODE

ACI BUILDING CODE SHALL MEAN ACI STANDARD "BUILDING CODE FOR REINFORCED CONCRETE",
ACI 318-63, WITH THE FOLLOWING MODIFICATION:

ALL REFERENCES TO THE "BUILDING OFFICIAL" AND THE "ENGINEER" SHALL MEAN THE
"CONTRACTING OFFICER".

---QUALIFICATIONS FOR CONCRETE TESTING SERVICE

CONCRETE TESTING SHALL BE PERFORMED BY A LABORATORY AND INSPECTION SERVICE
THOROUGHLY EXPERIENCED IN SAMPLING AND TESTING CONCRETE.

SUBMIT A WRITTEN DESCRIPTION OF PROPOSED CONCRETE TESTING SERVICE GIVING QUALIFI-
CATIONS OF PERSONNEL, LABORATORY EQUIPMENT AND FACILITIES, LISTS OF PROJECTS SIMILAR
IN SCOPE TO SPECIFIED WORK, AND OTHER INFORMATION AS MAY BE REQUIRED BY THE
CONTRACTING OFFICER.

---QUALIFICATIONS FOR READY-MIX CONCRETE MANUFACTURER

CONCRETE SHALL BE MANUFACTURED AND DELIVERED TO THE PROJECT SITE BY A READY-MIX
CONCRETE MANUFACTURER THOROUGHLY EXPERIENCED IN READY-MIX CONCRETE.

SUBMIT A WRITTEN DESCRIPTION OF PROPOSED READY-MIX CONCRETE MANUFACTURER GIVING
QUALIFICATIONS OF PERSONNEL, LOCATION OF BATCHING PLANT, LIST OF PROJECTS SIMILAR
IN SCOPE TO SPECIFIED WORK, AND OTHER INFORMATION AS MAY BE REQUESTED BY THE
CONTRACTING OFFICER.

---QUALIFICATIONS FOR WELDING WORK

NOTE: DELETE PARAGRAPH TITLE AND THE FOLLOWING
PARAGRAPH WHEN WELDING IS NOT REQUIRED.

ANY WELDING OF STEEL REINFORCEMENT SHALL BE DONE BY WELDING OPERATORS QUALIFIED
UNDER THE PROVISIONS OF AWS "STANDARD QUALIFICATION PROCEDURE" (AWS B3.0-41), OR
UNDER AN EQUIVALENT QUALIFICATION TEST APPROVED IN ADVANCE BY THE CONTRACTING
OFFICER. IN ADDITION TO THE ABOVE REQUIREMENTS, ALL TESTS SHALL BE PERFORMED ON
TEST PIECES IN POSITIONS AND WITH CLEARANCES EQUIVALENT TO THOSE ACTUALLY ENCOUNT-
ERED IN CONSTRUCTION. IF A TEST WELD FAILS TO MEET REQUIREMENTS, AN IMMEDIATE
RETEST OF 2 TEST WELDS SHALL BE MADE, AND EACH TEST WELD SHALL PASS. FAILURE IN
THE IMMEDIATE RETEST WILL REQUIRE THAT THE WELDER BE RETESTED AFTER FURTHER
PRACTICE OR TRAINING, AND A COMPLETE SET OF TEST WELDS SHALL BE MADE.

---PROOFS OF COMPLIANCE

SUBMIT PROOFS OF COMPLIANCE AS SPECIFIED IN THE "SUPPLEMENTARY GENERAL PROVISIONS"
AND AS FOLLOWS:

CERTIFICATES OF CONFORMANCE FOR ALL MATERIALS, EXCEPT MATERIALS REQUIRING A
LABORATORY TEST REPORT.

LABORATORY TEST REPORTS AS SPECIFIED IN THE ARTICLE ENTITLED "CONCRETE SAMPLING
AND TESTING".

CERTIFIED LABORATORY TEST REPORTS OF THE CHEMICAL REQUIREMENTS OF REINFORCING BARS
TO BE WELDED.

REPORTS OF CHEMICAL COMPOSITION, AND MECHANICAL, USABILITY AND SOUNDNESS TESTS, AS
SPECIFIED IN ASTM A233-64T, FOR ELECTRODES FOR MANUAL SHIELDED METAL-ARC WELDING.

---SHOP DRAWINGS AND DESCRIPTIVE DATA

SUBMIT SHOP DRAWINGS AND DESCRIPTIVE DATA AS SPECIFIED IN THE "SUPPLEMENTARY GENERAL
PROVISIONS" AND AS FOLLOWS:

SHOP DRAWINGS FOR REINFORCEMENT SHALL INDICATE DIMENSIONS AND DETAILS NECESSARY FOR
THE FABRICATION AND PLACING OF REINFORCEMENT AND ACCESSORIES, WITHOUT REFERENCE TO
THE PROJECT DRAWINGS.

NOTE: SHOP DRAWINGS FOR FORMWORK MAY BE REQUIRED
FOR UNUSUALLY COMPLICATED STRUCTURES, FOR STRU-
TURES WHOSE DESIGNS WERE PREDICTED ON A PARTI-
CULAR METHOD OF CONSTRUCTION, FOR STRUCTURES IN
WHICH THE FORMS IMPART A DESIRED ARCHITECTURAL
FINISH, FOR FOLDED PLATES, FOR THIN SHELLS, AND

3A- 2

```
                     FOR LONG-SPAN ROOF STRUCTURES.                              87 AG
                                                                                 87 AH
          MANUFACTUERER' PRINTED INSTALLATION INSTRUCTIONS OF THE FOLLOWING:     87
                                                                                 88
                    NOTE:  DELETE ANY OF THE FOLLOWING SUBPARAGRAPHS             89 AA
                    THAT ARE NOT APPLICABLE TO THE PROJECT.                      89 AB
                                                                                 89 AC
                                                                                 89 AD
                    AIR-ENTRAINING ADMIXTURE                                     90*
                                                                                 91
                    CONCRETE BONDING AGENT                                       92
                                                                                 93
                    EPOXY-RESIN ADHESIVE BINDER                                  94
                                                                                 95
                    WATERSTOPS                                                   96
                                                                                 97
                    LIQUID CHEMICAL FLOOR HARDENER                               98
                                                                                 99
                         NOTE:  DELETE THE FOLLOWING SUBPARAGRAPH WHEN           100 AA
                         HEAVY-DUTY FLOOR TOPPING IS NOT REQUIRED.               100 AB
                                                                                 100 AC
                    HEAVY-DUTY FLOOR TOPPING AGGREGATE MANUFACTURER'S PROPORTIONS OF TOPPING MIXTURE.  100
                                                                                 101
          ---SAMPLES                                                            102
                                                                                 103
                         NOTE:  DELETE PARAGRAPH TITLE AND THE FOLLOWING         104 AA
                         PARAGRAPHS AND SUBPARAGRAPHS WHEN SAMPLES WILL          104 AB
                         NOT BE REQUIRED.                                        104 AC
                                                                                 104
               SUBMIT SAMPLES AS SPECIFIED IN THE "SUPPLEMENTARY GENERAL PROVISIONS" OF THE  105
               FOLLOWING:                                                        106
                                                                                 107
                         NOTE:  DELETE ANY OF THE FOLLOWING SUBPARAGRAPHS        108 AA
                         THAT ARE NOT APPLICABLE TO THE PROJECT.  SPECIFY        108 AB
                         OTHER SAMPLES IF REQUIRED.                              108 AC
                                                                                 108 AD
                    ARCHITECTURAL CONCRETE AGGREGATE SAMPLES OF EACH TYPE OF AGGREGATE, AS REQUIRED  108
                    TO ILLUSTRATE COLOR, PARTICLE SHAPE, AND SIZE RANGE OF PARTICLES.  109
                                                                                 110
                    WATERSTOP SAMPLES, FULL SIZE BY 12 INCHES LONG.              111
                                                                                 112
          ---FIELD CONSTRUCTED SAMPLES                                          113
                                                                                 114
                         NOTE:  DELETE PARAGRAPH TITLE AND THE FOLLOWING PARAGRAPHS  115 AA
                         WHEN FIELD-CONSTRUCTED SAMPLES ARE NOT REQUIRED TO ESTABLISH  115 AB
                         THE STANDARD OF WORKMANSHIP FOR FINISHED WORK.  SPECIFY  115 AC
                         OTHER FIELD CONSTRUCTED SAMPLES IF REQUIRED.            115 AD
                                                                                 115 AE
               FIELD-CONSTRUCTED SAMPLES SHALL BE PROVIDED TO ESTABLISH THE STANDARD OF WORKMAN-  115
               SHIP FOR EXPOSED-TO-VIEW FINISHED SURFACES.  SUCH SAMPLES SHALL BE MADE WITH THE  116
               MATERIALS APPROVED FOR THE WORK AND USING THE CONSTRUCTION METHODS PROPOSED FOR THE  117
               WORK.  SAMPLE SECTIONS SHALL BE PROVIDED AS FOLLOWS:             118
                                                                                 119
                    WALL CORNER SECTION, APPROXIMATELY 4 FEET HIGH BY 3 FEET EACH SIDE BY 6 INCHES  120
                    THICK.  INCLUDE NOT LESS THAN 2 FORM TIES, 2 FORM PANEL INTERSECTIONS, ONE  121
                    VERTICAL CONSTRUCTION JOINT AND ONE HORIZONTAL CONSTRUCTION JOINT.  122
                                                                                 123
                    COLUMN SECTION, APPROXIMATELY 4 FEET HIGH BY AT LEAST 12 INCHES FACE DIMENSION.  124
                    CHAMFER THE EXPOSED EDGES OF RECTANGULAR OR SQUARE SAMPLE COLUMN, AS SPECIFIED.  125
                                                                                 126
                    SLAB SECTIONS, APPROXIMATELY 4 FEET SQUARE AND 6 INCHES IN THICKNESS.  PROVIDE  127
                    ONE CONSTRUCTION JOINT AND ONE CONTRACTION JOINT IN EACH SAMPLE SECTION.  128
                                                                                 129
               THE SAMPLE SECTIONS SHALL BE APPROVED BY THE CONTRACTING OFFICER BEFORE PLACING  130
               ANY CONCRETE WHICH WILL HAVE FINISHED SURFACES EXPOSED TO VIEW.  SAMPLE SECTIONS  131
               SHALL NOT BE REMOVED FROM THE PROJECT SITE UNTIL THE CONCRETE CONSTRUCTION IT  132
               REPRESENTS IS COMPLETED AND APPROVED BY THE CONTRACTING OFFICER.  133
                                                                                 134
          ---DELIVERY AND STORAGE OF MATERIALS (EXCEPT READY-MIX CONCRETE)      135
                                                                                 136
               PACKAGED MATERIALS SHALL BE DELIVERED TO THE PROJECT SITE IN THEIR ORIGINAL, UN-  137
               OPENED PACKAGE OR CONTAINER BEARING LABEL CLEARLY IDENTIFYING MANUFACTURER'S NAME,  138
               BRAND NAME, MATERIAL, WEIGHT OR VOLUME, AND OTHER PERTINENT INFORMATION.  PACKAGED  139
               MATERIALS SHALL BE STORED IN THEIR ORIGINAL, UNBROKEN PACKAGE OR CONTAINER IN A  140
               WEATHERTIGHT AND DRY PLACE, UNTIL READY FOR USE IN THE WORK.     141
                                                                                 142
               UNPACKAGED AGGREGATES SHALL BE STORED IN A MANNER TO AVOID EXCESSIVE SEGREGATION  143
               OR CONTAMINATION WITH OTHER MATERIALS OR WITH OTHER SIZES OF LIKE AGGREGATES, AND  144
               TO PROTECT FROM FREEZING.                                         145
                                                                                 146
               REINFORCEMENT AND OTHER METAL ITEMS SHALL BE PROTECTED FROM CORROSION, AND SHALL BE  147
               KEPT FREE FROM ICE, GREASE, AND OTHER COATINGS THAT WOULD DESTROY OR REDUCE BOND.  148
                                                                                 149
                                                                                 150
                                                                                 151
```

3A-   3

```
                                                ---CONCRETE MATERIALS---   152
                                                                           153
        ---CONCRETE AGGREGATES                                             154
                                                                           155
            CONCRETE AGGREGATES SHALL BE FINE AND COARSE AGGREGATES CONFORMING TO ASTM C33-67   156
            AND THE FOLLOWING:                                             157
                                                                           158
                WHERE THE CONCRETE WILL BE EXPOSED-TO-THE WEATHER, CONCRETE AGGREGATES SHALL MEET   159
                THE REQUIREMENTS OF ASTM C33-67  FOR FINE AGGREGATE SUBJECT TO ABRASION, FOR   160
                COARSE AGGREGATE SUBJECT TO SEVERE EXPOSURE, AND FOR ALL CONCRETE AGGREGATES WHERE   161
                SURFACE APPEARANCE OF THE CONCRETE IS IMPORTANT.           162
                                                                           163
                THE MAXIMUM SIZE OF COARSE AGGREGATE SHALL BE AS HEREINAFTER SPECIFIED IN THE   164
                ARTICLE ENTITLED "CLASSIFICATION AND QUALITY OF CONCRETE". 165
                                                                           166
                    NOTE:  DELETE THE FOLLOWING PARAGRAPH WHEN            167 AA
                    ARCHITECTURAL CONCRETE MADE OF THE SPECIFIED          167 AB
                    CONCRETE AGGREGATES IS NOT REQUIRED.  DELETE          167 AC
                    THE FOLLOWING PARAGRAPH, AND SPECIFY THE              167 AD
                    REQUIRED AGGREGATES, WHEN ARCHITECTURAL CON-          167 AE
                    CRETE MADE OF SPECIAL AGGREGATES, SUCH AS FOR         167 AF
                    EXPOSED-AGGREGATE FINISH, IS REQUIRED.  REFER         167 AG
                    TO SECTION 3B "PRECAST CONCRETE WALL PANELS",         167 AH
                    ARTICLE ENTITLED "CONCRETE MATERIALS".                167 AI
                                                                          167 AJ
            CONCRETE AGGREGATE FOR ARCHITECTURAL CONCRETE SHALL BE OBTAINED FROM A SINGLE SOURCE.   167
                                                                           168
        ---PORTLAND CEMENT                                                 169
                                                                           170
            PORTLAND CEMENT SHALL CONFORM TO ASTM C150-67, TYPE I OR III.  ONLY ONE BRAND AND   171
            TYPE OF PORTLAND CEMENT SHALL BE USED FOR ALL FORMED CONCRETE HAVING EXPOSED-TO-VIEW   172
            FINISHED SURFACES.                                             173
                                                                           174
        ---AIR-ENTRAINING ADMIXTURE                                       175
                                                                           176
            AIR-ENTRAINING ADMIXTURE FOR CONCRETE SHALL CONFORM TO ASTM C260-66T.   177
                                                                           178
        ---WATER FOR MIXING CONCRETE                                      179
                                                                           180
            WATER FOR MIXING CONCRETE SHALL MEET THE REQUIREMENTS OF AASHO T26-51   181
                                                                           182
        ---READY-MIX CONCRETE                                             183
                                                                           184
            READY-MIX CONCRETE SHALL MEET THE REQUIREMENTS OF ASTM C94-67  WITH THE FOLLOWING   185
            MODIFICATIONS:                                                 186
                                                                           187
                ASTM SECTION 4  "QUALITY OF CONCRETE".  DELETE ASTM SECTION 4  AND SUBSTITUTE THE   188
                FOLLOWING:  CONCRETE MATERIALS, PROPORTIONS, AND PROPERTIES SHALL BE AS SPECIFIED   189
                IN THE PROJECT SPECIFICATIONS.                             190
                                                                           191
                ASTM SECTION 5  "TOLERANCES IN SLUMP".  DELETE THE FIRST AND SECOND SENTENCES OF   192
                ASTM SECTION 5.1 AND SUBSTITUTE THE FOLLOWING:  THE SLUMP SHALL BE NOT MORE THAN   193
                THE VALUE SPECIFIED IN THE PROJECT SPECIFICATIONS.         194
                                                                           195
                ASTM SECTION 9.1.1.  "CENTRAL-MIXED CONCRETE".  DELETE REFERENCE TO NONAGITATING   196
                EQUIPMENT.  THE USE OF NONAGITATING EQUIPMENT WILL NOT BE PERMITTED.   197
                                                                           198
                ASTM SECTION 9.7.  DELETE ASTM SECTION 9.7 AND SUBSTITUTE THE FOLLOWING:  WHEN A   199
                TRUCK MIXER OR AGITATOR IS USED FOR MIXING OR DELIVERY OF CONCRETE, NO WATER   200
                FROM THE TRUCK-WATER SYSTEM OR ELSEWHERE SHALL BE ADDED AFTER THE INITIAL INTRO-   201
                DUCTION OF THE MIXING WATER FOR THE BATCH.  THE CONCRETE SHALL BE DELIVERED TO   202
                THE SITE OF THE WORK AND DISCHARGE SHALL BE COMPLETED WITHIN 1-1/2 HOURS, OR   203
                BEFORE THE DRUM HAS REVOLVED 300 REVOLUTIONS, WHICHEVER COMES FIRST, AFTER THE   204
                INTRODUCTION OF THE MIXING WATER TO THE CEMENT AND AGGREGATES OR THE INTRODUCTION   205
                OF THE CEMENT TO THE AGGREGATES, EXCEPT WHEN THE AIR TEMPERATURE IS ABOVE   206
                85 DEGREES FAHRENHEIT.  WHEN THE AIR TEMPERATURE IS BETWEEN 85 AND 90 DEGREES   207
                FAHRENHEIT, THE 1-1/2 HOURS MIXING AND DELIVERY TIME SHALL BE REDUCED TO 75 MIN-   208
                UTES, AND WHEN THE AIR TEMPERATURE IS ABOVE 90 DEGREES FAHRENHEIT, THE MIXING   209
                AND DELIVERY TIME SHALL BE FURTHER REDUCED TO 60 MINUTES.  WHEN A TRUCK MIXER IS   210
                USED FOR THE COMPLETE MIXING OF THE CONCRETE, THE MIXING OPERATION SHALL BEGIN   211
                WITHIN 30 MINUTES AFTER THE CEMENT HAS BEEN INTERMINGLED WITH THE AGGREGATES.   212
                                                                           213
                ASTM SECTION 14 "CERTIFICATES".  ADD TO ASTM SECTION 14  THE FOLLOWING:  WITH EACH   214
                LOAD OF CONCRETE DELIVERED TO THE SITE OF THE WORK THE READY-MIXED CONCRETE MANU-   215
                FACTURER SHALL FURNISH DUPLICATE DELIVERY TICKETS, ONE FOR THE CONTRACTING OFFICER   216
                AND ONE FOR THE CONTRACTOR.  IN ADDITION TO THE REQUIREMENTS OF ASTM SECTION 14.1,   217
                DELIVERY TICKETS SHALL PROVIDE THE FOLLOWING INFORMATION:  218
                                                                           219
                    TYPE AND BRAND OF CEMENT                               220
                                                                           221
                    CEMENT CONTENT IN 94 POUND BAGS PER CUBIC YARD OF CONCRETE   222
                                                                           223
```

3A-   4

CONCRETE PLACED IN FORMS SHALL BE DEPOSITED IN HORIZONTAL LAYERS NOT DEEPER THAN 18 INCHES IN A MANNER TO AVOID INCLINED HORIZONTAL LAYERS AND INCLINED CONSTRUCTION JOINTS.

TEMPORARY SPREADERS IN FORMS SHALL BE REMOVED WHEN THE CONCRETE PLACING HAS REACHED THE ELEVATION OF THE SPREADERS.

ALL CONCRETE PLACED IN FORMS SHALL BE CONSOLIDATED BY MECHANICAL VIBRATING EQUIPMENT SUPPLEMENTED BY HAND SPADING, RODDING OR TAMPING. VIBRATORS SHALL BE DESIGNED TO OPERATE WITH VIBRATORY ELEMENT SUBMERGED IN THE CONCRETE, AND SHALL MAINTAIN A SPEED OF NOT LESS THAN 6000 IMPULSES WHEN SUBMERGED IN THE CONCRETE. THE VIBRATING EQUIPMENT SHALL BE AT ALL TIMES ADEQUATE IN NUMBER OF UNITS AND POWER OF EACH UNIT TO PROPERLY CONSOLIDATE THE CONCRETE. VIBRATION OF FORMS AND REINFORCEMENT SHALL NOT BE PERMITTED. VIBRATORS SHALL NOT BE USED TO TRANSPORT CONCRETE INSIDE FORMS. VIBRATORS SHALL BE INSERTED AND WITHDRAWN VERTICALLY AT UNIFORMLY SPACED POINTS NOT FARTHER APART THAN THE VISIBLE EFFECTIVENESS OF THE MACHINE. THE VIBRATOR SHALL NOT BE INSERTED INTO LOWER COURSES OF CONCRETE THAT HAVE BEGUN TO SET. AT EACH INSERTION, THE DURATION OF VIBRATION SHALL BE LIMITED TO THE TIME NECESSARY TO CONSOLIDATE THE CONCRETE AND COMPLETE EMBEDMENT OF REINFORCEMENT AND OTHER EMBEDDED ITEMS WITHOUT CAUSING SEGREGATION OF THE CONCRETE MIX.

THE PLACING OF CONCRETE IN SUPPORTING ELEMENTS SHALL NOT BE STARTED UNTIL THE CONCRETE PREVIOUSLY PLACED IN COLUMNS AND WALLS IS NO LONGER PLASTIC.

---PLACING CONCRETE SLABS

CONCRETE FOR SLABS SHALL BE PLACED AND CONSOLIDATED IN A CONTINUOUS OPERATION, WITHIN THE LIMITS OF APPROVED CONSTRUCTION JOINTS, UNTIL THE PLACING OF A PANEL OR SECTION IS COMPLETED.

DURING CONCRETE PLACING OPERATIONS, THE CONCRETE SHALL BE CONSOLIDATED BY MECHANICAL VIBRATING EQUIPMENT SO THAT THE CONCRETE IS THOROUGHLY WORKED AROUND REINFORCEMENT AND OTHER EMBEDDED ITEMS AND INTO CORNERS. THE CONCRETE PLACED IN BEAMS AND GIRDERS OF SUPPORTED SLABS AND AGAINST THE BULKHEADS OF SLABS ON GROUND SHALL BE CONSOLIDATED BY MECHANICAL VIBRATORS AS SPECIFIED HEREINBEFORE IN THE PARAGRAPH ENTITLED "PLACING CONCRETE IN FORMS". THE CONCRETE IN THE REMAINDER OF THE SLABS SHALL BE CONSOLIDATED BY VIBRATING BRIDGE SCREEDS, ROLLER PIPE SCREEDS, OR OTHER APPROVED METHOD. CONSOLIDATION OPERATIONS SHALL BE LIMITED TO THE TIME NECESSARY TO OBTAIN CONSOLIDATION OF THE CONCRETE WITHOUT BRINGING AN EXCESS OF FINE AGGREGATE TO THE SURFACE. CONCRETE TO BE CONSOLIDATED SHALL BE AS DRY AS PRACTICABLE AND THE SURFACES THEREOF SHALL NOT BE MANIPULATED PRIOR TO THE FINISHING OPERATIONS. CONCRETE SHALL BE BROUGHT TO THE CORRECT LEVEL WITH A STRAIGHTEDGE AND STRUCK-OFF. BULL FLOATS OR DARBIES SHALL BE USED TO SMOOTH THE SURFACE, LEAVING IT FREE OF HUMPS OR HOLLOWS. NO SPRINKLING OF WATER ON PLASTIC SURFACE SHALL BE PERMITTED.

THE FINISH OF SLABS SHALL BE AS HEREINAFTER SPECIFIED IN THE ARTICLE ENTITLED "FINISHING OF MONOLITHIC SLABS".

---BONDING

THE SURFACES OF THE SET CONCRETE AT ALL JOINTS SHALL BE ROUGHENED, EXCEPT WHERE BONDING IS OBTAINED BY USE OF A CONCRETE BONDING AGENT, AND CLEANED FREE OF LAITANCE, COATINGS, LOOSE PARTICLES AND FOREIGN MATTER. SURFACES SHALL BE ROUGHENED IN A MANNER WHICH WILL EXPOSE THE AGGREGATE UNIFORMLY AND WILL NOT LEAVE LAITANCE, LOOSENED PARTICLES OF AGGREGATE, NOR DAMAGED CONCRETE AT THE SURFACE.

BONDING OF FRESH CONCRETE TO CONCRETE THAT HAS SET SHALL BE OBTAINED AS FOLLOWS:

AT JOINTS BETWEEN FOOTINGS AND WALLS OR COLUMNS, BETWEEN WALLS OR COLUMNS AND BEAMS OR SLABS THEY SUPPORT, AND ELSEWHERE UNLESS OTHERWISE SPECIFIED HEREINAFTER, THE ROUGHENED AND CLEANED SURFACE OF THE SET CONCRETE SHALL BE DAMPENED, BUT NOT SATURATED, IMMEDIATELY PRIOR TO THE PLACING OF FRESH CONCRETE.

AT JOINTS IN EXPOSED-TO-VIEW WORK; AT VERTICAL JOINTS IN WALLS; AT JOINTS NEAR THE MID POINT OF SPAN IN GIRDERS, BEAMS, SUPPORTED SLABS AND OTHER STRUCTURAL MEMBERS; AND AT JOINTS IN WORK DESIGNED TO CONTAIN LIQUIDS, THE ROUGHENED AND CLEANED SURFACE OF THE SET CONCRETE SHALL BE DAMPENED, BUT NOT SATURATED, AND THOROUGHLY COVERED WITH A CEMENT GROUT COATING.

THE CEMENT GROUT SHALL CONSIST OF EQUAL PARTS OF PORTLAND CEMENT AND FINE AGGREGATE BY WEIGHT AND NOT MORE THAN 6 GALLONS OF WATER PER SACK OF CEMENT. THE CEMENT GROUT SHALL BE APPLIED WITH A STIFF BROOM OR BRUSH TO A MINIMUM THICKNESS OF 1/16 INCH. THE FRESH CONCRETE SHALL BE DEPOSITED BEFORE THE CEMENT GROUT HAS ATTAINED ITS INITIAL SET.

INSTEAD OF AS SPECIFIED ABOVE, BONDING OF FRESH CONCRETE TO CONCRETE THAT HAS SET MAY BE OBTAINED BY THE USE OF CONCRETE BONDING AGENT. SUCH BONDING MATERIAL SHALL BE APPLIED TO THE CLEANED CONCRETE SURFACE IN ACCORDANCE WITH THE PRINTED INSTRUCTIONS OF THE BONDING MATERIAL MANUFACTURER.

WHERE FRESH CONCRETE WILL BE DEPOSITED ON OR AGAINST HARDENED CONCRETE OR EXISTING CONCRETE, BONDING SHALL BE OBTAINED BY THE USE OF EPOXY-RESIN ADHESIVE BINDER. INSTALLATION SHALL BE AS FOLLOWS:

EPOXY-RESIN ADHESIVE BINDER SHALL BE DELIVERED TO THE PROJECT SITE IN SUCH MANNER   1503
AS TO AVOID DAMAGE OR LOSS. STORAGE AREAS SHALL BE IN A WINDOWLESS AND WEATHER   1504
PROOF BUT VENTILATED, INSULATED, NONCOMBUSTIBLE BUILDING, WITH PROVISION NEARBY   1505
FOR CONDITIONING THE MATERIAL TO 70 TO 85 DEGREES FAHRENHEIT FOR A PERIOD OF 48   1506
HOURS BEFORE USE. THE AMBIENT TEMPERATURE IN THE STORAGE AREA OF THE EPOXY   1507
MATERIALS SHALL BE AT NO TIME HIGHER THAN 100 DEGREES FAHRENHEIT.   1508
                                                                                   1509
EPOXY-RESIN ADHESIVE BINDER SHALL BE MIXED IN THE PROPORTIONS RECOMMENDED BY THE   1510
MANUFACTURER. THE COMPONENTS SHALL BE CONDITIONED TO 70 TO 85 DEGREES FAHRENHEIT   1511
FOR 48 HOURS PRIOR TO MIXING. THE TWO EPOXY-RESIN ADHESIVE BINDER COMPONENTS   1512
SHALL BE MIXED WITH A POWER-DRIVEN EXPLOSION-PROOF STIRRING DEVICE IN A METAL OR   1513
POLYETHYLENE CONTAINER HAVING A HEMISPHERICAL BOTTOM FOR THE MIXING VESSEL. THE   1514
POLYSULFIDE-CURING AGENT COMPONENT SHALL BE ADDED GRADUALLY TO THE EPOXY-RESIN   1515
COMPONENT WITH CONSTANT STIRRING UNTIL A UNIFORM MIXTURE IS OBTAINED. THE RATE   1516
OF STIRRING SHALL BE SUCH THAT THE ENTRAINED AIR IS A MINIMUM.   1517
                                                                                   1518
PROTECTIVE CLOTHING, GLOVES, AND EYE PROTECTIVE DEVICES SHALL BE PROVIDED FOR ALL   1519
WORKMEN ENGAGED IN EPOXY-RESIN GROUT MIXING AND PLACING OPERATIONS.   1520
                                                                                   1521
ADEQUATE VENTILATION AND FIRE PROTECTION PRECAUTIONS SHALL BE MAINTAINED AT ALL   1522
MIXING AND PLACING OPERATIONS.   1523
                                                                                   1524
BEFORE DEPOSITING FRESH CONCRETE, THE SURFACES OF THE HARDENED CONCRETE OR EXIST-   1525
ING CONCRETE SHALL BE THOROUGHLY ROUGHENED AND CLEANED FREE OF DEBRIS AND LOOSE   1526
CONCRETE, AND THEN THOROUGHLY COATED WITH EPOXY-RESIN GROUT NOT LESS THAN 1/16   1527
INCH IN THICKNESS. PLACEMENT OF THE FRESH CONCRETE SHALL BE ACCOMPLISHED WHILE   1528
THE EPOXY-RESIN ADHESIVE BINDER IS STILL TACKY AND IN SUCH MANNER THAT THE GROUT   1529
COATING WILL NOT BE REMOVED.   1530
                                                                                   1531
INSTALLATION REQUIREMENTS NOT SPECIFIED HEREINBEFORE SHALL BE IN ACCORDANCE WITH   1532
THE EPOXY-RESIN ADHESIVE BINDER MANUFACTURER'S PRINTED INSTALLATION INSTRUCTIONS,   1533
AS APPROVED BY THE CONTRACTING OFFICER.   1534
                                                                                   1535
                                          ---FINISHING OF FORMED SURFACES---   1536
                                                                                   1537
        NOTE: THE FOLLOWING FINISHING OF FORMED SUR-   1538 AA
        FACES DO NOT INCLUDE SPECIAL ARCHITECTURAL   1538 AB
        FINISHES, SUCH AS EXPOSED AGGREGATE FINISH,   1538 AC
        TEXTURED FORM FINISH, SPECIAL PANEL FINISH, AND   1538 AD
        AGGREGATE TRANSFER FINISH. WHEN SPECIAL ARCHI-   1538 AE
        TECTURAL FINISHES ARE REQUIRED BY THE PROJECT,   1538 AF
        THE REQUIREMENTS FOR SUCH FINISHES SHOULD BE   1538 AG
        SPECIFIED. THE LOCATIONS OF SPECIAL ARCHITEC-   1538 AH
        TURAL FINISHES SHOULD BE INDICATED ON THE   1538 AI
        DRAWINGS.   1538 AJ
                                                                                  1538 AK
---REPAIRING AND PATCHING DEFECTIVE AREAS   1538
                                                                                   1539
    IMMEDIATELY AFTER REMOVAL OF FORMS, ALL DEFECTIVE AREAS SHALL BE REPAIRED AND PATCHED   1540
    WITH CEMENT MORTAR.   1541
                                                                                   1542
    HONEYCOMB, ROCK POCKETS, VOIDS OVER 1/2 INCH IN DIAMETER, AND HOLES LEFT BY TIE   1543
    RODS AND BOLTS SHALL BE CUT OUT TO SOLID CONCRETE; BUT IN NO CASE TO A DEPTH OF LESS   1544
    THAN 1 INCH. THE EDGES OF CUTS SHALL BE PERPENDICULAR TO THE SURFACE OF THE CONCRETE.   1545
    BEFORE PLACING THE CEMENT MORTAR, THE AREA TO BE PATCHED AND AT LEAST 6 INCHES   1546
    ADJACENT THERETO SHALL BE THOROUGHLY CLEANED, DAMPENED WITH WATER, AND BRUSH-COATED   1547
    WITH NEAT PORTLAND CEMENT GROUT. THE CEMENT MORTAR FOR PATCHING SHALL CONSIST OF ONE   1548
    PART STANDARD PORTLAND CEMENT TO 2 PARTS FINE AGGREGATE PASSING NO. 16 MESH SIEVE,   1549
    AND AS LITTLE WATER AS NECESSARY FOR HANDLING AND PLACING. WHERE THE CONCRETE SURFACE   1550
    WILL BE EXPOSED TO VIEW, THE PORTLAND CEMENT PORTION OF THE CEMENT MORTAR SHALL BE A   1551
    BLEND OF WHITE AND STANDARD PORTLAND CEMENT SO THAT, WHEN DRY, THE CEMENT MORTAR SHALL   1552
    MATCH THE SURROUNDING CONCRETE IN COLOR. THE CEMENT MORTAR SHALL BE THOROUGHLY COM-   1553
    PACTED IN PLACE AND STRUCK OFF SLIGHTLY HIGHER THAN THE SURROUNDING SURFACE. HOLES   1554
    EXTENDING THROUGH THE CONCRETE SHALL BE FILLED BY MEANS OF A PLUNGER TYPE GUN OR   1555
    OTHER SUITABLE DEVICE FROM THE UNEXPOSED FACE, USING A STOP HELD AT THE EXPOSED FACE   1556
    TO INSURE COMPLETE FILLING.   1557
                                                                                   1558
---STANDARD ROUGH FORM FINISH   1559
                                                                                   1560
    STANDARD ROUGH FORM FINISH SHALL BE THE CONCRETE SURFACE HAVING THE TEXTURE IMPARTED   1561
    BY THE FORM FACING MATERIAL USED, DEFECTIVE AREAS REPAIRED AND PATCHED AS SPECIFIED   1562
    HEREINBEFORE, AND ALL FINS AND OTHER PROJECTIONS EXCEEDING 1/4 INCH IN HEIGHT RUBBED   1563
    DOWN WITH WOOD BLOCKS.   1564
                                                                                   1565
    STANDARD ROUGH FORM FINISH SHALL BE GIVEN ALL CONCRETE FORMED SURFACES THAT ARE TO BE   1566
    CONCEALED BY OTHER CONSTRUCTION, UNLESS OTHERWISE SPECIFIED HEREINAFTER.   1567
                                                                                   1568
---STANDARD SMOOTH FINISH   1569
                                                                                   1570
    STANDARD SMOOTH FINISH SHALL BE THE AS-CAST CONCRETE SURFACE AS OBTAINED WITH THE   1571
    FORM FACING MATERIAL FOR STANDARD SMOOTH FINISH, DEFECTIVE AREAS REPAIRED AND PATCHED   1572
    AS SPECIFIED HEREINBEFORE, AND ALL FINS AND OTHER PROJECTIONS ON THE SURFACE COMPLETE-   1573
    LY REMOVED.   1574
                                                                                   1575

                                                                    3A- 23

ARCHITECTURAL WOODWORK GUIDE SPECIFICATIONS
Architectural Woodwork should, in all cases, be a separate section of Division 6.

The following is a suggested form for architectural woodwork specifications. Additions, deletions and changes should be made to conform with the specific requirements of the project. The schedules shown are an excellent supplement to the specifications.

GUIDE SPECIFICATION	NOTES TO SPECIFIER
1. GENERAL CONDITIONS	
1.01 The General Conditions of the contract are a part of this section of the specifications.	
2. SCOPE OF WORK	**2. SCOPE OF WORK** List briefly: Exterior trim; miscellaneous exterior millwork; exterior frames; interior trim; jambs; stairwork; casework (conventional); plastic covered casework; plastic tops and wall panels; laboratory tops (specify type); fire retardant treatment; doors; modular casework (wood factory finished or plastic covered).
2.01 All millwork shall be furnished and delivered as shown and/or specified, and as defined in applicable paragraphs of Section 2 of the latest edition of the Manual of Millwork as published by the Woodwork Institute of California.	
3. WORK NOT INCLUDED	**3. WORK NOT INCLUDED** Items listed are normally not included. If all or part are to be included, list them under 2.01 "Scope of Work."
3.01 Blocking, furring, grounds, reglets, cant strip, waste moulds, and structural members.	
3.02 Glass or glazing. (Local practices should determine if included or excluded.)	
3.03 Painting or priming.	
3.04 Cores for all metal covered work.	
3.05 Hardware, except hardware required in the fabrication of casework, miscellaneous specialty items shown in the interior of cases, and sash balances.	
3.06 Other items as desired.	
3.07 Installation of any kind.	
4. INSTALLATION	**4. INSTALLATION** If installation is required by manufacturer of millwork or casework, it shall be so specified and included under 2.01 "Scope of Work."
4.01 See Carpentry specifications for work in that division.	
5. SHOP DRAWINGS	**5. SHOP DRAWINGS** See: Section 1, Page 5, Manual of Millwork, listing minimum requirements for Architectural Shop Drawings including door schedules, profiles, wall paneling sections, and casework.
5.01 Mill shall prepare Shop Drawings as required in the execution of their work and submit drawings in duplicate to the architect for approval of general design only, as required by Section 1, Page 5 of the Manual of Millwork. After approval of details, mill shall furnish such copies of drawings as are required for distribution. The WIC Certified Compliance Grade Stamp indicating the grade specified shall be affixed to the casework shop drawings, certifying that the casework will be manufactured in accordance with the WIC grade specified.	
6. JOB MEASUREMENTS	**6. JOB MEASUREMENTS** If coordination with other trades is required, these trades or crafts should be noted under 4.01.
The mill shall take such field measurements as may be required for their work and be responsible for same. Report any major discrepancy between plan and field dimensions to the architect through proper channels.	

—1—

GUIDE SPECIFICATION

7. STANDARDS AND CERTIFICATION

7.01 All millwork shall be manufactured in accordance with the standards established in the latest edition of the Manual of Millwork of the Woodwork Institute of California in the Grade or Grades hereinafter specified or as shown on the drawings.

7.02 Before delivery to the jobsite, the millwork supplier shall issue a WIC Certified Compliance Certificate indicating the millwork products he will furnish for this job and certifying that they will fully meet all the requirements of the Grade or Grades specified.

7.03 Each unit of casework shall bear the WIC Certified Compliance Grade Stamp indicating the grade specified.

7.04 Each plastic laminate counter top shall bear the WIC Certified Compliance Grade Stamp indicating the grade specified.

7.05 Each laboratory counter top shall bear the WIC Certified Compliance Grade Stamp indicating the grade specified.

7.06 To assure quality as specified, the architect or his representative may inspect work in the process of manufacture or prior to delivery.

8. MATERIALS AND GRADES

Lumber and plywood shall be new, clean stock of the species and WIC grades shown below for the various uses.

—2—

312

GUIDE SPECIFICATION

(Grades and species shown are for illustration only and are not to be considered as suggestions or recommendations.)

		Species	WIC Grade	Finish
8.01	Exterior Trim	Redwood	Custom	Opaque
8.02	Exterior Miscellaneous Millwork	Redwood	Custom	Opaque
8.03	Exterior Frames	Redwood	Custom	Opaque
8.04	Interior Trim	Sel. R. Birch	Custom	Transparent
8.05	Interior Miscellaneous Millwork	Sel. R. Birch	Custom	Transparent
8.06	Interior Jambs	Sel. R. Birch	Custom	Transparent
8.07	Stairwork	Oak	Custom	Transparent
8.08	Sash and Windows— Wood	P. Pine	Custom	Opaque
8.09	Screens and Screen Doors	Douglas Fir	Custom	Opaque
8.10	Blinds and Shutters— Wood	Douglas Fir	Custom	Opaque

8.11 Preservative Treatment.

All _____ (designate items desired) shall be treated at the mill with wood preservative, in accordance with Section 18 of the Manual of Millwork.

NOTES TO SPECIFIER

8.01 Refer to Manual of Millwork, Section 7. Note if WIC grade, species or finish are not specified, WIC Economy Grade softwood intended for an opaque finish will be supplied. If species, grade or finish are not constant throughout the job, see suggested schedule contained in supplement to this Guide Specification.

8.02 Refer to Manual of Millwork, Section 8, and see note under 8.01 above.

8.03 Refer to Manual of Millwork, Section 9. If not shown on drawings, indicate whether flat jambs with applied stop, plowed jambs with "T" stop or rabbeted jambs are desired. See note under 8.01 above.

8.04 Refer to Manual of Millwork, Section 10. See note under 8.01 above.

8.05 Refer to Manual of Millwork, Section 11, specify any special matching of plywood desired and see note under 8. above.

If any miscellaneous interior millwork is to be covered with plastic laminate, see Section 16.

8.06 Refer to Manual of Millwork, Section 12. If not shown on drawings, indicate whether flat jambs with applied stop, plowed jambs with "T" stop or rabbeted jambs, and see note under 8.01 above.

8.07 Refer to Manual of Millwork, Section 13, and see note under 8.01 above.

8.08 Refer to Manual of Millwork, Section 21. Indicate if wood stops are desired. Indicate number and arrangement of cut up lights.

8.09 Refer to Manual of Millwork, Section 22. If species, grade and finish are not indicated, material will be WIC Economy Grade softwood intended for an opaque finish. Wire cloth shall be galvanized, 18 x 14 mesh.

8.10 Refer to Manual of Millwork, Section 23. See note on 8.01 above.

8.11 Refer to Manual of Millwork, Section 18. Specify the following:
a. All items of millwork to be preservative treated.

—3—

313

GUIDE SPECIFICATION

8.12   Casework, Conventional.

All casework shall be WIC _____ Grade (indicate grade).

All exposed portions shall be _____ (indicate species) intended for _____ finish (indicate transparent or opaque).

Construction shall be _____ (indicate face frame or flush overlay). If face frame construction, doors and drawers shall be _____ (lipped or flush).

Semi-exposed portions shall conform to the requirements of Section 14 for the grade or grades specified (if other material is desired, it must be so specified).

Cabinet doors shall be WIC type _____ (indicate type desired).

For flush overlay type construction, cabinet door hinges are furnished under the hardware Section _____ and shall be installed by the casework fabricator.

8.13   Casework, Conventional, Plastic Covered.

All plastic covered casework shall be WIC _____ Grade (indicate grade) (indicate brand, color, pattern numbers).

Cabinet hardware is furnished under Section _____ and shall be installed by the cabinet fabricator.

8.14   Laminated Plastic Counter Tops and Splashes.

All laminated plastic counter tops and splashes shall be WIC _____ Grade (indicate grade), with _____ edge covering (indicate type of edge covering) with _____ splash (indicate type of splash and height) (indicate brand, color, pattern numbers).

Each top shall bear the WIC Certified Compliance Grade Stamp indicating the grade specified, and the top fabricator shall furnish a WIC Certified Compliance Certificate certifying the tops he will furnish for this job fully meet all the requirements for the WIC grade specified.

NOTES TO SPECIFIER

8.12 Refer to Manual of Millwork, Section 14, and note on Page 3 the definitions of exposed, semi-exposed and concealed portions. If other material requirements are desired for semi-exposed portions, it must be so specified.

Note typical casework construction details, Pages 15, 16, 17 and 18 of Section 14.

If metal drawer slides are desired, they must be so specified. List acceptable choices by brand names and number.

Indicate WIC type of cabinet door desired. If not indicated, type of cabinet door shall be optional with the manufacturer within the limitations enumerated in Para. VII of Section 14. Unless otherwise indicated, cabinet doors shall be a minimum of 3/4" in thickness.

For counter tops, see Sections 16 and 17 of the Manual of Millwork.

See suggested casework schedule contained in supplement to this Guide Specification.

Indicate any desired modification from WIC standards.

8.13 Refer to Manual of Millwork, Section 15, and review definitions of exposed, semi-exposed and concealed portions.

See typical construction details Pages 3 and 4 of Section 15.

If metal drawer slides are desired, they must be so specified. List acceptable choices by brand names and number.

If counter tops are required, see Sections 16 and 17.

See suggested casework schedule contained in supplement to Guide Specification.

Indicate any desired modifications from WIC standards.

8.14 Refer to Manual of Millwork, Section 16. If WIC grade is not specified, counter tops shall be the same grade as that specified for casework.

If type of edge covering is not specified, self-edged will be furnished.

If type of back splash is not specified, an integral cove back splash will be furnished.

If type of top of back splash is not indicated, top edge of splash will be square with self-edge.

If height of back splash is not specified, height will be a minimum of 4" in height above the deck surface.

Indicate any desired modification from WIC standards.

—4—

314

GUIDE SPECIFICATION

8.15 Laminated Plastic Wall Paneling.

All laminated plastic wall paneling shall be _____ (indicate pattern, color) conforming to the requirements of Section 16, Para. VII of the Manual of Millwork.

8.16 Laboratory Tops and Splashes.

8.16.1 Laboratory Tops and Splashes—Acid Resistant Laminated Plastic.

All acid resistant laminated plastic tops and splashes shall be WIC _____ Grade (indicate grade) with _____ splash (indicate type of splash and height). Each top shall bear the WIC Certified Compliance Grade Stamp indicating the grade specified, and top fabricator shall furnish a WIC Certified Compliance Certificate certifying the tops he will furnish for this job fully meet all the requirements of the WIC grade specified.

(See Notes to Specifier for options.)

8.16.2 Laboratory Tops and Splashes—Composition Stone.

All composition stone laboratory tops and splashes shall be WIC _____ Grade (indicate grade). Each top shall bear the WIC Certified Compliance Grade Stamp indicating the grade specified, and top fabricator shall furnish a WIC Certified Compliance Certificate certifying the tops he will furnish for this job fully meet all the requirements of the WIC grade specified.

(See Notes to Specifier for options.)

NOTES TO SPECIFIER

8.15 Refer to Manual of Millwork, Section 16. Premium Grade is the only grade available. Indicate the location of furring strips and core material if desired. Indicate if other than textured surface laminate is desired. Indicate height of wainscote if other than 4'-0" above the floor is desired.

8.16 Laboratory Tops and Splashes.

8.16.1 Refer to Manual of Millwork, Section 17. Specify the following:

WIC grade or grades. (If not specified, counter tops of same grade as casework shall be furnished.)

Type of back splash, square butt or integral cove. (If not specified, integral cove back splash will be furnished.)

Top of back splash to be waterfall or square with self-edge. (If not specified, top of splash shall be square with self-edge.)

Height of back splash. (If not specified, splash shall be a minimum of 6" in height above deck surfaces unless job conditions do not permit.)

Type and size of sink desired.

Any modifications from WIC standards.

Refer to Page 3, Section 17 for details of acid resistant laminated plastic laboratory tops, and for acid resistance requirements see Page 4, Section 17.

8.16.2 Refer to Manual of Millwork, Section 17A. Specify the following:

WIC grade or grades.

If color other than standard charcoal gray is required.

If glazed tops and splashes are required.

If special water dam edge at fume hoods, drain grooves adjoining sink areas, or other special provisions.

Type and size of sink. If type is not specified, composition stone will be furnished.

Size and type of fixture required for sink drains.

If other than center drains in sinks are required.

If sealer or finish other than recommended by fabricator.

Height of splash. If not shown or specified, a minimum of 6" in height above the deck surface unless job conditions do not permit.

If scribe molds are required.

Refer to Page 2, Section 17A for Chemical Resistance Tests, and Page 3 for details of Composition Stone Tops.

—5—

315

GUIDE SPECIFICATION

8.16.3 Laboratory Tops and Splashes—Glass-Reinforced Polyester.

All glass-reinforced polyester tops shall conform to the requirements of Section 17B of the Manual of Millwork. Each top shall bear the WIC Certified Compliance Grade Stamp and the top fabricator shall furnish a WIC Certified Compliance Certificate certifying that the tops he will furnish will fully meet the WIC requirements.

(See Notes to Specifier for options.)

8.17 Doors—Wood.

Doors shall meet all the requirements of the WIC grade or grades hereinafter specified.

8.17.1 Flush Doors.

Flush doors shall be WIC _____ Grade (indicate grade), _____ (indicate species) intended for a _____ finish (indicate transparent or opaque).

Solid core doors shall be WIC Type _____ (indicate Type A or Type B) construction.

Laminated plastic face doors shall be WIC _____ Grade (indicate grade) with _____ plastic (give brand name, color, etc.).

Fire rated doors shall be _____ hour and shall bear UL Label (indicate 1-1/2, 1 or 3/4 hour). (Indicate if metal vision light frames are desired.) (Indicate type, size and location of metal vision light frames.)

Sound insulation doors shall have a sound transmission class of _____ (indicate class desired).

Transom panel construction shall be WIC Type _____ (indicate Type A or Type B) construction.

NOTES TO SPECIFIER

8.16.3 Refer to Manual of Millwork, Section 17B. Specify the following:

Location and dimensions of glass-reinforced polyester tops, sinks, splashes and shelves.

Type and size of sinks. If type is not specified, a glass-reinforced polyester sink will be furnished. If size is not indicated, sink will be a stock size as listed in the supplement to Section 17B, Manual of Millwork.

Tail pieces for sinks if required.

Color if other than standard light stone gray.

Height of back splash. If not specified, splashes will be a minimum of 6" in height above the deck surface, unless job conditions do not permit.

Any modifications from WIC standards.

Refer to Page 3, Section 17B for details, and Page 4 for Chemical Resistance Tests. See Page 6 for stock sink sizes.

8.17 Refer to Manual of Millwork, Section 20. WIC recommends that wood doors be included in same section of the specifications as all other architectural woodwork.

SPECIFY THE FOLLOWING:

8.17.1 All doors, transom panels, lights, louvers, astragals, edgings and hardware for doors that are required to comply with applicable state and local codes and statutes.

Where metal stops or metal vision light frames are required by codes or statutes, specify as to material, type, size and location.

Type of face veneer cut (plain sliced, rift cut, etc.).

If special type solid or hollow core is required, it must be specified. Otherwise, NWMA standards optional with the manufacturer will be furnished.

Where special hardware is specified such as kick plates, door closures, door hinges, panic hardware, special locks, etc., it is recommended that solid core doors be specified.

If hollow core construction is desired, the specifications must indicate special core construction if required to accommodate the hardware specified.

Type, size and location of lights, louvers, astragals, edgings and hardware.

(Continued)

—6—

316

GUIDE SPECIFICATION	NOTES TO SPECIFIER
	8.17.1 (Continued)
	Warranty.
	Underwriters Label for fire doors.
	Sound transmission class for sound insulating doors.
	Flashing if required for exterior doors.
	Book matching of face veneers. (Premium Grade contains this requirement.)
	Continuous grain matching of flush transom above flush doors if continuous grain matching through the door and transom is required. (Premium Grade contains this requirement.)
	Pairs of doors requiring sequence matching of face veneers. (Premium Grade contains this requirement.)
	Doors and adjacent panels requiring face veneers to be sequence matched.
	Overlay or other specialty faced doors.
	For allowable tolerances, see Page 6 of Section 20.
8.17.2 Stile and Rail Doors.	**8.17.2** Refer to Manual of Millwork, Section 20, Paragraphs VI and VII.
All stile and rail doors shall be WIC _____ (indicate grade), _____ (indicate species) for a _____ finish (indicate transparent or opaque), conforming to the requirements of Section 20 of the Manual of Millwork.	
8.17.3 All doors shall have light and louver cutouts sealed at the factory with one coat of exterior sealer.	**8.17.3** Require that all doors have top and bottom edges sealed with exterior sealer under the painting section of the specifications.
9. DELIVERY	**9.** If the project is located in an area of extreme weather and/or moisture conditions, extra precautions for the storage of millwork products should be required.
Do not deliver millwork of any kind to the job until notified by the general contractor that the building is in proper condition and arrangements are made to properly handle, store and protect such work.	

SUPPLEMENTAL SCHEDULES

Where species, WIC grades and finishes vary from room to room or throughout the project, a schedule or schedules similar to the following may prove of value in defining clearly what the requirements are under this section of the project.

Such schedules may be included in the specifications or drawn in the plans. If included in the plans, a reference should be made in the specifications.

–7–

317

SUPPLEMENTAL SCHEDULES

MILLWORK

ITEM	Douglas Fir	Ponderosa Pine	Redwood	Birch	Maple	Walnut	Teak	Oak	Opaque	Transparent	Economy	Custom	Premium
			SPECIES							FINISH	W.I.C. GRADE		
8.01 Exterior Trim													
8.02 Exterior Misc. Millwork													
8.03 Exterior Frames													
8.04 Interior Trim													
8.05 Interior Misc. Millwork													
8.06 Interior Jambs													
8.07 Stairwork													
8.08 Sash and Windows													
8.09 Screens and Screen Doors													
8.10 Blinds and Shutters													

CONVENTIONAL WOOD CASEWORK

8.12 Casework ROOM NO.	Face Frame	Lipped Doors & Drawers	Flush Doors & Drawers	Flush Overlay	Economy	Custom	Premium	Birch	Maple	Ash	Walnut	Plastic *	Wood	Type	Type	Opaque	Transparent
	TYPE				W.I.C. GRADE			SPECIES					TOPS		DOORS	FINISH	
1																	
2																	
3																	

CONVENTIONAL PLASTIC COVERED CASEWORK
(No Face Frame Construction)

8.13 Casework ROOM NO.	Economy	Custom	Premium	Brand or Trade Name	Stock or Design No.	Finish – Gloss, Satin, or Textured	Plastic *	Other (Specify)		
	W.I.C. GRADE			PLASTIC			TOPS			
1										
2										
3										

* If plastic tops are required, see Section 16, Manual of Millwork. —8—

C

SPECIFICATION REFERENCES

The documents contained in this Appendix are primarily illustrations of portions of major references used in almost every specification (see list below). One document is that of a major commercial testing and standards organization; the remainder are excerpts from governmentally published guide specifications and their index.

Tentative Specification for Sheet Material for Curing Concrete, American Society for Testing and Materials

Type Specification—Department of the Navy, Bureau of Yards and Docks

Federal Specification, Hardware, Builders: Locks and Door-trim, General Services Administration

Typical pages, Index to Federal Specifications, General Services Administration

Tentative Specification for

SHEET MATERIALS FOR CURING CONCRETE[1]

ASTM Designation: C 171 – 68 T

This Tentative Specification has been approved by the sponsoring committee and accepted by the Society in accordance with established procedures, for use pending adoption as standard. Suggestions for revisions should be addressed to the Society at 1916 Race St., Philadelphia, Pa. 19103.

1. Scope

1.1 This specification covers materials in sheet form used for covering the surfaces of hydraulic cement concrete to inhibit moisture loss during the curing period and, in the case of the white reflective type materials, to also reduce temperature rise in concrete exposed to radiation from the sun. The following types are included:

1.1.1 *Waterproof Paper:*
Regular
White

1.1.2 *Polyethylene Film:*
Clear
White Opaque

1.1.3 *White Burlap-Polyethylene Sheet.*

NOTE 1—The values stated in U.S. customary units are to be regarded as the standard. The metric equivalents of U.S. customary units given in the body of the standard may be approximate.

---

[1] Under the standardization procedure of the Society, this specification is under the jurisdiction of the ASTM Committee C-9 on Concrete and Concrete Aggregates. A list of members may be found in the ASTM Year Book.

Current edition accepted, June 26, 1968. Originally issued 1942. Replaces C 171 – 63.

2. Basis of Purchase

2.1 The purchaser shall specify the type of curing material to be furnished under this specification.

3. General Characteristics

3.1 The sheet materials furnished under this specification should be tough, strong, resilient, and capable of withstanding normal job use without puncturing or tearing.

4. Detail Requirements

4.1 Physical requirements of the sheet materials are prescribed in Table 1, and the following additional requirements are specified for the individual types:

4.1.1 Waterproof paper shall consist of two sheets of kraft paper cemented together with a bituminous material in which are embedded cords or strands of fiber running in both directions and not more than 1¼ in. (32 mm) apart. The paper shall be light in color, shall be free of visible defects, and shall have a uniform appearance. White paper shall have a white surface on at least one side.

4.1.2 Polyethylene film shall consist of a single sheet manufactured from

129

64–79

320

DEPARTMENT OF THE NAVY
BUREAU OF
YARDS AND DOCKS

TYPE
SPECIFICATION
TS-H15
21 December 1964

Type Specifications shall not be referenced but
are to be used as manuscripts in preparing
project specifications. APPROPRIATE CHANGES
AND ADDITIONS AS MAY BE NECESSARY AND AS REQUIRED
BY THE NOTES MUST BE MADE. Numbers in paren-
theses--e.g., "(4)"-- in right-hand margin refer
to corresponding notes at end of specification.
This section shall be included in Division 10 of
the new format. (Refer to TS-M129r for format).

SECTION   BUILDERS' HARDWARE

.1 Scope. This section includes all builders' hardware not
specified in other sections of this specification.

.2 Applicable documents. The following specifications and stan-   (4)
dards of the issues listed in this paragraph (including the amendments,
addenda, and errata designated), but referred to hereinafter by basic
designation only, form a part of this specification to the extent required by the references thereto. (See paragraph entitled "Specifications and standards" in Section 1A for additional information.)

.2.1 Federal specifications.

AA-C-30 ____   Cabinet, key, (boxes and racks, metal, and identi-
                       fication systems).

FF-H-106 ____   Hardware, builders'; locks and door trim.

FF-H-111 ____   Hardware, builders'; shelf and miscellaneous.

FF-H-116 ____   Hinges, hardware, builders'.

FF-H-121 ____   Hardware, builders', door-closing devices.

FF-P-101 ____   Padlocks.

.2.2 Non-Government documents.

~National Board of Fire Underwriters

80   Standard for the installation of fire doors and
                      windows; _____.

TS-H15
Sheet 1 of 8

FF-H-106a
<ins>23 NOVEMBER 1948</ins>
SUPERSEDING
Fed. Spec. FF-H-106
June 6, 1933.

FEDERAL SPECIFICATION

HARDWARE, BUILDERS'; LOCKS AND DOOR-TRIM

This specification was approved by the Director, Bureau of Federal Supply, for the use of all departments and establishments of the Government.

1. SCOPE AND CLASSIFICATION

1.1 Scope.—The hardware covered by this specification is that generally classified as builders' locks and lock-trim, or door-trim. It is not intended for marine use. (See definitions, 6.13, and index, p. 61.)

1.2 Types.—The hardware shall be of the types described in section 3, as specified.

2. APPLICABLE SPECIFICATIONS

2.1 Specifications.—The following Federal Specifications, of the issues in effect on date of invitation for bids, form a part of this specification:

FF-H-111—Hardware, Builders'; Shelf and Miscellaneous.

QQ-M-151—Metals; General Specification for Inspection of.

QQ-Z-363—Zinc-Base Alloy; Die Castings.

2.2 Specifications and publications applicable only to individual departments are listed in section 7.

3. REQUIREMENTS

CONTENTS OF SECTION 3

	Paragraph
Applicable requirements	3.1-3.1.1.
Materials	3.2-3.5.
Finishes	3.6-3.14.
Lock design and construction	3.15-3.29.
Workmanship, illustrations, dimensions	3.30-3.31.3.
Types of hardware	3.31.4 (pp. 6 to 51).

3.1 Applicable requirements.—The hardware shall conform (*a*) to all requirements given herein under the type number for which it is furnished, (*b*) to any other applicable requirements in this section, and (*c*) to any additional requirements specified in the invitation for bids in accordance with selective variations provided herein as to size, length, finish, etc. The hardware shall also meet any applicable tests in section 4.

3.1.1 *Supplier's options.*—Where variations are permitted herein as to materials, construction, appearance, or other characteristics, hardware conforming to any of the options thus provided, as well as to all other applicable requirements given herein, shall be considered as meeting this specification.

3.2 Materials, general.

3.2.1 *Optional materials.*—Where materials specified herein are designated as given below, the respective optional materials listed may be substituted. (This option does not apply to finish. See 3.6.1.)

Designated material:	*Optional material*
Brass	Bronze. (See 3.3.1.)
Brass, nickel-plated	White bronze (unplated).
Bronze	(See 3.3.2.)
Cast (nonferrous metal)	(See 3.2.2.)
Wrought (metal)	Rolled, forged, extruded, or pressure-cast forms of the metal specified.

3.2.2 *Substitution of wrought nonferrous metal for cast nonferrous metal.*—Where a cast nonferrous metal is specified, forged or extruded forms of the same nonferrous metal may be furnished, provided the forged or extruded items or parts are of substantially the same thickness or weight as commercially equivalent cast items or parts.

1

GPO - O - GSA 144

ALPHABETICAL LISTINGS OF FEDERAL AND INTERIM FEDERAL SPECIFICATIONS
(continued)

TITLE	NUMBER	FSC	PRICE (cents)
Card, index	UU-C-128d(1)	7530	5
Cardboard & railroad board (manila & wood)	UU-C-201f(1)	9310	5
Cardboard, bristol, (drafting)	UU-C-190	9310	10
Cardboard, bristol, (drafting)	UU-C-190 (Int. Amd. 1)	9310	
Cards, guide, file & card sets; guide, file	UU-C-95a	7530	5
Cards, guide, file (pressboard, card-size)	UU-C-93c	7530	10
Cards; tabulating	G-C-116d	7530	5
Carpet & rugs, velvet (nylon, wool & nylon) (see Carpets & rugs, wool, nylon, acrylic, modacrylic, DDD-C-95)			
Carpet-cushion (see Cushion (underlay), ZZ-C-811)			
Carpet, loop; & rug, loop (wool pile, knitted) (see Carpets & rugs, wool, DDD-C-95)			
Carpet, nonwoven, polypropylene, outdoor-indoor type	DCD-C-001173 (GSA-FSS)	7220	
Carpets & rugs; axminster (see Carpets & rugs, wool, nylon, DDD-C-95)			
Carpets & rugs, velvet, plain & twisted (see Carpets & rugs, wool, nylon, DDD-C-95)			
Carpets & rugs; Wilton (see Carpets & rugs, wool, nylon, DDD-C-95)			
Carpets & rugs, wool, nylon, acrylic, modacrylic	DDD-C-95	7220	15
Carpets & rugs, wool-nylon, loop pile, woven attached rubber cushioning (see Carpets & rugs, wool, nylon, acrylic, modacrylic, DDD-C-95)			
Carriage, dressing, surgical	AA-C-112a(1)	6530	15
Carriage, pail, CRM (frame, kick bucket)	GG-C-00126c (GSA-FSS)	6530	
Carriage, pail CRM (frame, kick bucket) (with conservation provision)	GG-C-126a(1)	6530	5
Carriers, amalgam (dental)	U-C-125	6520	5
Carriers, amalgam, dental	U-C-00125a (DSA-DM)	6520	
Carrots, canned	JJJ-C-76d(1)	8915	5
Carrots, fresh	HHH-C-81e(2)	8915	5
Carrots, frozen	HHH-C-0090 (AGR-AMS)	8915	
Cart, clinical chart holder (mobile)	GG-C-129	6530	10
Cart, clinical chart holder	GG-C-00129a (DSA-DS)	6520	
Cart, surgical dressing	AA-C-00112c (DSA-DM)	6530	
Carton, egg	UU-C-00225(1) (GSA-FSS)	8115	
Cartons, paper, folding (see Boxes, PPP-B-566)			
Cartridges, projectiles, gas and flare (and shells)	D-C-00115a(1) (GSA-FSS)	1310	
Carver, dental (amalgan & wax)	GG-C-001265 (DSA-DM)	6520	
Case, basic surgical instrument set	K-C-131b	6545	10
Case, dispatch, artificial leather (magnesium frame)	KK-C-001008 (GSA-FSS)	8460	
Case, dispatch, artificial leather (wood frame)	KK-C-00115a (GSA-FSS)	8460	
Case, filing, transfer, collapsible	UU-C-250a	7520	5
Case, filing, transfer, fiberboard	UU-B-255a	7520	5
Case, filing, transfer, steel	AA-C-121b	7125	5
Case, filing, transfer, wood or fiber	LLL-C-00110(2) (GSA-FSS)	7520	
Case, twist drill set; & stand, twist drill set--empty	GGG-C-116b(2)	5140	10
Case, twist drill set; & stand, twist drill set--empty	GGG-C-00116c (Ships)	5140	
Cases, brief, leather (see Brief case (leather), KK-B-650)			
Cases; mailing, dental (see Box, setup, mailing, dental, PPP-B-670).			
Cash box, steel	RR-C-140(1)	7520	5
Casserole, laboratory, porcelain	NNN-C-25	6640	5
Casseroles, porcelain (see Casserole, laboratory, porcelain, NNN-C-25)			
Cassette changer	GG-C-133	6525	10
Cassettes, radiographic film (medical)	GG-C-131	6525	5
Cassettes, radiographic film (medical)	GG-C-00131a (DSA-DM)	6525	
Casters, institutional duty	FF-C-77(1) (GSA-FSS)	5340	
Casters, rigid & swivel, industrial, heavy-duty	FF-C-88a(2)	5340	10
Casters, swivel, chair	FF-C-82b	5340	10
Casters, truck	FF-C-86	5340	5
Casters, truck, medium duty	FF-C-86(1) (GSA-FSS)	5340	
Castor oil, technical	JJJ-C-86(1)	8915	5
Catheters, ureteral, rubber	ZZ-C-101a(1)	6515	5
Catheters, urethral, rubber	ZZ-C-00101b (GSA-FSS)	6515	
Catheters, urethral, woven (braided)	GG-C-139	6515	10
Catheters, ureteral (x-ray, graduated)	GG-C-136b	6525	5
Catsup, tomato	JJJ-C-91d	8950	5
Cauliflower, fresh	HHH-C-101d	8915	5
Cauliflower, frozen	HHH-C-102a	8915	5
Caulking compound, oil & resin base type (for masonry & other structures)	TT-C-00598a(1) (GSA-FSS)	8030	
Cavity lining and thinner set, dental	U-C-133b	6520	5
Celery; fresh	HHH-C-191d(2)	8915	5
Celery, fresh	HHH-C-00191e (AGR-C&MS)	8915	

17

ALPHABETICAL LISTINGS OF FEDERAL AND INTERIM FEDERAL SPECIFICATIONS
(continued)

TITLE	NUMBER	FSC	PRICE (cents)
Cellophane (coated and noncoated regenerated cellulose film)	L-C-110c	8135	5
Cellophane (coated & noncoated regenerated cellulose film)	L-C-00110g(3)	8135	
Cellulose, absorbent, surgical	L-C-166a(1)	6570	5
Cellulose acetate plastic sheets (see Plastic sheet and film, L-P-504)			
Cement, bituminous, plastic	SS-C-153	5610	5
Cement, copper and zinc phosphates, dental	U-C-198a	6520	10
Cement, insulation; thermal, mineral-wool (see Cements, insulation, SS-C-160)			
Cement, iron & steel	QQ-C-100a	8030	5
Cement, Keene's	SS-C-161	5610	5
Cement, Keene's (see Plaster, gypsum (Keene's cement), SS-P-00410 (GSA-FSS))			
Cement, masonry	SS-C-181e(1)	5610	5
Cement, natural, (for use as a blend with portland cement)	SS-C-185a(1)	5610	5
Cement, plastic, fatty acid pitch base	SS-C-188	5610	10
Cement, portland	SS-C-192g(1)	5610	5
Cement, portland, blast-furnace slag	SS-C-197e(1)	5610	5
Cement, portland-pozzolan	SS-C-208c(1)	5610	5
Cement, rubber (artists' and photographers' and cold-patching)	ZZ-C-191a(3)	8040	5
Cement; silica (see Mortar, refractory, silica, HH-M-630a)			
Cement, silicate, and accessories (dental)	U-C-205a	6520	10
Cement, silicate (see Sodium-silicate, O-S-605a)			
Cement, slag	SS-C-218d(1)	5610	5
Cement, zinc oxide and eugenol, dental	U-C-208b	6520	10
Cement, zinc phosphate, dental	U-C-211a	6520	10
Cement, zinc phosphate, dental	U-C-00211b (GSA-FSS)	6520	
Cements, insulation, thermal	SS-C-160(1)	5640	5
Centrifuges, hand	GG-C-191	6640	5
Centrifuges, laboratory, clinical, and chemical, electric	GG-C-00195 (GSA-FSS)	6640	
Cereal, rolled oats	N-C-195(1)	8920	5
Cereal, rolled oats	N-C-00195a (Army-GL)	8920	
Cereals, (breakfast; prepared, ready-to-eat)	N-C-196g	8920	10
Cereals, (breakfast; prepared, ready-to-eat)	N-C-196d (Int. Amd. 1)	8920	
Cereals, wheat; uncooked	N-C-201d(1)	8920	10
Cervelat, chilled or frozen	PP-C-232a(1)	8905	10
Chains and attachments, welded, weldless, and roller chain	RR-C-271a(1)	4010	25
Chains and attachments, welded, weldless, and roller chain	RR-C-271a (Int. Amd. 2)	4010	
Chains, pot-cleaning (see Wireware, RR-W-456a)			
Chains; tire-anti-skid	RR-C-00281a(1) (GSA-FSS)	2540	
Chair, examining and treatment, surgical	AA-C-289	6530	10
Chair, folding, (steel)	AA-C-291e	7105	10
Chair, straight, tubular steel	AA-C-00297 (GSA-FSS)	7105	
Chair, student, metal and wood	AA-C-296	7110	10
Chair, student, wood	AA-C-298a	7110	30
Chair; wheel, invalid (nonfolding)	AA-C-346b(1)	6530	10
Chairs, aluminum, general office	AA-C-00275 (GSA-FSS)	7110	
Chairs, easy, executive office	AA-C-285(2)	7110	20
Chairs, easy, executive office	AA-C-285 (Int. Amd. 4)	7110	
Chairs, folding, wood, without arms	AA-C-00288a (GSA-FSS)	7105	
Chairs, operating, dental, motorless	AA-C-326a	6520	10
Chairs, rotary & straight, aluminum, office	AA-C-00275d (GSA-FSS)	7110	
Chairs, rotary & straight, wood, office (unitized furniture style)	AA-C-00400b(1) (GSA-FSS)	7110	
Chairs, rotary, steel tubular, special purpose	AA-C-295	7110	20
Chairs, rotary, steel tubular special purpose	AA-C-295 (Int. Amd. 3)	7110	
Chairs, rotary, steel, tubular, special purpose	AA-C-00295a(1) (GSA-FSS)	7110	
Chairs, steel, general office	AA-C-293(1)	7110	20
Chairs, steel, general office	AA-C-00293a(3) (GSA-FSS)	7110	
Chairs, wood, executive office	AA-C-300a(1)	7110	10
Chairs, wood, executive office	AA-C-300a (Int. Amd. 2)	7110	
Chairs, wood, executive office, traditional	AA-C-00300b(2) (GSA-FSS)	7110	
Chairs, wood, general office	AA-C-311b(1)	7110	35
Chairs, wood, general office	AA-C-311b (Int. Amd. 2)	7510	
Chalk, carpenters' and railroad	SS-C-255	7510	5
Chalk line & reel (self-chalking)	GGG-C-291a	5210	5
Chalk, marking, white & colored	SS-C-266d	7510	5
Chalk, marking, white & colored	SS-C-00266e (GSA-FSS)	7510	
Chambray	CCC-C-231a	8305	5
Chamois, leather, sheepskin, oil-tanned	KK-C-300b	8330	10
Chamois, leather, sheepskin, oil-tanned	KK-C-300b (Int. Amd. 1)	8330	
Charcoal	LLL-C-251	9110	5
Charge, fire extinguisher, antifreeze & charge, fire extinguisher, soda-acid	O-C-240d	4210	5

ALPHABETICAL LISTINGS OF FEDERAL AND INTERIM FEDERAL SPECIFICATIONS
(continued)

TITLE	NUMBER	FSC	PRICE (cents)
Ribbon, accounting machine	DDD-R-250e (Int. Amd. 3)	7510	
Ribbon; computing & recording machine	DDD-R-00271a(1) (GSA-FSS)	7510	
Ribbon, flagging, surveyor's plastic	L-R-00335a (GSA-FSS)	9330	
Ribbon, teletypewriter, record	DDD-R-00306a (GSA-FSS)	7510	
Ribbons; computing and recording-machine	DDD-R-271a	7510	5
Ribbons, teletypewriter	DDD-R-306(1)	7510	5
Ribbons, teletypewriter	DDD-R-306 (Int. Amd. 2)	7510	
Ribbons, typewriter	DDD-R-311d(3)	7510	10
Ribbons, typewriter	DDD-R-311d (Int. Amd. 6)	7510	
Ribbons, typewriter & composing machine, changeable type-plate style, carbon paper	UU-R-00350a(2) (GSA-FSS)	7510	
Ribbons, typewriter & composing machine, changeable type-plate style, polyethylene	L-R-00350(1) (G A-FSS)	7510	
Ribbons, typewriter fabric hectograph	DDD-R-291b	7510	5
Rice, brown	N-R-346a	8920	5
Rice, milled	N-R-351c	8920	5
Rice, milled	N-R-00351d (AGR-C&MS)	8920	
Ring buoy, life saving (cork)	GGG-R-351a	4220	5
Ring, cork, laboratory	NNN-R-350a	6640	5
Ring, laboratory apparatus support	NNN-R-370	6640	5
Ring, loose-leaf binder	RR-R-330a	7510	5
Rings; jar, rubber	ZZ-R-351(1)	8125	5
Rings; parachute vent, molded rubber	ZZ-R-371	1670	5
Rings, support, laboratory, metal (see Ring, laboratory apparatus, NNN-R-370)			
Rinse, additive, dishwashing	P-R-001272(1) (GSA-FSS)	7930	
Rinse additive, laundry	Q-R-001353 (GSA-FSS)	7930	
Rivet set, hand	GGG-R-400c	5120	5
Rivet sets, pneumatic tool	GGG-R-425a	5130	10
Rivet sets, pneumatic tool	GGG-R-425a (Int. Amd. 2)	5130	
Riveter, blind, hand & heads	GGG-R-00395(1) (GSA-FSS)	5120	
Riveter, pneumatic, jam and hammer; and holder-on, portable	OO-R-421a(4)	5130	10
Rivets, solid, small; rivets, split, small; rivets, tubular, small; & caps, rivets; general purpose	FF-R-556a(1)	5320	15
Rivets, taps (see Bolts, nuts, studs, FF-B-571a)			
Road and paving materials; methods of sampling and testing	SS-R-406c(1) (Part 2)	5610	55
Robes; bath	DDD-R-591b	8420	5
Rockers, hand blotter	UU-R-575(2)	7520	5
Rod, ground	W-R-00550 (GSA-FSS)	5975	
Rod, irrigator supporting	RR-R-00560 (DSA-DM)	6530	
Rod, stadia; folding	GG-R-550(1)	6675	10
Rod, stirring, laboratory	NNN-R-560a	6640	5
Rodenticide, anticoagulant, concentrates	O-R-00495b (INT-FWS)	6840	
Rodenticide, anticoagulant, universal, concentrate	O-R-00497b (INT-FWS)	6840	
Rodenticide, bait, anticoagulant	O-R-500	6840	10
Rodenticide; bait, anticoagulant	O-R-00500a (INT-FWS)	6840	
Rodenticide, calcium cyanide	O-R-501b	6840	5
Rodenticide, pivalyl, concentrates	O-R-503	6840	15
Rodenticide, pivalyl, water soluble	O-R-502	6840	10
Rodenticide, red squill, powder	O-R-505	6840	5
Rodenticide, sodium monofluoracetate	O-R-504	6840	5
Rodenticide, warfarin, concentrates	O-R-507a(1)	6840	5
Rodenticide, zinc phosphide	O-R-511c(1)	6840	5
Rods; glass stirring (see Rod, stirring, laboratory, NNN-R-560a)			
Rods, welding, aluminum & aluminum alloys	QQ-R-566a	3439	10
Rods, welding, copper & nickel alloys	QQ-R-571b	3439	5
Roll, absorbent cotton and roll, cellulose	GG-R-563b	6510	5
Roll, cotton-tape	DDD-R-630	6510	5
Roll, tools & accessories	GGG-R-615a	5140	5
Roller, bandage	GG-R-571b	6510	10
Roller, hand (rubber roller)	GGG-R-00620 (GSA-FSS)	5120	
Rolling pin (wood)	LLL-R-530a	7330	5
Rolls, brown & serve	EE-R-580a(2)	8920	5
Romaine, fresh	HHH-R-570c	8915	5
Roof-coating; asphalt, brushing-consistency	SS-R-451	5610	5
Roof coating; asphalt, brushing-consistency (see Asphalt, petroleum, roof coating, brushing consistency (SS-A-00694)			
Roofing and shingles; asphalt-prepared, etc. (see Shingles, asphalt, SS-S-300 and Roofing, felt, roll, SS-R-630).			
Roofing and siding (see Building-board SS-B-750)			
Roofing; asphalt and asbestos-prepared (see Roofing, felt, roll, etc. SS-R-630)			

71

325

ALPHABETICAL LISTINGS OF FEDERAL AND INTERIM FEDERAL SPECIFICATIONS
(continued)

TITLE	NUMBER	FSC	PRICE (cents)
Roofing felt (asbestos, asphalt saturated)	HH-R-590	5650	5
Roofing felt, asphalt-prepared, smooth surfaced	SS-R-00501c(1) (GSA-FSS)	5650	
Roofing felt (coal tar & asphalt saturated rag felts, rolls: for use in roofing & waterproofing	HH-R-595(1)	5650	5
Roofing felt, glass fiber, asphalt coated, (for flashing & roofing)	SS-R-620a(1)	5650	5
Roofing, felt, roll, asphalt-prepared, mineral-surfaced	SS-R-630	5650	5
Roofing felt (roll, asphalt-prepared, mineral surfaced)	SS-R-00630c (GSA-FSS)	5650	
Roofing, felt, roll (coal tar, asphalt, & pressure still tar saturated rag felt, for use in roofing & waterproofing) (see Roofing felt (coal tar & asphalt saturated rag felts, rolls; HH-R-595))			
Roofing, prepared; asphalt, smooth-surfaced	SS-R-501a(3)	5650	5
Roofing-slabs; concrete, precast	SS-R-531(3)	5650	5
Rope; cotton	T-R-571a	4020	5
Rope; cotton	T-R-00571b (Army-GL)	4020	
Rope, jute	T-R-592a	4020	5
Rope, manila & sisal	T-R-605b(2)	4020	5
Rope; mildew-resistant (see Treatment: mildew resistant, T-T-616)			
Rope, wire (see Wire, rope, RR-W-410a and Wire rope, steel, etc., RR-W-420)			
Rope, yarn, and twine; hemp	T-R-675(1)	4020	5
Rope, yarn, and twine; hemp	T-R-00675a (Army-QMC)	4020	
Rosin, gum; rosin, wood; and rosin, tall oil	LLL-R-626b	8810	10
Rouge sticks; dental	U-R-651	5350	5
Rowing machine	OO-R-581a	7830	5
Rubber band, four way	ZZ-R-00675 (GSA-FSS)	7510	
Rubber dam, dental	ZZ-R-690	6520	5
Rubber for mountings (unbounded-spool & compression types)	ZZ-R-768a	9320	5
Rubber gasket material, 35 durometer hardness	ZZ-R-710a	5330	5
Rubber sheet; cellular, hard board	ZZ-R-785a	9320	5
Rubber, silicone: low-&-high-temperature & tear resistant	ZZ-R-765a	9320	10
Rubber, silicone: low & high-temperature & tear resistant	ZZ-R-765a (Int. Amd. 1)	9320	
Rubber stamp, fixed type	ZZ-R-804	7520	5
Rubber stamps, band, fixed & removable, & fixed types	ZZ-R-00800(1) (GSA-FSS)	7520	
Rubbing compound (for lacquered surfaces)	TT-R-771	5350	5
Rubbing compound (for lacquered surfaces)	TT-R-00771a (GSA-FSS)	5350	
Rule, laboratory (measuring, plastic & wood)	NNN-R-770	6640	5
Rule, line guide	GG-R-00770a (GSA-FSS)	7510	
Ruler, plastic, desk	GG-R-001200 (GSA-FSS)	7510	
Ruler, wood (desk)	GG-R-791d	7510	5
Ruler, wood (desk)	GG-R-791d (Int. Amd. 1)	7510	
Rules, measuring	GGG-R-791f	5210	15
Rules, measuring (laboratory): plastic & wood (see Rule, laboratory (measuring, plastic & wood), NNN-R-770)			
Rules; parallel (see Parallel rulers, GG-P-118)			
Sacks, shipping, paper	UU-S-48d	8105	20
Sacks, shipping, paper	UU-S-48d (Int. Amd. 1)	8105	
Sacks, shipping, paper, (cushioned)	PPP-S-30(2)	8105	5
Sacks, shipping, paper, reinforced	PPP-S-50a	8105	10
Safe, dental x-ray film protective	AA-S-75	6525	5
Safe, office, fire resistant, burglary protection	AA-S-81b	7110	10
Safelight, darkroom, photographic	GG-S-86b	6740	10
Safety can, spring closing type	RR-S-30b	7240	10
Safety can, spring closing type	RR-S-0030c (Army-GL)	7240	
Safety equipment, climbing	RR-S-001301 (FAA)	4240	
Salad dressing (see Mayonnaise and salad, EE-M-131)			
Salad oil, vegetable	JJJ-S-30b(2)	8945	10
Salami, chilled or frozen, cooked	PP-S-76a	8905	10
Salami, chilled or frozen, cooked	PP-S-76a (Int. Amd. 1)	8905	
Salami, chilled or frozen, dry	PP-S-77a	8905	10
Salmon, canned	PP-S-31e	8905	5
Salt & pepper shakers, sugar dispensers (moisture resistant)	DD-S-0050a (GSA-FSS)	7350	
Salt, rock and evaporated (see Sodium chloride, SS-S-550)			
Salt, table	SS-S-31h	8950	10
Salt, table	SS-S-31h (Int. Amd. 1)	8950	
Salt, table	SS-S-00311 (Army-GL)	8950	
Salts; nickel (for electroplating and electrotyping (see Nickel salts, electrotyping, O-N-335)			
Sand; (for use in) sheet asphalt or bituminous concrete pavements	SS-S-71a	5610	5
Sander, disk, electric, portable, double insulated (shockproof), radio interference suppressed	OO-S-001116 (Navy-Ships)	5130	

72

GROUP LISTINGS OF FEDERAL AND INTERIM FEDERAL SPECIFICATIONS
(continued)
SS.- Continued

NUMBER	TITLE	FSC	PRICE (cents)	DATE
SS-A-00694a (GSA-FSS)	Asphalt, petroleum (roof coating, brushing & spraying consistency)	5610		Oct 7 64
SS-A-696(1)	Asphalt, petroleum, type PAF-1-25, (for) joint-filler (squeegee or puring method)	5610	5	Jun 17 37
SS-A-701	Asphalt-primer, (for) roofing and waterproofing	5610	5	Aug 1 33
SS-A-00701a (GSA-FSS)	Asphalt, petroleum (primer, roofing, & waterproofing)	5610		Jan 26 67
SS-A-706c	Asphalt, petroleum: road & pavement construction	5610	5	May 15 67
SS-B-00235(1) (GSA-FSS)	Bentonite, technical; with dye (forest fire retardant)	9390		Mar 15 65
SS-B-656b	Brick, building, common (clay or shale)	5620	5	Feb 18 66
SS-B-663b	Brick, building, concrete	5620	5	Jun 9 65
SS-B-668a	Brick, facing, clay, or shale	5620	5	Feb 15 66
SS-B-671c	Brick, paving	5620	5	Jun 2 65
SS-B-675a	Brick, rubbing	5345	5	Oct 9 61
SS-B-681b	Brick, building, sand-lime	5620	5	Dec 22 65
SS-B-691b	Brick, sewer, (clay or shale)	5620	5	Jun 9 65
SS-B-750b	Building board, asbestos-cement, corrugated	5640	5	Nov 23 60
SS-B-755a	Building board, asbestos-cement: flat & corrugated	5640	5	Mar 9 67
SS-C-153	Cement, bituminous, plastic	5610	5	Aug 1 33
SS-C-160(1)	Cements, insulation, thermal	5640	5	Sep 21 64
SS-C-161	Cement, Keene's	5610	5	Feb 7 33
SS-C-181e(1)	Cement, masonry	5610	5	Oct 18 65
SS-C-185a(1)	Cement, natural, (for use as a blend with portland cement)	5610	5	Oct 18 65
SS-C-188	Cement, plastic, fatty acid pitch base	5610	10	Feb 1 56
SS-C-192g(1)	Cement, portland	5610	5	Oct 18 65
SS-C-197e(1)	Cement, portland, blast-furnace slag	5610	5	Oct 18 65
SS-C-208c(1)	Cement, portland-pozzolan	5610	5	Oct 18 65
SS-C-218d(1)	Cement, slag	5610	5	Oct 18 65
SS-C-255	Chalk, carpenters' and railroad	7510	5	Aug 30 49
SS-C-266d	Chalk, marking, white and colored	7510	5	Jan 15 63
SS-C-00266e (GSA-FSS)	Chalk, marking, white & colored	7510		Jan 24 67
SS-C-450a	Cloth, impregnated (woven cotton cloth, asphalt impregnated; coat tar impregnated)	5650	5	Apr 10 67
SS-C-466e	Cloth, thread, & tape; asbestos	5640	10	Jul 2 64
SS-C-466e (Int. Amd. 1)	Cloth, thread, & tape; asbestos	5640		Jun 17 65
SS-C-540a	Coal tar (cutback) roof coating, brushing consistency)	5610	5	Mar 1 67
SS-C-560	Coating-material fatty acid pitch base, (nonbleeding) brushing and spraying consistency (for foundations, roofs, walls, etc.).	8010	10	Feb 1 56
SS-C-608(1)	Compound, jointing, sulfur (for bell-and-spigot cast-iron pipe)	8030	5	Jan 8 47
SS-C-614(2)	Compound, valve-grinding	5350	5	Jul 22 57
SS-C-618a	Concrete, ready-mixed	5610	5	Oct 12 59
SS-C-621(1)	Concrete-units, masonry, hollow	5620	5	May - 35
SS-C-00621a (GSA-FSS)	Concrete masonry unit, hollow (& solid, glazed & unglazed)	5620		Apr 18 66
SS-C-635b	Crayon assortment, drawing, colored	7510	5	Dec 7 66
SS-C-646b(2)	Crayon, marking, lumber	7510	5	Oct 31 63
SS-C-661(2)	Crayon, marking	7510	5	Apr 9 62
SS-C-001302 (GSA-FSS)	Concrete patching & leveling compound	5610		Mar 2 67
SS-F-111	Facings, foundry, carbon-base	3428	5	Nov 11 30
SS-F-001032 (GSA-FSS)	Floor covering, asphaltic felt (bituminous type surface)	7220		Oct 19 66
SS-G-659a	Graphite, dry (lubricating)	9620	5	Mar 1 67
SS-G-691(1)	Grindstones, natural, mounted	3415	5	Nov 29 43
SS-J-570a	Joint compound & tape, wallboard (for gypsum wallboard construction)	5640	5	Oct 24 66
SS-L-30c	Lath, sheathing, & wallboard, gypsum	5640	5	Mar 20 67
SS-L-351	Lime, hydrated (for) structural purposes	5610	5	Oct 14 30
SS-L-00351a (COM-NBS)	Lime: hydrated (for) structural purposes	5610		Aug 60
SS-L-361(1)	Lime, hydraulic, hydrated	5610	5	Apr 4 39
SS-M-51	Materials, (for) cushion course, brick, stone-block, or wood-block pavements (sand, slag, limestone, screenings, etc.).	5610	5	Jun 23 31
SS-M-351	Mineral-filler, (for) sheet asphalt or asphaltic concrete pavements (portland cement, limestone dust and dolomite dust).	5610	5	Jun 23 31
SS-P-155d	Pencil and lead, electrographic	7510	5	Feb 7 61
SS-P-155d (Int. Amd. 1)	Pencil & lead, electrographic	7510		Dec 19 66
SS-P-166d(3)	Pencils, lead	7510	5	Dec 7 62
SS-P-181a	Pencil, lead, drawing	7510	5	Oct 25 61
SS-P-183b	Pencil, lithographic	7510	5	Nov 15 60
SS-P-186d	Pencil, mechanical, (including leads & erasers	7510	10	Aug 10 65
SS-P-196c	Pencil; spiral-paper-form, wax, glass- and China-marking	7510	5	Jun 20 60
SS-P-201d	Pencil, nonmechanical, colored lead	7510	10	Feb 6 61

151

327

GROUP LISTINGS OF FEDERAL AND INTERIM FEDERAL SPECIFICATIONS
(continued)
SS.- Continued

NUMBER	TITLE	FSC	PRICE (cents)	DATE
SS-P-212(1)	Pencils and leads, refill; artists' and drafting	7510	5	Apr 13 54
SS-P-331c	Pipe, asbestos & cement: sewer, nonpressure	5630	5	Jun 28 67
SS-P-00340(1) (COM-PR)	Pipe, asbestos-cement, underdrain, perforated	5630		Aug 18 61
SS-P-345a	Pipe, bituminized-fiber, (sewer, laminated-wall, & fittings)	5630	10	Jul 11 63
SS-P-351a	Pipe, asbestos-cement	5640	5	Oct 7 53
SS-P-00351b (GSA-FSS)	Pipe & couplings, asbestos-cement, pressure	5630		Dec 7 66
SS-P-356	Pipe, bituminized-fiber, sewer, and fittings for same	5630	15	Apr 6 55
SS-P-358a	Pipe, bituminized fiber (perforated drainage), and fittings for same	5630		Feb 24 60
SS-P-359b	Pipe, clay, (perforated)	5630	10	Dec 27 60
SS-P-361b(3)	Pipe, clay, sewer	5630	5	Jan 22 62
SS-P-361b (Int. Amd. 5)	Pipe, clay, sewer	5630		Apr 8 63
SS-P-00361c (GSA-FSS)	Pipe, clay, (sewer)	5630		Dec 13 66
SS-P-371c	Pipe, concrete (nonreinforced, sewer)	5630	5	Jun 10 63
SS-P-372a	Pipe, concrete (nonreinforced, cast-in-place)	5630	5	Jan 11 66
SS-P-00372b (GSA-FSS)	Pipe, concrete (nonreinforced, cast-in-place)	5630		Dec 9 66
SS-P-375b	Pipe, concrete, (reinforced, sewer)	5630	5	Jun 10 63
SS-P-381	Pipe; pressure, reinforced concrete, pretensioned reinforcement (steel cylinder type)	5630	10	Sep 14 55
SS-P-385a	Pipe, steel, (cement-mortar lining & reinforced cement-mortar coating)	4710	10	Jan 31 64
SS-P-402(1)	Plaster; gypsum	5610	5	Jul 19 45
SS-P-00402a (GSA-FSS)	Plaster, gypsum	5610		Feb 16 65
SS-P-00410a (GSA-FSS)	Plaster, gypsum (Keene's cement)	5610		Dec 21 66
SS-P-446a	Plaster, orthopedic and dental	6520	5	Aug 27 55
SS-P-00450 (GSA-FSS)	Plaster, patching, gypsum, (spackling)	5610		Jul 31 64
SS-P-551b	Pencil pointer (abrasive paper)	7510	5	Jul 15 63
SS-P-551b (Int. Amd. 2)	Pencil pointer (abrasive paper)	7510		Feb 23 66
SS-P-00570 (COM-NBS)	Pozzolan (for use in Portland-cement concrete)	9620		Jun 27 67
SS-P-680	Priming-material, fatty acid pitch base, brushing and spraying consistency (for concrete, masonry, and other mineral surfaces).	8030	10	Mar 6 56
SS-P-821b	Pumice; ground, abrasive	5350	5	Aug 17 66
SS-P-001229 (GSA-FSS)	Pipe, clay (drain)	5620		Dec 12 66
SS-Q-351	Quicklime; (for) structural purposes	5610	5	Aug 19 30
SS-R-0044b (Army-GL)	Ranges, gas (domestic)	7310		May 22 64
SS-R-406c(1)(Part 2)	Road and paving materials; methods of sampling and testing	5610	55	Dec 1 58
SS-R-451	Roof-coating; asphalt, brushing-consistency	5610	5	Aug 1 33
SS-R-501a(3)	Roofing, prepared; asphalt, smooth-surfaced	5650	5	Apr 27 56
SS-R-00501c(1) (GSA-FSS)	Roofing felt, asphalt-prepared, smooth surfaced	5650		Aug 25 67
SS-R-531(3)	Roofing-slabs; concrete; precast	5650	5	Feb 9 55
SS-R-620a(1)	Roofing felt, glass fiber, asphalt coated, (for flashing & roofing)	5650	5	Oct 12 65
SS-R-630	Roofing, felt, roll, asphalt-prepared, mineral-surfaced	5650	5	Mar 1 61
SS-R-00630c (GSA-FSS)	Roofing felt (roll, asphalt-prepared, mineral surfaced)	5650		Jul 27 67
SS-S-31h	Salt, table	8950	10	Jun 25 64
SS-S-31h (Int. Amd. 1)	Salt, table	8950		Dec 10 65
SS-S-00311 (Army-GL)	Salt, table	8950		Sep 22 67
SS-S-71a	Sand; (for use in) sheet asphalt or bituminous concrete pavements	5610	5	Aug 28 42
SS-S-110a	Screen, window, metal (aluminum tubular frame, & tension)	5670	5	Oct 2 64
SS-S-111	Sound absorbing materials (trowel & spray applications)	5610	5	Sep 3 64
SS-S-00118 (GSA-FSS)	Sound absorbing materials (acoustical units, prefabricated)	5640		Jul 24 63
SS-S-156	Sealer; cold-application emulsion type, for joints in concrete	8030	5	Feb 11 52
SS-S-158a	Sealing compound; cold-application ready-mixed liquefier type, for joints in concrete	8030	5	Aug 28 58
SS-S-159b	Sealing compound; cold-application mastic multiple component type- for joints in concrete.	8030	5	Aug 28 58
SS-S-164(4)	Sealing compound; hot poured type, for joints in concrete	8030	5	Aug 18 64
SS-S-167b	Sealing compound, jet-fuel resistant, hot applied, concrete paving	8030	10	Dec 17 58
SS-S-168(2)	Sealing compound, sewer, bituminous, two-component, mineral-filled, cold-applied	5610	10	Apr 9 62
SS-S-169	Sealer; joint, sewer, mineral-filled, hot-pour	8030	5	Apr 20 54
SS-S-170	Sealing compound, two-components, jet fuel resistant, cold applied, concrete paving	8030	10	May 23 55
SS-S-171	Sealer; mineral-filled asphalt for joints in concrete	8030	5	Dec 4 51
SS-S-00195a(1) (CE)	Sealing compound; two-component, elastomeric, polymer type, cold-appli- ed, concrete paving joints	8030		Nov 25 66
SS-S-00200c(2) (Army-ME)	Sealing compound, two-component, elastomeric, polymer type, jet-fuel resistant, cold-applied, concrete paving	8030		Dec 15 66
SS-S-00210 (GSA-FSS)	Sealing compound, preformed plastic, for expansion joints & pipe joints	8030		Jul 26 65

152

GROUP LISTINGS OF FEDERAL AND INTERIM FEDERAL SPECIFICATIONS
(continued)
SS.- Continued

NUMBER	TITLE	FSC	PRICE (cents)	DATE
SS-S-291c	Shingles, asbestos cement, roofing	5650	10	Dec 21 56
SS-S-294a	Shingles, asphalt (mineral surfaced, uniform thickness, class A fire rating)	5650	5	Dec 7 66
SS-S-295a	Shingles, asphalt (mineral surfaced, uniform thickness, class B fire rating)	5650	5	Dec 7 66
SS-S-298b	Shingles, organic fiber, asphalt (mineral-surfaced) (thick-butt)	5650	5	Nov 26 62
SS-S-300b	Shingles, organic fiber, asphalt (mineral surfaced) (uniform thickness)	5650	5	Nov 26 62
SS-S-346b	Siding (shingles, clapboards, and sheets) asbestos-cement	5650	10	Dec 21 56
SS-S-360	Silica, pulverized, foundry mold wash	5650	10	Jun 17 55
SS-S-439	Slabs, roofing, precast, gypsum	5650	5	Jun 20 49
SS-S-445	Slag, stone, & gravel, crushed (for bituminous paving mixtures)	5610	5	Aug 12 66
SS-S-448	Slag & stone, crushed; gravel, crushed & uncrushed (for sewage trickling filter media)	5610	5	Aug 12 66
SS-S-448 (Int. Amd. 1)	Slag & stone, crushed; gravel, crushed & uncrushed (for sewage trickling filter media)	5610		Feb 28 67
SS-S-449	Slag & stone, crushed; gravel, crushed & uncrushed (for railroad ballast)	5610	5	Aug 8 66
SS-S-451	Slate; roofing	5650	5	Jun 26 32
SS-S-535a	Sodium borate, decahydrate, technical (borax)	6810	5	Jul 26 58
SS-S-550	Sodium chloride, technical, for water-softening units	6810	10	Jul 5 57
SS-S-550 (Int. Amd. 1)	Sodium chloride, technical, for water softening units	6810		Oct 22 63
SS-S-00550a (GSA-FSS)	Sodium chloride, technical for water softening units	6810		Mar 21 67
SS-S-721c	Stone, architectural, cast	5620	5	Nov 18 64
SS-S-721c (Int. Amd. 1)	Stone, architectural, cast	5620		Feb 27 67
SS-S-736b	Stones, sharpening	5345	10	Feb 25 65
SS-T-306b(1)	Tile, floor, asphalt	5620		Oct 1 51
SS-T-308b	Tile, floor, wall, and trim units, ceramic	5620	15	Nov 16 59
SS-T-310	Tile, drain; clay	5620	5	Jul 30 42
SS-T-312	Tile, floor; asphalt, rubber, vinyl, vinyl-asbestos	7220	5	Jun 2 66
SS-T-00315 (GSA-FSS)	Tile, gypsum (interior; floor & roof, precast)	5620		Dec 30 64
SS-T-316	Tile; partition, gypsum	5620	5	Mar 3 39
SS-T-00316a(GSA-FSS)	Tile; partition, gypsum	5620		Sep 10 53
SS-T-321(1)	Tile; structural, clay, floor	5620	5	Jan 36
SS-T-341a	Tile; structural, clay, load-bearing, wall	5620	5	Jan 21 43
SS-T-351a	Tile; structural, clay, non-load-bearing	5620	5	Jan 21 43
SS-T-665	Tripoli; dental	5350	5	Jul 14 48
SS-W-40a	Wall base: rubber, & vinyl plastic	7220	5	Mar 28 66
SS-W-110b	Water-repellent, colorless, silicone resin base	8030	5	Feb 7 63

TT.

NUMBER	TITLE	FSC	PRICE (cents)	DATE
TT-A-511b	Amyl acetate (for use in organic coatings)	6810	5	Aug 9 61
TT-A-516d	Amyl alcohol; secondary	6810	5	Aug 20 62
TT-A-580a(1)	Antiseize compound, white lead base, general purpose, (for threaded fittings)	8030	5	Jun 1 61
TT-A-00580c (GSA-FSS)	Antiseize compound, white lead base, general purpose (for threaded fittings)	8030		Aug 2 67
TT-B-838a	Butyl acetate; normal (for use in organic coatings)	6810	5	Aug 28 59
TT-B-840b	Butyl acetate: secondary (for use in organic coatings)	6810	5	Jan 5 60
TT-B-846b	Butyl alcohol: normal (butanol) (for use in organic coatings)	6810	5	Apr 20 60
TT-B-848b	Butyl alcohol: secondary (for use in organic coatings)	6810	5	Dec 7 59
TT-C-490	Cleaning methods and pretreatment of ferrous surfaces for organic coatings		10	Mar 30 61
TT-C-492a	Coating compound, paint antisweat	8010	10	May 23 66
TT-C-492a (Int. Amd. 1)	Coating compound, paint antisweat	8010		May 4 67
TT-C-494	Coating compound, bituminous, solvent type, acid resistant	8030	5	Mar 27 63
TT-C-495(2)	Coatings, exterior, for tinned food cans	8030	5	Dec 28 66
TT-C-00498a(1) (GSA-FSS)	Coating compound, bituminous, solvent type; asbestos filled & pigmented, low glare	8030		Jul 5 67
TT-C-00499(1) (GSA-FSS)	Coating compound, chemical resistant, clear	8010		Jan 27 67
TT-C-517a	Coating, strippable masking, (for spray booths & glass)	8030	5	Dec 31 64
TT-C-520a	Coating compound, bituminous, solvent type, underbody, (for motor vehicles)	8030	10	Jun 6 63
TT-C-530a	Coating compound, rust inhibitive, fish oil base	8030	5	Jul 25 62
TT-C-530a (Int. Amd. 1)	Coating compound, rust inhibitive, fish oil base	8030		Nov 8 66

153

329

GROUP LISTINGS OF FEDERAL AND INTERIM FEDERAL SPECIFICATIONS
(continued)
TT.- Continued

NUMBER	TITLE	FSC	PRICE (cents)	DATE
TT-C-535a	Coating, epoxy, two-component, for interior & exterior use of metal, wood, concrete & masonry	8010	5	Oct 23 64
TT-C-540b	Coating, polyurethane clear, linseed-oil, modified	8010	5	Sep 29 65
TT-C-00542a (GSA-FSS)	Coating, polyurethane, oil-free moisture-curing	8010		Apr 19 66
TT-C-00545b (HUD-HAA)	Coating, polyester-epoxy, two-component, low-odor, non-yellowing, acid resisting eggshell, finish (for interior use) white & light tints	8010		Oct 26 66
TT-C-550a	Coating system, glaze, interior, for masonry surfaces	8010	5	Oct 11 65
TT-C-00555 (Army-CE)	Coating system, textured (for interior & exterior masonry surfaces)	8010		Sep 24 65
TT-C-591(1)	Colors; (for) flag of the United States	8345	5	Oct 34
TT-C-598b	Calking compound, oil & resin base type (for masonry & other structures)	8030	10	Mar 12 65
TT-C-00607 (HHF-PHA)	Conditioner; exterior, for free chalking masonry surfaces			Sep 27 62
TT-C-621(2)	Correction-compound; stencil	7510	5	Mar 10 48
TT-C-00621a (POD-ORE)	Correction fluid, duplicating machine stencil	7510		Mar 31 66
TT-C-645a	Creosote, coal tar, technical	6810	5	Aug 3 61
TT-C-650b	Creosote-coal tar solution	6810	5	Oct 20 61
TT-C-655(1)	Creosote, technical, wood preservative (for) brush, spray, or open-tank treatment	6810	10	Aug 15 58
TT-C-655 (Int. Amd. 2)	Creosote, technical, wood preservative, (for) brush, spray, or open-tank treatment	6810		Jul 27 64
TT-C-00800(1) (GSA-FSS)	Curing compound, concrete, for new & existing surfaces	8030		Mar 1 67
TT-C-001079 (GSA-FSS)	Coating compound, bituminous, solvent type; asphalt base & aluminum pigmented, leafing type	8030		Sep 16 65
TT-C-001162 (HUD-HAA)	Coating, polyurethane alkyd-modified satin-finish (for interior & exterior use)	8010		Aug 5 66
TT-C-001226 (GSA-FSS)	Coating system, polyester, glaze, for interior surfaces	8010		Aug 15 67
TT-C-001227 (GSA-FSS)	Coating system, polyurethane, glaze, for interior surfaces	8010		Sep 13 67
TT-D-291b	Diamyl phthalate; plasticizer (for use in organic coatings)	6810	5	Apr 20 60
TT-D-301b	Dibutyl phthalate; plasticizer (for use in organic coatings)	6810	5	Apr 5 60
TT-D-376c	Dipentene, technical (for use in organic protective coatings)	6810	10	May 10 57
TT-D-643d	Drier, paint, naphthenate, liquid, concentrated	8010	5	Sep 17 65
TT-D-651e	Drier, paint, liquid	8010	5	Jun 9 65
TT-E-485e	Enamel, semigloss, rust-inhibiting	8010	10	Apr 29 66
TT-E-487b	Enamel; floor & deck	8010	5	Jun 2 65
TT-E-00488a(1) (GSA-FSS)	Enamel, primer coating, & clear lacquer (in pressurized dispensers)	8010		Aug 30 66
TT-E-489d(1)	Enamel, alkyd, gloss (for exterior & interior surfaces)	8010	15	Jul 21 66
TT-E-00490(2) (GSA-FSS)	Enamel, silicone alkyd copolymer semi-gloss exterior	8010		May 10 67
TT-E-491b	Enamel; gloss, synthetic, (for metal & wood hospital furniture)	8010	5	Mar 2 65
TT-E-496b	Enamel; heat-resisting (400°F.), black	8010	5	May 11 67
TT-E-505a(3)	Enamel, odorless, alkyd, interior, high gloss, white & light tints	8010	10	Aug 27 65
TT-E-506e(2)	Enamel, tints & white, gloss, interior	8010	5	Aug 20 65
TT-E-508b	Enamel; interior semigloss, tints & white	8010	5	Apr 12 67
TT-E-509b	Enamel, odorless, alkyd, interior, semigloss, white & tints	8010	5	Apr 12 67
TT-E-515(2)	Enamel, alkyd, lustreless, quick-drying	8010	10	Jun 13 66
TT-E-516	Enamel, lustreless, quick-drying styrenated alkyd type	8010	10	Dec 2 63
TT-E-522(1)	Enamel, phenolic, lusterless, outside	8010	5	Oct 11 66
TT-E-527b	Enamel, alkyd, lustreless	8010	10	Oct 12 64
TT-E-529b(1)	Enamel, alkyd, semigloss	8010	10	Sep 28 66
TT-E-543a	Enamel, interior, undercoat, tints & white	8010	5	Feb 24 66
TT-E-545a(2)	Enamel, odorless, alkyd, interior-undercoat, tints & white	8010	5	May 24 65
TT-E-751c	Ethyl acetate, technical	6810	5	Apr 13 67
TT-E-776b	Ethylene glycol monobutyl ether (for use in organic coatings)	6810	5	Apr 12 60
TT-E-781b	Ethylene glycol monoethyl ether, technical	6810	5	Nov 2 60
TT-E-001126a(1) (HUD-HAA)	Enamel, low-lustre thixotropic for interior use	8010		Oct 3 67
TT-F-00322(1) (Army-MR)	Filler, dent, cracks, small holes, two-component (polyester)	8010		Jun 28 66
TT-F-325a(1)	Filler, engraving, stamped marking	8010	5	Feb 23 66
TT-F-336b(1)	Filler, wood, paste	8010	10	Apr 28 60
TT-F-00336c (GSA-FSS)	Filler, wood, paste	8010		Feb 3 67
TT-F-340(3)	Filler, wood, plastic	8010	10	Oct 12 61
TT-F-00340a (GSA-FSS)	Filler, wood, plastic	8010		Mar 10 67
TT-F-001098a (HUD-HAA)	Filler, surface, styrene-butadiene, filler for porous surface (cinder block, concrete block, concrete, stucco, etc.)	8010		Oct 14 66
TT-G-00410c (GSA-FSS)	Glazing compound, sash (metal) for bedding & face glazing	8010		Aug 11 61
TT-G-00490a (Navy-Weps)	Granules; reflectorized	8010		Apr 22 63
TT-I-521(1)	Ink, copying and record	7510	5	Jan 30 40
TT-I-00521a(GPO)	Ink, copying and record	7510		May 20 59

NUMERICAL LISTINGS OF MILITARY SPECIFICATIONS AND STANDARDS *

NUMBER	TITLE		DATE
MIL-T-4D	Tire, pneumatic, & inner tube, pneumatic tire, tire with flap, tire with tube and flap, packaging and packing of		Nov 2 64
MIL-T-46D(1)	Tray, mess, compartmented 6 compartment, corrosion-resisting steel		May 18 64
MIL-C-102A	Coating compound, bituminous, solvent cut back, box and crate topcoating		May 21 54
MIL-C-104A(1)	Crates, wood; lumber and plywood sheathed, nailed and bolted		Mar 26 62
MIL-P-116E(3)	Preservation, methods of		Aug 18 67
MIL-B-117D	Bags & sleeves, interior packaging		Jun 30 67
MIL-B-121C(1)	Barrier material, greaseproofed, water-proofed, flexible		Aug 2 67
MIL-C-450B	Coating compound, bituminous, solvent type, black (for ammunition)		Nov 27 62
MIL-F-495C	Finish, chemical, black for copper alloys		Jun 9 66
MIL-C-675a(2)	Coating of glass optical elements (anti-reflection)		Oct 23 64
MIL-I-705C(1)	Ice cream mix		Mar 28 66
MIL-I-790B	Insulators, electric, porcelain		Feb 5 62
MIL-C-1058D(3)	Chicken or turkey, canned, boned		Jun 29 67
MIL-C-1283C	Can, gasoline, military, 5-gallon		Dec 7 64
MIL-P-1470D	Packaging, packing, labeling & marking of prepared (ready to eat) & uncooked breakfast cereals		Jul 22 65
MIL-L-1497D	Labeling of metal cans for subsistence items		Feb 7 66
MIL-L-2105B	Lubricating oil, gear, multi-purpose		Feb 19 62
MIL-R-2580C	Railroad board (for road signs)		Jun 29 66
MIL-B-2629	Bed-frame (Gatch)		Mar 26 51
MIL-I-3037C(1)	Insignia, service stripes, chevrons and bars (embroidered)		Jun 13 62
MIL-F-3069B	Frankfurters, canned		Mar 20 63
MIL-B-3149C	Baling of clothing and equipage		Apr 6 66
MIL-M-3171B(1)	Magnesium alloy, processes for pretreatment & prevention of corrosion on		Feb 26 65
MIL-I-3218	Ink, meat-stamping		May 31 50
MIL-C-3305A	Container, bait, rodent, paper		May 5 59
MIL-T-3338E(2)	Table, folding legs, field		Dec 29 66
MIL-R-3423A(1)	Roofing felt, in rolls, packaging of		May 12 65
MIL-W-3448A	Wallboard, packaging of		Aug 24 60
MIL-P-3453	Paper, chromatographic analysis		Mar 30 51
MIL-S-3534B	Surveying instruments and accessories, packaging of		Oct 16 59
MIL-R-3567A	Reconditioning of drums, metal, 55-gallon and cans, gasoline, Military, 5 gallon		Jul 21 53
MIL-R-3669A	Rubber stamps, fixed and removable types, food inspection, veterinary		Sep 27 57
MIL-C-3701A(1)	Cylinders, compressed gas; ICC-8 & ICC-8AL, acetylene, with valves		Oct 15 66
MIL-M-3722C	Milk, sterilized, whole		Apr 27 66
MIL-C-3885A(1)	Cable assemblies and cord assemblies, electrical (for use in electronic, communication, and associated electrical equipment)		Apr 26 62
MIL-B-4173A(1)	Benches, work, general purpose		Jun 19 64
MIL-H-6088D	Heat treatment of aluminum alloys		Mar 24 65
MIL-W-6110	Wood; determination of moisture content of		Apr 11 50
MIL-L-7178A(1)	Lacquer, cellulose nitrate, gloss, for aircraft use		Oct 26 56
MIL-C-7769A(2)	Cushioning material, uncompressed bound fiber for packaging		Apr 21 66
MIL-C-10023C	Celery salt		Jun 29 64
MIL-G-10024D(2)	Garlic salt		Jul 5 66
MIL-F-10089G	Furniture, composite metal & wood		Apr 26 66
MIL-S-10379A(1)	Suppression, radio interference general requirements for vehicles (and vehicular subassemblies)		Jul 23 52
MIL-L-10547D	Liners, case, & sheet, overwrap, water-vaporproof or waterproof, flexible		Mar 10 67
MIL-M-10578B	Metal conditioner and rust remover (phosphoric acid base)		Mar 16 56
MIL-C-10597C(1)	Cleaning compound with conditioner inhibitor for engine cooling systems		Aug 12 64
MIL-C-12000D(1)	Cable, cord, and wire, electric, packaging of		Mar 6 63
MIL-R-12294A(2)	Remover, paint and varnish (alkali-organic-solvent type)		Dec 30 55
MIL-F-14072(1)	Finishes for ground signal equipment		Nov 2 55
MIL-B-15228C(3)	Bed, bunk, steel, single and double deck (convertible type)		Feb 23 67
MIL-P-15328B(1)	Primer, pretreatment (formula No. 117 for metals)		Jun 3 66
MIL-C-1617D(1)	Corrosion preventive; compound solvent cut-back, cold application		Mar 17 67
MIL-G-16356B(1)	Gages, boiler-water, direct reading		Sep 28 65
MIL-G-16983A(1)	Gage, pressure, dial indicating		Oct 22 62
MIL-C-17435B(1)	Cushioning material, fibrous glass		Oct 29 56
MIL-P-20311 A	Paper, kraft, duplex, waterproof wrapping (for ammunition containers)		Jun 7 63

*A selected list of military specifications and standards which may be used by all federal agencies.
193

D

BIBLIOGRAPHY

Clough, Richard H., *Construction Contracting.* New York, N.Y.: Wiley Interscience (John Wiley & Sons, Inc.) 1969.

Colby, Edward E., *Practical Legal Advice for Builders and Contractors.* Englewood Cliffs, N.J.: Prentice-Hall Inc., 1972.

Construction Specifications Institute, *Manual of Practice,* Washington, D.C., 1972.

Construction Specifications Institute, *Uniform Construction Index*, Washington, D.C., 1972.

Douglas, Clarence D. and Elmer L. Munger, *Construction Management.* Englewood Cliffs, N.J.: Prentice-Hall, Inc., 1970.

Gale, D. W., *Specifying Building Construction.* New York, N.Y.: Reinhold Publishing Corp., 1963.

Hauf, Harold D., *Building Contracts for Design and Construction.* New York, N.Y.: John Wiley & Sons Inc., 1968.

Jessup, W. Edgar, Jr. and Walter E. Jessup, *Law and Specifications for Engineers and Scientists.* Englewood Cliffs, N.J.: Prentice-Hall, Inc., 1963.

Rosen, Harold J., *Principles of Specification Writing.* New York, N.Y.: Reinhold Publishing Corp., 1967.

Sweet, Justin, *Legal Aspects of Architecture, Engineering and the Construction Process.* St. Paul, Minn.: West Publishing Co., 1970.

Watson, Donald A., *Specifications Writing for Architects and Engineers.* New York, N.Y.: McGraw-Hill Book Co., 1964.

E

ORGANIZATIONS

The following list of organizations is included to help the beginning specifications writer, or experienced writer for that matter, to more easily find some sources providing specifications data in the form of masters or guide material. This is *not* a list of product manufacturers, since such lists are available elsewhere and direct contact may be made with them through distributors or representatives quite easily.

American Arbitration Association, 140 West 51st Street, New York, New York 10020

American Institute of Architects, 1735 New York Avenue, Washington, D.C. 20006

American Society for Testing and Materials, 1916 Race Street, Philadelphia, Pennsylvania 19103

Associated General Contractors of America Inc., 1957 E Street, NW, Washington, D.C. 20036

American National Standards Institute, 1430 Broadway, New York, New York 10018

Construction Specifications Institute, 1150 Seventeenth Street, NW, Washington, D.C. 20036

Federal Housing Authority, Superintendent of Documents, Government Printing Office, Washington, D.C. 20402

General Services Administration, Superintendent of Documents, Government Printing Office, Washington, D.C. 20402

Pacific International Computer Corporation, 50 Beale Street, San Francisco, California 94119

Production Systems for Architects and Engineers, 1785 Massachusetts Avenue NW, Washington, D.C. 20036

Underwriters Laboratories Inc., 207 East Ohio Street, Chicago, Illinois 60611

INDEX

A

Acceptance, Uniform System, 86
Addenda, 115, 118
Alternates, 115, 116
American Society for Testing
    and Materials (ASTM), 25
Announcements, 65
"Any," use of, 59
Architect, 18
Associations, 38, 329
Association specifications, 311

B

Bibliography, 333
Bid form, 70
Binding for specifications, 138
Blueprinting, 137
"Boilerplate," 63
Bond forms, 71
Broadscope, 78
Building codes, 39
Building departments, 21
Building openings, 12

C

Carbon paper, 132
Catalogs:
    local, 31
    manufacturers', 32
    product, 28
Catalog retrieval, 125
Change order, 115, 120
Check-and-recheck, 102
Checking drawings, 20
Check list, 242
Clients, who are, 158
Closed specification, 43, 44
Codes, 39, 40
Color coding, 138
Commercial standards, 37
Computers, 128, 137
COMSPEC, 150, 277
Conditions:
    general, 67
    special, 69
    supplemental general, 68
Consultants, 155
Consultants' consultants, 160
Consultants' fee, 159
Consultant's office, 158
Construction Specifications Institute, 75
Contractor, 18, 57
Cost accounting guide, 83
Cross referencing, 14
C's, three, 55
Cut-and-paste master, 143

D

Description of project, 66
Details, 18
Deviations, 16
Dimensions, 12
DIVISION, the, 77, 79
Drafting notes, 19

Drafting scale, 13
Drafting symbols, 10

E

"Either," use of, 59
Electrostatic duplicating, 134
Engineers, Corps of (U.S. Army), 36
Escape clauses, 58
"Etc.," use of, 59
Exact word meaning, 60

F

Federal Housing Authority (FHA), 37
Federal specifications, 35, 47, 105, 320, 322
Fees, consultants', 159
Filing system, the, 82
Final specifications, 92, 100
FORMAT, CSI, 76
Forms, 64, 70, 72
"Front-end" documents, 63
Future, the, 165

G

General conditions, 67
Government masters, 147
Government sources, information from, 34
Government work, 112

H

Hatching, 11
Highway Commissions, 40

I

Index of key words, 83
Insurance companies, 40
"Intent," use of, 59
Invitation to bid, 66

K

Key word, index of, 83

L

Language, specifications, 55
Last Look, the, 102

M

Mandatory construction, 56
Manufacturer–contractor, 84
Manufacturer–distributor, 109
Manufacturers' catalogs, 32
Manufacturer's specifications, 46, 311
Material, indication of, 10
Material methods research, 101
MASTERSPEC, 149, 293
Master specifications, 143, 151
Military specifications, 36, 331
Mimeograph duplicating, 134
"Must," use of, 59

N

Narrowscope, 78
NASA specifications, 305

Navy Bureau of Yards and Docks, 36
Nonstandard items, federal, 112

O

Office master, 145
Open specifications, 43, 44
"Or equal" clause, 45

P

Page arrangement, 99
Page identification, 99
Paragraph, numbering, 98
PDE (Project Design Engineer), 105
Performance specification, 49
Pre-bid qualification, 67
Preliminary review, 89
Preliminary specification, 91
Preliminary submittal, 107
Preliminary survey, 106
Preprinted material, 140
Printing specifications, 136
Product catalogs, 28
Project, description of, 66
Punctuation, 58
Purchased masters, 149

Q

Qualification, pre-bid, 67

R

Reference drawings, 19
Reproduction, methods of, 131

Researcher, the, 161
Research, material-methods, 101

S

Sample specifications, 255, 256, 270
Scales, drafting, 13
Schedules, 15
SECTION, the, 78, 79, 93
"Some said," use of, 59
SPEC-DATA, 32, 33, 216
Special Conditions, 69
Specifications, 16, 43, 217, 231
    commercial, 48, 256
    consultant, 155
    federal, 110, 111, 270
    mechanizations of, 123
    preliminary, 217
Specifications covers, 140
Specifications language, 55
Spirit duplication, 133
Standard details, 18
Streamlined specifications, 50
Sub-contractors, list of, 71
Supplemental General Conditions, 68
Survey, preliminary, 106
Sweet's Information Service, 29
Systems approach, 124
Symbols, drafting, 10

T

Tabulation specifications, 52
Testing, 24

Testing, private laboratories, 28
Three-part section, 93
"To be," use of, 59
"Topsy" masters, 144
Trade associations, 38
Training and experience, 157
"Type" specifications, 321
Typewriter, automatic, 126

U

Underwriters Laboratories Inc., 27
Uniform System, 30, 75, 86, 169
Unit prices, 118
Use permit, 21

W

Wage scales, 70
Waiting period, 108
Woodwork Institute of California, 311
Words and phrases, 59

Y

Yards and Docks, Bureau of (U.S. Navy),
    36, 321